interchange

FOURTH EDITION

Jack C. Richards

With Jonathan Hull and Susan Proctor

1

CAMBRIDGE
UNIVERSITY PRESS

TEACHER'S EDITION

CAMBRIDGE UNIVERSITY PRESS
Cambridge, New York, Melbourne, Madrid, Cape Town,
Singapore, São Paulo, Delhi, Mexico City

Cambridge University Press
32 Avenue of the Americas, New York, NY 10013-2473, USA

www.cambridge.org
Information on this title: www.cambridge.org/9781107699175

First published 1995
Second edition 2000
Third edition 2005
2nd printing 2013

Printed in Hong Kong, China, by Golden Cup Printing Company Limited

A catalog record for this publication is available from the British Library.

ISBN 978-1-107-64867-8 Student's Book 1 with Self-study DVD-ROM
ISBN 978-1-107-69443-9 Student's Book 1A with Self-study DVD-ROM
ISBN 978-1-107-67396-0 Student's Book 1B with Self-study DVD-ROM
ISBN 978-1-107-64872-2 Workbook 1
ISBN 978-1-107-61687-5 Workbook 1A
ISBN 978-1-107-69959-5 Workbook 1B
ISBN 978-1-107-69917-5 Teacher's Edition 1 with Assessment Audio CD/CD-ROM
ISBN 978-1-107-64725-1 Class Audio CDs 1
ISBN 978-1-107-67993-1 Full Contact 1 with Self-study DVD-ROM
ISBN 978-1-107-61136-8 Full Contact 1A with Self-study DVD-ROM
ISBN 978-1-107-63780-1 Full Contact 1B with Self-study DVD-ROM

For a full list of components, visit www. cambridge.org/interchange

Art direction, book design, layout services, and photo research: Integra
Audio production: CityVox, NYC

Contents

Plan of Book 1

Titles/Topics	Speaking	Grammar
UNIT 1 — PAGES 2–7		
Please call me Beth. Introductions and greetings; names, countries, and nationalities	Introducing yourself; introducing someone; checking information; exchanging personal information; saying hello and good-bye	Wh-questions and statements with *be*; questions with *what, where, who,* and *how*; yes/no questions and short answers with *be*; subject pronouns; possessive adjectives
UNIT 2 — PAGES 8–13		
What do you do? Jobs, workplaces, and school; daily schedules; clock time	Describing work and school; asking for and giving opinions; describing daily schedules	Simple present Wh-questions and statements; question: *when*; time expressions: *at, in, on, around, early, late, until, before,* and *after*
PROGRESS CHECK — PAGES 14–15		
UNIT 3 — PAGES 16–21		
How much is it? Shopping and prices; clothing and personal items; colors and materials	Talking about prices; giving opinions; discussing preferences; making comparisons; buying and selling things	Demonstratives: *this, that, these, those; one* and *ones*; questions: *how much* and *which*; comparisons with adjectives
UNIT 4 — PAGES 22–27		
I really like hip-hop. Music, movies, and TV programs; entertainers; invitations and excuses; dates and times	Talking about likes and dislikes; giving opinions; making invitations and excuses	Yes/no and Wh-questions with *do*; question: *what kind*; object pronouns; modal verb *would*; verb + *to* + verb
PROGRESS CHECK — PAGES 28–29		
UNIT 5 — PAGES 30–35		
I come from a big family. Families; typical families	Talking about families and family members; exchanging information about the present; describing family life	Present continuous yes/no and Wh-questions, statements, and short answers; quantifiers: *all,* nearly *all, most, many, a lot of, some, not many,* and *few*; pronoun: *no one*
UNIT 6 — PAGES 36–41		
How often do you exercise? Sports, fitness activities, and exercise; routines	Asking about and describing routines and exercise; talking about frequency; discussing sports and athletes; talking about abilities	Adverbs of frequency: *always, almost always, usually, often, sometimes, hardly ever, almost never,* and *never*; questions: *how often, how long, how well,* and *how good*; short answers
PROGRESS CHECK — PAGES 42–43		
UNIT 7 — PAGES 44–49		
We had a great time! Free-time and weekend activities	Talking about past events; giving opinions about past experiences; talking about vacations	Simple past yes/no and Wh-questions, statements, and short answers with regular and irregular verbs; past of *be*
UNIT 8 — PAGES 50–55		
What's your neighborhood like? Stores and places in a city; neighborhoods; houses and apartments	Asking about and describing locations of places; asking about and describing neighborhoods; asking about quantities	*There is/there are; one, any,* and *some*; prepositions of place; quantifiers; questions: *how many* and *how much*; count and noncount nouns
PROGRESS CHECK — PAGES 56–57		

Pronunciation/Listening	Writing/Reading	Interchange Activity
Linked sounds Listening for names and countries	Writing questions requesting personal information "What's in a Name?": Reading about popular names	"Getting to know you": Collecting personal information about classmates PAGE 114
Syllable stress Listening to descriptions of jobs and daily routines	Writing a biography of a classmate "Why Do You Need a Job?": Reading about people who need jobs	"Common ground": Finding similarities in classmates' daily schedules PAGE 115
Sentence stress Listening to people shopping; listening for items, colors, and prices	Writing a comparison of prices in different countries "Tools for Better Shopping": Reading about electronic tools for shopping	"Flea market": Buying and selling things PAGES 116–117
Intonation in questions Identifying musical styles; listening for likes and dislikes	Writing a text message "Fergie of the Black Eyed Peas": Reading about a famous entertainer	"Are you free this weekend?": Making plans; inviting and giving excuses PAGE 118
Intonation in statements Listening for family relationships	Writing an email about family "Stay-at-Home Dads": Reading about three fathers	"Family facts": Finding out information about classmates' families PAGE 119
Intonation with direct address Listening to people talking about free-time activities; listening to descriptions of sports participation	Writing about favorite activities "Health and Fitness Quiz": Reading about and taking a quiz	"Do you dance?": Finding out about classmates' abilities PAGE 120
Reduction of *did you* Listening to descriptions and opinions of past events and vacations	Writing an online post "Vacation Posts": Reading about different kinds of vacations	"Thinking back": Playing a board game PAGE 121
Reduction of *there is/there are* Listening for locations and descriptions of places	Writing a "roommate wanted" ad "The World in One Neighborhood": Reading about a Toronto neighborhood	"Where Am I?": describing and guessing locations PAGE 122

Authors' acknowledgments

A great number of people contributed to the development of *Interchange Fourth Edition*. Particular thanks are owed to the reviewers using *Interchange, Third Edition* in the following schools and institutes – their insights and suggestions have helped define the content and format of the fourth edition:

Ian Geoffrey Hanley, **The Address Education Center**, Izmir, Turkey

James McBride, **AUA Language Center**, Bangkok, Thailand

Jane Merivale, **Centennial College**, Toronto, Ontario, Canada

Elva Elena Peña Andrade, **Centro de Auto Aprendizaje de Idiomas**, Nuevo León, Mexico

José Paredes, **Centro de Educación Continua de la Escuela Politécnica Nacional** (CEC-EPN), Quito, Ecuador

Chia-jung Tsai, **Changhua University of Education**, Changhua City, Taiwan

Kevin Liang, **Chinese Culture University**, Taipei, Taiwan

Roger Alberto Neira Perez, **Colegio Santo Tomás de Aquino**, Bogotá, Colombia

Teachers at **Escuela Miguel F. Martínez**, Monterrey, Mexico

Maria Virgínia Goulart Borges de Lebron, **Great Idiomas**, São Paulo, Brazil

Gina Kim, **Hoseo University**, Chungnam, South Korea

Heeyong Kim, Seoul, South Korea

Elisa Borges, **IBEU-Rio**, Rio de Janeiro, Brazil

Jason M. Ham, **Inha University**, Incheon, South Korea

Rita de Cássia S. Silva Miranda, **Instituto Batista de Idiomas**, Belo Horizonte, Brazil

Teachers at **Instituto Politécnico Nacional**, Mexico City, Mexico

Victoria M. Roberts and Regina Marie Williams, **Interactive College of Technology**, Chamblee, Georgia, USA

Teachers at **Internacional de Idiomas**, Mexico City, Mexico

Marcelo Serafim Godinho, **Life Idiomas**, São Paulo, Brazil

J. Kevin Varden, **Meiji Gakuin University**, Yokohama, Japan

Rosa Maria Valencia Rodrìguez, Mexico City, Mexico

Chung-Ju Fan, **National Kinmen Institute of Technology**, Kinmen, Taiwan

Shawn Beasom, **Nihon Daigaku**, Tokyo, Japan

Gregory Hadley, **Niigata University of International and Information Studies**, Niigata, Japan

Chris Ruddenklau, **Osaka University of Economics and Law**, Osaka, Japan

Byron Roberts, **Our Lady of Providence Girls' High School**, Xindian City, Taiwan

Simon Banha, **Phil Young's English School**, Curitiba, Brazil

Flávia Gonçalves Carneiro Braathen, **Real English Center**, Viçosa, Brazil

Márcia Cristina Barboza de Miranda, **SENAC**, Recife, Brazil

Raymond Stone, **Seneca College of Applied Arts and Technology**, Toronto, Ontario, Canada

Gen Murai, **Takushoku University**, Tokyo, Japan

Teachers at **Tecnológico de Estudios Superiores de Ecatepec**, Mexico City, Mexico

Teachers at **Universidad Autónoma Metropolitana–Azcapotzalco**, Mexico City, Mexico

Teachers at **Universidad Autónoma de Nuevo León**, Monterrey, Mexico

Mary Grace Killian Reyes, **Universidad Autónoma de Tamaulipas**, Tampico Tamaulipas, Mexico

Teachers at **Universidad Estatal del Valle de Ecatepec**, Mexico City, Mexico

Teachers at **Universidad Nacional Autónoma de Mexico – Zaragoza**, Mexico City, Mexico

Teachers at **Universidad Nacional Autónoma de Mexico – Iztacala**, Mexico City, Mexico

Luz Edith Herrera Diaz, Veracruz, Mexico

Seri Park, **YBM PLS**, Seoul, South Korea

Self-assessment charts revised by Alex Tilbury

Grammar plus written by Karen Davy

A letter from the authors

Dear teachers and colleagues,

Together with Cambridge University Press, we have always been committed to ensuring that the *Interchange* series continues to provide you and your students with the best possible teaching and learning resources. This means we always seek ways to add new features to the course to make sure it reflects the best practices in language teaching. We are delighted to tell you that we have now prepared a new edition of the series to make sure it continues to be the market leader in English language teaching today.

Here are some of the things you can look forward to in the fourth edition:

- a fresh **new design, new illustrations** and **photos,** and **updated content**
- a new **Self-study DVD-ROM** in the back of each Student's Book that provides additional skills and video viewing practice
- a revised **Teacher's Edition** now with an **Assessment Audio CD/CD-ROM** that features ready-to-print PDFs and customizable Microsoft Word tests
- an array of **new technology** components to support teaching and enhance learning both inside and outside of the classroom
- the all-new *Interchange Video Program* and accompanying Video Resource materials

In addition, the features that have made *Interchange* the world's most popular and successful English course continue to be the hallmarks of the fourth edition:

- the same **trusted methodology** and proven approach
- **flexibility** for use in any teaching situation
- a wealth of resources for teacher training and professional development

We look forward to introducing you to the fourth edition of *Interchange*.

With best wishes and warmest regards,

Jack C. Richards
Jonathan Hull
Susan Proctor

The new edition

Interchange Fourth Edition is a fully revised edition of *Interchange Third Edition*, the world's most successful series for adult and young adult learners of English.

The course has been thoroughly updated, and it remains the innovative series teachers and students have grown to love, while incorporating suggestions from teachers and students all over the world. There is new content in every unit, additional grammar practice, as well as opportunities to develop speaking and listening skills.

What's new

Content – more than half of the readings are new and many others have been updated.

Grammar plus – the self-study section at the back of the Student's Book provides additional grammar practice that students can do in class or as homework. An answer key is also included at the back of the book, so students can check their work.

Progress checks – the Self-assessment charts have been revised to reflect student outcomes, and the statements are aligned with the Common European Framework of Reference (CEFR). This allows students to assess their ability to communicate effectively rather than focus on mastery of grammar.

Student's self-study DVD-ROM – contains brand new content at each level of the Student's Book. The interactive activities provide students with extra practice in vocabulary, grammar, listening, speaking, and reading. It also contains the complete video program with activities that allow students to check their comprehension themselves.

Assessment Audio CD / CD-ROM – contains eight oral and written quizzes plus a midterm and final exam. The quizzes are available in two formats – as ready-to-print PDFs and in Microsoft Word. The audio program, audio scripts, and answer keys are also included on this disc.

Core series components

Interchange Fourth Edition has a variety of components to help you and your students meet their language learning needs. Here is a list of the core components.

COMPONENT	DESCRIPTION
Student's Book with *NEW!* **Self-study DVD-ROM**	The Student's Book is intended for classroom use and contains 16 six-page units. The Self-study DVD-ROM provides additional vocabulary, grammar, listening, speaking, reading, and full class video–viewing practice.
Class Audio CDs	The Class Audio CDs are intended for classroom use. The CDs provide audio for all the audio sections in the Student's Book.
Teacher's Edition with *NEW!* **Assessment Audio CD / CD-ROM**	The interleaved Teacher's Edition with Assessment Audio CD / CD-ROM includes: • Page-by-page teaching notes with step-by-step lesson plans • Audio scripts and answer keys for the Student's Book, Workbook, and DVD • Language summaries of the new vocabulary and expressions in each unit • Supplementary Resource Overviews that make it easy to plan what to teach for each unit • A complete assessment program, including oral and written quizzes, as well as review unit tests in printable PDF and Microsoft Word formats
Workbook	The Workbook's six-page units can be used in class or for homework. Each unit provides students with additional grammar, vocabulary, and writing practice.
NEW! **Online Workbook**	The Online Workbook is an online version of the print workbook, optimized for online practice. The Online Workbook provides instant feedback for hundreds of activities as well as simple tools to monitor progress.
NEW! **Video Program**	Videos for each unit offer entertaining free-standing sequences that reinforce and extend the language presented in the Student's Book. Video Resource Books include step-by-step comprehension and conversation activities and detailed teaching suggestions.
NEW! **Classware Presentation Software**	Classroom Presentation Software can be used on an interactive whiteboard, portable interactive software technology, or with a computer or projector. This software is intended for classroom use and presents the Student's Book, audio, and video.
NEW! **Animated Presentations**	Student's Book pages are reproduced digitally in MS PowerPoint format, allowing teachers to complete activities in front of the classroom using only a computer and a projector.
NEW! Interchange **Arcade**	*Interchange* Arcade is a free self-study website offering fun, interactive, self-scoring activities for each unit. The *Interchange* Arcade includes activities that help students practice listening, vocabulary, grammar, and reading skills. MP3s of the class audio program can also be found here.
Placement Test	The placement test provides three versions of the placement test and four achievement tests for each level of the Student's Book, as well as for *Passages* 1 and 2.

For a complete list of components, visit www.cambridge.org/interchange or contact your local Cambridge University Press representative.

Student's Book overview

Every unit in *Interchange Fourth Edition* contains two cycles, each of which has a specific topic, grammar point, and function. The units in Level 1 contain a variety of exercises, including a Snapshot, Conversation, Grammar focus, Pronunciation, Discussion (or Speaking / Role Play), Word power, Listening, Writing, Reading, and Interchange activity. The sequence of these exercises differs from unit to unit. Here is a sample unit from Level 1.

Cycle 1 (Exercises 1–8)

Topic: leisure activities
Grammar: simple past
Function: talk about the weekend

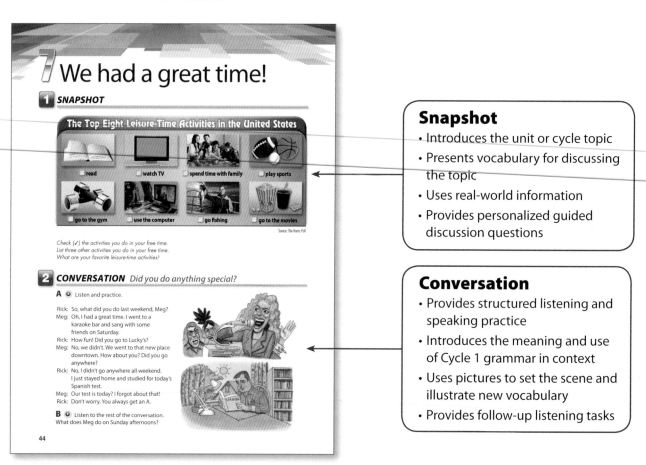

Snapshot
- Introduces the unit or cycle topic
- Presents vocabulary for discussing the topic
- Uses real-world information
- Provides personalized guided discussion questions

Conversation
- Provides structured listening and speaking practice
- Introduces the meaning and use of Cycle 1 grammar in context
- Uses pictures to set the scene and illustrate new vocabulary
- Provides follow-up listening tasks

Grammar focus

- Summarizes the Cycle 1 grammar
- Includes audio recordings of the grammar
- Provides controlled grammar practice in realistic contexts, such as short conversations
- Provides freer, more personalized speaking practice

Pronunciation

- Provides controlled practice in recognizing and producing sounds linked to the cycle grammar
- Promotes extended or personalized pronunciation practice

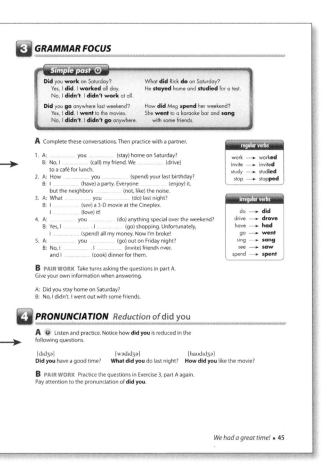

3 GRAMMAR FOCUS

Simple past

Did you **work** on Saturday?	What **did** Rick **do** on Saturday?
Yes, I **did**. I **worked** all day.	He **stayed** home and **studied** for a test.
No, I **didn't**. I **didn't work** at all.	
Did you **go** anywhere last weekend?	How **did** Meg **spend** her weekend?
Yes, I **did**. I **went** to the movies.	She **went** to a karaoke bar and **sang**
No, I **didn't**. I **didn't go** anywhere.	with some friends.

A Complete these conversations. Then practice with a partner.

1. A: .... you .... (stay) home on Saturday?
   B: No, I .... (call) my friend. We .... (drive) to a café for lunch.
2. A: How .... you .... (spend) your last birthday?
   B: I .... (have) a party. Everyone .... (enjoy) it, but the neighbors .... (not, like) the noise.
3. A: What .... you .... (do) last night?
   B: I .... (see) a 3-D movie at the Cineplex. I .... (love) it!
4. A: .... you .... (do) anything special over the weekend?
   B: Yes, I .... I .... (go) shopping. Unfortunately, I .... (spend) all my money. Now I'm broke!
5. A: .... you .... (go) out on Friday night?
   B: No, I .... I .... (invite) friends over, and I .... (cook) dinner for them.

regular verbs

work	→	work**ed**
invite	→	invit**ed**
study	→	stud**ied**
stop	→	stop**ped**

irregular verbs

do	→	**did**
drive	→	**drove**
have	→	**had**
go	→	**went**
sing	→	**sang**
see	→	**saw**
spend	→	**spent**

B PAIR WORK Take turns asking the questions in part A. Give your own information when answering.

A: Did you stay home on Saturday?
B: No, I didn't. I went out with some friends.

4 PRONUNCIATION Reduction of did you

A Listen and practice. Notice how **did you** is reduced in the following questions.

[dɪdʒə]
Did you have a good time?

[wədɪdʒə]
What did you do last night?

[haʊdɪdʒə]
How did you like the movie?

B PAIR WORK Practice the questions in Exercise 3, part A again. Pay attention to the pronunciation of **did you**.

We had a great time! ▪ 45

Word power

- Presents vocabulary related to the unit topic
- Provides practice with collocations and categorizing vocabulary
- Promotes freer, more personalized practice

Discussion

- Provides communicative tasks that help develop oral fluency
- Recycles grammar and vocabulary in the cycle
- Includes pair work, group work, and class activities

Listening

- Provides pre-listening focus tasks or questions
- Develops a variety of listening skills, such as listening for main ideas and details
- Includes post-listening speaking tasks

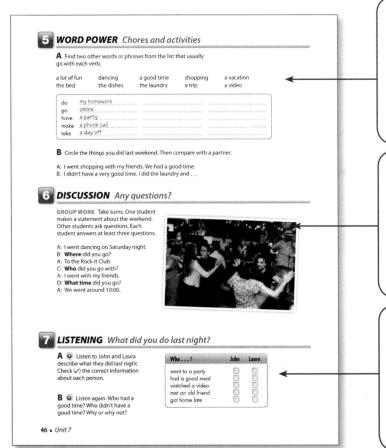

5 WORD POWER Chores and activities

A Find two other words or phrases from the list that usually go with each verb.

a lot of fun	dancing	a good time	shopping	a vacation
the bed	the dishes	the laundry	a trip	a video

do	my homework	....	....
go	online	....	....
have	a party	....	....
make	a phone call	....	....
take	a day off	....	....

B Circle the things you did last weekend. Then compare with a partner.

A: I went shopping with my friends. We had a good time.
B: I didn't have a very good time. I did the laundry and . . .

6 DISCUSSION Any questions?

GROUP WORK Take turns. One student makes a statement about the weekend. Other students ask questions. Each student answers at least three questions.

A: I went dancing on Saturday night.
B: **Where** did you go?
A: To the Rock-it Club.
C: **Who** did you go with?
A: I went with my friends.
D: **What time** did you go?
A: We went around 10:00.

7 LISTENING What did you do last night?

A Listen to John and Laura describe what they did last night. Check (✓) the correct information about each person.

Who . . . ?	John	Laura
went to a party	☐	☐
had a good meal	☐	☐
watched a video	☐	☐
met an old friend	☐	☐
got home late	☐	☐

B Listen again. Who had a good time? Who didn't have a good time? Why or why not?

46 ▪ Unit 7

Topic: vacations
Grammar: past of *be*
Function: talk about vacations

Conversation

- Provides structured listening and speaking practice
- Introduces the meaning and use of Cycle 2 grammar in context
- Uses pictures to set the scene and illustrate new vocabulary
- Introduces useful expressions and discourse features

Grammar focus

- Summarizes the Cycle 2 grammar
- Presents examples from the previous conversation
- Provides controlled grammar practice in realistic contexts, such as short conversations

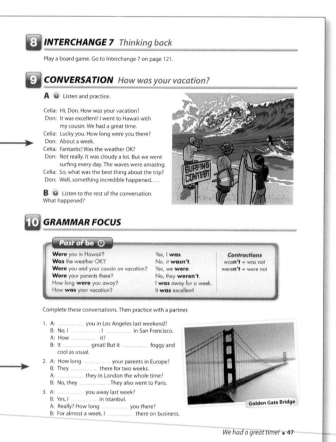

8 INTERCHANGE 7 Thinking back

Play a board game. Go to Interchange 7 on page 121.

9 CONVERSATION How was your vacation?

A Listen and practice.

Celia: Hi, Don. How was your vacation?
Don: It was excellent! I went to Hawaii with my cousin. We had a great time.
Celia: Lucky you. How long were you there?
Don: About a week.
Celia: Fantastic! Was the weather OK?
Don: Not really. It was cloudy a lot. But we went surfing every day. The waves were amazing.
Celia: So, what was the best thing about the trip?
Don: Well, something incredible happened. . . .

B Listen to the rest of the conversation. What happened?

10 GRAMMAR FOCUS

Past of be ⊙

Were you in Hawaii?	Yes, I **was**.	**Contractions**
Was the weather OK?	No, it **wasn't**.	wasn't = was not
Were you and your cousin on vacation?	Yes, we **were**.	weren't = were not
Were your parents there?	No, they **weren't**.	
How long **were** you away?	I **was** away for a week.	
How **was** your vacation?	It **was** excellent!	

Complete these conversations. Then practice with a partner.

1. A: .... you in Los Angeles last weekend?
   B: No, I .... I .... in San Francisco.
   A: How .... it?
   B: It .... great! But it .... foggy and cool as usual.

2. A: How long .... your parents in Europe?
   B: They .... there for two weeks.
   A: .... they in London the whole time?
   B: No, they .... They also went to Paris.

3. A: .... you away last week?
   B: Yes, I .... in Istanbul.
   A: Really? How long .... you there?
   B: For almost a week. I .... there on business.

Golden Gate Bridge

We had a great time! ▪ 47

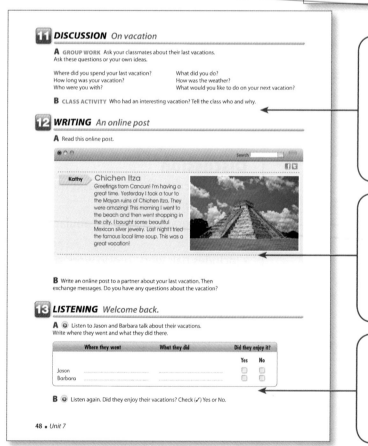

11 DISCUSSION On vacation

A GROUP WORK Ask your classmates about their last vacations. Ask these questions or your own ideas.

Where did you spend your last vacation?
How long was your vacation?
Who were you with?

What did you do?
How was the weather?
What would you like to do on your next vacation?

B CLASS ACTIVITY Who had an interesting vacation? Tell the class who and why.

12 WRITING An online post

A Read this online post.

Search

Kathy Chichen Itza
Greetings from Cancun! I'm having a great time. Yesterday I took a tour to the Mayan ruins of Chichen Itza. They were amazing! This morning I went to the beach and then went shopping in the city. I bought some beautiful Mexican silver jewelry. Last night I tried the famous local lime soup. This was a great vacation!

B Write an online post to a partner about your last vacation. Then exchange messages. Do you have any questions about the vacation?

13 LISTENING Welcome back.

A Listen to Jason and Barbara talk about their vacations. Write where they went and what they did there.

	Where they went	What they did	Did they enjoy it?	
			Yes	No
Jason			☐	☐
Barbara			☐	☐

B Listen again. Did they enjoy their vacations? Check (✓) Yes or No.

48 ▪ *Unit 7*

Discussion

- Provides communicative tasks that help develop oral fluency
- Recycles grammar and vocabulary in the cycle
- Includes pair work, group work, and class activities

Writing

- Provides a model writing sample
- Develops skills in writing different texts, such as postcards and email messages
- Reinforces the vocabulary and grammar in the cycle or unit

Listening

- Provides pre-listening focus tasks or questions
- Develops a variety of listening skills, such as listening for main ideas and details

Reading

- Presents a variety of text types
- Introduces the text with a pre-reading task
- Develops a variety of reading skills, such as reading for main ideas, reading for details, and inferencing
- Promotes discussion that involves personalization and analysis

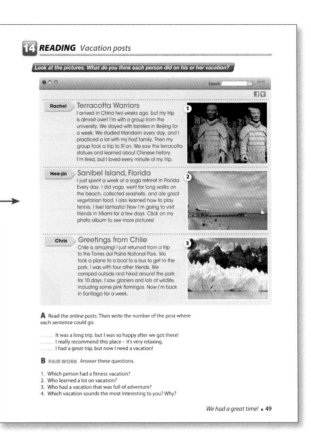

14 READING *Vacation posts*

Look at the pictures. What do you think each person did on his or her vacation?

Rachel — Terracotta Warriors
I arrived in China two weeks ago, but my trip is almost over! I'm with a group from the university. We stayed with families in Beijing for a week. We studied Mandarin every day, and I practiced a lot with my host family. Then my group took a trip to Xi'an. We saw the terracotta statues and learned about Chinese history. I'm tired, but I loved every minute of my trip.

Hee-jin — Sanibel Island, Florida
I just spent a week at a yoga retreat in Florida. Every day, I did yoga, went for long walks on the beach, collected seashells, and ate great vegetarian food. I also learned how to play tennis. I feel fantastic! Now I'm going to visit friends in Miami for a few days. Click on my photo album to see more pictures!

Chris — Greetings from Chile
Chile is amazing! I just returned from a trip to the Torres del Paine National Park. We took a plane to a boat to a bus to get to the park. I was with four other friends. We camped outside and hiked around the park for 10 days. I saw glaciers and lots of wildlife, including some pink flamingos. Now I'm back in Santiago for a week.

A Read the online posts. Then write the number of the post where each sentence could go.

.... It was a long trip, but I was so happy after we got there!
.... I really recommend this place – it's very relaxing.
.... I had a great trip, but now I need a vacation!

B PAIR WORK Answer these questions.

1. Which person had a fitness vacation?
2. Who learned a lot on vacation?
3. Who had a vacation that was full of adventure?
4. Which vacation sounds the most interesting to you? Why?

We had a great time! ▪ 49

In the back of the book

Interchange activity

- Expands on the unit topic, vocabulary, and grammar
- Provides opportunities to consolidate new language in a creative or fun way
- Promotes fluency with communicative activities such as discussions, information gaps, and games

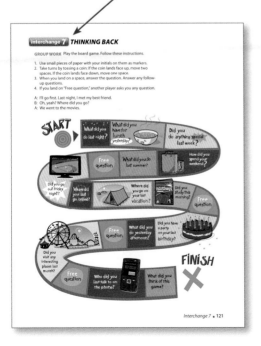

interchange 7 *THINKING BACK*

GROUP WORK Play the board game. Follow these instructions.

1. Use small pieces of paper with your initials on them as markers.
2. Take turns by tossing a coin. If the coin lands face up, move two spaces. If the coin lands face down, move one space.
3. When you land on a space, answer the question. Answer any follow-up questions.
4. If you land on "Free question," another player asks you any question.

A: I'll go first. Last night, I met my best friend.
B: Oh, yeah? Where did you go?
A: We went to the movies.

Interchange 7 ▪ 121

Grammar plus

- Explores the unit grammar in greater depth
- Practices the grammar with controlled exercises
- Can be done in class or assigned as homework

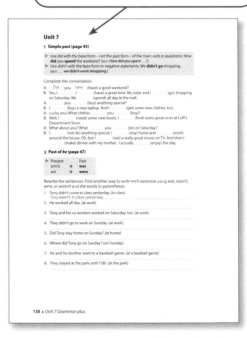

Unit 7

1 Simple past (page 45)

▸ Use *did* with the base form – not the past form – of the main verb in questions: How **did** you **spend** the weekend? (NOT: How did you spent...?)
▸ Use *didn't* with the base form in negative statements: We **didn't go** shopping. (NOT: ... we didn't went shopping.)

Complete the conversation.

A: *Did* you *have* (have) a good weekend?
B: Yes, I .... I .... (have) a great time. My sister and I .... (go) shopping on Saturday. We .... (spend) all day at the mall.
A: .... you .... (buy) anything special?
B: I .... (buy) a new laptop. And I .... (get) some new clothes, too.
A: Lucky you! What clothes .... you .... (buy)?
B: Well, I .... (need) some new boots. I .... (find) some great ones at Luff's Department Store.
A: What about you? What .... you .... (do) on Saturday?
B: I .... (not do) anything special. I .... (stay) home and .... (work) around the house. Oh, but I .... (see) a really good movie on TV. And then I .... (make) dinner with my mother. I actually .... (enjoy) the day.

2 Past of be (page 47)

Present		Past
am/is	→	was
are	→	were

Rewrite the sentences. Find another way to write each sentence using *was, wasn't, were,* or *weren't* and the words in parentheses.

1. Tony didn't come to class yesterday. (in class)
   Tony wasn't in class yesterday.
2. He worked all day. (at work)
3. Tony and his co-workers worked on Saturday, too. (at work)
4. They didn't go to work on Sunday. (at work)
5. Did Tony stay home on Sunday? (at home)
6. Where did Tony go on Sunday? (on Sunday)
7. He and his brother went to a baseball game. (at a baseball game)
8. They stayed at the park until 7:00. (at the park)

138 ▪ Unit 7 Grammar plus

Self-study DVD-ROM overview

Interchange Fourth Edition Self-study DVD-ROM in the back of the Student's Book provides students with hundreds of additional exercises to practice the language taught in the Student's Book on their own, in the classroom, or in the lab.

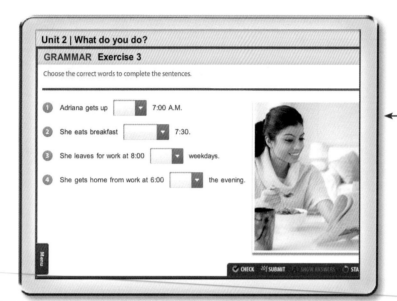

Interactive exercises

Hundreds of interactive exercises provide hours of additional:

- vocabulary practice
- grammar practice
- listening practice
- speaking practice
- reading practice

The complete *Interchange* video program

The entire *Interchange* video program for this level is included on the DVD-ROM with new exercises that allow the students to watch and check comprehension themselves.

Interchange Arcade overview

Interchange Arcade is a free self-study website for students that offers fun, interactive, self-scoring activities for each unit of each level of *Interchange Fourth Edition*. Using animated characters, sound effects, and illustrations, *Interchange* Arcade includes activities that help students practice listening, vocabulary, grammar, and reading skills.

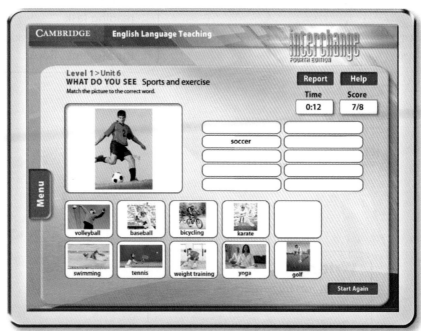

Workbook overview

Interchange Fourth Edition provides students with additional opportunities to practice the language taught in the Student's Book outside of the classroom by using the Workbook that accompanies each level.

Vocabulary
Provides vocabulary practice based on the unit topic

Grammar
Reinforces the unit grammar through controlled practice

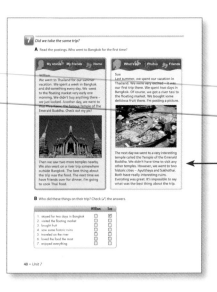

Reading
- Gives additional reading practice based on the theme of the unit
- Introduces the text with a pre-reading task
- Reinforces reading skills used in the Student's Book

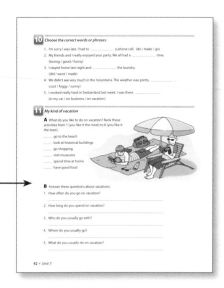

Writing
- Promotes freer, more personalized practice
- Reinforces the vocabulary and grammar in the unit

Online Workbook overview

Each level of the *Interchange Fourth Edition Online Workbooks* provides additional activities to reinforce what is presented in the corresponding Student's Book. They provide all the familiarity of a traditional print workbook with the ease of online delivery. Each *Online Workbook* includes:

- A variety of interactive activities which correspond to each Student's Book lesson, allowing students to interact with workbook material in a fresh, lively way.
- Instant feedback for hundreds of activities, challenging students to focus on areas for improvement.
- Simple tools for teachers to monitor students' progress such as scores, attendance, and time spent online, providing instant information, saving valuable time for teachers.
- Intuitive navigation and clear, easy-to-follow instructions, fostering independent study practice.

The *Interchange Fourth Edition Online Workbooks* can be purchased in a variety of ways:
- directly online; using a credit card,
- as an institutional subscription,
- as a stand-alone access card, or
- as part of a Student's Book with Online Workbook Pack.

Please contact your local Cambridge representative for more details.

Teacher's Edition overview

The Teacher's Editions provide complete support for teachers who are using *Interchange Fourth Edition*. They contain Supplementary Resources Overview charts to help teachers plan their lessons (for more information see page xxiv), Language summaries, Workbook answer keys, Audio scripts, Fresh ideas, and Games. They also include detailed teaching notes for the units and Progress checks in the Student's Books.

Unit preview

Previews the topics, grammar, and functions in each unit

Teaching notes

- Includes the Learning objectives for each exercise
- Provides step-by-step lesson plans
- Provides stimulating and fun Games to review or practice skills such as grammar and vocabulary.
- Includes Answers and Vocabulary definitions
- Provides Tips that promote teacher training and development

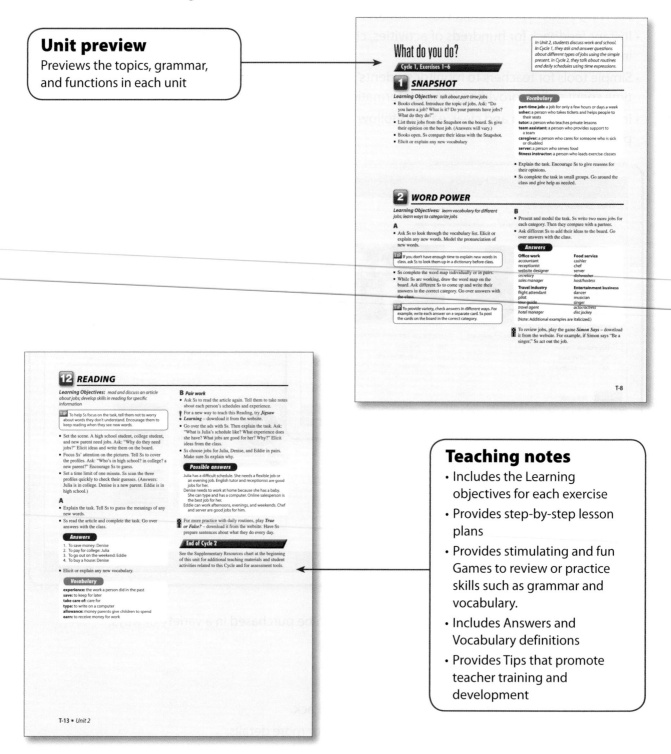

Teaching notes

- Suggests Options for alternative presentations or expansions
- Includes Audio scripts
- Provides alternative ways to present and review exercises in the Fresh ideas

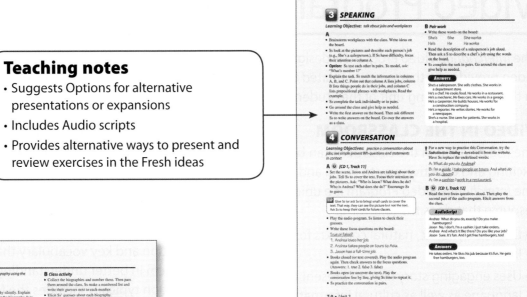

End-of-cycle

- Provides suggestions for further practice in other *Interchange Fourth Edition* components and online
- Provides suggestions for regular assessment using quizzes and tests

Assessment Audio CD / CD-ROM

- Contains oral and written quizzes and tests
- Ready-to-print PDFs of all quizzes and mid-term and final tests make teacher preparation easy
- Microsoft Word formats of all quizzes and tests give teachers the option to customize the material
- Provides support audio, audio scripts, and answer keys

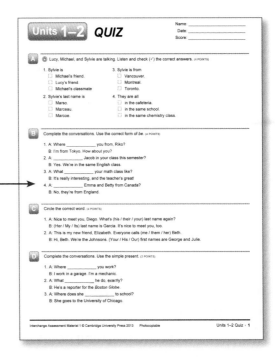

For more information on the Placement Test Program see page xxvi.

Video Program overview

The *Interchange* Video Program is designed to complement the Student's Books. Each video provides further practice related to the topics, language, and vocabulary introduced in the corresponding unit of the Student's Book.

VIDEO IN THE CLASSROOM

The use of video in the classroom can be an exciting and effective way to teach and learn. The *Interchange* Video Program is a unique resource that does the following:

- Depicts dynamic, natural contexts for language use.
- Uses engaging story lines to present authentic language as well as cultural information about speakers of English.
- Enables learners to use visual information to enhance comprehension.
- Allows learners to observe the gestures, facial expressions, and other aspects of body language that accompany speech.

PROGRAM COMPONENTS

Video

The sixteen videos in each level's video program complement Units 1 through 16 of the corresponding Student's Book. There are a variety of genres: dramatized stories, documentaries, interviews, profiles, and travelogues.

Video Resource Book

The Video Resource Book contains the following:

- engaging **photocopiable worksheets** for students
- detailed **teaching notes** for teachers
- answer keys for the student worksheets
- complete video transcripts

TEACHING A TYPICAL VIDEO SEQUENCE

The **worksheets** and **teaching notes** for each video are organized into four sections: *Preview, Watch the video, Follow-up*, and *Language*

close-up. The unit-by-unit teaching notes in the Video Resource Book give detailed suggestions for teaching each unit.

Preview

The *Preview* activities build on each other to provide students with relevant background information and key vocabulary that will assist them in better understanding the video. This section typically includes the following elements.

- **Culture**: activities to introduce the topics of the video sequences and provide important background and cultural information
- **Vocabulary**: activities to introduce and practice the essential vocabulary of the videos through a variety of interesting tasks
- **Guess the facts / Guess the story**: activities in which students make predictions about characters and their actions by watching part of the video, by watching all of the video with the sound off, or by looking at photos in the worksheets. These schema-building activities improve students' comprehension when they watch the full video with sound.

Watch the video

The carefully sequenced Watch the video activities first help students focus on gist and then guide them in identifying important details and language. These tasks also prepare them for *Follow-up* speaking activities.

- **Get the picture:** initial viewing activities first help students gain a global understanding of the videos by focusing on gist. Activity types vary from unit to unit, but typically involve watching for key information needed to complete a chart, answer questions, or arrange events in sequential order.

- **Watch for details**: activities in which students focus on more detailed meaning by watching and listening for specific information to complete the tasks
- **What's your opinion?**: activities in which students make inferences about the characters' actions, feelings, and motivations, or state their own opinions about topics in the video

Follow-up

The *Follow-up* speaking activities encourage students to extend and personalize information by voicing their opinions or carrying out communicative tasks.

- **Role play, interview, and other expansion activities**: communicative activities based on the videos in which students extend and personalize what they have learned. Students can use new language to talk about themselves and their ideas as they complete the tasks.

Language close-up

Students finish with the *Language close-up*, examining and practicing the particular language structures and functions presented in the video.

- **What did they say?**: cloze activities that aim to develop bottom-up listening skills by having students focus on the specific language in the videos and then fill in missing words.
- **Grammar and functional activities**: activities which reflect the structural and functional focus of a particular unit as presented in the videos.

OPTIONS FOR THE CLASSROOM

Once teachers feel comfortable with the basic course procedures, they can try other classroom techniques for presenting and working with the videos. Here are several proven techniques.

Fast-forward viewing For activities in which students watch the video with the sound off, play the entire sequence on fast-forward and have students list all of the things they see. Nearly all of the activities designed to be completed with the sound off can be done in this manner.

Information gap Play approximately the first half of a video, and then have students work in pairs or groups to predict what will happen next. Play the rest of the sequence so that students can check their predictions.

Act it out All of the videos provide an excellent basis for role plays and drama activities. Select a short scene, and have students watch it several times. Then have pairs or groups act out the scene, staying as close as possible to the actions and expressions of the characters. Have pairs or groups act out their scenes in front of the class.

What are they saying? Have students watch a short segment of a video in which two people are talking, but without sound. Then have pairs use the context to predict what the people might be saying to each other. Have pairs write out sample dialogs and share their work with the class.

Freeze-frame Freeze a frame of a video and have students call out information about the scene: the objects they can see, what the people are doing, the time and place – whatever is appropriate to the scene or the learning situation.

Teacher Support Site overview

This website offers a variety of materials to assist with your teaching of the series. It includes practical articles, author video and audio casts on methodology, correlations, language summaries, overviews of supplementary materials, ideas for games and extra activities, as well as a number of downloadable worksheets for projects and extra practice of vocabulary, grammar, listening, writing, and speaking.

Author videocasts

Provide useful information on methodology and practical tips

Professor Jack C. Richards

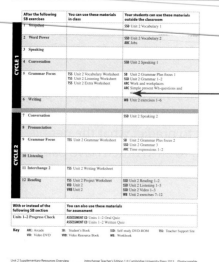

Unit 2 Supplementary Resources Overview

	After the following SB exercises	You can use these materials in class	Your students can use these materials outside the classroom
CYCLE 1	1 Snapshot		SSD Unit 2 Vocabulary 1
	2 Word Power		SSD Unit 2 Vocabulary 2 / ARC Jobs
	3 Speaking		
	4 Conversation		SSD Unit 2 Speaking 1
	5 Grammar Focus	TSS Unit 2 Vocabulary Worksheet / TSS Unit 2 Listening Worksheet / TSS Unit 2 Extra Worksheet	SB Unit 2 Grammar Plus focus 1 / SSD Unit 2 Grammar 1–2 / ARC Work and workplaces / ARC Simple present Wh-questions and statements
	6 Writing		WB Unit 2 exercises 1–6
CYCLE 2	7 Conversation		SSD Unit 2 Speaking 2
	8 Pronunciation		
	9 Grammar Focus	TSS Unit 2 Grammar Worksheet	SB Unit 2 Grammar Plus focus 2 / SSD Unit 2 Grammar 3 / ARC Time expressions 1–2
	10 Listening		
	11 Interchange 2	TSS Unit 2 Writing Worksheet	
	12 Reading	TSS Unit 2 Project Worksheet / VID Unit 2 / VRB Unit 2	SSD Unit 2 Reading 1–2 / SSD Unit 2 Listening 1–3 / SSD Unit 2 Video 1–3 / WB Unit 2 exercises 7–12

With or instead of the following SB section	You can also use these materials for assessment
Units 1–2 Progress Check	ASSESSMENT CD Units 1–2 Oral Quiz / ASSESSMENT CD Units 1–2 Written Quiz

Key ARC: Arcade SB: Student's Book SSD: Self-study DVD-ROM TSS: Teacher Support Site
VID: Video DVD VRB: Video Resource Book WB: Workbook

Unit 2 Supplementary Resources Overview   Interchange Teacher's Edition 1 © Cambridge University Press 2013 Photocopiable

Supplementary Resources Overviews

Indicate all the activities available in the various ancillary components that can be used after each exercise in the Student's Book units for extra practice, review, and assessment.

Downloadable worksheets

- Offer extra speaking opportunities
- Provide guidance for projects and extra practice of grammar, vocabulary, listening, and writing

1 THIS IS ME!

Plan

Get to know your classmates. Use these questions and your own questions.

What's your name?
What do people call you?
Where are you from?
What's your last name?
How do you spell it?
Other questions:

Prepare

Pair work Interview your partner. Then make a poster. Use magazines, pictures, and your own words to describe your partner.

Present

Class activity Introduce your partner to the class. Show your poster and explain why you chose the pictures and words.

© Cambridge University Press **Photocopiable**   *Projects: Unit 1* • 69

Classroom Presentation Software overview

Interchange Classroom Presentation Software combines the contents of the Student's Book, the class audio, and the video program for each level of the series into a convenient one-stop presentation solution. It can be used with all types of interactive whiteboards or with just a projector and a computer to present *Interchange* core materials in the classroom in a lively and engaging way.

The software provides an effective medium to focus students' attention on the content being presented and practiced. It can also help promote their participation and interaction with the material in a more dynamic way.

This component simplifies several of the teaching tasks that take place in the classroom. You can use the software to play audio or video without having to use a separate CD or DVD player, display the answers for the exercises in an uncomplicated way, zoom in on a page to more efficiently focus students' attention on an activity or image, and even annotate pages for future lessons.

Animated Presentations overview

The *Interchange Fourth Edition* Animated Presentations contain the digitally reproduced Student's Book pages in PowerPoint format, allowing teachers to display answers in the classroom using only a computer and a projector. Please contact your local Cambridge University Press representative for more details.

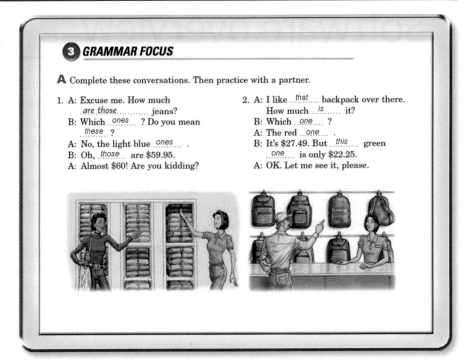

Placement Test Program overview

The *Interchange* and *Passages* Placement Test Program provides three versions of an Objective Placement Test with Listening, three versions of a Placement Essay Test, and Placement Speaking Assessment. An audio program, audio scripts, answer keys, and guidelines for administering the tests are included. Please contact your local Cambridge University Press representative for more details.

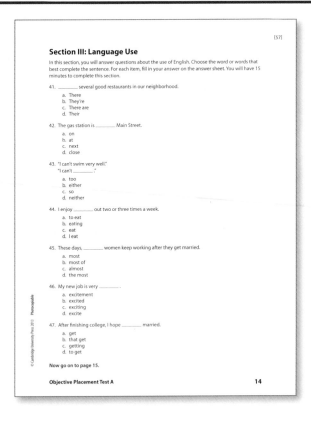

Introduction to the CEFR

Introduction to the Common European Framework of Reference (CEFR)

The overall aim of the Council of Europe's Common European Framework of Reference (CEFR) is to provide objective criteria for describing and assessing language proficiency in an internationally comparable manner. The Council of Europe's work on the definition of appropriate learning objectives for adult language learners dates back to the '70s. The influential Threshold series (J. A. van Ek and J. L. M. Trim, Cambridge University Press, 1991) provides a detailed description in functional, notional, grammatical, and sociocultural terms, of what a language user needs to be able to do in order to communicate effectively in the sort of situations commonly encountered in everyday life. Three levels of proficiency are identified, called Waystage, Threshold, and Vantage (roughly corresponding to Elementary, Intermediate, and Upper Intermediate).

The Threshold series was followed in 2001 by the publication of the Common European Framework of Reference, which describes six levels of communicative ability in terms of competences or "can do" statements: A1 (Breakthrough), A2 (Waystage), B1 (Threshold), B2 (Vantage), C1 (Effective Operational Proficiency), and C2 (Mastery). Based on the CEFR descriptors, the Council of Europe also developed the European Language Portfolio, a document that enables learners to assess their language ability and to keep an internationally recognized record of their language learning experience.

Interchange Fourth Edition and the Common European Framework of Reference

The table below shows how *Interchange Fourth Edition* correlates with the Council of Europe's levels and with some major international examinations.

	CEFR	Council of Europe	Cambridge ESOL	IELTS	TOEFL iBT	TOEIC
Interchange						
Level Intro	A1	Breakthrough				120+
Level 1	A2	Waystage				225+
Level 2						
Level 3	B1	Threshold	KET (Key English Test)	4.0–5.0	57–86	550+
			PET (Preliminary English Test)			
Passages						
Level 1	B2	Vantage	FCE (First Certificate in English)	5.5–6.5	87–109	785+
Level 2	C1	Effective Operational Efficiency	CAE (Certificate in Advanced English)	7.0–8.0	110–120	490+ (Listening) 445+ (Reading)

Sources: http://www.cambridgeesol.org/about/standards/cefr.html
http://www.ets.org/Media/Research/pdf/CEFR_Mapping_Study_Interim_Report.pdf
http://www.sprachenmarkt.de/fi leadmin/sprachenmarkt/ets_images/TOEIC_Can-do-table_CEFR_2008.pdf

Essential teaching tips

Classroom management

Error correction

- During controlled practice accuracy activities, correct students' wrong use of the target language right away, either by correcting the error yourself or, whenever possible, having the student identify and / or correct the error. This way, the focus is on accuracy, and students can internalize the correct forms, meaning, and use of the language.
- During oral fluency activities, go around the room and take notes on errors you hear. Do not interrupt students. Instead, take notes of their errors in the use of target language and write these errors on the board. Encourage students to correct them first. Be sure to point out and praise students for language used correctly as well.

Grouping students

It is good to have students work in a variety of settings: individually, in pairs, in groups and as a class. This creates a more student-centered environment and increases student talking time.

- The easiest and quickest way to put students in pairs is to have two students sitting close to one another work together. This is good for when students need to have a quick discussion or check answers.
- To ensure students don't always work with the same partner and / or for longer activities, pair students by name, e.g., Maria work with Javier.
- One way to put students in groups is to give them a number from 1 to 4, and then have all number 1s work together, all number 2s work together, and so forth.

Instructions

- Give short instructions and model the activity for the students.
- Check your instructions, but avoid asking, Do you understand? Instead ask concept questions such as, Are you going to speak or write when you do this activity?

Monitoring

- Make sure you go around the room and check that the students are doing the activity and offer help as necessary.
- Monitor closely during controlled practice, but don't make yourself too accessible during fluency activities; otherwise, students may rely on you to answer questions rather than focus on communicating their ideas to their partner or group.

Teaching lower-level students

- Teach the Classroom Language on page xxix and put useful language up in the classroom, so the students get used to using English.
- Don't rush. Make sure all the students have had enough time to practice the material.
- Do a lot of repetition and drilling of the new target language.
- Encourage students to practice and review target language by doing activities in the Workbook, and Self-study DVD-ROM.
- Elicit answers from your students and involve them in the learning process. Even though they are beginners, they may have a passive knowledge of English. Find out what they already know by asking them questions.
- Use the optional activities within the Teaching Notes and the Supplementary Resources Overview charts at the beginning of each unit in this Teacher's Edition to add variety to your lessons.

Teaching reading and listening

- Reading and Listening texts are meant to help the students become better readers / listeners, not to test them. Explain to your students why they need to read or listen to a text several times.
- Adapt the reading speed to the purpose of the reading. When the students read for gist, encourage them to read quickly. When students read for detail, give them more time.

CLASSROOM LANGUAGE *Student questions*

Unit 1 Supplementary Resources Overview

	After the following SB exercises	You can use these materials in class	Your students can use these materials outside the classroom
CYCLE 1	1 Conversation		**SSD** Unit 1 Speaking 1 **WB** Unit 1 exercise 1
	2 Speaking		
	3 Conversation	**TSS** Unit 1 Extra Worksheet	**SSD** Unit 1 Speaking 2
	4 Pronunciation		
	5 Grammar Focus	**TSS** Unit 1 Vocabulary Worksheet	**SB** Unit 1 Grammar Plus focus 1 **SSD** Unit 1 Grammar 1–2 **ARC** Statements with *be*; possessive adjectives **ARC** Pronouns and contractions **ARC** Wh-questions with *be* **WB** Unit 1 exercises 2–6
CYCLE 2	6 Snapshot		
	7 Conversation		**SSD** Unit 1 Speaking 3
	8 Grammar Focus	**TSS** Unit 1 Grammar Worksheet **TSS** Unit 1 Listening Worksheet	**SB** Unit 1 Grammar Plus focus 2 **SSD** Unit 1 Grammar 3 **ARC** Yes/No questions and short answers with *be*
	9 Word Power		**SSD** Unit 1 Vocabulary 1–2 **ARC** Hello and good-bye
	10 Listening		
	11 Interchange 1	**TSS** Unit 1 Writing Worksheet	
	12 Reading	**TSS** Unit 1 Project Worksheet **VID** Unit 1 **VRB** Unit 1	**SSD** Unit 1 Reading 1–2 **SSD** Unit 1 Listening 1–3 **SSD** Unit 1 Video 1–3 **WB** Unit 1 exercises 7–12

Key **ARC**: Arcade **SB**: Student's Book **SSD**: Self-study DVD-ROM **TSS**: Teacher Support Site
VID: Video DVD **VRB**: Video Resource Book **WB**: Workbook

My Plan for Unit 1

Use the space below to customize a plan that fits your needs.

With the following SB exercises	I am using these materials in class	My students are using these materials outside the classroom

With or instead of the following SB section	I am using these materials for assessment

1 Please call me Beth.

CONVERSATION *Where are you from?*

▶ Listen and practice.

David: Hello, I'm David Garza. I'm a new club member.

Beth: Hi. My name is Elizabeth Silva, but please call me Beth.

David: OK. Where are you from, Beth?

Beth: Brazil. How about you?

David: I'm from Mexico.

Beth: Oh, I love Mexico! It's really beautiful.

Beth: Oh, good. Sun-hee is here.

David: Who's Sun-hee?

Beth: She's my classmate. We're in the same math class.

David: Where's she from?

Beth: South Korea. Let's go and say hello. Sorry, what's your last name again? Garcia?

David: Actually, it's Garza.

Beth: How do you spell that?

David: G-A-R-Z-A.

2 **SPEAKING** *Checking information*

A ▶ Match the questions with the responses. Listen and check. Then practice with a partner. Give your own information.

1. I'm sorry. What's your name again? ....   a. S-I-L-V-A.
2. What do people call you? ....   b. It's Elizabeth Silva.
3. How do you spell your last name? ....   c. Everyone calls me Beth.

B **GROUP WORK** Introduce yourself with your full name. Use the expressions in part A. Make a list of names for your group.

A: Hi! I'm Yuriko Noguchi.
B: I'm sorry. What's your last name again? . . .

2

Please call me Beth.

Cycle 1, Exercises 1–5

> In Unit 1, students discuss personal information. In Cycle 1, they introduce themselves and others using *be* and possessive adjectives. In Cycle 2, they talk about themselves using yes/no questions and short answers with *be*.

1 CONVERSATION

Learning Objectives: *practice a conversation between two people who just met; see statements with* be *and possessive adjectives in context*

TIP To learn your Ss' names, have them make name cards. Each S folds a piece of paper in thirds and writes his or her name on one side. Then they place the name cards on their desks.

Beth

▶ **[CD 1, Track 1]**

- Focus Ss' attention on the picture. Ask: "Where are the people? Who are they? How old are they?" Encourage Ss to make guesses.
- Set the scene. David is a new member of a club for international students. He's meeting Beth for the first time.
- Books closed. Write these questions on the board:
  1. Where is Beth from?
  2. Where is David from?
- Play the first part of the audio program. Elicit Ss' answers. (Answers: 1. Brazil 2. Mexico)

- Write this on the board for the next task:

  First name   Last name
  Beth
  David
- Play the first part of the audio program again. Ss listen to find out Beth's and David's last names. Then elicit the answers and write them on the board. (Answers: Silva, Garza)
- Books open. Play the first part of the audio program again. Ss listen and read silently.
- Ss stand up and practice the conversation in pairs. Go around the class and give help as needed.
- **Option:** Ss use their own information to practice the first part of the conversation. Before they start, ask Ss to underline the names and countries, so they know what information to substitute.
- Ask: "Where is Sun-hee from?" Play the rest of the audio program and elicit the answer. (Answer: South Korea)
- Ss practice the conversation in pairs.

2 SPEAKING

Learning Objectives: *introduce oneself; check information about other people*

A ▶ [CD 1, Track 2]

- Explain that sometimes people misunderstand information, so it's important to ask polite questions to check information.
- Have Ss match the questions and responses individually or in pairs. Then play the audio program. Ss listen and check their answers.

Answers

1. b   2. c   3. a

- Play the audio program again. Focus Ss' attention on the intonation of the questions.
- Tell Ss to ask you the questions. Respond with information about yourself. Then Ss use their own information to ask and answer the questions in pairs.
- **Option:** Review the letters of the alphabet.

B Group work

- Model the task with a few Ss. Ask them their names. Then check the information before writing it on the board.
- Ss complete the task in small groups.

3 CONVERSATION

Learning Objectives: *practice a conversation between three people who just met; see statements with* be *in context*

A *[CD 1, Track 3]*

- Books closed. Set the scene. Beth is introducing Sun-hee to David. Ask: "What is Sun-hee's last name?" Play the audio program and elicit the answer. (Answer: Park)
- Books open. Focus Ss' attention on the Conversation title. Elicit or explain the meaning of *What's . . . like?* Ask the class: "Where is David from? What's it like?" Ss check answers in the Conversation on page 2. (Answers: Mexico, beautiful)
- Play the audio program again. Ss listen and read the conversation silently. Then they practice it.

❗ For a new way to practice this Conversation, try *Look Up and Speak!* – download it from the website.

B *[CD 1, Track 4]*

- Elicit names of cities in Mexico (e.g., *Mexico City, Acapulco*). Then read the two focus questions.
- Play the audio program. Ss listen to find the answers to the questions. Elicit the answers.

> **AudioScript**

Sun-hee So David, where are *you* from?
David I'm from Mexico.
Sun-hee Really? What city?
David Mexico City.
Sun-hee Wow! What's it like there?
David Well, it's a big city, and very busy, but I like it a lot.

> **Answers**

David is from Mexico City. It's big and very busy.

4 PRONUNCIATION

Learning Objective: *learn to sound natural by linking words*

 [CD 1, Track 5]

- Explain that some English words sound unnatural when pronounced separately. Therefore, native speakers usually link these words.

- Play the audio program. Point out the linked sounds. Ask Ss to practice the sentences.
- **Option:** Play the audio program for the Conversation on page 3 again. Then tell Ss to practice linking sounds in selected sentences (e.g., *This is David.*).

5 GRAMMAR FOCUS

Learning Objectives: *practice statements with* be, *contractions of* be, *and possessive adjectives; ask and answer questions with* be

 [CD 1, Track 6]

Statements with be *and contractions of* be

- Introduce yourself ("I'm . . ."). Explain that it's common to use contractions (e.g., *I'm*) when speaking. Tell Ss to go around the room and introduce themselves.
- Go over the contractions in the Grammar Focus box. Close your thumb and first finger to show how the pronouns + *be* become contractions. For example, your thumb (*you*) and first finger (*are*) contract to become *you're*.

Possessive adjectives

- Explain the difference between subject pronouns and possessive adjectives by writing this on the board:

  I am David.   My name is David.

  You are Beth.   Your name is Beth.

- Play the audio program for the first Grammar Focus box.

🎲 For more practice with possessive adjectives, try the *Chain Game* – download it from the website.

A

- Ss complete the sentences individually or in pairs. Go over answers with the class.

> **Answers**

1. **My** name is Mariko Kimura. **I'm** from Japan. **My** family is in Osaka. **My** brother is a university student. **His** name is Kenji.
2. **My** name is Antonio. **I'm** from Buenos Aires. **It's** a really nice city. **My** sister is a student here, too. **Our** parents are in Argentina right now.
3. **I'm** Katherine, but everyone calls me Katie. **My** last name is Martin. **I'm** a student at City College. **My** parents are on vacation this week. **They're** in Los Angeles.

3 CONVERSATION *What's Seoul like?*

A Listen and practice.

Beth: Sun-hee, this is David Garza. He's a new club member from Mexico.

Sun-hee: Nice to meet you, David. I'm Sun-hee Park.

David: Hi. So, you're from South Korea?

Sun-hee: That's right. I'm from Seoul.

David: That's cool. What's Seoul like?

Sun-hee: It's really nice. It's a very exciting city.

B Listen to the rest of the conversation. What city is David from? What's it like?

4 PRONUNCIATION *Linked sounds*

Listen and practice. Notice how final consonant sounds are often linked to the vowels that follow them.

I'm a new club member.   Sun-hee is over there.   My name is Elizabeth Silva.

5 GRAMMAR FOCUS

Statements with be; possessive adjectives

Statements with be	Contractions of be	Possessive adjectives
I**'m** from Mexico.	I**'m** = I am	my
You**'re** from Brazil.	you**'re** = you are	your
He**'s** from Japan.	he**'s** = he is	his
She**'s** a new club member.	she**'s** = she is	her
It**'s** an exciting city.	it**'s** = it is	its
We**'re** in the same class.	we**'re** = we are	our
They**'re** my classmates.	they**'re** = they are	their

A Complete these sentences. Then tell a partner about yourself.

1. ...My... name is Mariko Kimura. .... from Japan. .... family is in Osaka. .... brother is a university student. .... name is Kenji.

2. .... name is Antonio. .... from Buenos Aires. .... a really nice city. .... sister is a student here, too. .... parents are in Argentina right now.

3. .... Katherine, but everyone calls me Katie. .... last name is Martin. .... a student at City College. .... parents are on vacation this week. .... in Los Angeles.

B Complete these questions. Then practice with a partner.

1. A: ...._Who's_........ that?
   B: Oh, that's Miss West.

2. A: .... she from?
   B: She's from Miami.

3. A: .... her first name?
   B: It's Celia.

4. A: .... the two students over there?
   B: Their names are Jeremy and Karen.

5. A: .... they from?
   B: They're from Vancouver, Canada.

6. A: .... they .... ?
   B: They're shy, but very friendly.

C GROUP WORK Write five questions about your classmates. Then ask and answer the questions.

> What's your last name?
> Where's Ming from?

6 SNAPSHOT

GREETINGS from around the world

- a handshake — the United States
- a kiss on the cheek
- a bow
- a hug
- a pat on the back
- a fist bump

Sources: www.familyeducation.com; www.time.com

Which greetings are typical in your country?
Can you write the name of a country for each greeting?
What are other ways to greet people?

[CD 1, Track 7]

Wh-questions with **be**

- Write these questions and answers on the board:

Questions	Answers
Where's your friend?	She's my classmate.
Who's Sun-hee?	It's a very exciting
What's Seoul like?	city.
Where are you and	He's in class.
Luisa from?	They're really nice.
How are your classes?	We're from Brazil.
What are your classmates	They're pretty
like?	interesting.

Books closed. Ask Ss to match the questions and answers on the board.

- Books open. Ss check answers with the Grammar Focus box. Answer any questions.
- Play the audio program.
- **Option:** Divide the class into two groups. Group A asks the questions and Group B answers. Then change roles.

B
- Ss complete the questions individually. Go over answers with the class.

Answers

1. **Who is/Who's** that?
2. **Where is/Where's** she from?
3. **What is/What's** her first name?
4. **Who are** the two students over there?
5. **Where are** they from?
6. **What are** they **like**?

- Explain the task. Ss practice the conversations in

Cycle 2, Exercises 6–12

6 SNAPSHOT

Learning Objective: learn about greetings used around the world

- Go around the class, shake Ss' hands, and say "hello" or "hi."
- Focus Ss' attention on the pictures. Point out that a handshake is a common way to greet people in the U.S. and Canada. Read the first question: "Which greetings are typical in your country?" If Ss are from different countries, ask them to demonstrate how they greet people.
- Go over the second and third questions. Ss answer them in pairs or small groups.

pairs. Model the task with a strong S and then with another S.
- Ss complete the task in pairs.

C Group work

- Explain the task. Elicit possible Wh-questions.
- **Option:** Ss look at the Conversations on pages 2 and 3 for examples of Wh-questions with *be*. (Answers: Where are you from? Who's Sun-hee? Where's she from? What's your last name again? What's Seoul like?)
- Ss write five Wh-questions individually. Go around the class and give help as needed.
- Ss work in small groups. They take turns asking and answering their questions.
- Go around the class and write down any errors. Then write the questions or answers with errors on the board. Ss correct the errors as a class.

End of Cycle 1

See the Supplementary Resources chart at the beginning of this unit for additional teaching materials and student activities related to this Cycle.

Possible answers

a handshake: the United States, Canada, Peru
a kiss on the cheek: Brazil, France, Venezuela
a bow: Korea, Japan, Indonesia
a hug: the United States, Denmark, Egypt
a pat on the back: Greece, Russia, Mexico
a fist bump: the United States, Canada

TIP To encourage Ss to use the Classroom Language on page v of the Student's Book, write the expressions on cards. Then put the cards on the walls.

7 CONVERSATION

Learning Objectives: *practice a conversation between two people who know each other; see yes/no questions and short answers with* be *in context*

 [CD 1, Track 8]

- Introduce the Conversation title. Ask: "How's it going?" Help Ss with responses (e.g., *fine, not bad*).
- Set the scene. A few days after the International Club party, Sun-hee sees David and starts a conversation.
- Write these questions on the board:

  1. Are David's classes interesting this semester?
  2. Are David and Beth in the same chemistry class?
  3. Is Sun-hee on her way to class?
  4. Is Sun-hee free?

8 GRAMMAR FOCUS

Learning Objective: *practice yes/no questions and short answers with* be

 [CD 1, Track 9]

Yes/No questions

- Write several statements with *be* about David and Sun-hee or your own Ss on the board. For example:

  David is a student.

  Julia and Elena are sisters.

- Focus Ss' attention on the statements. Point out that statements begin with a subject + verb.

  David <u>is</u> a student.
    S V

  <u>Julia and Elena</u> <u>are</u> sisters.
       S   V

- **Option:** If you don't want to teach the terms *subject* and *verb*, use the numbers 1 and 2 instead.

- Explain that yes/no questions begin with a verb + subject. For example:

  <u>Is</u> <u>David</u> a student?
  V   S

  <u>Are</u> <u>Julia and Elena</u> sisters?
   V   S

- Ask Ss to change any remaining statements on the board to yes/no questions. Give help as needed.
- Ss study the Grammar Focus box questions.

Short answers with be

- Present the short answers in the Grammar Focus box. Point out that there are two ways of saying "no" for each pronoun, except for *I*.

- Elicit or explain any new vocabulary.

- Books closed. Play the audio program twice. Elicit answers to the questions on the board. (Answers: 1. yes 2. no 3. no 4. yes)
- Books open. Play the audio program again. Ss look at the picture and read the conversation silently.
- Ss stand up and practice the conversation in pairs.

- Ask yes/no questions with *be* about Ss in the class. Ss respond with short answers.
- Play the audio program. Focus Ss' attention on the stress in short answers (e.g., *Yes, I am. No, I'm not.*).

A

- Ss complete the conversations individually. Go over answers with the class.

Answers

1. A: **Is** Ms. Gray from the United States?
   B: Yes, she **is. She's** from Chicago.
2. A: **Is** English class at 10:00?
   B: No, **it isn't. It's** at 11:00.
3. A: **Are** you and Monique from France?
   B: Yes, we **are. We're** from Paris.
4. A: **Are** Mr. and Mrs. Tavares American?
   B: No, they **aren't. They're** Brazilian.

- Model the first conversation with a strong S and the second conversation with a different S. Then Ss practice the conversations in pairs.

B

- Explain the task. Ss write answers to the questions individually. Then they ask and answer the questions in pairs.

C Group work

- Model the task with the first question. Ss write questions individually. Then they ask their questions.
- **Option:** Ss write questions in small groups. Collect the questions and give them to different groups. Ss take turns asking and answering the questions.

7 CONVERSATION *How's it going?*

▶ Listen and practice.

Sun-hee: Hey, David. How's it going?
David: Fine, thanks. How are you?
Sun-hee: Pretty good. So, are your classes interesting this semester?
David: Yes, they are. I really love chemistry.
Sun-hee: Chemistry? Are you and Beth in the same class?
David: No, we aren't. My class is in the morning. Her class is in the afternoon.
Sun-hee: Listen, I'm on my way to the cafeteria now. Are you free?
David: Sure. Let's go.

8 GRAMMAR FOCUS

Yes/No questions and short answers with be ▶

Are you free?	Yes, I **am**.	No, I**'m not**.
Is David from Mexico?	Yes, he **is**.	No, he**'s not**./No, he **isn't**.
Is Beth's class in the morning?	Yes, it **is**.	No, it**'s not**./No, it **isn't**.
Are you and Beth in the same class?	Yes, we **are**.	No, we**'re not**./No, we **aren't**.
Are your classes interesting?	Yes, they **are**.	No, they**'re not**./No, they **aren't**.

A Complete these conversations. Then practice with a partner.

1. A: ___Is___ Ms. Gray from the United States?
   B: Yes, she .... from Chicago.

2. A: .... English class at 10:00?
   B: No, it .... at 11:00.

3. A: .... you and Monique from France?
   B: Yes, we .... from Paris.

4. A: .... Mr. and Mrs. Tavares American?
   B: No, they .... Brazilian.

B Answer these questions. If you answer "no," give the correct information. Then ask your partner the questions.

1. Are you from the United States? ....
2. Is your teacher from Canada? ....
3. Is your English class in the morning? ....
4. Are you and your best friend the same age? ....

C GROUP WORK Write five questions about your classmates. Then ask and answer the questions.

> Are Cindy and Brian from Los Angeles?

9 WORD POWER Hello and good-bye

A Do you know these expressions? Which ones are "hellos" and which ones are "good-byes"? Complete the chart. Add expressions of your own.

✓ Bye.
✓ Good morning.
  Good night.
  Have a good day.
  Hey.
  Hi.

How are you?
How's it going?
See you later.
See you tomorrow.
Talk to you later.
What's up?

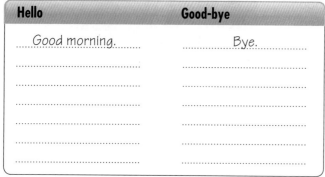

Hello	Good-bye
Good morning.	Bye.

B Match each expression with the best response.

1. Have a good day.
2. Hi. How are you?
3. What's up?
4. Good morning.

a. Oh, not much.
b. Thank you. You, too.
c. Good morning.
d. Pretty good, thanks.

C CLASS ACTIVITY Practice saying hello. Then practice saying good-bye.

A: Hi, Aki. How's it going?
B: Pretty good, thanks. How are you?

10 LISTENING What's your last name again?

 Listen to the conversations. Complete the information about each person.

	First name	Last name	Where from?
1.	Chris		
2.		Sanchez	
3.	Min-ho		

11 INTERCHANGE 1 Getting to know you

Find out about your classmates. Go to Interchange 1 on page 114.

9 WORD POWER

Learning Objective: *learn different ways to say hello and good-bye*

TIP To show Ss the purpose of an activity, write the learning objective on the board. At the end of the activity, point out what Ss have achieved.

A

- Explain the task. Ss write the expressions they know in the chart.
- Copy the chart from the Student's Book on the board.
- Go over each expression. Then elicit more expressions and have Ss write them in the chart on the board.

Answers

Hello	Good-bye
Good morning.	Bye.
Hey.	Good night.
Hi.	Have a good day.
How are you?	See you later.

How's it going?	See you tomorrow
What's up?	Talk to you later.
Good afternoon.	*See you.*
Good evening.	*Later.*

(Note: Additional expressions are italicized.)

B

- Model the first greeting and response with a few Ss.
- Ss match the greetings and responses.

Answers

1. b   2. d   3. a   4. c

C *Class activity*

- Model the conversation with a S.
- Ss stand up and go around the room to practice greeting their classmates using expressions from the *Hello* column in part A. Then they practice using expressions from the *Good-bye* column.

10 LISTENING

Learning Objective: *develop skills in listening for detail*

 **[CD 1, Track 10]**

- Explain the task and the information in the chart. Ask the class: "What is Chris' last name? What else do we need to find out about him?"
- Play the first conversation in the audio program. Ss listen to for Chris's last name and where he's from.
- Play the rest of the audio program. As Ss listen and complete the chart, draw the chart on the board.
- Elicit answers and have Ss write them in the chart on the board. Do not correct wrong answers.
- Play the audio program again. Stop after each conversation and discuss the answers on the board.

AudioScript

1.
Man Chris, this is my friend Lucy. We're in the same English class.
Chris Hi, Lucy. I'm Christopher Olsen. But everyone calls me Chris.
Lucy Nice to meet you, Chris. What's your last name again?
Chris It's Olsen. O-L-S-E-N.
Lucy And where are you from, Chris?

Chris I'm from here, the United States – originally from Los Angeles.
Lucy Wow! How do you like Los Angeles?
Chris Oh, I love it. It's my favorite city.
2.
Clerk OK, Ms. Sanchez. Let me just check this information. Is your first name spelled I-S-A-B-E-L?
Isabela No, it's not. My first name is Isabela. It's spelled I-S-A-B-E-L-A.
Clerk OK. Thanks. And you're from Argentina, right?
Isabela Um, no, I'm not from Argentina. I'm from Mexico.
Clerk Oh, sorry. Mexico. But you are studying English.
Isabela Actually, I'm not. I'm a business student.
Clerk Business. OK. Got it.
3.
Man Excuse me. Are you Hee-young Kim?
Hee-young Yes, I am.
Man Is your brother Min-ho Kim?
Hee-young Yes, he is.
Man Tell me, is Min-ho still here at the university?
Hee-young No, he's not. He's at home in South Korea.
Man Oh, he's in Korea. Is he in school there?
Hee-young Yeah. He's at Seoul University this semester.

Answers

First name	Last name	Where from?
Chris	Olsen	the United States
Isabela	Sanchez	Mexico
Min-ho	Kim	South Korea

11 INTERCHANGE 1

See page T-114 for teaching notes.

12 READING

> **TIP** Explain that in real life people read in different ways for different purposes. For example, they read manuals or recipes slowly and in detail, but they skim magazines or scan telephone books more quickly.

- Ask: "What English names do you like? Why?" Elicit answers.
- Focus Ss' attention on the title of the reading. Ask: "What do you think this article is about?" Elicit ideas.
- Ss scan the text quickly to find examples of names. Ask: "Do you know any people with these names? What are they like?"
- Point out that in the last paragraph *Georges* and *Bettys* are simply plurals of *George* and *Betty*. This refers to all people with those names.

A

- Explain the task. Read the statements.
- Ss read the article individually. Then they complete the task. Go over answers with the class.

Answers

True statements: 1, 2, 4, and 5.

B

- Elicit or explain any adjectives from the reading.

Vocabulary

average: like everybody else
creative: making or using new or unusual ideas
athletic: good at sports
nerdy: smart, but without good social skills
old-fashioned: having old ideas; not modern
independent: able to do things without help
adventurous: liking excitement and new things
plain: not very good-looking
ordinary: not special
intelligent: smart

- Explain the task. Give one or two examples.
- Ss complete the task individually. As Ss work, draw the chart on the board.
- Ask Ss who finish first to write their answers in the chart on the board. Then check answers as a class.

Answers

Positive names		Negative names	
Jacob	Michael	George	Stanley
Emma	Nicole	Betty	Jane

C Pair work

- Ss discuss the questions in pairs.
- **Option:** Each pair joins another pair to compare ideas.

For more practice with introductions and the alphabet, play **Line Up!** – download it from the website. Have Ss line up alphabetically according to first names.

End of Cycle 2

See the Supplementary Resources chart at the beginning of this unit for additional teaching materials and student activities related to this Cycle.

What's in a Name?

Look at the names in the article. Do you know any people with these names? What are they like?

Your name is very important. When you think of yourself, you probably think of your name first. It is an important part of your identity.

Right now, the two most popular names for babies in the United States are "Jacob" for boys and "Emma" for girls. Why are these names popular? And why are other names unpopular?

Names can become popular because of famous actors, TV or book characters, or athletes. Popular names suggest very positive things. Unpopular names suggest negative things. Surprisingly, people generally agree on the way they feel about names. Here are some common opinions about names from a recent survey.

HELLO
my name is

_ _ _ _ _ _ _ _ _ _ _ _

Boys' names

George: average, boring
Jacob: creative, friendly
Michael: good-looking, athletic
Stanley: nerdy, serious

Girls' names

Betty: old-fashioned, average
Emma: independent, adventurous
Jane: plain, ordinary
Nicole: beautiful, intelligent

So why do parents give their children unpopular names? One reason is tradition. Many people are named after a family member. Of course, opinions can change over time. A name that is unpopular now may become popular in the future. That's good news for all the Georges and Bettys out there!

A Read the article. Then check (✓) the statements that are true.

1. Your name is part of your identity.
2. People often feel the same way about a particular name.
3. Boys' names are more popular than girls' names.
4. People are often named after family members.
5. Opinions about names can change.

B According to the article, which names suggest positive things? Which suggest negative things? Complete the chart.

Positive names		Negative names	
....	....	....	....
....	....	....	....

C **PAIR WORK** What names are popular in your country? Why are they popular?

Unit 2 Supplementary Resources Overview

After the following SB exercises	You can use these materials in class	Your students can use these materials outside the classroom
CYCLE 1		
1 Snapshot		**SSD** Unit 2 Vocabulary 1
2 Word Power		**SSD** Unit 2 Vocabulary 2 **ARC** Jobs
3 Speaking		
4 Conversation		**SSD** Unit 2 Speaking 1
5 Grammar Focus	**TSS** Unit 2 Vocabulary Worksheet **TSS** Unit 2 Listening Worksheet **TSS** Unit 2 Extra Worksheet	**SB** Unit 2 Grammar Plus focus 1 **SSD** Unit 2 Grammar 1–2 **ARC** Work and workplaces **ARC** Simple present Wh-questions and statements
6 Writing		**WB** Unit 2 exercises 1–6
CYCLE 2		
7 Conversation		**SSD** Unit 2 Speaking 2
8 Pronunciation		
9 Grammar Focus	**TSS** Unit 2 Grammar Worksheet	**SB** Unit 2 Grammar Plus focus 2 **SSD** Unit 2 Grammar 3 **ARC** Time expressions 1–2
10 Listening		
11 Interchange 2	**TSS** Unit 2 Writing Worksheet	
12 Reading	**TSS** Unit 2 Project Worksheet **VID** Unit 2 **VRB** Unit 2	**SSD** Unit 2 Reading 1–2 **SSD** Unit 2 Listening 1–3 **SSD** Unit 2 Video 1–3 **WB** Unit 2 exercises 7–12

With or instead of the following SB section	You can also use these materials for assessment
Units 1–2 Progress Check	**ASSESSMENT CD** Units 1–2 Oral Quiz **ASSESSMENT CD** Units 1–2 Written Quiz

Key   **ARC**: Arcade   **SB**: Student's Book   **SSD**: Self-study DVD-ROM   **TSS:** Teacher Support Site
         VID: Video DVD   **VRB:** Video Resource Book   **WB:** Workbook

My Plan for Unit 2

Use the space below to customize a plan that fits your needs.

With the following SB exercises	I am using these materials in class	My students are using these materials outside the classroom

With or instead of the following SB section	I am using these materials for assessment

2 What do you do?

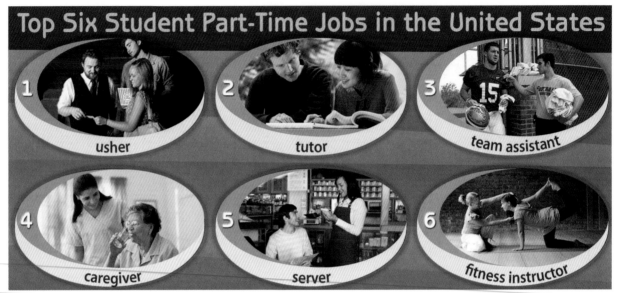

Top Six Student Part-Time Jobs in the United States

1 usher
2 tutor
3 team assistant
4 caregiver
5 server
6 fitness instructor

Source: www.snagajob.com

Which jobs are easy? Which are difficult? Why?
What's your opinion? Are these good jobs for students?
What are some other student jobs?

2 WORD POWER

A Complete the word map with jobs from the list.

✓ accountant
✓ cashier
  chef
✓ dancer
✓ flight attendant
  musician
  pilot
  receptionist
  server
  singer
  tour guide
  website designer

Office work
accountant

Food service
cashier

Jobs

Travel industry
flight attendant

Entertainment business
dancer

B Add two more jobs to each category. Then compare with a partner.

8

What do you do?

> In Unit 2, students discuss work and school. In Cycle 1, they ask and answer questions about different types of jobs using the simple present. In Cycle 2, they talk about routines and daily schedules using time expressions.

1 SNAPSHOT

Learning Objective: *talk about part-time jobs*

- Books closed. Introduce the topic of jobs. Ask: "Do you have a job? What is it? Do your parents have jobs? What do they do?"
- List three jobs from the Snapshot on the board. Ss give their opinion on the best job. (Answers will vary.)
- Books open. Ss compare their ideas with the Snapshot.
- Elicit or explain any new vocabulary

Vocabulary

part-time job: a job for only a few hours or days a week
usher: a person who takes tickets and helps people to their seats
tutor: a person who teaches private lessons
team assistant: a person who provides support to a team
caregiver: a person who cares for someone who is sick or disabled
server: a person who serves food
fitness instructor: a person who leads exercise classes

- Explain the task. Encourage Ss to give reasons for their opinions.
- Ss complete the task in small groups. Go around the class and give help as needed.

2 WORD POWER

Learning Objectives: *learn vocabulary for different jobs; learn ways to categorize jobs*

A

- Ask Ss to look through the vocabulary list. Elicit or explain any new words. Model the pronunciation of new words.

> **TIP** If you don't have enough time to explain new words in class, ask Ss to look them up in a dictionary before class.

- Ss complete the word map individually or in pairs.
- While Ss are working, draw the word map on the board. Ask different Ss to come up and write their answers in the correct category. Go over answers with the class.

> **TIP** To provide variety, check answers in different ways. For example, write each answer on a separate card. Ss post the cards on the board in the correct category.

B

- Present and model the task. Ss write two more jobs for each category. Then they compare with a partner.
- Ask different Ss to add their ideas to the board. Go over answers with the class.

Answers

Office work	Food service
accountant	cashier
receptionist	chef
website designer	server
secretary	*dishwasher*
sales manager	*host/hostess*

Travel industry	Entertainment business
flight attendant	dancer
pilot	musician
tour guide	singer
travel agent	*actor/actress*
hotel manager	*disc jockey*

(Note: Additional examples are italicized.)

To review jobs, play the game *Simon Says* – download it from the website. For example, if Simon says "Be a singer," Ss act out the job.

3 SPEAKING

Learning Objective: *talk about jobs and workplaces*

A

- Brainstorm workplaces with the class. Write ideas on the board.
- Ss look at the pictures and describe each person's job (e.g., She's a *salesperson*.). If Ss have difficulty, focus their attention on column A.
- **Option:** Ss test each other in pairs. To model, ask: "What's number 1?"
- Explain the task. Ss match the information in columns A, B, and C. Point out that column A lists jobs, column B lists things people do in their jobs, and column C lists prepositional phrases with workplaces. Read the example.
- Ss complete the task individually or in pairs.
- Go around the class and give help as needed.
- Write the first answer on the board. Then ask different Ss to write answers on the board. Go over the answers as a class.

B *Pair work*

- Write these words on the board:

  She's   She   She works

  He's   He   He works

- Read the description of a salesperson's job aloud. Then ask a S to describe a chef's job using the words on the board.
- Ss complete the task in pairs. Go around the class and give help as needed.

Answers

She's a salesperson. She sells clothes. She works in a department store.
He's a chef. He cooks food. He works in a restaurant.
He's a mechanic. He fixes cars. He works in a garage.
He's a carpenter. He builds houses. He works for a construction company.
He's a reporter. He writes stories. He works for a newspaper.
She's a nurse. She cares for patients. She works in a hospital.

4 CONVERSATION

Learning Objectives: *practice a conversation about jobs; see simple present Wh-questions and statements in context*

A [CD 1, Track 11]

- Set the scene. Jason and Andrea are talking about their jobs. Tell Ss to cover the text. Focus their attention on the pictures. Ask: "Who is Jason? What does he do? Who is Andrea? What does she do?" Encourage Ss to guess.

> **TIP** Give Ss (or ask Ss to bring) small cards to cover the text. That way, they can see the picture but not the text. Ask Ss to keep their cards for future classes.

- Play the audio program. Ss listen to check their guesses.
- Write these focus questions on the board:

  True or false?

  1. Andrea loves her job.
  2. Andrea takes people on tours to Asia.
  3. Jason has a full-time job.

- Books closed (or text covered). Play the audio program again. Then check answers to the focus questions. (Answers: 1. true 2. false 3. false)
- Books open (or uncover the text). Play the conversation line by line, giving Ss time to repeat it.
- Ss practice the conversation in pairs.

❗ For a new way to practice this Conversation, try the **Substitution Dialog** – download it from the website. Have Ss replace the underlined words:

A: What do you do, Andrea?

B: I'm a guide. I take people on tours. And what do you do, Jason?

A: I'm a cashier. I work in a restaurant.

B ▶ [CD 1, Track 12]

- Read the two focus questions aloud. Then play the second part of the audio program. Elicit answers from the class.

AudioScript

Andrea What do you do, exactly? Do you make hamburgers?
Jason No, I don't. I'm a cashier. I just take orders.
Andrea And what's it like there? Do you like your job?
Jason Sure. It's fun. And I get free hamburgers, too!

Answers

He takes orders. He likes his job because it's fun. He gets free hamburgers, too.

3 SPEAKING Work and workplaces

A Look at the pictures. Match the information in columns A, B, and C.

A	B	C
a salesperson	builds houses	in a restaurant
a chef	cares for patients	for a construction company
a mechanic	writes stories	in a hospital
a carpenter	cooks food	in a garage
a reporter	fixes cars	in a department store
a nurse	sells clothes	for a newspaper

B **PAIR WORK** Take turns describing each person's job.

A: She's a salesperson. She sells clothes. She works in a department store.
B: And he's a chef. He . . .

4 CONVERSATION Where do you work?

A ▶ Listen and practice.

Jason: Where do you work, Andrea?
Andrea: I work at Thomas Cook Travel.
Jason: Oh, really? What do you do there?
Andrea: I'm a guide. I take people on tours to countries in South America, like Peru.
Jason: How interesting!
Andrea: Yeah, it's a great job. I really love it. And what do you do?
Jason: Oh, I'm a student. I have a part-time job, too.
Andrea: Where do you work?
Jason: In a fast-food restaurant.
Andrea: Which restaurant?
Jason: Hamburger Heaven.

B ▶ Listen to the rest of the conversation. What does Jason do, exactly? How does he like his job?

5 GRAMMAR FOCUS

Simple present Wh-questions and statements ⊙

What do you **do**?	I'**m** a student. I **have** a part-time job, too.
Where do you **work**?	I **work** at Hamburger Heaven.
Where do you **go** to school?	I **go** to the University of Texas.
What does Andrea **do**?	She's a guide. She **takes** people on tours.
Where does she **work**?	She **works** at Thomas Cook Travel.
How does she **like** it?	She **loves** it.

I/You	He/She
work	works
take	takes
study	studies
teach	teaches
do	does
go	goes
have	has

A Complete these conversations. Then practice with a partner.

1. A: What ....*do*.... you ....*do*.... ?
   B: I'm a full-time student. I study the violin.
   A: And .... do you .... to school?
   B: I .... to the New York School of Music.
   A: Wow! .... do you like your classes?
   B: I .... them a lot.

2. A: What .... Tanya do?
   B: She's a teacher. She .... an art class
      at a school in Denver.
   A: And what about Ryan? Where .... he work?
   B: He .... for a big computer company in
      San Francisco.
   A: .... does he do, exactly?
   B: He's a website designer. He .... fantastic
      websites.

B **PAIR WORK** What do you know about these jobs?
Complete the chart. Then write sentences about each job.

A reporter	A flight attendant	A teacher
works for a newspaper	....	....
interviews people	....	....
writes stories	....	....

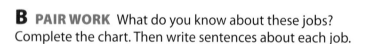

A reporter works for a newspaper, interviews people, and writes stories.

C **PAIR WORK** Ask your partner questions like these about work
and school. Take notes to use in Exercise 6.

What do you do?	Do you go to school?	How do you like . . . ?
Where do you live?	Do you have a job?	What's your favorite . . . ?

5 GRAMMAR FOCUS

Learning Objective: *practice simple present Wh-questions and statements*

▶ *[CD 1, Track 13]*

Simple present statements

- Books closed. Write these sentences on the board, allowing space between lines:

  I'm a guide.
  I work at Thomas Cook Travel.
  I take people on tours.
  I love my job.

- Books open. **Ask:** "Who said this?" (Answer: Andrea) Ask Ss to describe her job. Write the new version below the original:

  She's a guide.
  She works at Thomas Cook Travel.
  She takes people on tours.
  She loves her job.

- Point out that the verbs for *he, she,* and *it* end in *-s.*

- **Option:** Repeat the activity with sentences about Jason.

> **TIP** Write the letter *s* on a card. Every time Ss forget to use the final *-s,* hold up the card. Write the word *does* on a separate card for the same purpose.

- Focus Ss' attention on the third column in the Grammar Focus box. Point out the spelling changes that occur with *he/she.*

Simple present Wh-questions

- Draw a chart with five columns on the board. Number the columns from 1 to 5.

- Focus Ss' attention on the Conversation on page 9. Ask Ss to find two questions with the word *do* in part A. Then read the two questions about Jason in part B. Write them in the chart:

1	2	3	4	5
Where	do	you	work,	Andrea?
What	do	you	do	there?
What	does	Jason	do,	exactly?
How	does	he	like	his job?

- Focus Ss' attention on the questions in the chart and in the Grammar Focus box. Elicit the rule for forming Wh-questions in the simple present:
  Wh- + *do/does* + subject + verb

- Ask Ss the questions in the Grammar Focus box. Ss use their own information for the first three questions.

- Play the audio program. Ss listen and repeat.

A

- Ss complete the task individually. Then they compare answers with a partner.

> **TIP** To build Ss' confidence, have them compare answers in pairs or groups before you check answers as a class.

- Go over answers with the class. Then Ss practice the conversations in pairs.

Answers

1. A: What **do** you **do**?
   B: I'm a full-time student. I study the violin.
   A: And **where** do you **go** to school?
   B: I **go** to the New York School of Music.
   A: Wow! **How** do you like your classes?
   B: I **like** them a lot.
2. A: What **does** Tanya do?
   B: She's a teacher. She **teaches** an art class at a school in Denver.
   A: And what about Ryan? Where **does** he work?
   B: He **works** for a big computer company in San Francisco.
   A: **What** does he do, exactly?
   B: He's a website designer. He **designs** fantastic websites.

B *Pair work*

- Explain the task. While Ss complete the task in pairs, copy the chart on the board.

- Ask different Ss to write their answers in the chart on the board.

Possible answers

A reporter	A flight attendant	A teacher
works for a newspaper	works for an airline	works in a school
interviews people	assists passengers	teaches classes
writes stories	serves drinks	helps students

C *Pair work*

- Model the task. Ask a S a few of the questions, and take notes on the board.

- Ss complete the task in pairs. Go around the class and check for use of the simple present.

6 WRITING

Learning Objective: *write a biography using the simple present*

A

- Tell Ss to read the model biography silently. Explain any new vocabulary. Point out that the biography does not have the person's name.
- Ss write their biographies. Go around the class and give help as needed.
- **Option:** Ss write the biographies for homework.

Cycle 2, Exercises 7–12

7 CONVERSATION

Learning Objectives: *practice a conversation about daily schedules; see time expressions in context*

A ▶ *[CD 1, Track 14]*

- Point out the title and the picture. Ask: "What is this conversation about?" Elicit ideas.
- Books closed (or text covered). Ask: "What does Allie do?" Play the audio program. Ss listen for the answer. (Answer: She's a chef.)
- Write these questions on the board:

  1. What time does Allie get home at night?
  2. Where does she work?

- Play the audio program again. Ss listen for the answers. (Answers: 1. at midnight 2. at the Pink Elephant)
- Books open. Play the audio program again. Ss read the conversation silently. Then they practice in pairs.
- **Option:** To review the simple present, ask Ss to describe Allie's daily routine from memory.

8 PRONUNCIATION

Learning Objective: *notice and use correct syllable stress*

A ▶ *[CD 1, Track 16]*

- Explain that some syllables have more stress. Read the examples, clapping on the stressed syllable.
- Play the audio program. Ss clap on stressed syllables.

B *Class activity*

- Collect the biographies and number them. Then pass them around the class. Ss make a numbered list and write their guesses next to each number.
- Elicit Ss' guesses about each biography.

End of Cycle 1

See the Supplementary Resources chart at the beginning of this unit for additional teaching materials and student activities related to this Cycle.

B ▶ *[CD 1, Track 15]*

- Read the two focus questions.
- Play the audio program. Elicit answers from the class.

AudioScript

Allie And what about you, Kevin? What's your day like?
Kevin Well, right now I'm in school, so I just have a part-time job. But I'm pretty busy. I get up at 6:00 on weekdays. I have class from 7:00 to 9:00, and then I come here to the gym. I work from 11:00 to 2:00. Then I have classes in the afternoon.
Allie So where do you work?
Kevin At the Hungry Student restaurant, near the university. I'm a dishwasher.
Allie Really? Say, do you want to work at the Pink Elephant?

Answers

Kevin gets up around 6:00. He starts work at 11:00.

B ▶ *[CD 1, Track 17]*

- Ss complete the chart individually.
- Play the audio program. Ss listen and check their answers. Go over answers with the class.

Answers

- ● ○ dancer, server, tutor
- ● ● ○ salesperson, carpenter, caregiver
- ○ ● ○ accountant, musician, reporter

6 WRITING A biography

A Use your notes from Exercise 5 to write a biography of your partner. Don't use your partner's name. Use *he* or *she* instead.

> My partner is a student. She lives near the university. She studies fashion design at the Fashion Institute. Her favorite class is History of Design. She has a part-time job in a clothing store. She loves her job and . . .

B CLASS ACTIVITY Pass your biographies around the class. Guess who each biography is about.

7 CONVERSATION I start work at five.

A Listen and practice.

Kevin: So, do you usually come to the gym in the morning?

Allie: Yeah, I do. I usually come here at 10:00.

Kevin: Really? What time do you go to work?

Allie: Oh, I work in the afternoon. I start work at five.

Kevin: Wow, that's late. When do you get home at night?

Allie: I usually get home at midnight.

Kevin: Midnight? That *is* late. What do you do, exactly?

Allie: I'm a chef. I work at the Pink Elephant.

Kevin: That's my favorite restaurant! By the way, I'm Kevin. . . .

B Listen to the rest of the conversation. What time does Kevin get up? start work?

8 PRONUNCIATION Syllable stress

A ⊙ Listen and practice. Notice which syllable has the main stress.

⬤ ◦	⬤ ◦ ◦	◦ ⬤ ◦
dancer	salesperson	accountant
....	....	....
....	....	....

B ⊙ Which stress pattern do these words have? Add them to the columns in part A. Then listen and check.

carpenter   caregiver   musician   reporter   server   tutor

Time expressions ⊙

				Expressing clock time
I get up	**at** 6:00	**in** the morning	**on** weekdays.	6:00
I go to bed	**around** ten	**in** the evening	**on** weeknights.	six
I leave work	**early**	**in** the afternoon	**on** weekends.	six o'clock
I get home	**late**	**at** night	**on** Fridays.	6:00 A.M. = 6:00 in the morning
I stay up	**until** midnight	**on** Saturdays.		6:00 P.M. = 6:00 in the evening
I exercise	**before** noon	**on** Saturdays.		
I wake up	**after** noon	**on** Sundays.		

A Circle the correct words.

1. I get up **at** / **until** six **at** / **on** weekdays.
2. I have lunch **at** / **early** 11:30 **in** / **on** Mondays.
3. I have a little snack **in** / **around** 10:00 **in** / **at** night.
4. **In** / **On** Fridays, I leave school **early** / **before**.
5. I stay up **before** / **until** 1:00 A.M. **in** / **on** weekends.
6. I sleep **until** / **around** noon **in** / **on** Sundays.

B Rewrite the sentences in part A so that they are true for you. Then compare with a partner.

C **PAIR WORK** Take turns asking and answering these questions.

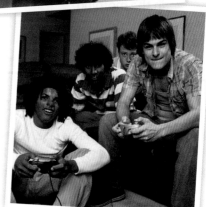

1. Which days do you get up early? late?
2. What's something you do before 8:00 in the morning?
3. What's something you do on Saturday evenings?
4. What do you do only on Sundays?

10 **LISTENING** Daily schedules

A ⊙ Listen to Greg, Megan, and Lori talk about their daily schedules. Complete the chart.

	Job	Gets up at . . .	Gets home at . . .	Goes to bed at . . .
Greg	mechanic			
Megan		7:00 a.m.		
Lori				

B **CLASS ACTIVITY** Who do you think has the best daily schedule? Why?

11 **INTERCHANGE 2** Common ground

Find out about your classmates' schedules. Go to Interchange 2 on page 115.

GRAMMAR FOCUS

Learning Objective: *practice time expressions such as prepositions of time and adverbs of time*

 [CD 1, Track 18]

***Prepositions of time:* at/in/on + time**

- Draw these prepositions and three large circles on the board:

 at   *in*   *on*

- Focus Ss' attention on the Grammar Focus box. Ask: "What words follow *at, in,* and *on*?" Different Ss write the words inside the circles on the board.

- Elicit or explain the rules:
  at + times of day; *night*
  in + parts of day (except *night*)
  on + days of the week

 For more practice with prepositions of time, play *Run For It!* – download it from the website.

Adverbs of time

- Elicit or explain the meanings of *early, late, around, until, before,* and *after*. Then play the audio program.

A

- Ss complete the task individually or in pairs.
- Go around the class and give help as needed. Go over answers with the class.

> **Answers**
>
> 1. I get up **at** six **on** weekdays.
> 2. I have lunch **at** 11:30 **on** Mondays.
> 3. I have a little snack **around** 10:00 **at** night.
> 4. **On** Fridays, I leave school **early**.
> 5. I stay up **until** 1:00 **on** weekends.
> 6. I sleep **until** noon **on** Sundays.

B

- Model the task. Rewrite one or two sentences on the board so that they are true for you.
- Ss work individually. Then they go over their answers in pairs.

C *Pair work*

- Model the task. First, Ss ask you the questions. Then Ss complete the task in pairs.

---

10 **LISTENING**

Learning Objective: *develop skills in listening for specific information*

A **[CD 1, Track 19]**

- Set the scene. Then play the audio program, stopping after each person talks about his or her schedule. Ss complete the chart individually.
- Play the audio program again.
- Go over answers with the class.

> **AudioScript**
>
> *Megan* What do you do, Greg?
> *Greg* I'm a mechanic.
> *Megan* Oh, yeah? So, what are your work hours like?
> *Greg* They're OK. I work in the mornings and afternoons. I get up around 6:00 A.M., and I work from 7:00 A.M. until 3:00 P.M. I get home pretty early, about 4:00 P.M. I go to bed at 10:00. And what do you do, Megan?
> *Megan* Well, I'm a receptionist. It's a regular nine-to-five office job, so I get up at 7:00 A.M. and get home around 6:00 P.M. That's OK, though, because I like to go out

at night. I go to bed around midnight on weekdays.
Greg What about you, Lori?
Lori Well, my hours are a bit different – I'm a nurse. I start work at 11:00 at night. I work until 7:00 A.M.
Megan Wow! So what time do you get up?
Lori I get home at 8:00 and go to bed at about 8:30. And I sleep until 4:00 P.M.
Greg And what do you do in the evenings?
Lori Oh, you know. I have dinner, watch TV, see friends. It's a great schedule for me.

> **Answers**
>
> | | Job | Gets up at . . . | Gets home at . . . | Goes to bed at . . . |
> |---|---|---|---|---|
> | Greg | mechanic | 6 A.M. | 4 P.M. | 10 P.M. |
> | Megan | receptionist | 7 A.M. | 6 P.M. | midnight |
> | Lori | nurse | 4 P.M. | 8 A.M. | 8:30 A.M. |

B *Class activity*

- Elicit Ss' responses. Then take a class vote.

---

11 **INTERCHANGE 2**

See page T-115 for teaching notes.

12 READING

Learning Objectives: *read and discuss an article about jobs; develop skills in reading for specific information*

> **TIP** To help Ss focus on the task, tell them not to worry about words they don't understand. Encourage them to keep reading when they see new words.

- Set the scene. A high school student, college student, and new parent need jobs. Ask: "Why do they need jobs?" Elicit ideas and write them on the board.

- Focus Ss' attention on the pictures. Tell Ss to cover the profiles. Ask: "Who's in high school? in college? a new parent?" Encourage Ss to guess.

- Set a time limit of one minute. Ss scan the three profiles quickly to check their guesses. (Answers: Julia is in college. Denise is a new parent. Eddie is in high school.)

A

- Explain the task. Tell Ss to guess the meanings of any new words.

- Ss read the article and complete the task. Go over answers with the class.

Answers

1. To save money: Denise
2. To pay for college: Julia
3. To go out on the weekend: Eddie
4. To buy a house: Denise

- Elicit or explain any new vocabulary.

Vocabulary

experience: the work a person did in the past
save: to keep for later
take care of: care for
type: to write on a computer
allowance: money parents give children to spend
earn: to receive money for work

B *Pair work*

- Ask Ss to read the article again. Tell them to take notes about each person's schedules and experience.

! For a new way to teach this Reading, try *Jigsaw Learning* – download it from the website.

- Go over the ads with Ss. Then explain the task. Ask: "What is Julia's schedule like? What experience does she have? What jobs are good for her? Why?" Elicit ideas from the class.

- Ss choose jobs for Julia, Denise, and Eddie in pairs. Make sure Ss explain why.

Possible answers

Julia has a difficult schedule. She needs a flexible job or an evening job. English tutor and receptionist are good jobs for her.
Denise needs to work at home because she has a baby. She can type and has a computer. Online salesperson is the best job for her.
Eddie can work afternoons, evenings, and weekends. Chef and server are good jobs for him.

For more practice with daily routines, play *True or False?* – download it from the website. Have Ss prepare sentences about what they do every day.

End of Cycle 2

See the Supplementary Resources chart at the beginning of this unit for additional teaching materials and student activities related to this Cycle and for assessment tools.

Why do you need a job?

Scan the profiles. Who is in high school? Who is in college? Who is a new parent?

These people need jobs. Read about their schedules, experience, and why they need a job.

Julia Brown

I study French and want to be a teacher someday. I have classes all day on Monday, Tuesday, and Thursday, and on Wednesday and Friday afternoons. I usually study on weekends. I need a job because college is really expensive! I don't have any experience, but I'm a fast learner.

Eddie Chen

I'm 16 now, and my parents don't give me an allowance anymore. I want to earn some money because I like to go out with my friends on the weekend. I go to school at 8:00 and get home around 4:30. My parents own a restaurant, so I know a little about restaurant work.

Denise Parker

My husband is an accountant and makes good money, but we don't save very much. We live in a small apartment, and we have a new baby. We want to save money to buy a house. I take care of the baby, so I need a job I can do at home. I can type well, and I have a new computer.

A Read the article. Why do these people need jobs? Check (✓) the correct boxes.

	Julia	Denise	Eddie
1. To save money	☐	☐	☐
2. To pay for college	☐	☐	☐
3. To go out on the weekend	☐	☐	☐
4. To buy a house	☐	☐	☐

B PAIR WORK Choose the best job for each person. Explain why.

Chef	**English Tutor**	**Caregiver**
French and Italian cooking *Weekends only*	*Flexible work hours* *$10 an hour*	*Work with children* *Earn great money*

Server	**Receptionist**	**Online Salesperson**
Evenings only *Experience a plus*	*Mornings and afternoons* *No experience necessary*	*Work at home* *Earn up to $20 an hour*

Units 1–2 Progress check

SELF-ASSESSMENT

How well can you do these things? Check (✓) the boxes.

I can	Very well	OK	A little
Make an introduction and use basic greeting expressions (Ex. 1)	☐	☐	☐
Show I didn't understand and ask for repetition (Ex. 1)	☐	☐	☐
Ask and answer questions about myself and other people (Ex. 2)	☐	☐	☐
Ask and answer questions about work (Ex. 3, 4)	☐	☐	☐
Ask and answer questions about habits and routines (Ex. 5)	☐	☐	☐

 ROLE PLAY *Introductions*

A PAIR WORK You are talking to someone at school. Have a conversation.

A: Hi. How are you?
B: . . .
A: By the way, my name is . . .
B: I'm sorry. What's your name again?
A: . . .
B: I'm . . . . Are you a student here?
A: . . . And how about you?
B: . . .
A: Oh, really? And where are you from?

B GROUP WORK Join another pair.
Introduce your partner.

 SPEAKING *Interview*

Write questions for these answers. Then use the questions to interview a classmate.

1.	What's _____	?	My name is Keiko Kawakami.
2.	_____	?	I'm from Osaka, Japan.
3.	_____	?	Yes, my classes are very interesting.
4.	_____	?	My favorite class is English.
5.	_____	?	No, my teacher isn't American.
6.	_____	?	My classmates are very nice.
7.	_____	?	My best friend is Maria.

Units 1–2 Progress check

SELF-ASSESSMENT

Learning Objectives: *reflect on one's learning; identify areas that need improvement*

- Ask: "What did you learn in Units 1 and 2?" Elicit Ss' answers.

- Ss complete the Self-assessment. Encourage them to be honest, and point out they will not get a bad grade if they check (✓) *a little.*

- Ss move on to the Progress check exercises. You can have Ss complete them in class or for homework, using one of these techniques:

  1. Ask Ss to complete all the exercises.

  2. Ask Ss: "What do you need to practice?" Then assign exercises based on their answers.

  3. Ask Ss to choose and complete exercises based on their Self-assessment.

ROLE PLAY

Learning Objectives: *assess one's ability to make an introduction and use basic greeting and leave-taking expressions; assess one's ability to ask for repetition for clarification*

A Pair work

- Read the instructions aloud and focus Ss' attention on the picture. Explain that Ss should pretend they don't know their partners in this role play.

- Model the role play with a S. Explain how to use the conversation cues.

- Ss role-play the conversation in pairs. Encourage Ss to use appropriate body language and gestures, add follow-up questions, and ask for clarification where appropriate.

- **Option:** Ss introduce themselves without referring to the example conversation.

B Group work

- Each pair joins another pair. Ss introduce their partners to the other pair and ask follow-up questions.

> **TIP** If you don't have enough class time for the speaking activities, assign each S a speaking partner. Then have Ss complete the activities with their partners for homework.

SPEAKING

Learning Objective: *assess one's ability to ask and answer questions about myself and other people*

- Explain the task and model the first question. Ss should consider if the questions are Wh- or yes/no questions.

- Ss work individually to write the seven questions. Point out that there may be more than one correct question for each answer.

- Go over Ss' questions with the class.

Possible answers

1. What's your name?
2. Where are you from?
3. Are your classes interesting?
4. What's your favorite class?
5. Is your teacher American?
6. What are your classmates like?
7. Who is your best friend?

- Ss work in pairs. They take turns using the questions to interview each other. Encourage Ss to add follow-up questions.

- **Option:** Each S uses the questions to interview another S.

3 SPEAKING

Learning Objective: *assess one's ability to ask and answer questions about work*

A

- Explain the task. Then elicit things a receptionist does and write them on the board.
- Ss complete the task individually or in pairs.

4 LISTENING

Learning Objectives: *assess one's ability to understand descriptions of work and school; assess one's ability to ask and answer questions about work*

A *[CD 1, Track 20]*

- Set the scene. James and Lindsey are talking about work and school at a party.
- Play the audio program once or twice. Ss listen and complete the chart.

AudioScript

James [doorbell rings] Hey, Nick. How are you?
Nick I'm great, James. Welcome to my house. Oh, James, this is my friend Lindsey.
James Hi, Lindsey. It's nice to meet you.
Lindsey Nice to meet you, too, James.
Nick [doorbell rings again] Excuse me.
Lindsey So how do you know Nick?
James Oh, we work in the same office.
Lindsey Really? What do you do?
James I'm a website designer.
Lindsey That's exciting! Where do you work?
James At Central Computers.
Lindsey Central Computers, huh? How do you like your job?
James It's OK. I work late a lot. I usually finish at 10:30 and get home at 11:00.

B *Group work*

- Ss compare their lists in small groups. Encourage Ss to ask Wh-questions about the jobs (e.g., *What does a receptionist do? Where does a receptionist work?*).
- Go around the class and check Ss' use of the simple present.

Lindsey That *is* late!
James Yeah. After work, I usually go to bed right away. What about you? What do you do?
Lindsey Oh, I'm a student. I study dance.
James Wow! Now *that's* exciting! Where do you study?
Lindsey At New York Dance.
James How do you like your classes?
Lindsey I love them. I dance all day long. It's wonderful.
James What do you do after school?
Lindsey I have a part-time job. I work in an office.
James Where is the office?
Lindsey Actually, I work in your office! At Central Computers.
James You do? Well, stop by and say hello sometime.
Lindsey OK.

Answers

James	Lindsey
website designer	dance student
Central Computers	New York Dance
OK	loves them
goes to bed	works in an office

B *Pair work*

- Explain the task. Ss take turns asking and answering the questions in part A.

5 SURVEY

Learning Objective: *assess one's ability to ask and answer questions about habits and routines*

A

- Elicit or explain the meaning of *a perfect day*. Model the task by having a S ask you the questions.

WHAT'S NEXT?

Learning Objective: *become more involved in one's learning*

- Focus Ss' attention on the Self-assessment again. Ask: "How well can you do these things now?"

- Ss complete the task individually.

B *Pair work*

- Ss take turns describing their perfect day in pairs. Encourage Ss to ask follow-up questions.

- Ask Ss to underline one thing they need to review. Ask: "What did you underline? How can you review it?"
- If needed, plan additional activities or reviews based on Ss' answers.

3 SPEAKING What a job!

A What do you know about these jobs? List three things each person does.

receptionist

tour guide

cashier

teacher

takes messages

....
....
....

B GROUP WORK Compare your lists. Take turns asking about the jobs.

4 LISTENING Work and school

A ▶ Listen to James and Lindsey talk at a party. Complete the chart.

	James	Lindsey
What do you do?	....	....
Where do you work/study?	....	....
How do you like your job/classes?	....	....
What do you do after work/school?	....	....

B PAIR WORK Practice the questions in part A. Answer with your own information.

5 SURVEY My perfect day

A Imagine your perfect day. Complete the chart with your own answers.

What time do you get up?	....
What do you do after you get up?	....
Where do you go?	....
What do you do in the evening?	....
When do you go to bed?	....

B PAIR WORK Talk about your perfect day. Answer any questions.

WHAT'S NEXT?

Look at your Self-assessment again. Do you need to review anything?

Unit 3 Supplementary Resources Overview

	After the following SB exercises	You can use these materials in class	Your students can use these materials outside the classroom
CYCLE 1	1 Snapshot		**SSD** Unit 3 Vocabulary 1
	2 Conversation		**SSD** Unit 3 Speaking 1
	3 Grammar Focus	**TSS** Unit 3 Extra Worksheet	**SB** Unit 3 Grammar Plus focus 1 **ARC** Demonstratives; *one, ones*
	4 Pronunciation		
	5 Role Play		
	6 Listening		
	7 Interchange 3	**TSS** Unit 3 Listening Worksheet	**WB** Unit 3 exercises 1–5
CYCLE 2	8 Word Power	**TSS** Unit 3 Vocabulary Worksheet	**SSD** Unit 3 Vocabulary 2 **ARC** Colors and materials
	9 Conversation		**SSD** Unit 3 Speaking 2
	10 Grammar Focus	**TSS** Unit 3 Grammar Worksheet	**SB** Unit 3 Grammar Plus focus 2 **SSD** Unit 3 Grammar 1–2 **ARC** Demonstratives and preferences **ARC** Preferences; comparisons with adjectives
	11 Writing	**TSS** Unit 3 Writing Worksheet	
	12 Reading	**TSS** Unit 3 Project Worksheet **VID** Unit 3 **VRB** Unit 3	**SSD** Unit 3 Reading 1–2 **SSD** Unit 3 Listening 1–2 **SSD** Unit 3 Video 1–3 **WB** Unit 3 exercises 6–10

Key   **ARC**: Arcade   **SB:** Student's Book   **SSD:** Self-study DVD-ROM   **TSS:** Teacher Support Site
         VID: Video DVD   **VRB:** Video Resource Book   **WB:** Workbook

My Plan for Unit 3

Use the space below to customize a plan that fits your needs.

With the following SB exercises	I am using these materials in class	My students are using these materials outside the classroom

With or instead of the following SB section	I am using these materials for assessment

3 How much is it?

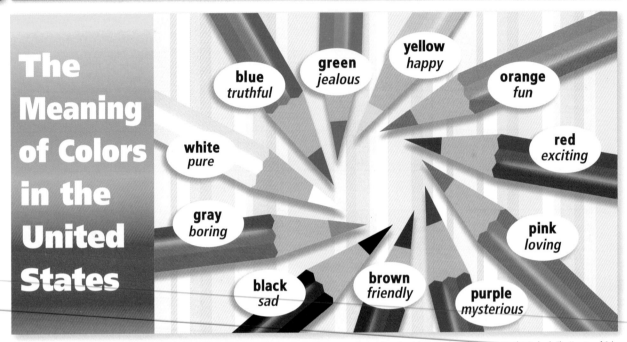

The Meaning of Colors in the United States

- **blue** *truthful*
- **green** *jealous*
- **yellow** *happy*
- **orange** *fun*
- **white** *pure*
- **red** *exciting*
- **gray** *boring*
- **pink** *loving*
- **black** *sad*
- **brown** *friendly*
- **purple** *mysterious*

Sources: Based on information from Think Quest; Hewlett-Packard, *The Meaning of Color*

Which words have a positive meaning? Which have a negative meaning?
What meanings do these colors have for you?
What does your favorite color make you think of?

2 CONVERSATION *It's really pretty.*

A ▶ Listen and practice.

Salesclerk: Can I help you?
Customer: Yes, thank you. How much are these gloves?
Salesclerk: The gray ones? They're $18.
Customer: Oh, that's not bad. Do they come in black?
Salesclerk: No, sorry, just gray.
Customer: OK. Um, how much is that scarf?
Salesclerk: Which one? The blue and orange one?
Customer: No, the yellow one.
Salesclerk: Let's see . . . it's $24.95.
Customer: It's really pretty. I'll take it.

B ▶ Listen to the rest of the conversation. What else does the customer look at? Does she buy it?

How much is it?

> *In Unit 3, students discuss money, especially with regard to shopping. In Cycle 1, they talk about prices using demonstratives and the pronouns one/ones. In Cycle 2, they talk about preferences using comparisons with adjectives.*

1 SNAPSHOT

Learning Objective: *read about and discuss the meaning of colors*

- Books closed. Ask several Ss: "What is your favorite color?" Write the colors on the board. Help with vocabulary for colors as needed.
- Ask several Ss to choose between pairs of adjectives for colors. For example, ask: "Is red exciting or sad?" "Is white dirty or pure?"
- Books open. Explain that colors have different meanings in different countries. Discuss the meanings in the Snapshot. Elicit or explain any new vocabulary.

Vocabulary

truthful: honest
jealous: unhappy because you want someone's things
mysterious: strange and difficult to understand
friendly: nice to other people; sociable
pure: very clean

- Focus Ss' attention on the first two questions. Draw this chart on the board:

Positive meanings	Negative meanings
pure	sad

- Ask different Ss to add adjectives from the Snapshot to the chart. Does everyone agree on the placement of *exciting*? of *mysterious*?
- Ss discuss the last two questions in pairs. Allow about five minutes. Then discuss the questions as a class.
- **Option:** Select three colors. In pairs or groups, Ss make lists of all the things in the room with those colors.

2 CONVERSATION

Learning Objective: *practice a conversation about shopping; see demonstratives and* one/ones *in context*

A ▶ [CD 1, Track 21]

- To set the scene, focus Ss' attention on the picture. Ask: "Where are they? What are they doing?"
- Write this focus question on the board:
  What color scarf does she buy?
- Books closed (or text covered). Play the audio program. Ss listen for the answer. (Answer: yellow)
- **Option:** Write these focus questions on the board:
  1. How much are the gray gloves?
  2. Why does she buy the scarf?
- Then play the audio again. Ss check answers. (Answers: 1. $18 2. It's really pretty.)
- Books open (or uncover the text). Play the audio program again. Ss listen and read along silently.
- Elicit or explain any new vocabulary.

Vocabulary

That's not bad.: They aren't too expensive.
Hmm: a sound people make when they're thinking
Let's see.: Allow me to look (at the price).
I'll take it.: I'll buy it.

- Ss practice the conversation in pairs.
- ❗ For a new way to practice this Conversation, try the **Onion Ring** technique – download it from the website.

B ▶ [CD 1, Track 22]

- Read the two focus questions aloud. Then play the audio program. Elicit answers from the class.

AudioScript

Salesclerk We have some nice hats over here.
Customer Oh, yeah? I need a new hat.
Salesclerk They're on sale today only.
Customer Oh, they *are* nice. This red one is pretty. How much is it?
Salesclerk It's $26.50.
Customer Hmm . . . I don't think so. Thanks anyway.

Answers

She looks at a hat. She doesn't buy it.

3 GRAMMAR FOCUS

Learning Objective: *practice demonstratives and one/ones*

⏵ **[CD 1, Track 23]**

Demonstratives

- Books closed. Point to Ss' things and make statements with *this* and *these* (e.g., "This is Peter's pen. This is Jane's necklace. These are Dan's glasses.").

- Hold some things close to show how we use *this* or *these* for nearby things. Explain that *this* refers to a singular thing, while *these* refers to plurals.

- ▪ *Option:* Ss place their things in a bag. Each S takes out something and says whose it is (e.g., "This is Mary's pen.").

- Place some thing far away to show how we use *that* and *those*. Ss point to things and make statements (e.g., "That is Bill's book. Those are Mike's keys."). Explain that *that* refers to a singular thing, while *those* refers to plural things.

- To check Ss' understanding of demonstratives and review colors, ask about things in the room (e.g., "What color is this pen? What color are those books?").

One/Ones

- Focus Ss' attention on the Conversation on page 16. Ask Ss to find examples of *one* and *ones*.

- For each example, ask: "What noun does *one* replace?" (Answers: the blue and orange scarf or the yellow scarf) Elicit the rule: *One* replaces a singular noun, and *ones* replaces a plural noun.

- Play the first part of the audio program.

> **TIP** To raise awareness of both the meaning and form of a new structure, always link the Grammar Focus to the Conversation.

Saying prices

- Play the rest of the audio program. Ss repeat the prices. Present additional examples as needed.

▦ For practice in listening for prices, play **Bingo** using prices instead of words – download it from the website.

A

- Model the first line of the first conversation.
- Ss complete the task individually. Go over answers with the class.

Answers

1. A: Excuse me. How much are **those** jeans?
   B: Which **ones**? Do you mean **these**?
   A: No, the light blue **ones**.
   B: Oh, **those** are $59.95.
   A: Wow! That's expensive.
2. A: How much is **that** backpack?
   B: Which **one**?
   A: The red **one**.
   B: It's $36.99. But **this** green **one** is only $22.25.
   A: That's not bad. Can I see it, please?

- Ss practice the conversations in pairs.
- ▪ *Option:* Bring in two different pairs of sunglasses, pens, necklaces, or hats. Then Ss practice the conversations again using these things.

B *Pair work*

- Explain the task. Ss work in pairs to choose prices for the sunglasses, phones, and scarves.
- Model the example conversation with a S. Then Ss take turns asking and answering questions about the items. Go around the class to check for the use of demonstratives and *one* or *ones*.
- ▪ *Option:* If you live in an English-speaking environment, have Ss go to a store to ask the prices of three things in English.
- ▪ *Option:* Bring in clothing catalogs. Ss use them to practice the conversations.

❗ For a new way to practice this Conversation, try the *Substitution Dialog* – download it from the website.

3 GRAMMAR FOCUS

Demonstratives; one, ones ▶

How much is	**this** scarf?	**that** scarf?	Which **one**?	**It's** $24.95.
	this one?	**that one**?	The yellow **one**.	
How much are	**these** gloves?	**those** gloves?	Which **ones**?	**They're** $18.
	these?	**those**?	The gray **ones**.	

saying prices ▶

79¢	= seventy-nine cents
$18	= eighteen dollars
$24.95	= twenty-four ninety-five

A Complete these conversations. Then practice with a partner.

1

A: Excuse me. How much
   are ....*those*.... jeans?
B: Which .... ? Do you
   mean .... ?
A: No, the light blue ....
B: Oh, ... are $59.95.
A: Wow! That's expensive!

2

A: How much is .... backpack?
B: Which .... ?
A: The red ....
B: It's $36.99. But ....
   green .... is only $22.25.
A: That's not bad. Can I see it, please?

B PAIR WORK Add prices to the items. Then ask and answer questions.

A: How much are these sunglasses?
B: Which ones?
A: The pink ones.
B: They're $86.99.
A: That's expensive!

useful expressions

That's cheap.
That's reasonable.
That's OK/not bad.
That's expensive.

4 PRONUNCIATION Sentence stress

A ▶ Listen and practice. Notice that the important words in a sentence have more stress.

Excuse me.   That's expensive.   I'll take it.   Do you mean these?

B **PAIR WORK** Practice the conversations in Exercise 3, part B again. Pay attention to the sentence stress.

5 ROLE PLAY Can I help you?

A **PAIR WORK** Put items "for sale" on your desk, such as notebooks, watches, phones, or bags.

Student A: You are a salesclerk. Answer the customer's questions.

Student B: You are a customer. Ask the price of each item. Say if you want to buy it.

A: Can I help you?
B: Yes. I like these sunglasses. How much are they?
A: Which ones?

B Change roles and try the role play again.

6 LISTENING Look at this!

A ▶ Listen to two friends shopping. Write the color and price for each item.

Item	Color	Price	Do they buy it?	
			Yes	No
1. phone	....	....	☐	☐
2. watch	....	....	☐	☐
3. sunglasses	....	....	☐	☐
4. T-shirt	....	....	☐	☐

B ▶ Listen again. Do they buy the items? Check (✓) Yes or No.

7 INTERCHANGE 3 Flea market

See what kinds of deals you can make as a buyer and a seller.
Go to Interchange 3 on pages 116–117.

4 PRONUNCIATION

Learning Objectives: *notice sentence stress; learn to sound natural using sentence stress*

A *[CD 1, Track 24]*

- Remind Ss that in each word, one syllable has more stress. Explain that important words in a sentence also have more stress.

- Read the examples, clapping on the stressed words.
- Play the audio program. Ss clap on each stressed word.
- Play the audio program again. Pause for Ss to repeat the sentences, stressing important words.

B *Pair work*

- Ss practice the conversations in part A of Exercise 3 again. Correct Ss' use of sentence stress as needed.

5 ROLE PLAY

Learning Objective: *role-play a conversation between a salesclerk and a customer*

A *Pair work*

- Place several items of different colors on your desk. Use things such as notebooks, phones or bags.

- Model the task with a S.
- Ss work in pairs. Tell Ss to ask about the price of more than one item.

B

- Ss change roles and try the role play again.

6 LISTENING

Learning Objective: *develop skills in listening for details*

A *[CD 1, Track 25]*

- Set the scene. Two people are shopping. They want to know the prices of four things.
- Play the audio program. Ss listen and complete the *Color* and *Price* columns in their books.

AudioScript

1.
A Look at this! It's so cool - and it's purple!
B It's nice. But you have a cell phone. How much is it?
A Let's see . . . Wow, it's expensive! It's $399. I guess I don't really *need* it. Let's go.

2.
B Here's a great watch for you!
A Which one? That white one?
B No, this one. This black one.
A Oh, that's nice. Is it expensive?
B Not really. It's only $9.95.
A That's reasonable. I think I'll get it.

3.
B What do you think of these sunglasses?
A They're . . . interesting. How much are they?
B They're only $11.50. That's cheap.
A Try them on. They look great. Green is a good color on you.
B OK. I'll get them.

4.
A I love these T-shirts! Do you like them?
B Yeah, I do. Why don't you get one?
A Hmm, they're pretty expensive. I only have $20.
B Hey! These T-shirts aren't bad. They're only $12.
A Oh, those are nice, too.
B So, what color? How about this red and yellow one? Do you like it?
A Not really. Hey, *all* these shirts are red and yellow. I think that's why they're on sale.
B So do you want one?
A No, let's go. I'm hungry. It's time for lunch.

Answers

Item	Color	Price	Do they buy it?
1. phone	purple	$399	No
2. watch	black	$9.95	Yes
3. sunglasses	green	$11.50	Yes
4. T-shirt	red & yellow	$12	No

B *[CD 1, Track 26]*

- Play the audio program again. Ss listen to find out if the people buy the things.
- Go over answers with the class.

7 INTERCHANGE 3

See pages T-116 and T-117 for teaching notes.

See the Supplementary Resources chart at the beginning of this unit for additional teaching materials and student activities related to this Cycle.

End of Cycle 1

WORD POWER

Learning Objective: *learn vocabulary for clothes and materials*

A

- If possible, bring in one thing made of each material: cotton, rubber, gold, silk, leather, silver, plastic, and wool. Write the names of the materials on cards. Put the items on your desk with the cards next to them.
- Say the word for each material. Ss repeat the word.
- Explain the task. Ss work individually to complete the exercise. Go around the class and give help. Make sure that Ss do not add *-s* to the adjectives (e.g., NOT *wools socks, rubbers boots*).
- Go over answers with the class.

Answers

1. a **silk** tie
2. a **plastic** bracelet
3. a **gold** ring
4. a **cotton** shirt
5. a **leather** jacket
6. **silver** earrings
7. **rubber** boots
8. **wool** socks

B *Pair work*

- Write the names of the eight things in part A across the top of the board. Ask the question in the book.

- Ask different Ss to write possible materials below each thing on the board. For example, under *socks* they can write *wool, cotton,* or *silk.*
- **Option:** Use the materials word cards. Ask Ss to place the cards next to other items in the classroom made of these materials.

> **TIP** Ss usually forget about 80 percent of new words after 24 hours. To help them remember more, recycle or review new vocabulary the next class.

C *Class activity*

- Model the sentence for the class.
- Ss make as many statements as possible. Point out that they can use other patterns (e.g., "I'm wearing . . .").
- **Option:** Ss write four sentences about what they have or what they're wearing on a piece of paper. Collect the papers and read the sentences aloud. Then Ss guess who wrote the sentences.

For more practice with vocabulary for materials, play ***Change Chairs*** – download it from the website. Give the first command: "Change chairs if you have a leather jacket."

 # CONVERSATION

Learning Objectives: *practice a conversation about preferences; see comparisons with adjectives in context*

A 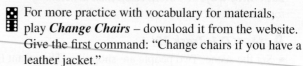 [CD 1, Track 27]

- Elicit ideas and vocabulary based on the picture.
- Set the scene. Brett and Lisa are shopping. Ask Ss to listen for answers to these focus questions:
    1. What are they shopping for?
    2. Which color sweater does Brett prefer?
    3. Does Brett buy a wool sweater?
- Books closed. Play the audio program. Then check answers to the focus questions. (Answers: 1. wool sweaters 2. blue 3. no)
- Books open. Play the audio program again. Ss listen and read along silently. Elicit or explain any new vocabulary.
- Ss practice the conversation in pairs.

For a new way to teach this Conversation, try ***Say It with Feeling!*** – download it from the website.

B [CD 1, Track 28]

- Read the two focus questions aloud. Then play the audio program. Elicit answers from the class.

AudioScript

Brett Wow! That sweater is really expensive. I don't want to spend that much money.
Lisa Oh, look. There are some things on sale over there.
Brett Oh, you're right. These shirts are really nice. And they're cheap, too. I like this one. Is it cotton?
Lisa Let's see . . . Yes, it is. It looks nice on you. The colors are really cool.
Brett Great! I'll take it.

Answers

Brett buys a cotton shirt. Lisa likes it.

8 WORD POWER Materials

A What are these things made of? Label each one. Use the words from the list.

cotton   gold   leather   plastic
rubber   silk   silver   wool

1. a ....silk.... tie   2. a .... bracelet   3. a .... ring   4. a .... shirt

5. a .... jacket   6. .... earrings   7. .... boots   8. .... socks

B PAIR WORK What other materials are the things in part A sometimes made of? Make a list.

C CLASS ACTIVITY Which materials can you find in your classroom?

"Pedro has a cotton shirt, and Ellen has leather shoes."

9 CONVERSATION *I prefer the blue one.*

A ▶ Listen and practice.

Brett: These wool sweaters are really nice. Which one do you like better?
Lisa: Let's see . . . I like the green one more.
Brett: The green one? Why?
Lisa: It looks warmer.
Brett: That's true, but I think I prefer the blue one. It's more stylish than the green one.
Lisa: Hmm. There's no price tag.
Brett: Excuse me. How much is this sweater?
Clerk: It's $139. Would you like to try it on?
Brett: Uh, no. That's OK. But thanks anyway.
Clerk: You're welcome.

B ▶ Listen to the rest of the conversation. What does Brett buy? What does Lisa think of it?

10 GRAMMAR FOCUS

Preferences; comparisons with adjectives ▶

Which sweater do you **prefer**?
   I **prefer** the blue one.   It's **nicer than** the green one.
Which one do you **like more**?
   I **like** the blue one **more**.   It's **prettier than** the green one.
Which one do you **like better**?
   I **like** the blue one **better**. It's **more stylish than** the green one.

Spelling
cheap ⟶ cheaper
nice ⟶ nicer
pretty ⟶ prettier
big ⟶ bigger

A Complete these conversations. Then practice with a partner.

1. A: Which of these jackets do you like more?
   B: I prefer the leather one. The design is .... (nice), and it looks .... (expensive) the wool one.

2. A: These T-shirts are nice. Which one do you prefer?
   B: I like the green and white one better. The colors are .... (pretty). It's .... (attractive) the gray and black one.

3. A: Which earrings do you like better?
   B: I like the silver ones more. They're .... (big) the gold ones. And they're .... (cheap).

B **PAIR WORK** Compare the things in part A. Give your own opinions.

A: Which jacket do you like more?
B: I like the wool one better. The color is prettier.

useful expressions

The color is prettier.
The design is nicer.
The style is more attractive.
The material is better.

11 WRITING Comparing prices

How much do these things cost in your country? Complete the chart.
Then compare the prices in your country with the prices in the U.S.

	Price in my country	Price in the U.S.
a cup of coffee	....	$1.40
a movie ticket	....	$12.50
a paperback novel	....	$8.95
a video game	....	$50.00

Many things are more expensive in my country than in the United States. For example, a cup of coffee costs about $2.00 at home. In the U.S., it's cheaper. It's only $1.40. A movie ticket costs . . .

10 GRAMMAR FOCUS

Learning Objective: *practice preferences and comparisons with adjectives*

▶ **[CD 1, Track 29]**

Preferences

- Bring some items to class that are similar (e.g., two rings, two ties, two pens, two T-shirts).
- Focus Ss' attention on the Conversation on page 19. Ask: "Which sweaters do Brett and Lisa prefer? Why?" Write the answers on the board and underline the words *likes* and *better*:

  Lisa <u>likes</u> the green one <u>better</u>. It looks warmer.

  Brett <u>likes</u> the blue one <u>better</u>. It's more stylish than the green one.

- Point out that *like better* means *prefer*.
- Hold up two similar items (e.g., two ties). Ask two or three Ss: "Which one do you prefer?" Elicit the response: "I prefer . . ." or "I like . . . better." Repeat with other pairs of items.
- **Option:** Use two pairs of similar items to review *ones*.

Comparisons with adjectives

- Underline *warmer* and *more stylish* in the sentences on the board. Then draw two columns on the board, like this:

1	2
warmer	more expensive
nicer	more stylish
prettier	more beautiful

> **TIP** To help Ss see the differences in grammar forms, use different colors on the board.

- Point out that column 1 has two one-syllable adjectives (*warm, nice*) and one two-syllable adjective that ends in -*y* (*pretty*). The comparative forms of these adjectives end in -*er*.
- Point out that column 2 has adjectives of two or more syllables (e.g., *expensive*). The comparative forms of these start with *more*.

- Elicit more comparative adjectives for both columns. Ask different Ss to write them on the board.
- Point out the spelling rules in the Grammar Focus box. A final -*y* changes to -*i* when we add -*er* (*prettier*), and a single vowel + consonant doubles the consonant (*bigger*).
- Present the irregular forms: *good – better* and *bad – worse*. Then play the audio program.
- Hold up two items again. Ask: "Which . . . do you prefer? Why do you prefer it/them?" Elicit answers.
- **Option:** Ask Ss to look back over previous units to find more adjectives. (See pages 7 and 16.) Elicit the comparative forms and ask different Ss to write them in column 1 or 2.

A

- Explain the task. Remind Ss to look at the pictures when answering.
- Ss complete the task individually. Then go over answers with the class.

Answers

1. A: Which of these jackets do you like more?
   B: I prefer the leather one. The design is **nicer**, and it looks **more expensive than** the wool one.
2. A: These T-shirts are nice. Which one do you prefer?
   B: I like the green and white one better. The colors are **prettier**. It's **more attractive than** the gray and black one.
3. A: Which earrings do you like better?
   B: I like the silver ones more. They're **bigger than** the gold ones. And they're **cheaper**.

- Ss practice the conversations in pairs.

B *Pair work*

- Focus Ss' attention on the pictures in part A. Model the conversation with a S. Go over the useful expressions.
- Ss work in pairs. They talk about the items, giving their opinions.

 For more practice making comparative forms, play *Tic-Tac-Toe* – download it from the website.

11 WRITING

Learning Objective: *write a paragraph comparing prices*

- Have Ss read the directions, chart, and sample paragraph. Allow three minutes.
- Ask: "What does the chart show? What are you going to add to the chart?" (Answers: prices in the U.S., prices in my country)

- Ss work individually. First they complete the chart. Then they write a paragraph comparing prices.
- Ss read each other's paragraphs and make suggestions.
- **Option:** Ss write a paragraph in class and then revise it for homework.

12 READING

Learning Objective: *read and discuss an article about online shopping; develop skills in scanning and differentiating fact and opinion*

TIP To help Ss understand what reading strategy to use, focus their attention on the purpose of the task. For example: "Today we're going to practice scanning a text to find specific information."

- Set the scene. Ask: "How often do you go shopping? Do you like shopping? Do you ever buy things on the Internet?"
- Explain that this article is about famous websites where people shop online.
- **Option:** If Ss have access to the Internet, tell them to look at the websites Facebook, Twitter, Shopzilla, and Google before they read. If Ss have smartphones, have them look at any shopping applications they may have.
- Point out the pre-reading questions. Ss guess the answers. Then they scan the text quickly to check their guesses.

Answers

Facebook, Twitter, Shopzilla, Google

- Elicit or explain any new vocabulary.

Vocabulary

online: using the Internet
social networking: connecting with people through websites
smartphone: a cell phone with computer features
bargain: something you get for a good price

A

- Explain the task. Ss read the article. Remind Ss not to worry about words they don't know. Ss then answer the questions individually.
- **Option:** Ss work in pairs. One S answers questions a and b, while the other S answers questions c and d. Then they share their answers.
- Ss compare answers in pairs or small groups.

Answers

4 a. Shopzilla and Google compare prices, give reviews, and find stores near you with the best bargains.
2 b. Twitter users are called *Twitterers*.
3 c. You can type in the item number and check prices.
1 d. Two social networking sites are Facebook and Twitter.

B

- Explain the task. Model the first example. First, find the information in the article. (Answer: paragraph 2) Then find the names of the websites. (Answer: Facebook, Twitter)
- Ss work individually. Go around the class and give help as needed.
- Ss compare answers in pairs. Then go over answers with the class.

Answers

	Face-book	Twitter	Smart-phone	Shop-zilla	Google
1. get opinions from friends	x	x			
2. find product reviews		x	x	x	x
3. compare prices			x	x	x
4. find stores with items you want		x	x	x	x
5. buy items directly					x

C *Pair work*

- Read the two questions. Then Ss discuss the questions in pairs.
- Discuss the questions as a class.

End of Cycle 2

See the Supplementary Resources chart at the beginning of this unit for additional teaching materials and student activities related to this Cycle and for assessment tools.

12 *READING*

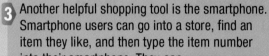

Tools for Better Shopping

Scan the article. Find the names of popular websites. Do you use any of them for shopping?

1 Do you like to shop online? Like millions of people, you want to find the best things for the best price. There are so many choices that it can be difficult to find the things you need and want. Here's where technology comes in! Popular websites like Facebook and Twitter aren't just for social networking anymore.

2 The websites Facebook and Twitter are popular because people can connect to friends and get their most recent news. But people also use these sites as powerful shopping tools. Members can ask about an item and then get opinions from people they trust. Twitterers can also search for news from other users and then find stores nearby that sell the item.

3 Another helpful shopping tool is the smartphone. Smartphone users can go into a store, find an item they like, and then type the item number into their smartphone. They can compare prices, read reviews, and make better decisions about their purchase. Many people find a better price online or at another store. People often want to see and touch an item before they buy. They can do just that – and pay a lower price, too.

4 But you don't have to be a Facebook or Twitter member or have a smartphone to find a bargain. Websites like Shopzilla compare prices, give reviews, and find stores near you with the best bargains. Google does all these things but also lets you buy items directly through its site. Be a smart shopper. The information you need is at your fingertips!

A Read the article. Answer these questions. Then write the number of the paragraph where you find each answer.

.... a. How are Shopzilla and Google similar? ....
.... b. What are Twitter users called? ....
.... c. How do smartphones help find bargains? ....
.... d. What are two social networking sites? ....

B According to the article, which shopping tools do these things? Check (✓) the correct boxes.

	Facebook	Twitter	Smartphone	Shopzilla	Google
1. get opinions from friends	☐	☐	☐	☐	☐
2. find product reviews	☐	☐	☐	☐	☐
3. compare prices	☐	☐	☐	☐	☐
4. find stores with items you want	☐	☐	☐	☐	☐
5. buy items directly	☐	☐	☐	☐	☐

C **PAIR WORK** Do you shop mostly in stores or online? How do you find good prices?

How much is it? ▪ **21**

Unit 4 Supplementary Resources Overview

	After the following SB exercises	You can use these materials in class	Your students can use these materials outside the classroom
CYCLE 1	1 Snapshot		
	2 Word Power	**TSS** Unit 4 Extra Worksheet	**SSD** Unit 4 Vocabulary 1–2 **ARC** Entertainment
	3 Conversation		**SSD** Unit 4 Speaking 1
	4 Grammar Focus		**SB** Unit 4 Grammar Plus focus 1 **SSD** Unit 4 Grammar 1
	5 Pronunciation		**ARC** Simple present questions; short answers 1–2
	6 Speaking	**TSS** Unit 4 Vocabulary Worksheet **TSS** Unit 4 Writing Worksheet	
	7 Listening		**WB** Unit 4 exercises 1–6
CYCLE 2	8 Conversation	**TSS** Unit 4 Listening Worksheet	**SSD** Unit 4 Speaking 2
	9 Grammar Focus	**TSS** Unit 4 Grammar Worksheet	**SB** Unit 4 Grammar Plus focus 2 **SSD** Unit 4 Grammar 2 **ARC** Simple present questions and *Would*
	10 Writing		**ARC** Text message abbreviations
	11 Interchange 4		
	12 Reading	**TSS** Unit 4 Project Worksheet **VID** Unit 4 **VRB** Unit 4	**SSD** Unit 4 Reading 1–2 **SSD** Unit 4 Listening 1–3 **SSD** Unit 4 Video 1–3 **WB** Unit 4 exercises 7–12

With or instead of the following SB section	You can also use these materials for assessment
Units 3–4 Progress Check	**ASSESSMENT CD** Units 3–4 Oral Quiz **ASSESSMENT CD** Units 3–4 Written Quiz

Key
ARC: Arcade	**SB**: Student's Book	**SSD**: Self-study DVD-ROM	**TSS:** Teacher Support Site
VID: Video DVD	**VRB**: Video Resource Book	**WB**: Workbook	

My Plan for Unit 4

Use the space below to customize a plan that fits your needs.

With the following SB exercises	I am using these materials in class	My students are using these materials outside the classroom

With or instead of the following SB section	I am using these materials for assessment

4 I really like hip-hop.

1 SNAPSHOT

Music Sales in the United States

Rock	Other	Classical	Jazz	Gospel	Hip-hop	R&B	Pop	Country	New Age
32%	15%	2%	1%	7%	11%	10%	9%	12%	1%

Source: The Recording Industry Association of America, *2008 Consumer Profile*

▶ Listen and number the musical styles from 1 to 9.
Which of these styles of music are popular in your country?
What other kinds of music are popular in your country?

2 WORD POWER

A Complete the word map with words from the list.

action   reality show
electronic   reggae
game show   salsa
heavy metal   science fiction
horror   soap opera
musical   talk show

B Add two more words to each category.
Then compare with a partner.

C **GROUP WORK** Number the items
in each list from 1 (you like it the most)
to 6 (you like it the least). Then compare
your ideas.

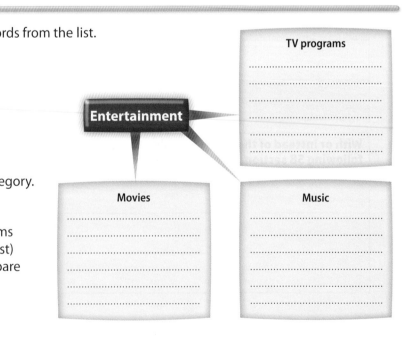

TV programs

Entertainment

Movies

Music

I really like hip-hop.

In Unit 4, students discuss entertainment and personal likes and dislikes. In Cycle 1, they talk about music using yes/no and Wh-questions with do. In Cycle 2, they make invitations and excuses using would and verb + to + verb.

1 SNAPSHOT

Learning Objective: *discuss types of music*

 [CD 1, Track 30]

- Books closed. Ask: "What kind of music is popular in your country?" Help with vocabulary as needed. Write answers on the board.
- Books open. Point out the percentage signs. Ask: "What is this symbol called? What does this chart show?" (Answers: percent, music sales in the U.S.)
- Read out the names of the music styles. Ask: "What kind of music is popular in the U.S.? What music is unpopular? Does anything surprise you about the information?" Elicit answers.
- Elicit or explain any new vocabulary.

Vocabulary

hip-hop: music of African American origin, with rhyming words and a strong beat
R&B: rhythm and blues
country: country-and-western
new age: a type of music which is intended to produce a calm and peaceful state of mind

gospel: a kind of Christian religious music
jazz: music of African American origin, with a strong rhythm

- Brainstorm with Ss what the "other" category might include (e.g., *reggae, salsa*).
- Explain that Ss will hear nine short pieces of music in different styles. Ss listen and number the musical styles from 1 to 9.
- Play the audio program. Ss complete the task individually. Then they compare answers in pairs.
- **Option:** If Ss have difficulty, do the activity with the whole class.

Answers

1. jazz	4. classical	7. rock
2. pop	5. hip-hop	8. R&B
3. gospel	6. country	9. new age

- Go over the two discussion questions. Ss discuss them in small groups. Then elicit answers from the class.
- **Option:** What kind of music does the class like best? Take a poll.

2 WORD POWER

Learning Objective: *learn vocabulary for types of entertainment*

A

- Explain the task. Ss work in pairs or small groups. Allow them to use dictionaries.
- Draw the word map on the board. Ask different Ss to write the answers on the board. Model the pronunciation of the words as you check answers.

B

- Ss add two more words to each category. Then they compare answers in pairs.
- Ask different Ss to write their new words on the board. Go over their answers and model the pronunciation.

Answers

TV programs	Movies	Music
game show	action	electronic
reality show	horror	heavy metal
soap opera	musical	reggae
talk show	science fiction	salsa
cartoon	*adventure*	*classical*
documentary	*comedy*	*opera*
news	*drama*	*pop*
sports event	*western*	*hip-hop*

(Note: Additional examples are italicized.)

- **Option:** To help Ss remember the words in the categories, add names of popular TV programs, movies, and songs or musicians.

C *Group work*

- Explain the task. Ss work individually to rank their items from 1 to 6.
- **Option:** Review language for preferences from Unit 3.
- Ss compare their ideas in small groups.

3 CONVERSATION

Learning Objectives: *practice a conversation about likes and dislikes; see yes/no and Wh-questions with* do *in context*

A [CD 1, Track 31]

- Set the scene. Marissa and Brian are talking about music. Ask: "Who do you see in the pictures?" (Answers: Taylor Swift, Jay-Z)
- Books closed. Write these statements on the board:
  1. I'm a big fan of Taylor Swift.
  2. I don't like it very much.
  3. I really like hip-hop.
  4. I don't like hip-hop very much.
- Ask: "Who says these things – Marissa or Brian?" Play the audio program and Ss listen for the answers. Then elicit the answers. (Answers: 1. Marissa 2. Brian 3. Brian 4. Marissa)
- Point out the expressions *I'm a big fan of . . .* , *I really like . . .* , and *I don't like . . . very much.* Ask: "What do you think of Taylor Swift? Jay-Z?"
- Books open. Play the audio program again. Ss listen and read silently.
- Ask these comprehension questions: "Who is Brian's favorite singer? What does Marissa think of Jay-Z?" Elicit Ss' answers. (Answers: Jay-Z. She doesn't like him.)

- Ss practice the conversation in pairs. Go around the class and give help as needed.
- **!** For a new way to practice this Conversation, try **Say It with Feeling!** – download it from the website.

B [CD 1, Track 32]

- Read the focus questions aloud. Play the audio program once or twice.
- Ss compare answers in small groups. Go over answers with the class.

AudioScript

Marissa What about groups, Brian? Who do you like?
Brian Oh, I like a lot of different groups. I guess my favorite group is Green Day.
Marissa Green Day? Really?
Brian Why? Don't you like them?
Marissa No, I don't. I guess they have some good songs, but they're very . . . noisy.

Answers

His favorite group is Green Day. No, because she thinks their music is very noisy.

4 GRAMMAR FOCUS

Learning Objective: *practice yes/no and Wh-questions with* do

 [CD 1, Track 33]

Yes/No and Wh-questions with do

- Ask Ss to find four questions with *do* or *does* in the Conversation in Exercise 3. Write the questions on the board, in columns:

1	2	3	4	5
	Do	you	like	country music?
	Does	she	play	the guitar?
What kind of . . .	do	you	like?	
	Do	you	like	him?

- Focus Ss' attention on the questions on the board. Elicit the rule for forming questions with *do*: Wh-question + *do/does* + subject + verb?
- Elicit new questions from Ss and write them in the columns on the board.
- Point out the language in the Grammar Focus box. Play the audio program for the first and second columns.

Object pronouns

- Go over the object pronouns in the Grammar Focus box. Play the audio program for the third column.
- Ask Ss to find and circle examples of object pronouns in the Conversation in Exercise 3. (Answers: it, her, him) Ask: "What does . . . refer to?" (Answers: it = country music, her = Taylor Swift, him = Jay-Z)
- Explain the task. Model the first answer.
- Ss complete the task individually. Then Ss compare answers with a partner. Go over the answers with the class.

Answers

1. A: I like the Kings of Leon a lot. **Do** you know **them**?
   B: Yes, I **do**, and I love this song. Let's download **it**.
2. A: **Do** you like science fiction movies?
   B: Yes, I **do**. I like **them** very much.
3. A: **Do** Kevin and Emma like soap operas?
   B: Kevin **does**, but Emma **doesn't**. She hates **them**.
4. A: What kind of music **does** Noriko like?
   B: Classical music. She loves Yo-Yo Ma.
   A: Yeah, he's amazing. I like **him** a lot.

- Ss practice the conversations in pairs.

3 CONVERSATION *Who's your favorite singer?*

A ▶ Listen and practice.

Marissa: Do you like country music, Brian?
Brian: No, I don't like it very much. Do you?
Marissa: Yeah, I do. I'm a big fan of Taylor Swift.
Brian: I think I know her. Does she play the guitar?
Marissa: Yes, she does. She's a really good musician. So, what kind of music do you like?
Brian: I really like hip-hop.
Marissa: Oh, yeah? Who's your favorite singer?
Brian: Jay-Z. Do you like him?
Marissa: No, I don't. I don't like hip-hop very much.

B ▶ Listen to the rest of the conversation. Who is Brian's favorite group? Does Marissa like them?

4 GRAMMAR FOCUS

Simple present questions; short answers ▶

		Object pronouns
Do you **like** country music?	**What kind of** music **do** you **like**?	me
Yes, I **do**. I love it.	I really like hip-hop.	you
No, I **don't**. I don't like it very much.		him
Does she **play** the piano?	**What does** she **play**?	her
Yes, she **does**. She plays very well.	She plays the guitar.	it
No, she **doesn't**. She doesn't play an instrument.		us
Do they **like** Green Day?	**Who do** they **like**?	them
Yes, they **do**. They like them a lot.	They like Coldplay.	
No, they **don't**. They don't like them at all.		

Complete these conversations. Then practice with a partner.

1. A: I like Kings of Leon a lot. .... you know .... ?
   B: Yes, I ...., and I love this song. Let's download ....
2. A: .... you like science fiction movies?
   B: Yes, I .... I like .... very much.
3. A: .... Kevin and Emma like soap operas?
   B: Kevin ...., but Emma .... She hates ....
4. A: What kind of music .... Noriko like?
   B: Classical music. She loves Yo-Yo Ma.
   A: Yeah, he's amazing. I like .... a lot.

Kings of Leon

PRONUNCIATION *Intonation in questions*

A Listen and practice. Yes/No questions usually have rising intonation. Wh-questions usually have falling intonation.

Do you like pop music?   What kind of music do you like?

B **PAIR WORK** Practice these questions.

Do you like TV?   What programs do you like?
Do you like video games?   What games do you like?
Do you play a musical instrument?   What instrument do you play?

6 **SPEAKING** *Entertainment survey*

A **GROUP WORK** Write five questions about entertainment and entertainers. Then ask and answer your questions in groups.

What kinds of . . . do you like?
   (music, TV programs, video games)
Do you like . . . ?
   (reggae, game shows, action movies)
Who's your favorite . . . ?
   (singer, actor, athlete)

B **GROUP WORK** Complete this information about your group. Ask any additional questions.

Our Group Favorites
What's your favorite kind of . . . ?
music ....
movie ....
TV program ....
What's your favorite . . . ?
song ....
movie ....
video game ....
Who's your favorite . . . ?
singer ....
actor ....
athlete ....

Utada Hikaru

reality show

Cristiano Ronaldo

3-D movie

C **CLASS ACTIVITY** Read your group's list to the class. Find out the class favorites.

5 PRONUNCIATION

Learning Objective: *notice and use intonation in questions; learn to sound natural when asking questions*

A [CD 1, Track 34]

- Books closed. Use your voice and gestures to demonstrate intonation. Explain that intonation is the rise and fall of the voice.
- Play the audio program. After each question, ask: "Is the voice going up or down?"
- Elicit or explain the rule. Yes/no questions have rising intonation, and Wh-questions have falling intonation.
- Books open. Play the audio program again. Ss repeat the questions. Ask different Ss to read the questions and check their intonation.

> **TIP** If Ss repeat things as a group, it's hard to hear if they're using correct pronunciation or intonation. Therefore, check some individual Ss' pronunciation.

B *Pair work*

- Explain the task. Model the questions using correct intonation.
- Ss work in pairs. Go around the class and check individual Ss' use of intonation.
- **Option:** Ss look back at the Conversation on page 23 and mark (with arrows) rising or falling intonation above the questions. Ss then practice the conversation again in pairs, paying special attention to intonation.

6 SPEAKING

Learning Objective: *talk about entertainment; discuss likes and dislikes*

A *Group work*

- Write two example questions on the board, e.g.:
  Do you like TV?
  What kind of TV programs do you like?
- Ask different Ss to answer the questions.
- Explain the task. Ss work individually to write five questions. Go around the class and give help as needed.
- Ss take turns asking their questions in small groups. Set a time limit of five to seven minutes.
- Go around the class and listen to Ss' responses.
- **Option:** Encourage Ss to give longer responses (e.g., *No, I don't, but I love . . . , I'm a big fan of . . . , I prefer . . .*).

B *Group work*

- Ss work in small groups. One S leads the discussion to make sure everybody speaks (e.g., *What's your favorite . . . ? What about you, . . . ? What do you think, . . . ? It's your turn to ask a question.*). Another S records the answers.

- The S who recorded the answers reads the responses, and the group decides the favorites. Then the Ss complete their charts.

> **TIP** Assigning each S in the group a role (e.g., *note-taker, leader, English monitor, reporter*) encourages all Ss to participate.

C *Class activity*

- Write these expressions on the board:
  Our favorite . . . is . . .
  We all like . . .
  We don't agree on . . .
- Explain that Ss can use these expressions to report their group's favorites.
- One S from each group reports the results to the class. Another S from each group writes the results on the board.
- Discuss the favorites as a class.
- For more practice with yes/no questions, play *Twenty Questions* – download it from the website.

7 LISTENING

Learning Objective: *develop skills in listening for detail*

A ▶ *[CD 1, Track 35]*

- Set the scene. Linda is on a game show. The hostess is going to interview three men. Linda will choose one for a date.
- Play the audio program. Pause after every few lines to give Ss time to complete the chart.

> **TIP** If an audio program is long and contains many details, break it into parts. Pause the audio program after each part.

- Ss compare answers in pairs.

AudioScript

Hostess [*applause*] Welcome to *Who's My Date?* Today, Linda is going to meet Bill, John, and Tony. So, let's start with the first question . . . on music. Bill, what kind of music do you like?
Bill Oh, classical music.
Hostess Classical. OK. And how about you, John?
John Well, I like jazz.
Hostess And you, Tony?
Tony My favorite music is rock.
Hostess How about you, Linda?
Linda Well, I like pop music. I don't like jazz or classical music very much. [*applause*]
Hostess OK. Now let's talk about movies. Bill, what kind of movies do you like?
Bill I like action movies.
Hostess And how about you, John?
John Oh, I like musicals.
Hostess And how about you, Tony?
Tony I love horror movies.
Hostess And what about you, Linda?

Cycle 2, Exercises 8–12

8 CONVERSATION

Learning Objectives: *practice making plans; see* would *and verb + to + verb in context*

A ▶ *[CD 1, Track 36]*

- Ask: "What do you see in the picture?" Then play the audio program. Ss look at the pictures and read the conversation silently.
- Ss practice the conversation in pairs.

B ▶ *[CD 1, Track 37]*

- Read the focus question aloud. Then play the audio program. Elicit answers from the class.

Linda I really like horror movies, too. [*applause*]
Hostess And now for question number three. Bill, what kind of TV programs do you like?
Bill Well, I like to watch reality shows.
Hostess John?
John Uh, well, you know, I really like talk shows.
Hostess And, Tony, how about you?
Tony I like game shows a lot.
Hostess And, Linda, what do you like?
Linda Well, I like talk shows and game shows.
Hostess [*buzzer*] OK! Time is up! Now, who's the best date for Linda? [*applause*]

Answers

	Music	**Movies**	**TV programs**
Bill	classical	action	reality shows
John	jazz	musicals	talk shows
Tony	rock	horror movies	game shows
Linda	pop	horror movies	talk shows and game shows

B Class activity

- Ss discuss the best date for Linda as a class.

Possible answers

Tony is the best date because he and Linda like horror movies and game shows. They all disagree about music.

End of Cycle 1

See the Supplementary Resources chart at the beginning of this unit for additional teaching materials and student activities related to this Cycle.

AudioScript

Dave [*crowd cheering*] Yes! That's *another* goal for the Ducks! That's the Ducks 3, the Frogs 0.
Susan You really are a Ducks fan, Dave.
Dave I know. They're my favorite team.
Susan They're OK, but I like the Frogs a lot better, especially Mario Sanchez.
Dave He *is* very talented. It's too bad he's not playing today.

Answers

Dave likes the Ducks. Susan likes the Frogs.

7 LISTENING *Who's my date?*

A Listen to four people on a TV game show. Three men want to invite Linda on a date. What kinds of things do they like? Complete the chart.

	Music	Movies	TV programs
Bill			
John			
Tony			
Linda			

B CLASS ACTIVITY Who do you think is the best date for Linda? Why?

8 CONVERSATION *An invitation*

A ◉ Listen and practice.

Dave: I have tickets to the soccer match on Friday night. Would you like to go?

Susan: Thanks. I'd love to. What time does it start?

Dave: At 8:00.

Susan: That sounds great. So, do you want to have dinner at 6:00?

Dave: Uh, I'd like to, but I have to work late.

Susan: Oh, that's OK. Let's just meet at the stadium before the match, around 7:30.

Dave: OK. Why don't we meet at the gate?

Susan: That sounds fine. See you there.

B ◉ Listen to Dave and Susan at the soccer match. Which team does each person like?

9 GRAMMAR FOCUS

Would; verb + to + verb ⊙

Would you **like to go** out on Friday?
  Yes, I **would**.
  Yes, I'**d love to**. Thanks.

Would you **like to go** to a soccer match?
  I'**d like to**, but I **have to work** late.
  I'**d like to**, but I **need to save** money.
  I'**d like to**, but I **want to visit** my parents.

Contraction
I'**d** = I would

A Respond to three invitations. Then write three invitations for the given responses.

1. A: I have tickets to the baseball game
   on Saturday. Would you like to go?
  B: ....

2. A: Would you like to come over for dinner
   tomorrow night?
  B: ....

3. A: Would you like to go to a pop concert
   with me this weekend?
  B: ....

4. A: ....
   ....
  B: Yes, I'd love to. Thank you!

5. A: ....
   ....
  B: Well, I'd like to, but I have to study.

6. A: ....
   ....
  B: Yes, I would. They're my favorite band.

B **PAIR WORK** Ask and answer the questions in part A. Give your own responses.

C **PAIR WORK** Think of three things you would like to do. Then invite a partner
to do them with you. Your partner responds and asks follow-up questions like these:

When is it?   What time does it start?   When does it end?   Where is it?

10 WRITING A text message

A What does this text message say?

text message abbreviations			
M = am		L8	= late
U = you		W8	= wait
R = are		GR8	= great
C = see		THX	= thanks
4 = for		LUV	= love
2 = to		NITE	= night

B **GROUP WORK** Write a text message to each person in your group.
Then exchange messages. Write a response to each message.

11 INTERCHANGE 4 Are you free this weekend?

Make weekend plans with your classmates. Go to Interchange 4 on page 118.

9 GRAMMAR FOCUS

Learning Objective: *practice* would *and* verb + to + verb

 [CD 1, Track 38]

Would

- Refer Ss to the Conversation on page 25. Ask: "How does Dave invite Susan?" Write his question on the board: Would you like to go?
- Explain that we use *Would you like to . . . ?* for polite invitations. It is more polite than *Do you want to . . . ?*
- Ask Ss to find Susan's response. Ask: "What does she say?" Write it on the board:
  Thanks. I'd love to.
- Point out that *I'd = I would.* Explain that there are different ways to accept an invitation. Susan uses one. Add two more to the board:
  Yes, I would.
  Yes, I'd really like to (go).
- Play the audio program for the first column in the Grammar Focus box. Ss read silently.

Verb + to + verb

- Refer Ss again to the Conversation on page 25. Susan invites Dave to have dinner at 6:00, but he doesn't accept. Ask: "What were his words?" Write them on the board: Uh, I'd like to but I <u>have to work</u> late.

- Explain that we often use the structure *verb + to + verb* when making excuses. Focus Ss' attention on the Grammar Focus box. Elicit examples.
- Play the audio program for the second and third columns.

A

- Explain the task. Questions 1–3 require an acceptance or a refusal. Questions 4–6 require an invitation.
- Ss work individually. Go around the class and check their answers. If you notice common problems, stop and go over them with the class.

B *Pair work*

- Explain the task. Ss work in pairs. They take turns asking and answering the questions.

C *Pair work*

- Explain the task. With Ss, brainstorm three things to do. Model inviting a S to do one of those things. Your S partner uses some of the follow-up questions.
- Have Ss first think of three real or imaginary things they would like to do. Then they practice inviting each other. Remind Ss to use *Would you like to . . . ?* and to include follow-up questions.

10 WRITING

Learning Objective: *write and respond to text messages*

A

- Point out that Ss practiced oral invitations. Now they will make text message invitations.
- Focus Ss' attention on the text message. Ask Ss to guess its meaning. (Answer: Would you like to see a movie tonight?)
- Discuss abbreviations. Explain that people use the abbreviations because there is very little space on cell phone screens. Elicit the words the text message abbreviations stand for. (Answers: 2 = to, c = see, 2nite = tonight).
- Ask the class: "Do you ever write text messages? Who do you write to? What do you write about?"

B *Group work*

- Ss work in groups of three. Ss work individually to write a message to the other two Ss in their group.
- Ss exchange messages with the other Ss in the group. They read each message and write a response (e.g., *sounds GR8!*). Then they return the responses. (Note: If Ss can't think of an invitation, encourage them to look at the Grammar Focus or Conversation on page 25 for ideas.)
- *Option:* In Ss' responses, they write questions asking for more information. They continue to exchange and return responses, answering questions and asking for more information until they accept or refuse the invitations.
- *Option:* If Ss have cell phones, they can practice sending text messages in class or for homework.

11 INTERCHANGE 4

See page T-118 for teaching notes.

12 READING

Learning Objectives: *read and discuss an article about a singer; develop skills in scanning a time line*

- Books closed. Draw these diagrams on the board:

FERGIE OF THE BLACK EYED PEAS

We know   We'd like to know

- Ss brainstorm ideas in pairs. If they have difficulty, suggest possible topics (e.g., *hit songs, age, full/real name, nationality*). Then Ss come to the board and write things they know or would like to know in the correct diagram. Don't correct Ss if they are wrong. Just correct their language.

- Books open. Point out that the time line shows the history of Fergie's life.

- Focus Ss' attention on the pictures. Ask different Ss to read the captions aloud.

- Allow Ss two minutes to scan the article quickly and find the dates for the pictures. (Answers: 2010, 1984, 2004) Remind Ss not to read the whole article but to look quickly for key words (e.g., *World Cup, TV show* Kids Incorporated, *Black Eyed Peas*).

! For a new way to introduce this Reading, try
• *Cloud Prediction* – download it from the website.

A

- Explain the task. Focus Ss' attention on the first event on the time line. Tell Ss to find the sentence in part A that matches this event. (Answer: b)

- Elicit or explain any new vocabulary.

Vocabulary

hit: a very popular song
single: one song
fans: people who love a celebrity
rapper: someone who performs rap music
highlights: important events
album: a collection of songs on a CD
Grammy Award: a set of prizes given to people who work in the music industry
performs: sings or acts

- Ss complete the task individually. Go around the class and give help as needed.

- Ss compare answers in pairs. Then go over answers with the class.

Answers

a. 8	e. 3
b. 1	f. 2
c. 7	g. 6
d. 4	h. 5

TIP If your Ss speak languages that have similar vocabulary to English, encourage them to look for cognates, or words with similar forms and meanings (e.g., *glamorous, celebration*).

- Focus Ss' attention on the diagrams on the board. Ask: "What did you learn? What do you still want to know? Where can you find this information?"

- **Option:** Books closed. Ask: "How much can you remember about Fergie?" Ss work in pairs to list facts.

B Pair work

- Read the questions aloud. Ss discuss their favorite musicians in pairs. Then ask Ss to share information with the class.

To review vocabulary from this Reading, play *Picture It!* – download it from the website.

End of Cycle 2

See the Supplementary Resources chart at the beginning of this unit for additional teaching materials and student activities related to this Cycle and for assessment tools.

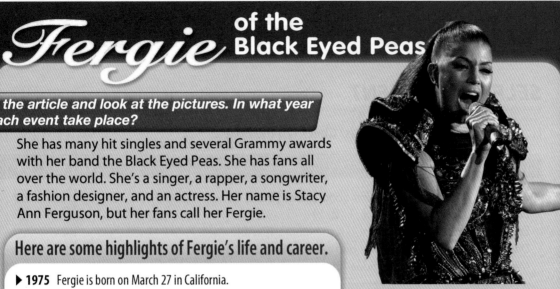

Fergie of the Black Eyed Peas

Scan the article and look at the pictures. In what year did each event take place?

She has many hit singles and several Grammy awards with her band the Black Eyed Peas. She has fans all over the world. She's a singer, a rapper, a songwriter, a fashion designer, and an actress. Her name is Stacy Ann Ferguson, but her fans call her Fergie.

▲ performing at the World Cup

Here are some highlights of Fergie's life and career.

▶ **1975** Fergie is born on March 27 in California.

▶ **1984** Fergie starts acting, doing the voice of Sally in the *Peanuts* cartoons. She also stars in the popular TV show *Kids Incorporated,* with actress Jennifer Love Hewitt.

▶ **1991** Fergie forms the all-female band Wild Orchid.

▶ **2003** Fergie records a song with the band Black Eyed Peas. The band likes her, and she records five more songs on the album.

▶ **2004** Fergie joins the Black Eyed Peas.

▶ **2005** Fergie and the Black Eyed Peas win their first Grammy award for "Let's Get It Started."

▶ **2006** Fergie makes a solo album and has six big hits. "Big Girls Don't Cry" is her first worldwide number one single.

▶ **2008** Fergie records "That Ain't Cool" with Japanese R&B singer Kumi Koda. She becomes famous in Japan.

▶ **2009** Fergie acts and sings in the movie *Nine*.

▶ **2010** Fergie and the Black Eyed Peas perform five songs at the 2010 World Cup celebration concert in South Africa.

▲ on the TV show *Kids Incorporated*

Fergie says she's the "luckiest girl in the world. " Why? Her song "Glamorous" says it all: "All the fans, I'd like to thank. Thank you really though, 'cause I remember yesterday when I dreamed about the days when I'd rock on MTV. . . ."

▲ on stage with the Black Eyed Peas

A Read the article. Then number these sentences from 1 (first event) to 8 (last event).

.... a. She sings at the World Cup concert.
.... b. She is born in California.
.... c. She acts and sings in a movie.
.... d. Her band wins its first Grammy.

.... e. She forms her first band.
.... f. She is on TV with Jennifer Love Hewitt.
.... g. She becomes very popular in Japan.
.... h. She has her first worldwide number one song.

B **PAIR WORK** Who is your favorite musician? What do you know about his or her life?

I really like hip-hop. ▪ **27**

Units 3–4 Progress check

SELF-ASSESSMENT

How well can you do these things? Check (✓) the boxes.

I can	Very well	OK	A little
Give and understand information about prices (Ex. 1)	☐	☐	☐
Say what I like and dislike (Ex. 1, 2, 3)	☐	☐	☐
Explain what I like or dislike about something (Ex. 2)	☐	☐	☐
Describe and compare objects and possessions (Ex. 2)	☐	☐	☐
Make and respond to invitations (Ex. 4)	☐	☐	☐

1 LISTENING *Weekend sale*

A Listen to a commercial for Dave's Discount Store. Circle the correct prices.

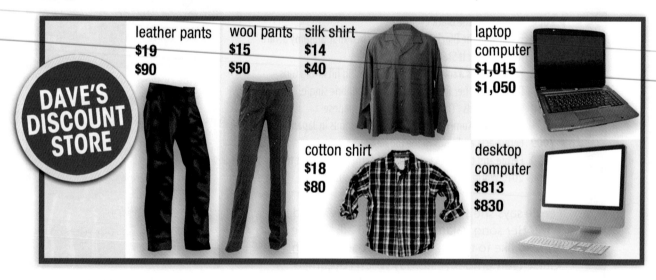

DAVE'S DISCOUNT STORE

leather pants
$19
$90

wool pants
$15
$50

silk shirt
$14
$40

laptop computer
$1,015
$1,050

cotton shirt
$18
$80

desktop computer
$813
$830

B **PAIR WORK** What do you think of the items in part A? Give your own opinions.

2 ROLE PLAY *Shopping trip*

Student A: Choose things from Exercise 1 for your family. Ask for Student B's opinion.

Student B: Help Student A choose presents for his or her family.

> A: I want to buy a computer for my parents. Which one do you like better?
> B: Well, I like the laptop better. It's nicer, and . . .

Change roles and try the role play again.

Units 3-4 Progress check

SELF-ASSESSMENT

Learning Objectives: *reflect on one's learning; identify areas that need improvement*

- Ask: "What did you learn in Units 3 and 4?" Elicit Ss' answers.
- Ss complete the Self-assessment. Encourage them to be honest, and point out they will not get a bad grade if they check (✓) *a little*.

- Ss move on to the Progress check exercises. You can have Ss complete them in class or for homework, using one of these techniques:
  1. Ask Ss to complete all the exercises.
  2. Ask Ss: "What do you need to practice?" Then assign exercises based on their answers.
  3. Ask Ss to choose and complete exercises based on their Self-assessment.

LISTENING

Learning Objectives: *assess one's ability to understand information about prices; assess one's ability to give opinions about what one likes and dislikes*

A ▶ [CD 1, Track 39]

- Set the scene. Dave's Discount Store is having a sale today. Ss will hear the prices of six items.
- Play the audio program once or twice. Ss listen and circle the correct price of each item.

AudioScript

Announcer Come in to Dave's today! Everything is on sale – for one day only. Here are some of our terrific sale prices. First, in the clothing department, we have great sales on both men's and women's pants. We have leather pants for only $90. That's right! All our stylish leather pants are only $90. And wool pants are on sale for $50. Just $50 for wool pants. Amazing! But that's not all. Every style and color of shirt is on sale. Designer silk shirts are now only $40. Again, that's $40 for a silk shirt. And cotton shirts are on sale for just $18. Unbelievable!

Finally, in the electronics department, we have a great selection of computers. We have laptop computers for only $1,015. And we have desktop computers for $830. A complete computer system for only $830. What a deal!
Remember, these prices are for today only, so come in and save at our one-day sale. Get everything you need . . . at Dave's!

Answers

leather pants: $90	cotton shirt: $18
wool pants: $50	laptop computer: $1,015
silk shirt: $40	desktop computer: $830

B *Pair work*

- Explain the task. Ss talk about the items in part A and give their own opinions about them in pairs. Are the things expensive, reasonable, or cheap?

ROLE PLAY

Learning Objectives: *assess one's ability to give opinions about what one likes and dislikes; assess one's ability to talk about preferences and make comparisons*

- Focus Ss' attention on the pictures in Exercise 1 and explain the task. Ss work in pairs. Student A wants to buy presents for his or her family at Dave's Discount Store. Student B is helping Student A choose presents.

- Model the example conversation with a S. Elicit other expressions and comparisons to use in the role plays.
- Ss practice the role play in pairs. Then they change roles. Go around the class and give help as needed.
- **Option:** Have Ss give the items different prices and try the role play again.

3 SURVEY

Learning Objective: *assess one's ability to ask and answer questions about entertainment using the simple present*

A

- Ss work individually. They write answers to the questions in the *Me* column.

B Class activity

- Explain and model the task. Say: "I usually watch TV at (7:00). When do you usually watch TV?" Ask different Ss until someone gives the same answer.

- Explain that you will write that person's name in the *My classmate* column. Point out that Ss should write a classmate's name only once.

- Ss go around the class and ask questions to complete the activity. Note any grammar, vocabulary, or pronunciation errors.

- **Option:** Go over any grammar, vocabulary, or pronunciation errors after Ss complete the activity.

4 SPEAKING

Learning Objective: *check one's ability to make invitations and excuses with* would like to + *verb*

A

- Explain the task. Then ask a S to read the example invitation in the book.

- Elicit suggestions for other interesting activities and write them on the board.

- Hand out three index cards to each S. Explain the task. Ss write three different invitations individually (one per card). Point out that they should not put their names on the cards.

- Ss complete the task. Go around the class and give help as needed.

B

- Ask different Ss to read the three response cards. Elicit other ways of accepting or refusing an invitation. Encourage Ss to suggest silly or unusual excuses for refusals.

- Hand out three index cards to each S. Explain the task. Ss write one acceptance and two refusals. The acceptance cards should include a question about where or when to meet. Point out that they should not put their names on the cards.

- Ss complete the task. Go around the class and give help as needed.

C Group work

- Ss work in small groups. One S collects all the invitation cards, shuffles them, and puts them in a pile.

- A different S collects all the response cards, shuffles them, and puts them in a different pile.

- Explain the task. Each S takes three invitation cards and three response cards. Then they read them silently.

- Model the task. Read an invitation card aloud. Ss accept or refuse the invitation by reading a response card.

- Ss take turns completing the task.

WHAT'S NEXT?

Learning Objective: *become more involved in one's learning*

- Focus Ss' attention on the Self-assessment again. Ask: "How well can you do these things now?"

- Ask Ss to underline one thing they need to review. Ask: "What did you underline? How can you review it?"

- If needed, plan additional activities or reviews based on Ss' answers.

3 SURVEY *Likes and dislikes*

A Write answers to these questions.

	Me	My classmate
When do you usually watch TV?	....	....
What kinds of TV programs do you like?	....	....
Do you like game shows?	....	....
Do you listen to the radio?	....	....
Who is your favorite singer?	....	....
What do you think of heavy metal?	....	....
What is your favorite movie?	....	....
Do you like musicals?	....	....
What kinds of movies do you dislike?	....	....

B **CLASS ACTIVITY** Find someone who has the same answers. Go around the class. Write a classmate's name only once!

4 SPEAKING *What an excuse!*

A Make up three invitations to interesting activities. Write them on cards.

> *I want to see the frog races tomorrow. They're at the park at 2:00. Would you like to go?*

B Write three response cards. One is an acceptance card, and two are refusals. Think of silly or unusual excuses.

> *That sounds great! What time do you want to meet?*

> *I'd like to, but I have to wash my cat tomorrow.*

> *I'd love to, but I want to take my bird to a singing contest.*

C **GROUP WORK** Shuffle the invitation cards together and the response cards together. Take three cards from each pile. Then invite people to do the things on your invitation cards. Use the response cards to accept or refuse.

WHAT'S NEXT?

Look at your Self-assessment again. Do you need to review anything?

Unit 5 Supplementary Resources Overview

	After the following SB exercises	You can use these materials in class	Your students can use these materials outside the classroom
CYCLE 1	1 Word Power	**TSS** Unit 5 Vocabulary Worksheet	**SSD** Unit 5 Vocabulary 1–2 **ARC** Family
	2 Listening		
	3 Conversation	**TSS** Unit 5 Listening Worksheet	**SSD** Unit 5 Speaking 1
	4 Pronunciation		
	5 Grammar Focus	**TSS** Unit 5 Extra Worksheet	**SB** Unit 5 Grammar Plus focus 1 **SSD** Unit 5 Grammar 1–2 **ARC** Present continuous 1–2
	6 Discussion		
	7 Interchange 5		**WB** Unit 5 exercises 1–6
CYCLE 2	8 Snapshot		
	9 Conversation		**SSD** Unit 5 Speaking 2
	10 Grammar Focus	**TSS** Unit 5 Grammar Worksheet **TSS** Unit 5 Writing Worksheet	**SB** Unit 5 Grammar Plus focus 2 **SSD** Unit 5 Grammar 3 **ARC** Quantifiers 1–2
	11 Writing		
	12 Reading	**TSS** Unit 5 Project Worksheet **VID** Unit 5 **VRB** Unit 5	**SSD** Unit 5 Reading 1–2 **SSD** Unit 5 Listening 1–3 **SSD** Unit 5 Video 1–3 **WB** Unit 5 exercises 7–11

Key

ARC: Arcade	**SB:** Student's Book	**SSD:** Self-study DVD-ROM	**TSS:** Teacher Support Site
VID: Video DVD	**VRB:** Video Resource Book	**WB:** Workbook	

My Plan for Unit 5

Use the space below to customize a plan that fits your needs.

With the following SB exercises	I am using these materials in class	My students are using these materials outside the classroom

With or instead of the following SB section	I am using these materials for assessment

5 I come from a big family.

WORD POWER *Family*

A Look at Sam's family tree. How are these people related to him?
Add the words to the family tree.

cousin
daughter
father
grandmother
niece
sister-in-law
uncle
wife

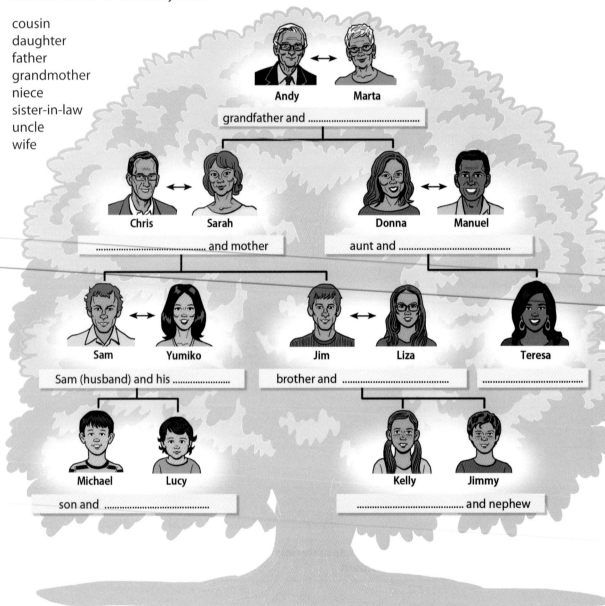

Andy ↔ Marta

grandfather and ....

Chris ↔ Sarah   Donna ↔ Manuel

.... and mother   aunt and ....

Sam ↔ Yumiko   Jim ↔ Liza   Teresa

Sam (husband) and his ....   brother and ....

Michael   Lucy   Kelly   Jimmy

son and .... and nephew

B Draw your family tree (or a friend's family tree). Then take turns talking
about your families. Ask follow-up questions to get more information.

A: There are five people in my family. I have two brothers and a sister.
B: How old is your sister?

I come from a big family.

Cycle 1, Exercises 1–7

In Unit 5, students discuss families, typical families, and family life. In Cycle 1, they talk about their own and other families using the present continuous. In Cycle 2, they discuss facts about families using quantifiers.

1 WORD POWER

Learning Objective: *learn vocabulary for discussing the family*

A

- Write the word *family* in a circle on the board. Then write the words *mother* and *father* around the circle.
- In pairs, Ss brainstorm words for family members and make a list. Then they compare lists with another pair. Go around the class and note the words on their lists.

> **TIP** To avoid teaching words Ss already know, start by asking Ss the words they know. Then teach any remaining vocabulary.

- Ask Ss to find Sam and circle his picture. Then ask: "Who is Yumiko?" (Answer: his wife) Ask Ss to write *wife* under Yumiko's picture and check (✓) *wife* in the vocabulary list.
- Ss complete the exercise in pairs. Go over the answers with the class and check pronunciation.

Answers

grandfather and **grandmother** (Marta)
father (Chris) and mother
aunt and **uncle** (Manuel)
Sam (husband) and his **wife** (Yumiko)
brother and **sister-in-law** (Liza)
cousin (Teresa)
son and **daughter** (Lucy)
niece (Kelly) and nephew

- As needed, teach other family words (e.g., *great-grandfather, great-grandmother, grandson, granddaughter, son, stepbrother, stepsister, only child, twins, parents, ex-wife, ex-husband*). Use pictures to present additional vocabulary.
- **Option:** For more practice, ask questions about another person in the family tree (e.g., *Donna*). Possible questions include: *Who is Donna's husband? Who is her sister-in-law?*

B

- Explain the task. Ss draw their family trees individually. Point out that single Ss can include their grandparents, parents, brothers, and sisters, while married Ss can include their husband or wife, children, and grandchildren.
- Draw your family tree on the board while Ss complete the task.
- Model the task by describing your own family. Then encourage Ss to ask you questions. If needed, present or review words such as *married, single, divorced, widowed,* or *deceased.*
- Ss complete the task in pairs or small groups. Go around the room and encourage Ss to ask follow-up questions (e.g., *How old is he? What does he do?*).
- Elicit interesting things Ss learned about their partners.
- **Option:** Ask Ss to bring in pictures of their family. Ss show each other family photos in small groups. Encourage them to add two pieces of information for each photo (e.g., *This is my brother. He's 27, and he's a lawyer.*).

> **TIP** To personalize the class and make the language more meaningful, encourage Ss to bring their own materials to class.

To review the vocabulary of family, try **Picture Dictation** – download it from the website. Ask Ss to draw a family tree while you say: "Amanda has one brother and one sister. Her brother, Edward, is married to Jean. They have three children. Amanda's sister, Mary, is married to Mike. They have one daughter. Amanda has a husband. His name is Charlie."

For more practice matching words for family members with their meanings, play **Concentration** – download it from the website.

2 LISTENING

Learning Objective: develop skills in listening for specific information

⏵ [CD 1, Track 40]

- Focus Ss' attention on the pictures. Ask: "How are the people related?" Encourage Ss to make guesses.
- Play the audio program. Ss listen and complete the task.
- Go over answers with the class.

AudioScript

1.
Woman Who are you listening to, Adam?
Adam Oh, it's Coldplay. They're my favorite band. Chris Martin has a cool voice.
Woman Yeah, they're pretty good. Do you know who his wife is?
Adam His wife? No.
Woman The actress Gwyneth Paltrow. They make an interesting couple.
2.
Man What are you reading, Pete?
Pete An article about Francis Ford Coppola. He has a new movie out.
Man Who?
Pete Francis Ford Coppola. You know, the director of The Godfather and The Godfather: Part II.
Man Oh, right.
Pete Do you know who his nephew is? The actor Nicholas Cage.
Man Really?
3.
Mom Are you downloading a song, Cindy?
Cindy Oh, hi, Mom. Yeah, I am. It's the new Miley Cyrus song.
Mom Miley Cyrus . . . is she related to Billy Ray Cyrus?
Cindy I have no idea. Who's he?
Mom He's a country singer and an actor. Here, let's look it up. [*pause, typing*] Yes, Billy Ray is her father.
4.
Woman So . . . what movie do we want to watch? Oh, here's one with Casey Affleck.
Man Oh, I like him. He's really good in dramas.
Woman I like his sister-in-law, too.
Man Who's that?
Woman Jennifer Garner, the actress.
Man Oh, right. She's married to Ben Affleck, Casey's brother.

Answers

1. wife   2. nephew   3. father   4. sister-in-law

3 CONVERSATION

Learning Objectives: practice a conversation about families; see the present continuous in context

A ⏵ [CD 1, Track 41]

- Set the scene. Rita is asking about Sue's family. Focus Ss' attention on the pictures. Ask: "How do you think they are related to Sue?" Elicit ideas.
- Books closed. Explain the task. One S listens for information about the woman and one listens for information about the man. Play the audio program and Ss complete the task.
- Books open. Play the audio program again. Ss listen and read silently.
- Ss practice the conversation in pairs.

B ⏵ [CD 1, Track 42]

- Read the two focus questions aloud. Play the audio program once or twice.
- Go over answers with the class.

AudioScript

Sue So, what about your parents, Rita? Where do they live?
Rita They live in Texas.
Sue Oh, where in Texas?
Rita In Austin. It's a small city, but it's very nice.
Sue Are they still working?
Rita Oh, yes. My mother is teaching at a university there, and my father is a carpenter.

Answers

They live in Austin, Texas. Her mother teaches at a university, and her father is a carpenter.

4 PRONUNCIATION

Learning Objectives: notice and use intonation in statements; sound natural when making statements

A ⏵ [CD 1, Track 43]

- Play the audio program. Point out the falling intonation. Ss repeat the statements. Ask different Ss to say the statements to check their intonation.

B *Pair work*

- Explain the task. Ss work in pairs. Go around the class and check Ss' intonation.

2 LISTENING *How are they related?*

▶ Listen to four conversations about famous people. How is the second person related to the first person?

1.

Chris Martin

Gwyneth Paltrow

....

2.
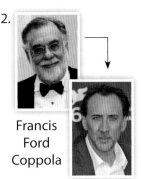
Francis Ford Coppola

Nicholas Cage

....

3.
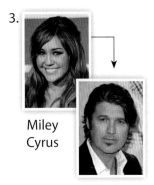
Miley Cyrus

Billy Ray Cyrus

....

4.
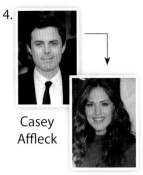
Casey Affleck

Jennifer Garner

....

3 CONVERSATION *Asking about families*

A ▶ Listen and practice.

Rita: Tell me about your brother and sister, Sue.
Sue: Well, my sister works for the government.
Rita: Oh, what does she do?
Sue: I'm not sure. She's working on a very secret project right now.
Rita: Wow! And what about your brother?
Sue: He's a wildlife photographer.
Rita: What an interesting family! Can I meet them?
Sue: Sure, but not now. My sister's away. She's not working in the United States this month.
Rita: And your brother?
Sue: He's traveling in the Amazon.

B ▶ Listen to the rest of the conversation. Where do Rita's parents live? What do they do?

4 PRONUNCIATION *Intonation in statements*

A ▶ Listen and practice. Notice that statements usually have falling intonation.

He's traveling in the Amazon.

She's working on a very secret project.

B **PAIR WORK** Practice the conversation in Exercise 3 again. Pay attention to the intonation in the statements.

Present continuous ▶

Are you **living** at home now?	Yes, I **am**.	No, I**'m not**.
Is your sister **working** for the government?	Yes, she **is**.	No, she**'s not**./No, she **isn't**.
Are Ed and Jill **taking** classes this year?	Yes, they **are**.	No, they**'re not**./No, they **aren't**.

Where **are** you **working** now?	I**'m not working**. I need a job.
What **is** your brother **doing**?	He**'s traveling** in the Amazon.
What **are** your friends **doing** these days?	They**'re studying** for their exams.

A Complete these phone conversations using the present continuous.

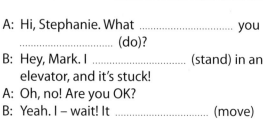

A: Hi, Stephanie. What .... you
.... (do)?

B: Hey, Mark. I .... (stand) in an
elevator, and it's stuck!

A: Oh, no! Are you OK?

B: Yeah. I – wait! It .... (move)
now. Thank goodness!

A: Marci, how .... you and Justin
.... (enjoy) your shopping trip?

B: We .... (have) a lot of fun.

A: .... your brother
.... (spend) a lot of money?

B: No, Mom. He .... (buy) only
one or two things. That's all!

B **PAIR WORK** Practice the phone conversations with a partner.

 DISCUSSION *Is anyone . . . ?*

GROUP WORK Ask your classmates about people in their families. What are
they doing? Ask follow-up questions to get more information.

A: Is anyone in your family traveling right now?
B: Yes, my dad is. He's in South Korea.
C: What's he doing there?

topics to ask about	
traveling	going to high school or college
living abroad	moving to a new home
taking a class	studying a foreign language

5 GRAMMAR FOCUS

Learning Objectives: *practice the present continuous; ask and answer questions using the present continuous*

 [CD 1, Track 44]

Simple present vs. present continuous

- Draw this chart on the board:

	Usually	Right now
Sue's sister		
Sue's brother		

- Focus Ss' attention on the Conversation on page 31. Ask: "What does Sue's sister do? What is she doing right now?" (Answers: She works for the government. She's working on a secret project.) Complete the chart. Repeat the procedure for Sue's brother. (Answers: He's a wildlife photographer. He's traveling in the Amazon.)

- Elicit or explain the difference between the two tenses (simple present = habitual actions; present continuous = actions that are happening right now).

- Compare the formation of the two tenses:
  She works. (subject + verb)
  She is working. (subject + *be* + verb + *-ing*)

Present continuous questions and statements

- Focus Ss' attention on the Conversation on page 31. Ask: "Why can't Rita meet Sue's family?" Elicit the answers, and write them on the board:

  Sue's sister is not working in the U.S. this month.
  Sue's brother is traveling in the Amazon right now.

- Focus Ss' attention on the Grammar Focus box. Elicit the rule for forming yes/no and Wh-questions in the present continuous:
  Be + subject + verb + *-ing*?
  (Wh-question) + *be* + subject + verb + *-ing*?

- Ask Ss to underline the time expressions in the Grammar Focus box that show the action is temporary or current: *this year, now, these days.*

- Play the audio program.

A

- Explain the task and model the first question.
- Ss complete the task individually. Encourage Ss to use contractions in statements. Review contractions as needed.
- Ss go over their answers in pairs. Then go over answers with the class.

Answers

1. A: Hi, Stephanie. What **are** you **doing**?
   B: Hey, Mark. I**'m standing** in an elevator, and it's stuck!
   A: Oh, no! Are you OK?
   B: Yeah. I – wait! It**'s moving** now. Thank goodness!
2. A: Marci, how **are** you and Justin **enjoying** your shopping trip?
   B: We**'re having** a lot of fun.
   A: **Is** your brother **spending** a lot of money?
   B: No, Mom. He**'s buying** only one or two things. That's all!

B *Pair work*

- Ss practice the phone conversations.
- **Option:** Ss practice the conversations sitting back-to-back or with their cell phones.

6 DISCUSSION

Learning Objectives: *discuss families using the present continuous; develop the skill of asking follow-up questions*

Group work

- Explain the task and go over the topics in the box. Explain any new vocabulary and elicit other possible discussion topics.
- Model the conversation with one or two Ss. Encourage Ss to add follow-up questions and introduce new topics.

- Give Ss a few minutes to prepare things to say about their families.
- Ss complete the task in small groups. Go around the class and note any common errors. Then go over them with the class.

> **TIP** To help you decide if additional controlled grammar practice is necessary, watch the Ss' performance during the speaking activities.

7 INTERCHANGE 5

See page T-119 for teaching notes.

End of Cycle 1

Cycle 2, Exercises 8–12

See the Supplementary Resources chart at the beginning of this unit for additional teaching materials and student activities related to this Cycle.

8 SNAPSHOT

Learning Objective: *compare and discuss statistics about families in different countries*

- Books closed. Write these questions on the board:

  1. What percentage of homes in Mexico have a TV set?
     a. 83%   b. 85%   c. 93%

  2 What percentage of husbands and wives in Canada share the housework?
     a. 31%   b. 45%   c. 70%

- Review percentages if needed. Ask Ss to guess the answers to these questions. Then elicit their guesses.

- Books open. Ss read the Snapshot to find the answers. (Answers: 1. c 2. b) Ask: "Who was right? Do these two facts seem positive or negative? Why?"

- Go over the facts about the countries. Ss then discuss if each fact is positive or negative in small groups.

- Ss discuss how they think their country compares to the facts as a class.

9 CONVERSATION

Learning Objectives: *practice a conversation about family size; see quantifiers in context*

A ▶ [CD 1, Track 45]

- Ask the class: "How many brothers do you have? How many sisters?" Elicit answers.

- Draw this chart on the board:

	Where from?	Number of brothers/sisters?	Typical?
1. Mei-li			
2. Marcos			

- Books closed. Set the scene. Marcos and Mei-li are talking about their families.

- Play the audio program. Ss listen for the answers. Ask Ss to complete the chart on the board if they know the answers. Play the audio program again as needed and ask Ss to add to or change the information in the chart. (Answers: 1. China, no brothers or sisters, yes 2. Peru, three brothers and two sisters, no)

- Books open. Play the audio program again. Ss look at the picture and read the conversation silently.

- Ss practice the conversation in pairs.

❗For a new way to practice this Conversation, try the **Disappearing Dialog** – download it from the website.

B ▶ [CD 1, Track 46]

- Ask: "Why does Marcos like having a big family?" (Answer: Because he gets lots of birthday presents.)

- Read the focus question aloud. Ask Ss to make predictions and write them on the board.

- Play the audio program. Ss listen to find out if any prediction on the board is correct.

AudioScript

Marcos So, do you like being an only child?
Mei-li Of course. I get all my parents' attention.
Marcos Yeah, I share my parents' attention with five other people.
Mei-li But sometimes I want a brother or a sister.
Marcos Do you ever feel lonely?
Mei-li Sure. But it's OK. I have a lot of friends.

Answers

She gets all her parents' attention.

INTERCHANGE 5 *Family facts*

Find out about your classmates' families. Go to Interchange 5 on page 119.

8 SNAPSHOT

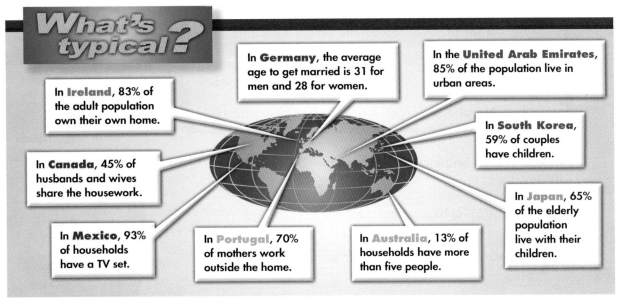

What's typical?

In **Ireland**, 83% of the adult population own their own home.

In **Germany**, the average age to get married is 31 for men and 28 for women.

In the **United Arab Emirates**, 85% of the population live in urban areas.

In **Canada**, 45% of husbands and wives share the housework.

In **South Korea**, 59% of couples have children.

In **Mexico**, 93% of households have a TV set.

In **Portugal**, 70% of mothers work outside the home.

In **Australia**, 13% of households have more than five people.

In **Japan**, 65% of the elderly population live with their children.

Source: nationmaster.com

Which facts surprise you? Why?
Which facts seem like positive things? Which seem negative?
How do you think your country compares?

9 CONVERSATION *Is that typical?*

A Listen and practice.

Marcos: How many brothers and sisters do you have, Mei-li?
 Mei-li: Actually, I'm an only child.
Marcos: Really?
 Mei-li: Yeah, a lot of families in China have only one child these days.
Marcos: I didn't know that.
 Mei-li: What about you, Marcos?
Marcos: I come from a big family. I have three brothers and two sisters.
 Mei-li: Wow! Is that typical in Peru?
Marcos: I'm not sure. Many families are smaller these days. But big families are great because you get a lot of birthday presents!

B Listen to the rest of the conversation. What does Mei-li like about being an only child?

10 GRAMMAR FOCUS

Quantifiers ▶

100%	**All** **Nearly all** **Most**	families have only one child.
	Many **A lot of** **Some**	families are smaller these days.
	Not many **Few**	couples have more than one child.
0%	**No one**	gets married before the age of 18.

A Rewrite these sentences using quantifiers. Then compare with a partner.

1. In the U.S., 75% of high school students go to college.

   ....

2. Seven percent of the people in Brazil are age 65 or older.

   ....

3. In India, 0% of the people vote before the age of 18.

   ....

4. Forty percent of the people in Sweden live alone.

   ....

5. In Singapore, 23% of the people speak English at home.

   ....

B **PAIR WORK** Rewrite the sentences in part A so that they are true about your country.

> In . . . , many high school students go to college.

11 WRITING An email about your family

A Write an email to your e-pal about your family.

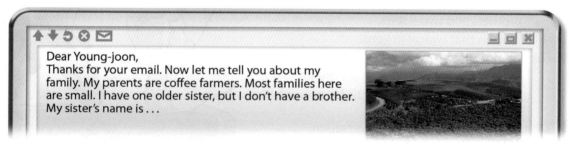

Dear Young-joon,
Thanks for your email. Now let me tell you about my family. My parents are coffee farmers. Most families here are small. I have one older sister, but I don't have a brother. My sister's name is . . .

B **GROUP WORK** Take turns reading your emails. Ask questions to get more information.

10 GRAMMAR FOCUS

Learning Objectives: *practice quantifiers; present facts using quantifiers*

 [CD 1, Track 47]

- Explain that when people don't know the exact percentage of something, they use words like *most* or *some*. Point out the quantifiers in the Grammar Focus box.
- Explain that all these quantifiers come before plural nouns except one. Ask Ss which one does not. (Answer: no one)
- Play the audio program.
- Ask Ss to find two sentences with quantifiers in the Conversation on page 33. (Answers: A lot of families in China . . ., Many families . . .)
- Ask: "Who is from a big family? Raise your hand." Then elicit a statement about the class that starts with a quantifier (e.g., *Most students in the class are from big families.*). Ask more questions and elicit more statements with quantifiers (e.g., *Are you single? Do you live at home? Are you an only child?*).

A
- Explain the task. Model the first answer.

- Ss rewrite the sentences individually. Point out that more than one quantifier may be possible. Then Ss go over their answers in pairs.
- Go over answers with the class.

Possible answers

1. In the U.S., many high school students go to college.
2. Few people in Brazil are age 65 or older.
3. In India, no one votes before the age of 18.
4. Some people in Sweden live alone.
5. In Singapore, not many people speak English at home.

B *Pair work*
- Explain the task and elicit the first answer. Write it on the board.
- Ss complete the task in pairs. Go around the class and give help as needed. Then each pair joins another pair to compare answers.
- **Option:** Ss make statements about the facts in the Snapshot on page 33 using quantifiers instead of percentages.
- For more practice with quantifiers, play *Tic-Tac-Toe* – download it from the website.

11 WRITING

Learning Objective: *write an email describing one's family*

A
- Ss describe their family to a partner. Then they read the example email silently.
- Elicit information Ss can include in a description of their family (e.g., names, ages, jobs, where they live). Write all ideas on the board.

- For a new way to prepare for this Writing, try *Mind Mapping* – download it from the website.
- Ss write emails about their family. Encourage them to use quantifiers.

B *Group work*
- Ss read each other's emails in small groups and ask each other for more information.

12 READING

Learning Objectives: *read an article about dads who stay at home with their children; develop skills in reading topic sentences*

- Books closed. Ask: "Why do men decide to stay at home with their children? What happens to the children when both parents work?" Elicit ideas.
- Books open. Read the title and the pre-reading task.
- Explain that the first sentence of a paragraph usually gives you its main idea. This is called a "topic sentence."
- Ss read the topic sentences of the paragraphs. Ask: "Which question from the pre-reading task will the article answer?" (Answer: Why do men decide to stay at home with their children?)

A

- Go over the five questions. Then Ss read the article silently and answer the questions.
- Elicit or explain any new vocabulary.

Vocabulary

housework: work people do to take care of the home, such as cleaning

- Ss compare their answers in groups. Go around the class and give help as needed.
- Go over answers with the class.

Answers

Who . . . ?	William	Daniel	Roberto
has more than two children?	X		
has an only child			X
had a stressful career	X		X
thinks it's hard to stay at home		X	
has a wife with a great job?		X	

B *Pair work*

- Read the three questions. Then Ss discuss the questions in pairs.
- Go over the answers with the class. Then elicit ideas from the pairs.

Possible answers

Likes: one-on-one time with daughter, play with kids, spend time with kids while they're young, freedom from work, no stressful job

Challenges: no time for self, do housework, it's hard work

Other reasons: able to work from home, paying for childcare too expensive

End of Cycle 2

See the Supplementary Resources chart at the beginning of this unit for additional teaching materials and student activities related to this Cycle.

Stay-at-Home Dads

Read the title of the article. Then check (✓) the question you think the interviews will answer. ☐ *Why do men decide to stay at home with their children?* ☐ *What happens when both parents work?*

Families in the U.S. are changing. One important change is that many fathers are staying home with their children. They take care of the kids, and their wives go to work. *Modern Family* magazine asked three stay-at-home dads the question "What's it like being a stay-at-home dad?"

William Chan: I'm having a great time! When the kids are in school, I do housework. Our youngest child goes to school part-time. When I pick her up, I love the one-on-one time with her. Then, when my two sons get home from school, we all play together. Why do I stay home? Well, I wasn't happy at my job. It was pretty stressful, in fact.

Daniel Evans: It's a challenge. We have two young children. They don't go to school yet. I never have time for myself! That's not easy. But my kids are growing up so fast. I really want to spend time with them when they're young. Also, my wife loves her job. I think most stay-at-home dads say the same thing: It's hard, but it's worth it.

Roberto Garcia: In my neighborhood, there aren't many dads in the park with their kids on weekdays. Nearly all of the parents are moms. I had a stressful job before and didn't have a lot of free time. I hated it. We have a daughter, and now I'm spending more time with her. I love that. I'm enjoying my freedom from work, but I'm also working very hard!

A Read the interviews. Check (✓) the correct names.

Who . . . ?	William	Daniel	Roberto
1. has more than two children	☐	☐	☐
2. has an only child	☐	☐	☐
3. had a stressful career	☐	☐	☐
4. thinks it's hard to stay at home	☐	☐	☐
5. has a wife with a great job	☐	☐	☐

B **PAIR WORK** What do the dads like about staying at home? What challenges are they having? What are some other reasons dads stay at home?

Unit 6 Supplementary Resources Overview

	After the following SB exercises	You can use these materials in class	Your students can use these materials outside the classroom
CYCLE 1	1 Snapshot		**SSD** Unit 6 Vocabulary 1
	2 Word Power	**TSS** Unit 6 Vocabulary Worksheet	**SSD** Unit 6 Vocabulary 2 **ARC** Sports and exercise 1–2
	3 Conversation		**SSD** Unit 6 Speaking 1
	4 Grammar Focus	**TSS** Unit 6 Listening Worksheet	**SB** Unit 6 Grammar Plus focus 1 **SSD** Unit 6 Grammar 1 **ARC** Adverbs of frequency
	5 Pronunciation		
	6 Speaking		
	7 Listening		
	8 Discussion	**TSS** Unit 6 Extra Worksheet	
	9 Writing	**TSS** Unit 6 Writing Worksheet	**WB** Unit 6 exercises 1–6
CYCLE 2	10 Conversation		**SSD** Unit 6 Speaking 2
	11 Grammar Focus	**TSS** Unit 6 Grammar Worksheet	**SB** Unit 6 Grammar Plus focus 2 **SSD** Unit 6 Grammar 2–3 **ARC** Adverbs of frequency and Questions with *how* **ARC** Questions with *do* and *how*
	12 Listening		
	13 Interchange 6		
	14 Reading	**TSS** Unit 6 Project Worksheet **VID** Unit 6 **VRB** Unit 6	**SSD** Unit 6 Reading 1–2 **SSD** Unit 6 Listening 1–3 **SSD** Unit 6 Video 1–3 **WB** Unit 6 exercises 7–11

With or instead of the following SB section	You can also use these materials for assessment
Units 5–6 Progress Check	**ASSESSMENT CD** Units 5–6 Oral Quiz **ASSESSMENT CD** Units 5–6 Written Quiz

Key **ARC**: Arcade   **SB**: Student's Book   **SSD**: Self-study DVD-ROM   **TSS:** Teacher Support Site
VID: Video DVD   **VRB:** Video Resource Book   **WB:** Workbook

Unit 6 Supplementary Resources Overview   *Interchange* Teacher's Edition 1 © Cambridge University Press 2013   Photocopiable

My Plan for Unit 6

Use the space below to customize a plan that fits your needs.

With the following SB exercises	I am using these materials in class	My students are using these materials outside the classroom

With or instead of the following SB section	I am using these materials for assessment

6 How often do you exercise?

1 SNAPSHOT

The Top Five Sports and Fitness Activities in the United States

Sports	Fitness Activities
☐ basketball	☐ walking
☐ baseball	☐ weight training
☐ soccer	☐ treadmill
☐ football	☐ stretching
☐ softball	☐ jogging

Source: SGMA International, *Sports Participation in America*

Do people in your country enjoy any of these sports or activities?
Check (✓) the sports or fitness activities you enjoy.
Make a list of other sports or activities you do. Then compare with the class.

2 WORD POWER *Sports and exercise*

A Which of these activities are popular with the following age groups?
Check (✓) the activities. Then compare with a partner.

	Children	Teens	Young adults	Middle-aged people	Older people
aerobics	☐	☐	☐	☐	☐
bicycling	☐	☐	☐	☐	☐
bowling	☐	☐	☐	☐	☐
golf	☐	☐	☐	☐	☐
karate	☐	☐	☐	☐	☐
swimming	☐	☐	☐	☐	☐
tennis	☐	☐	☐	☐	☐
volleyball	☐	☐	☐	☐	☐
yoga	☐	☐	☐	☐	☐

B **PAIR WORK** Which activities in part A are used with *do, go,* or *play*?

do aerobics ....   go bicycling ....   play golf ....

....

....

How often do you exercise?

In Unit 6, students discuss sports, exercise, and leisure activities. In Cycle 1, they talk about sports and exercise using adverbs of frequency. In Cycle 2, they talk about leisure activities using questions with how and short answers.

SNAPSHOT

Learning Objectives: *talk about sports and fitness; learn sports and fitness vocabulary*

- Books closed. Introduce the topics of sport and fitness. Ss brainstorm sports and fitness activities. Write Ss' ideas in two columns on the board:

Sports	Fitness activities
baseball	jogging
soccer	weight training
basketball	walking

> **TIP** To make new vocabulary easy for your Ss to copy, make a vocabulary list on one side of the board. Add new words to the list throughout the class.

- Ask Ss to guess the sports and fitness activities people from the U.S. like best. (Answers: basketball, walking)
- Books open. Ss look at the Snapshot and compare their guesses. Ask: "Who guessed right?"

- Elicit or explain any new vocabulary. Help Ss with the pronunciation of difficult words (e.g., *weight*, *treadmill*). If needed, explain that American football is different from international football. Players use their hands, throw and run with the ball, and wear safety equipment. In the U.S, international football is called *soccer*.

Vocabulary

softball: a sport similar to baseball but with a bigger, softer ball
weight training: lifting weights to become stronger
treadmill: a machine for walking or running
stretching: extending or making your arms and legs longer

- Go over the discussion questions and tasks.
- Ss complete the tasks individually. Go around the class and give help as needed. Then elicit Ss' answers.

WORD POWER

Learning Objectives: *Discuss types of sports and exercise; learn collocations with* do, go, *and* play

A

- Go over the activities in the chart. In pairs, Ss match the activities to the icons. Give help as needed.
- Explain and model the task. Ask: "What age groups like aerobics?" Point out that there is no correct answer.
- While Ss complete the task individually, write this conversation on the board:
  A: What age groups like (aerobics)?
  B: I think it's popular with (young adults).
  A: I agree OR I don't really agree. I think it's popular with (teens).
- Model the conversation with one or two Ss. Then Ss use the model conversation to compare answers in pairs.

B *Pair work*

- Present the rules for these collocations:
  go + activities ending in *-ing*, except *weight training*
  play + games, such as sports played with a ball
  do + fitness activities and individual exercises
- Ss complete the task in pairs. To check answers, write the verbs *do*, *go*, and *play* on the board. Ask different Ss to write the answers. Give help as needed.

Answers

do	go	play
aerobics	bicycling	golf
karate	bowling	tennis
yoga	swimming	volleyball

- **Option:** Ss circle the activities and sports they enjoy. Then they compare with a partner.

- For more practice with sports and exercise vocabulary, play *Sculptures* – download it from the website.

T-36

3 CONVERSATION

Learning Objectives: *practice a conversation about exercise; see adverbs of frequency in context*

A ▶ [CD 2, Track 1]

- Use the picture to set the scene. Ask: "Where are Paul and Marie? What are they doing? What do you think they like to do in their free time?"
- Books closed. Write these sentences on the board:
  1. *Paul goes bicycling often.*
  2. *Marie exercises every day.*

  Ask: "Are these sentences true or false?" Play the audio program and elicit the answers. (Answers: 1. false 2. false) Elicit the correct answers. (Answers: 1. swimming 2. hardly ever)
- Elicit or explain any new vocabulary.

Vocabulary

Seriously?: Really?
couch potato: a person who watches a lot of TV and is not very active

- Books open. Play the audio program again. Ss listen and read silently. Ask: "Are you more like Marie or Paul?" Elicit Ss' answers.
- Ss practice the conversation in pairs.
- ! For a new way to practice this Conversation, try the *Moving Dialog* – download it from the website.

B ▶ [CD 2, Track 2]

- Read the focus question aloud. Ask Ss to make guesses. Write their ideas on the board.
- Play the audio program. Then elicit the answer.

AudioScript

Marie What else do you like to do, Paul?
Paul Well, I like video games a lot. I play them every day. It drives my mom crazy!
Marie Hey, I play video games all the time, too.
Paul Well, listen, I have some great new games. Why don't we play some after class today?
Marie OK!

Answers

He plays video games.

4 GRAMMAR FOCUS

Learning Objectives: *practice adverbs of frequency; ask and answer questions using adverbs of frequency*

 [CD 2, Track 3]

Adverbs of frequency

- Write these sentences on the board:

  I _____ get up early
  I _____ go swimming.
  I _____ exercise
  I _____ just watch TV.

- Ask Ss to find the missing words in the Conversation in Exercise 3 and write them on the board. (Answers: almost always, often, hardly ever, usually) Explain that these are adverbs of frequency. Point out that they go before most verbs. Focus Ss' attention on the second column of the Grammar Focus box.
- On the board, write: *I'm always late.* Point out that adverbs of frequency go after the verb *be.*
- Point out the third column. Explain that percentages show how often something happens.
- Now focus Ss' attention on the first column. Ask: "Where do these adverbs go?" (Answer: at the end of a statement or question)
- Play the audio program.

A

- Explain the task. Model the first example. Ss complete the task individually.
- Ss practice the conversations in pairs.

Answers

1. A: Do you **ever** play sports?
   B: Sure. I play soccer **twice a week**.
2. A: What do you **usually** do on Saturday mornings?
   B: Nothing much. I **almost always** sleep until noon.
3. A: Do you **often** do aerobics at the gym?
   B: No, I **hardly ever** do aerobics.
4. A: Do you **always** exercise on Sundays?
   B: No, I **never** exercise on Sundays.
5. A: What do you **usually** do after class?
   B: I go out with my classmates **about three times a week**.

B Pair work

- Explain the task. Ss ask and answer the questions in part A in pairs, using their own information.
- For more practice with adverbs of frequency, play *Tic-Tac-Toe* – download it from the website. Write different adverbs of frequency in the nine boxes.

3 CONVERSATION *I hardly ever exercise.*

A 🔘 Listen and practice.

Marie: You're really fit, Paul. Do you exercise a lot?
Paul: Well, I almost always get up early, and I lift weights for an hour.
Marie: Seriously?
Paul: Sure. And then I often go swimming.
Marie: Wow! How often do you exercise like that?
Paul: About five times a week. What about you?
Marie: Oh, I hardly ever exercise. I usually just watch TV in my free time. I guess I'm a real couch potato!

B 🔘 Listen to the rest of the conversation. What else does Paul do in his free time?

4 GRAMMAR FOCUS

Adverbs of frequency 🔘

How often do you exercise?	Do you **ever** watch TV in the evening?	**100%** **always**
I lift weights **every day**.	Yes, I **often** watch TV after dinner.	**almost always**
I go jogging **once a week**.	I **sometimes** watch TV before bed.	**usually**
I play soccer **twice a month**.	**Sometimes** I watch TV before bed.*	**often**
I swim about **three times a year**.	I **hardly ever** watch TV.	**sometimes**
I don't exercise very **often/much**.	No, I **never** watch TV.	**hardly ever**
Usually I exercise before work.*		**almost never**
	***Usually** *and* **sometimes** *can begin a sentence.*	**0%** **never**

A Put the adverbs in the correct place. Then practice with a partner.

1. A: Do you play sports? (ever)
   B: Sure. I play soccer. (twice a week)

2. A: What do you do on Saturday mornings? (usually)
   B: Nothing much. I sleep until noon. (almost always)

3. A: Do you do aerobics at the gym? (often)
   B: No, I do aerobics. (hardly ever)

4. A: Do you exercise on Sundays? (always)
   B: No, I exercise on Sundays. (never)

5. A: What do you do after class? (usually)
   B: I go out with my classmates. (about three times a week)

B **PAIR WORK** Take turns asking the questions in part A. Give your own information when answering.

5 PRONUNCIATION *Intonation with direct address*

A ▶ Listen and practice. Notice these statements with direct address.
There is usually falling intonation and a pause before the name.

You're really fit, Paul.   You look tired, Marie.   I feel great, Dr. Lee.

B **PAIR WORK** Write four statements using direct address.
Then practice them.

6 SPEAKING *Fitness poll*

A **GROUP WORK** Take a poll in your group. One person takes notes.
Take turns asking each person these questions.

1. Do you have a regular fitness program? How often do you exercise?

2. Do you ever go to a gym? How often do you go? What do you do there?

3. Do you play any sports? Which ones? How often do you play them?

4. Do you ever take long walks? How often? Where do you go?

5. What else do you do to keep fit?

B **GROUP WORK** Study the results of the poll. Who in your group
has a good fitness program?

7 LISTENING *In the evening*

A ▶ Listen to three people discuss what they like to do in the evening.
Complete the chart.

	Activity	How often?
Justin	....	....
Carrie	....	....
Marcos	....	....

B ▶ Listen again. Who is most similar to you – Justin, Carrie, or Marcos?

5 PRONUNCIATION

Learning Objectives: *notice intonation with direct address; learn to sound natural when using direct address*

A *[CD 2, Track 4]*

- Play the audio program. Use gestures to demonstrate falling intonation. Elicit or explain that direct address statements end with falling intonation.
- Play the audio program again. Ss repeat the statements individually.

B *Pair work*

- Explain the task and model it by writing an example statement.
- Ss write four statements in pairs. Then they practice them. Go around the class and check Ss' intonation.

6 SPEAKING

Learning Objective: *talk about fitness using* How often *and adverbs of frequency*

A *Group work*

- Focus Ss' attention on the title. Explain that a poll has two parts. First everyone answers the same questions. Then you compare and summarize the answers.

- In small groups, Ss take turns asking each other questions. One S takes notes. Go around the class and give help as needed.

B *Group work*

- Ss compare the results of their poll and decide who has a good fitness program. Then one S in each group reports the information to the class.

7 LISTENING

Learning Objective: *develop skills in listening for key words and specific information*

A *[CD 2, Track 5]*

- Set the scene. Three people are talking about their favorite evening activities. Have Ss brainstorm things people do in the evening.
- Explain the task. Ss listen only for favorite activities and complete the first column in the chart. Write the chart on the board.
- Play the audio program. Ss complete the task individually and compare their answers in pairs. Ask different Ss to write the answers on the board.
- Explain the task. Ss listen only for how often Justin, Carrie, and Marcos do the activities. Ss complete the second column.
- Play the audio program again. Ss complete the task individually and compare their answers in pairs. Ask different Ss to write the answers on the board.

> **TIP** If Ss have difficulty understanding the audio program, try to find out where they have difficulty. Replay that part of the program and ask what they hear.

AudioScript

Carrie So, what do you usually do in the evening, Justin?
Justin I exercise a lot. I like to go swimming after work.
Carrie Yeah? How often do you go swimming?
Justin Twice a week – on Tuesdays and Thursdays.

Carrie Well, you are in great shape.
Justin Thanks!
Marcos You're in great shape, too, Carrie.
Carrie Oh, thanks, Marcos. I usually go to the gym and do yoga in the evenings. I love it! My friends and I take a yoga class there.
Justin How often do you go?
Carrie Three times a week. And what about you, Marcos? Do you ever go to the gym in the evenings?
Marcos Actually, I don't exercise very much. But I go bowling about twice a month. But I'm not very good.

Answers

	Favorite activity	How often?
Justin	swimming	twice a week
Carrie	yoga	three times a week
Marcos	bowling	twice a month

B *[CD 2, Track 6]*

- Play the audio program. Ss listen to find out who is most similar to them. Then they discuss their answers in pairs or small groups.

8 DISCUSSION

Learning Objective: *discuss sports and athletes using adverbs of frequency*

Group work

- Focus Ss' attention on the picture. Ask: "Who is he? What is he doing? Who is she? What is she doing?" (Answers: Lionel Messi, playing soccer; Serena Williams, playing tennis)

- Explain that you want Ss to discuss the questions for ten minutes. Point out that it's important to speak fluently, so it's OK to make errors.

- Ss take turns asking and answering the questions in small groups. Go around the class and ask follow-up questions.

9 WRITING

Learning Objective: *write about favorite activities using the simple present and adverbs of frequency*

A

- Explain the task. Point out that Ss can write about any favorite activities, not just sports. Ss read the example paragraph silently.

- Ss make notes about favorite activities individually.

- Ss write a paragraph based on their notes. Remind Ss to include one false piece of information.

! For a new way to teach this Writing, try **Pass the**
• **Paper** download it from the website.

B Group work

- Explain the task and read the example question. Ss read each other's descriptions and write guesses about which activity is false. Then they ask each other to check their guesses.

End of Cycle 1

See the Supplementary Resources chart at the beginning of this unit for additional teaching materials and student activities related to this Cycle.

Cycle 2, Exercises 10–14

10 CONVERSATION

Learning Objectives: *practice a conversation about fitness; see questions with* how *and short answers in context*

A ⊙ [CD 2, Track 7]

- Ss cover the text and look at the picture. Elicit ideas and vocabulary.

- Write this focus question on the board:
  Do Ruth and Keith usually play tennis together?

- Then play the audio program and elicit the answer. (Answer: no)

- Write these focus questions on the board:
  1. How often does Keith do aerobics?
  2. How well does Keith play tennis?
  3. How good is Ruth at tennis?

- Play the audio program again and elicit the answers. (Answers: 1. twice a week 2. pretty well 3. not very good)

- **Option:** Have Ss close their eyes as they listen to the audio program.

- Ss read the conversation silently. Then they practice the conversation in pairs.

B ⊙ [CD 2, Track 8]

- Read the focus question and ask Ss to guess who wins. Then play the audio program. Ss listen to find the answer.

AudioScript

Ruth Good game, Keith.
Keith Thanks. You, too. And congratulations on the win. You play pretty well.
Ruth Oh, no, not really.
Keith How often do you play?
Ruth Once or twice a year. I'm just lucky today, I guess. Want to play another game?
Keith Um . . . sure. After a five-minute break.

Answers

Ruth is the winner.

8 DISCUSSION *Sports and athletes*

GROUP WORK Take turns asking and answering these questions.

Who's your favorite male athlete? Why?
Who's your favorite female athlete? Why?
Who are three famous athletes in your country?
What's your favorite sports team? Why?
Do you ever watch sports on TV? Which ones?
Do you ever watch sports live? Which ones?
What are two sports you don't like?
What sport or activity do you want to try?

9 WRITING *About favorite activities*

A Write about your favorite activities. Include one activity that is false.

> I love to exercise! I usually work out every day. I get up early in the morning and go jogging for about 30 minutes. Then I often go to the gym and do yoga. Sometimes I play tennis in the afternoon. I play . . .

B **GROUP WORK** Take turns reading your descriptions. Can you guess the false information?

"You don't play tennis in the afternoon. Right?"

10 CONVERSATION *I'm a real fitness freak.*

A Listen and practice.

Ruth: You're in great shape, Keith.
Keith: Thanks. I guess I'm a real fitness freak.
Ruth: How often do you work out?
Keith: Well, I do aerobics twice a week. And I play tennis every week.
Ruth: Tennis? That sounds like a lot of fun.
Keith: Oh, do you want to play sometime?
Ruth: Uh, . . . how well do you play?
Keith: Pretty well, I guess.
Ruth: Well, all right. But I'm not very good.
Keith: No problem. I'll give you a few tips.

B Listen to Keith and Ruth after their tennis match. Who's the winner?

11 GRAMMAR FOCUS

> ### Questions with how; short answers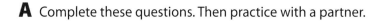
>
> **How often** do you work out?
>   **Every day**.
>   **Twice a week**.
>   **Not very often**.
>
> **How long** do you spend at the gym?
>   **Thirty minutes a day**.
>   **Two hours a week**.
>   **About an hour on weekends**.
>
> **How well** do you play tennis?
>   **Pretty well**.
>   **About average**.
>   **Not very well**.
>
> **How good** are you at sports?
>   **Pretty good**.
>   **OK**.
>   **Not so good**.

A Complete these questions. Then practice with a partner.

1. A: .... at volleyball?
   B: I guess I'm pretty good. I often play on weekends.

2. A: .... spend online?
   B: About an hour after dinner. I like to chat with my friends.

3. A: .... play chess?
   B: Once or twice a month. It's a good way to relax.

4. A: .... swim?
   B: Not very well. I need to take swimming lessons.

B **GROUP WORK** Take turns asking the questions in part A.
Give your own information when answering.

12 LISTENING *I'm terrible at sports.*

Listen to Dan, Jean, Sally, and Phil discuss sports and exercise.
Who is a couch potato? a fitness freak? a sports nut? a gym rat?

a couch potato	**a fitness freak**	**a sports nut**	**a gym rat**
1.	2.	3.	4. ....

13 INTERCHANGE 6 *Do you dance?*

Find out what your classmates can do. Go to Interchange 6 on page 120.

11 GRAMMAR FOCUS

Learning Objective: *practice questions with* how *and short answers*

 [CD 2, Track 9]

Questions with **how**

- Books closed. Write these questions and answers on the board in two columns:

A	B
How often do you work out?	Pretty well.
How long do you spend at the gym?	Twice a week.
How well do you play tennis?	Not very good.
How good are you at sports?	Two hours a week.

- Ss match the questions in A with the answers in B.
- Books open. Ss check their answers in the Grammar Focus box.
- Focus Ss' attention on the first column of the Grammar Focus box. Elicit or explain the difference between *how often* and *how long* (*how often* = with what frequency, *how long* = in how much time).
- Focus Ss' attention on the second column. Ask: "How are *how well* and *how good* different?" (They have the same meaning, but *good* is an adjective and *well* is an adverb. Use *how good* with *be* and *how well* with other verbs.)

Short answers

- Point out that answering in complete sentences sounds unnatural. Therefore, people use short answers.
- Play the audio program.

A

- Explain the task. Ss work individually to complete the questions. Check Ss' work as they finish. Ask Ss with correct questions to write them on the board.
- Ss check answers against the board. Then they practice the conversations in pairs.

Answers

1. A: **How good are you** at volleyball?
2. A: **How long do you** spend online?
3. A: **How often do you** play chess?
4. A: **How well can you** swim?

B *Group work*

- Explain the task. Ss take turns asking and answering the questions in small groups.

---

 12 LISTENING

Learning Objective: *develop skills in listening for details and inferencing*

 [CD 2, Track 10]

- Books closed. Set the scene. Four friends (Dan, Jean, Sally, and Phil) are talking about sports and exercise.
- Play the audio program.
- Books open. Focus Ss' attention on the pictures and read the captions aloud. Ask: "What do you think each type of person is like?"
- Play the audio program again. Have Ss identify the four people.
- Go over answers with the class.

AudioScript

Jean How good are you at sports, Dan?
Dan Are you kidding? I'm terrible! But I love to watch sports. I go to baseball games all the time. My favorite team is the Tigers. And I buy three or four different sports magazines every week.

Jean Wow!
Phil Do you like sports, Jean?
Jean Oh, yes. I like to exercise. But I don't watch sports very much, and I never buy sports magazines.
Phil How much time do you spend exercising?
Jean Well, I guess I exercise about two or three hours a day. I do aerobics at home three times a week, and the other days I go swimming. Oh, and sometimes I go bicycling.
Phil That's great! Sally, you're in great shape, too.
Sally Thanks. I go to the gym six days a week.
Jean Six days a week? Wow!
Sally I love the gym. I run on the treadmill and then do weight training for about an hour.
Dan And what about you, Phil?
Phil Oh, I'm too lazy to play sports – I really hate exercising. And I almost never go to any sporting events. In my free time, I like to sit with my feet up and watch my favorite TV shows.

Answers

1. Phil   2. Jean   3. Dan   4. Sally

---

13 INTERCHANGE 6

See page T-120 for teaching notes.

14 READING

Learning Objectives: *read and complete a health and fitness quiz; develop skills in skimming and making inferences*

- Read the title. Ask: "What is this? How is it different from a quiz in class?" Elicit ideas.
- Tell Ss to look over the quiz. Ask: "Where can you find this kind of quiz? What is the quiz about?" (Answers: in a magazine or newspaper, health and fitness)
- Point out the pre-reading question. Then Ss skim the questions in the quiz. Ask Ss to write down the score they think they're going to get.

A

- Explain the task. Read the first question and ask Ss to check (✓) the answer that is true for them.
- Ss read the quiz individually and check (✓) their answers.
- **Option:** Ss work in pairs and take turns asking each other the questions. They complete the quiz for each other.
- Go around the class and elicit or explain any new vocabulary.

Vocabulary

meal: breakfast, lunch, or dinner
servings: portions of food
junk food: food that is not good for you
vitamins: nutritional supplements, usually in a pill
average: medium; usual

- Ss add up their points. Then they read the *Rate yourself* section.
- Ask: "Are the points the same as you guessed? More than you guessed? Fewer than you guessed? Do you agree with your score? Why or why not?"
- **Option:** Ss give the quiz to friends or family members for homework. Then they share the results in class.

B Group work

- Ss compare their scores in small groups. Ask Ss to list five things they can do to improve their health and fitness. Point out that they can use ideas from the quiz.
- Each group joins another group and shares ideas. Then elicit ideas from the groups.

End of Cycle 2

See the Supplementary Resources chart at the beginning of this unit for additional teaching materials and student activities related to this Cycle and for assessment tools.

Health and Fitness Quiz

How healthy and fit do you think you are? Skim the questions below.
Then guess your health and fitness score from 0 (very unhealthy) to 50 (very healthy).

Your Food and Nutrition

1. How many meals do you eat each day?

	Points
Four or five small meals	5
Three meals	3
One or two big meals	0

2. How often do you eat at regular times during the day?

	Points
Almost always	5
Usually	3
Hardly ever	0

3. How many servings of fruits or vegetables do you eat each day?

Five or more	5
One to four	3
None	0

4. How much junk food do you eat?

Very little	5
About average	3
A lot	0

5. Do you take vitamins?

Yes, every day	5
Sometimes	3
No	0

Your Fitness

6. How often do you exercise or play a sport?

	Points
Three or more days a week	5
One or two days a week	3
Never	0

7. Which best describes your exercise program?

	Points
Both weight training and aerobic exercise	5
Either weight training or aerobic exercise	3
None	0

8. How important is your fitness program to you?

Very important	5
Fairly important	3
Not very important	0

Your Health

9. How often do you get a physical exam?

	Points
Once a year	5
Every two or three years	3
Rarely	0

10. How often do you sleep well?

Always	5
Usually or sometimes	3
Hardly ever or never	0

Rate yourself

TOTAL POINTS

42 to 50: Excellent job! Keep up the good work!
28 to 41: Good! Your health and fitness are above average.
15 to 27: Your health and fitness are a little below average.
14 or below: You can improve your health and fitness.

A Take the quiz and add up your score. Is your score similar to your original guess? Do you agree with your quiz score? Why or why not?

B GROUP WORK Compare your scores. Who is the healthiest and fittest? What can you do to improve your health and fitness?

Units 5–6 Progress check

SELF-ASSESSMENT

How well can you do these things? Check (✓) the boxes.

I can	Very well	OK	A little
Ask about and describe present activities (Ex. 1, 2, 3)	☐	☐	☐
Describe family life (Ex. 3)	☐	☐	☐
Ask for and give personal information (Ex. 3)	☐	☐	☐
Give information about quantities (Ex. 3)	☐	☐	☐
Ask and answer questions about free time (Ex. 4)	☐	☐	☐
Ask and answer questions about routines and abilities (Ex. 4)	☐	☐	☐

1 LISTENING *What are they doing?*

A ▶ Listen to people do different things.
What are they doing? Complete the chart.

B **PAIR WORK** Compare your answers.

A: In number one, someone is watching TV.
B: I don't think so. I think someone is . . .

What are they doing?
1. ....
2. ....
3. ....
4. ....

2 GAME *Memory test*

GROUP WORK Choose a person in the
room, but don't say who! Other students
ask yes/no questions to guess the person.

A: I'm thinking of someone in the classroom.
B: Is it a woman?
A: Yes, it is.
C: Is she sitting in the front of the room?
A: No, she isn't.
D: Is she sitting in the back?
A: Yes, she is.
E: Is she wearing jeans?
A: No, she isn't.
B: Is it . . . ?

The student with the correct guess
has the next turn.

Units 5–6 Progress check

SELF-ASSESSMENT

Learning Objectives: *reflect on one's learning; identify areas that need improvement*

- Ask: "What did you learn in Units 5 and 6?" Elicit Ss' answers.

- Ss complete the Self-assessment. Encourage them to be honest, and point out they will not get a bad grade if they check (✓) a *little*.

- Ss move on to the Progress check exercises. You can have Ss complete them in class or for homework, using one of these techniques:
  1. Ask Ss to complete all the exercises.
  2. Ask Ss: "What do you need to practice?" Then assign exercises based on their answers.
  3. Ask Ss to choose and complete exercises based on their Self-assessment.

LISTENING

Learning Objective: *assess one's ability to understand and describe present activities*

A ▶ [CD 2, Track 11]

- Explain the task. Ss will hear four sounds of people doing different things. Ss guess what the person is doing and write sentences using the present continuous.

- Model the task. Ask Ss to close their eyes. Then do something that makes a distinctive sound (e.g., write on the board, sharpen your pencil). Ask: "What am I doing?" Ss answer in the present continuous (e.g., *You're writing on the board.*).

- Play the audio program once or twice. Ss listen and complete the chart. Help with vocabulary as needed.

Possible answers

1. Someone is playing a video game.
2. Someone is exercising.
3. Someone is bowling.
4. Someone is driving.

B *Pair work*

- Explain the task. Model the example conversation with a S. Elicit different ways of agreeing and disagreeing.

- Ss compare answers in pairs. Go around the class and check Ss' use of the present continuous.

GAME

Learning Objectives: *assess one's ability to ask and answer questions about present activities; assess one's ability to describe present activities*

Group work

- Explain the task. Ss work in small groups. One S chooses a person in the room. The other Ss take turns asking present continuous yes/no questions until they guess the person's identity. The S who guesses correctly has the next turn.

- Model the example conversation. Take the role of Student A and ask other Ss to take the roles of Students B, C, D, and E.

- Ss play the game in small groups.

SURVEY

Learning Objectives: *assess one's ability to describe present activities; assess one's ability to describe family life; assess one's ability to ask for and give personal information; assess one's ability to give information about quantities*

A *Group work*

- Explain the task and read the instructions aloud.
- Ss read the questions in small groups. Then, as a group, they add two more yes/no questions about family life. Encourage Ss to use both the simple present and the present continuous.
- Explain the task. Ss take turns asking and answering the questions. They write the number of *yes* and *no* answers in the correct columns. Remind Ss to include their own answers.

B *Group work*

- Explain the task. For each question, Ss add up the number of yes/no responses in their group. Then they write a sentence to describe the group's responses using determiners (e.g., *most, some, a few, all*).
- Ss complete the task in groups. Then they read their sentences to the class.
- **Option:** Complete the activity as a class.

DISCUSSION

Learning Objectives: *assess one's ability to ask and answer questions about free time; assess one's ability to ask and answer questions about routines and abilities*

Group work

- Explain the task. Ss choose three questions and check (✓) them individually. Then they ask each other the questions in small groups. When someone answers "yes," the S must add at least one follow-up question, including *how* questions (e.g., *how well, how often, how good*).

- **Option:** Ss think of their own questions beginning with *Do you ever . . . ?*
- Ask four Ss to read the example conversation. Elicit other possible follow-up questions.
- Ss complete the task. Go around the class and check for use of follow-up questions.

WHAT'S NEXT?

Learning Objective: *become more involved in one's learning*

- Focus Ss' attention on the Self-assessment again. Ask: "How well can you do these things now?"

- Ask Ss to underline one thing they need to review. Ask: "What did you underline? How can you review it?"
- If needed, plan additional activities or reviews based on Ss' answers.

3 SURVEY *Family life*

A **GROUP WORK** Add two more yes/no questions about family life to the chart. Then ask and answer the questions in groups. Write down the number of "yes" and "no" answers. (Remember to include yourself.)

	Number of "yes" answers	Number of "no" answers
1. Are you living with your family?	....	....
2. Do your parents both work?	....	....
3. Do you eat dinner with your family?	....	....
4. Are you working these days?	....	....
5. Are you married?	....	....
6. Do you have any children?	....	....
7.	....	....
8.	....	....

B **GROUP WORK** Write up the results of the survey. Then tell the class.

> 1. In our group, most people are living with their family.
> 2. Few of our parents both work.

4 DISCUSSION *Routines and abilities*

GROUP WORK Choose three questions. Then ask your questions in groups. When someone answers "yes," think of other questions to ask.

Do you ever . . . ?
- ☐ sing karaoke
- ☐ listen to English songs
- ☐ chat online
- ☐ do weight training
- ☐ play golf
- ☐ play video games
- ☐ cook for friends
- ☐ go swimming
- ☐ watch old movies

A: **Do you ever** sing karaoke?
B: Yes, I often do.
C: **What** song do you like to sing?
B: "I Love Rock 'n' Roll."
A: **When** do you sing karaoke?
B: In the evenings.
C: **How often** do you go?
B: Every weekend!
D: **How well** do you sing?
B: Not very well. But I have a lot of fun!

WHAT'S NEXT?

Look at your Self-assessment again. Do you need to review anything?

Unit 7 Supplementary Resources Overview

	After the following SB exercises	You can use these materials in class	Your students can use these materials outside the classroom
CYCLE 1	1 Snapshot		**SSD** Unit 7 Vocabulary 1
	2 Conversation		**SSD** Unit 7 Speaking 1
	3 Grammar Focus		**SB** Unit 7 Grammar Plus focus 1 **SSD** Unit 7 Grammar 1–2 **ARC** Simple past 1–2
	4 Pronunciation		
	5 Word Power	**TSS** Unit 7 Vocabulary Worksheet	**SSD** Unit 7 Vocabulary 2
	6 Discussion		
	7 Listening		
	8 Interchange 7		**WB** Unit 7 exercises 1–6
CYCLE 2	9 Conversation		**SSD** Unit 7 Speaking 2
	10 Grammar Focus	**TSS** Unit 7 Grammar Worksheet **TSS** Unit 7 Listening Worksheet **TSS** Unit 7 Extra Worksheet	**SB** Unit 7 Grammar Plus focus 2 **SSD** Unit 7 Grammar 3 **ARC** Past of *be*
	11 Discussion		**ARC** Simple past and Descriptions of vacations
	12 Writing	**TSS** Unit 7 Writing Worksheet	
	13 Listening		
	14 Reading	**TSS** Unit 7 Project Worksheet **VID** Unit 7 **VRB** Unit 7	**SSD** Unit 7 Reading 1–2 **SSD** Unit 7 Listening 1–2 **SSD** Unit 7 Video 1–3 **WB** Unit 7 exercises 7–11

Key

ARC: Arcade	**SB:** Student's Book	**SSD:** Self-study DVD-ROM	**TSS:** Teacher Support Site
VID: Video DVD	**VRB:** Video Resource Book	**WB:** Workbook	

My Plan for Unit 7

Use the space below to customize a plan that fits your needs.

With the following SB exercises	I am using these materials in class	My students are using these materials outside the classroom

With or instead of the following SB section	I am using these materials for assessment

7 We had a great time!

SNAPSHOT

The Top Eight Leisure-Time Activities in the United States

☐ read   ☐ watch TV   ☐ spend time with family   ☐ play sports

☐ go to the gym   ☐ use the computer   ☐ go fishing   ☐ go to the movies

Source: The Harris Poll

Check (✓) the activities you do in your free time.
List three other activities you do in your free time.
What are your favorite leisure-time activities?

2 CONVERSATION *Did you do anything special?*

A ▶ Listen and practice.

Rick: So, what did you do last weekend, Meg?
Meg: Oh, I had a great time. I went to a karaoke bar and sang with some friends on Saturday.
Rick: How fun! Did you go to Lucky's?
Meg: No, we didn't. We went to that new place downtown. How about you? Did you go anywhere?
Rick: No, I didn't go anywhere all weekend. I just stayed home and studied for today's Spanish test.
Meg: Our test is today? I forgot about that!
Rick: Don't worry. You always get an A.

B ▶ Listen to the rest of the conversation.
What does Meg do on Sunday afternoons?

We had a great time!

In Unit 7, students discuss daily, leisure, and vacation activities. In Cycle 1, they talk about daily and leisure activities using the simple past with both regular and irregular verbs. In Cycle 2, they talk about vacations using the past tense of be.

1 SNAPSHOT

Learning Objective: *learn vocabulary for discussing leisure activities*

- Books closed. Ask: "What do you do in your free time?" Help with vocabulary as needed. Write Ss' responses on the board.
- **Option:** Ask Ss to guess the top eight leisure activities in the U.S. Later, Ss compare their ideas with the Snapshot.
- Books open. Ask different Ss to read the leisure activities aloud. Point out that these are the top eight leisure activities in the U.S. Elicit or explain any new vocabulary.

- Ask: "Does anything on this list surprise you? What?" Elicit Ss' answers.
- Read and explain the three tasks. Point out that, for the last task, Ss should list the activities starting with their favorite.
- Ss complete the tasks individually. Go around the class and give help as needed.
- Elicit Ss' responses.
- **Option:** Use Ss' responses to make a list of the top eight activities for the class.
- For a new way to practice the Snapshot vocabulary, try **Vocabulary Steps** – download it from the website.

2 CONVERSATION

Learning Objectives: *practice a conversation about weekend activities; see the simple past in context*

A ⏵ [CD 2, Track 12]

- Set the scene. Rick and Meg are talking about their weekends. Ask Ss to use the pictures to predict what each person did. Elicit or explain vocabulary in the pictures (e.g., *karaoke*).
- **Option:** Ss list all the words they can see in the pictures. Find out who has the most words.
- Books closed. Write these focus questions on the board:

  1. What did Meg do on Saturday?
  2. What did Rick do?

- Play the audio program. Ss listen for the answers. Then elicit the answers. (Answers: 1. She went to a karaoke bar and sang with some friends. 2. He stayed home all weekend and studied for the Spanish test.)
- Books open. Play the audio program again. Ss listen and read silently.
- Ss practice the conversation in pairs. Go around the class and give help as needed.
- For a new way to practice this Conversation, try the **Disappearing Dialog** – download it from the website.

B ⏵ [CD 2, Track 13]

- Read the focus question aloud. Ask Ss to guess. Write some of their ideas on the board.
- Play the audio program. Ss work individually. Then go over the answer with the class.

AudioScript

Rick So, Meg, what did you do on Sunday?
Meg I stayed home in the morning. I just watched TV and read.
Rick How about in the afternoon?
Meg Oh, I worked. I have a part-time job at the university bookstore.
Rick I didn't know you had a job.
Meg Yeah, I'm a cashier there. I work every Sunday from 2:00 to 5:00.

Answers

She stayed home in the morning. She watched TV and read. She worked in the afternoon.

- For more practice talking about last weekend's activities, play the **Chain Game** – download it from the website.

> **TIP** To help Ss who are weak at listening, write the answers on the board. That way, they can *see* the answers.

3 GRAMMAR FOCUS

Learning Objective: *practice simple past questions, short answers, and regular and irregular verbs*

⏵ **[CD 2, Track 14]**

Simple past questions with **did**

- Focus Ss' attention on the Conversation on page 44. Ask Ss to find three questions with *did*. Then write them on the board. (Answers: What did you do last weekend? Did you go to Lucky's? Did you go anywhere?)

> **TIP** Use a different color for target features (e.g., *did* + verb). This helps Ss visualize the grammar pattern.

- Point out the questions in the Grammar Focus box. Elicit the rules for forming yes/no and Wh-questions in the simple past:
  Did + subject + verb?
  Wh-question + *did* + subject + verb?
- Elicit more examples and write them on the board.
- Play the audio program. Have Ss repeat the questions and responses.

Regular and irregular verbs

- Point out the regular and irregular verbs to the right of part A. Then draw this chart on the board:

Regular verbs	Irregular verbs
work – work<u>ed</u>	do – <u>did</u>
invite – invit<u>ed</u>	drive – <u>drove</u>

- Focus Ss' attention on the Conversation on page 44 again. Ask Ss to find the simple past forms of *stay* and *study*. (Answers: stayed, studied) Ask a S to write them on the board in the *Regular* column. Then ask Ss to find and circle the simple past of *sing* and *forget*. (Answers: sang, forgot) Ask a different S to write them in the *Irregular* column.
- Have Ss turn to the appendix at the back of the book. Tell them to use this list as needed.
- **Option:** Ask Ss to look for patterns in the list of irregular verbs (e.g., *i → a: sit → sat, swim → swam, drink → drank*).

4 PRONUNCIATION

Learning Objective: *notice the reduction of did you; learn to sound natural when asking did you questions*

A ⏵ [CD 2, Track 15]

- Play the audio program. Ss listen for the reduction of *did* you.
- Play the audio program again. Ss practice saying the questions with reductions.

> **TIP** Some Ss like to repeat things aloud. Others prefer to mouth words or sentences silently. Help Ss find learning styles they prefer.

A

- Explain the task. Model the first conversation with a strong S. Then model it with a different S.
- Ss complete the task individually. Go over answers with the class.

Answers

1. A: **Did** you **stay** home on Saturday?
   B: No, I **called** my friend. We **drove** to a café for lunch.
2. A: How **did** you **spend** your last birthday?
   B: I **had** a party. Everyone **enjoyed** it, but the neighbors **didn't like** the noise.
3. A: What **did** you **do** last night?
   B: I **saw** a 3-D movie at the Cineplex. I **loved** it!
4. A: **Did** you **do** anything special over the weekend?
   B: Yes, I **did**. I **went** shopping. Unfortunately, I **spent** all my money. Now I'm broke!
5. A: **Did** you **go** out on Friday night?
   B: No, I **didn't**. I **invited** friends over, and I **cooked** dinner for them.

- Ss practice the conversations in pairs.

B Pair work

- Explain the task. Then model it by asking different Ss to ask you the questions in part A. Give your own responses.
- Point out that Ss can avoid answering a question by saying *I'd rather not say*. They can also make up answers.
- Ss complete the task in pairs.

 For more practice with regular and irregular verbs, play *Bingo* – download it from the website.

- Tell different Ss to ask the questions. Check their use of reduced forms.

B Pair work

- Explain and model the task. Ss complete the task in pairs. Go around the class and check Ss' use of reductions.

3 GRAMMAR FOCUS

Simple past ▶

Did you **work** on Saturday?
Yes, I **did**. I **worked** all day.
No, I **didn't**. I **didn't work** at all.

Did you **go** anywhere last weekend?
Yes, I **did**. I **went** to the movies.
No, I **didn't**. I **didn't go** anywhere.

What **did** Rick **do** on Saturday?
He **stayed** home and **studied** for a test.

How **did** Meg **spend** her weekend?
She **went** to a karaoke bar and **sang**
with some friends.

A Complete these conversations. Then practice with a partner.

1. A: .... you .... (stay) home on Saturday?
   B: No, I .... (call) my friend. We .... (drive)
      to a café for lunch.
2. A: How .... you .... (spend) your last birthday?
   B: I .... (have) a party. Everyone .... (enjoy) it,
      but the neighbors .... (not, like) the noise.
3. A: What .... you .... (do) last night?
   B: I .... (see) a 3-D movie at the Cineplex.
      I .... (love) it!
4. A: .... you .... (do) anything special over the weekend?
   B: Yes, I .... I .... (go) shopping. Unfortunately,
      I .... (spend) all my money. Now I'm broke!
5. A: .... you .... (go) out on Friday night?
   B: No, I .... I .... (invite) friends over,
      and I .... (cook) dinner for them.

regular verbs	
work	→ work**ed**
invite	→ invite**d**
study	→ stud**ied**
stop	→ stop**ped**

irregular verbs	
do	→ **did**
drive	→ **drove**
have	→ **had**
go	→ **went**
sing	→ **sang**
see	→ **saw**
spend	→ **spent**

B **PAIR WORK** Take turns asking the questions in part A.
Give your own information when answering.

A: Did you stay home on Saturday?
B: No, I didn't. I went out with some friends.

4 PRONUNCIATION *Reduction of* did you

A ▶ Listen and practice. Notice how **did you** is reduced in the
following questions.

[dɪdʒə]
Did you have a good time?

[wədɪdʒə]
What did you do last night?

[haʊdɪdʒə]
How did you like the movie?

B **PAIR WORK** Practice the questions in Exercise 3, part A again.
Pay attention to the pronunciation of **did you**.

WORD POWER Chores and activities

A Find two other words or phrases from the list that usually
go with each verb.

a lot of fun	dancing	a good time	shopping	a vacation
the bed	the dishes	the laundry	a trip	a video

do	my homework	....	....
go	online	....	....
have	a party	....	....
make	a phone call	....	....
take	a day off	....	....

B Circle the things you did last weekend. Then compare with a partner.

A: I went shopping with my friends. We had a good time.
B: I didn't have a very good time. I did the laundry and . . .

DISCUSSION Any questions?

GROUP WORK Take turns. One student
makes a statement about the weekend.
Other students ask questions. Each
student answers at least three questions.

A: I went dancing on Saturday night.
B: **Where** did you go?
A: To the Rock-it Club.
C: **Who** did you go with?
A: I went with my friends.
D: **What time** did you go?
A: We went around 10:00.

LISTENING What did you do last night?

A ◉ Listen to John and Laura
describe what they did last night.
Check (✓) the correct information
about each person.

B ◉ Listen again. Who had a
good time? Who didn't have a
good time? Why or why not?

Who . . . ?	John	Laura
went to a party	☐	☐
had a good meal	☐	☐
watched a video	☐	☐
met an old friend	☐	☐
got home late	☐	☐

5 WORD POWER

Learning Objectives: *learn vocabulary for chores and activities; learn collocations with* do, go, have, make, *and* take

A

- Copy the chart onto the board. Explain the task.
- Ss complete the task in pairs. Go around the class and give help with new vocabulary.
- **Option:** Allow Ss to use dictionaries.
- Ask different Ss to write their answers on the board. Give help with any collocations they don't know.

Answers

do	my homework	the dishes	the laundry
go	online	dancing	shopping
have	a party	a good time	a lot of fun
make	a phone call	the bed	a video
take	a day off	a trip	a vacation

B

- Explain the task. Model the conversation with a S. Then Ss complete the task and compare with a partner.

6 DISCUSSION

Learning Objectives: *discuss activities using the simple past; develop the skill of asking follow-up questions*

Group work

- Model the example discussion with four Ss.
- Point out that a good listener shows interest in a conversation by asking follow-up questions.

- Ss complete the activity in groups. Remind Ss to use reduced forms of *did you*.
- **Option:** The Ss get one point for each follow-up question they ask. The Ss with the most points in each group win.

7 LISTENING

Learning Objective: *develop skills in listening for main ideas and details*

A ▶ [CD 2, Track 16]

- Write two columns on the board, one with the heading *Good* and one with the heading *Boring*.
- Set the scene. Ask: "Did you have a good time or a boring time last night? What did you do?" List Ss' activities in the correct columns.
- Explain the task. Play the audio program and Ss complete the chart.
- Ss compare answers in pairs. Then go over answers with the class.

AudioScript

Laura So, what did you do last night, John?
John Uh, I went to my boss's house. He invited me over for dinner.
Laura Really? How was it?
John Oh, the food was excellent, but he talked about football all night, and I hate football. Then we watched a boring sports video.
Laura How awful! I know how you feel about sports.
John I didn't get home until after midnight.
Laura That doesn't sound like much fun. I had a great time last night!
John Oh, yeah? What did you do?

Laura I went to a party and met an old school friend of mine. We went to high school together. We had lots to talk about. I stayed out until about 1:00 A.M., so I got home really late, too.
John Hmm, it sounds like you had a better time than I did.
Laura Yeah. I guess you're right.

Answers

Who . . . ?	John	Laura
went to a party		✓
had a good meal	✓	
watched a video	✓	
met an old friend		✓
got home late	✓	✓

B ▶ [CD 2, Track 17]

- Explain the task. Read the questions aloud.
- Play the audio program.
- Go over the answers with the class.

Answers

Had a good time: Laura
Reason: went to a party and met an old friend
Didn't have a good time: John
Reason: his boss talked about football all night, and John hates football. They also watched a boring video.

8 INTERCHANGE 7

See page T-121 for teaching notes.

End of Cycle 1

Cycle 2, Exercises 9–14

See the Supplementary Resources chart at the beginning of this unit for additional teaching materials and student activities related to this Cycle.

9 CONVERSATION

Learning Objectives: *practice a conversation about a vacation; see the past of* be *in context*

A *[CD 2, Track 18]*

- Books closed. Set the scene. Celia and Don are talking about Don's vacation. Write these focus questions on the board:
  1. Did Don enjoy his vacation?
  2. Where did he go?
  3. How long was he there?

- Play the audio program. Elicit Ss' answers to the focus questions. (Answers: 1. yes 2. Hawaii 3. about a week) Go over any expressions Ss don't understand.

- Books open. Play the audio program again. Ss listen and read the conversation silently.

- Ss practice the conversation in pairs.

B *[CD 2, Track 19]*

- Ask Ss to predict what happened. Write their ideas on the board.
- Play the audio program. Ss listen to find out if any prediction was correct.

AudioScript

Celia So, tell me! What happened?
Don Well, like I said, I went surfing every day. One day, I entered a contest and I won. I got first prize!
Celia Wow! Congratulations!
Don But that's not all. Someone made a video of me surfing and posted it online. Do you want to see it?
Celia Sure!

Answers

Don went surfing. He won a contest. Someone made a video of him surfing and posted it online.

10 GRAMMAR FOCUS

Learning Objective: *practice the past of* be *in questions and short answers*

 [CD 2, Track 20]

Past of **be** *questions*

- Write these questions from the Conversation in Exercise 9 on the board, with *was* or *were* underlined:
  1. <u>Was</u> the weather OK?
  2. What <u>was</u> the best thing about the trip?
  3. How <u>was</u> your vacation?
  4. How long <u>were</u> you there?

- Focus Ss' attention on the underlined words on the board and elicit the rules for yes/no and Wh-questions:
  Was/Were + subject + verb?
  Wh-question + *was/were* + subject + verb?

Was/Were and contractions

- Elicit when to use *was* and *were*. Focus Ss' attention on the Grammar Focus box if they aren't sure.

- Use the audio program to present the questions, short answers, and contractions.
- Explain the task. Model the first conversation with a S.
- Ss complete the task individually. Then Ss practice the conversations in pairs.

Answers

1. A: **Were** you in Los Angeles last weekend?
   B: No, I **wasn't**. I **was** in San Francisco.
   A: How **was** it?
   B: It **was** great! But it **was** foggy and cool as usual.
2. A: How long **were** your parents in Europe?
   B: They **were** there for two weeks.
   A: **Were** they in London the whole time?
   B: No, they **weren't**. They also went to Paris.
3. A: **Were** you away last week?
   B: Yes, I **was** in Istanbul.
   A: Really? How long **were** you there?
   B: For almost a week. I **was** there on business.

8 INTERCHANGE 7 Thinking back

Play a board game. Go to Interchange 7 on page 121.

9 CONVERSATION How was your vacation?

A ▶ Listen and practice.

Celia: Hi, Don. How was your vacation?
Don: It was excellent! I went to Hawaii with my cousin. We had a great time.
Celia: Lucky you. How long were you there?
Don: About a week.
Celia: Fantastic! Was the weather OK?
Don: Not really. It was cloudy a lot. But we went surfing every day. The waves were amazing.
Celia: So, what was the best thing about the trip?
Don: Well, something incredible happened. . . .

B ▶ Listen to the rest of the conversation. What happened?

10 GRAMMAR FOCUS

> ### Past of be ▶
>
> | | | |
> |---|---|---|
> | **Were** you in Hawaii? | Yes, I **was**. | **Contractions** |
> | **Was** the weather OK? | No, it **wasn't**. | was**n't** = was not |
> | **Were** you and your cousin on vacation? | Yes, we **were**. | were**n't** = were not |
> | **Were** your parents there? | No, they **weren't**. | |
> | How long **were** you away? | I **was** away for a week. | |
> | How **was** your vacation? | It **was** excellent! | |

Complete these conversations. Then practice with a partner.

1. A: .... you in Los Angeles last weekend?
   B: No, I .... I .... in San Francisco.
   A: How .... it?
   B: It .... great! But it .... foggy and cool as usual.

2. A: How long .... your parents in Europe?
   B: They .... there for two weeks.
   A: .... they in London the whole time?
   B: No, they .... They also went to Paris.

3. A: .... you away last week?
   B: Yes, I .... in Istanbul.
   A: Really? How long .... you there?
   B: For almost a week. I .... there on business.

Golden Gate Bridge

We had a great time! ▪ **47**

11 DISCUSSION On vacation

A GROUP WORK Ask your classmates about their last vacations.
Ask these questions or your own ideas.

Where did you spend your last vacation?
How long was your vacation?
Who were you with?

What did you do?
How was the weather?
What would you like to do on your next vacation?

B CLASS ACTIVITY Who had an interesting vacation? Tell the class who and why.

12 WRITING An online post

A Read this online post.

Search [   ] Go

Kathy

Chichen Itza

Greetings from Cancun! I'm having a great time. Yesterday I took a tour to the Mayan ruins of Chichen Itza. They were amazing! This morning I went to the beach and then went shopping in the city. I bought some beautiful Mexican silver jewelry. Last night I tried the famous local lime soup. This was a great vacation!

B Write an online post to a partner about your last vacation. Then exchange messages. Do you have any questions about the vacation?

13 LISTENING Welcome back.

A Listen to Jason and Barbara talk about their vacations.
Write where they went and what they did there.

	Where they went	What they did	Did they enjoy it?	
			Yes	No
Jason	....	....	☐	☐
Barbara	....	....	☐	☐

B Listen again. Did they enjoy their vacations? Check (✓) Yes or No.

11 DISCUSSION

Learning Objectives: *discuss vacations using the past tense; develop the skill of retelling a story*

A Group work

- Books closed. Ss work in small groups. Assign different groups the topics *transportation, weather,* and *food.* Groups brainstorm words related to the topics.
- Ask a S from each group to write their words on the board. For example:

Transportation	Weather	Food
car, bus	rainy, sunny	good, bad

- Books open. Explain the task and read the example questions. Ask Ss to think of more questions related to vacations. Write their questions on the board.

- Model the task by describing a vacation you took.
- Ss take turns talking about their vacations in small groups. Go around the class and note any errors.
- Write any errors you noted on the board. Ss try to correct them as a class.

> **TIP** It's best not to interrupt Ss during a discussion or fluency activity. Instead, listen and note any errors you hear. Go over the most common ones after the activity.

B Class activity

- Ss in each group vote for the most interesting vacation. Then one S from each group tells the class about it. Encourage other Ss to ask questions.

12 WRITING

Learning Objectives: *learn postcard-writing skills; use the past tense to write a postcard about a vacation*

A

- Ss read the postcard silently. Elicit or explain any new vocabulary.

B

- Explain the task. Tell Ss to use the questions in Exercise 11 for ideas about the topic.

- Ss write postcards in pairs. Remind Ss to include the greeting, body, signature, and their partner's address. Go around the class and check Ss' work. Then Ss exchange postcards.
- **Option:** Bring in real postcards for Ss to use.
- ❗ For a new way to teach this Writing, try **Pass the Paper** – download it from the website.

13 LISTENING

Learning Objective: *develop skills in listening for main ideas and details*

A [CD 2, Track 21]

- Set the scene. Two friends, Jason and Barbara, are talking about their vacations.
- Play the audio program. Ask Ss to listen to find out their vacation places and if they enjoyed them. They write those answers in the chart.

AudioScript

Barbara Jason! Hi! Welcome back. You were away last week, right?
Jason Yeah, I was on vacation.
Barbara Where did you go?
Jason I went to San Francisco.
Barbara Nice! How was it?
Jason Oh, I loved it! It's a really pretty city.
Barbara So . . . why San Francisco?
Jason Oh, my sister lives there. I stayed with her. She loves to shop, so we went shopping every day. Look, I got this sweater.

Barbara Nice! I didn't go anywhere on my last vacation. I didn't have enough money to go anywhere.
Jason Oh, that's too bad.
Barbara Oh, not really. I actually enjoyed my vacation a lot. A friend from college stayed with me for a week. We just talked and watched a lot of old movies.
Jason That sounds fun, too.

B 🔘 [CD 2, Track 22]

- Play the audio program again. Ss list the reasons they enjoyed or didn't enjoy their vacations.
- Go over answers with the class.

Answers

	Vacation place	What they did	Enjoyed it?
Jason	San Francisco	went shopping	yes
Barbara	home	talked and watched old movies	yes

Learning Objectives: *read and discuss vacation postcards; develop skills in reading for main ideas and supporting details*

- **Option:** Ask Ss to bring in recent vacation photos or postcards. In pairs or small groups, Ss talk about the places.
- Ask Ss to cover the writing on the postcards and look at the pictures. Ask: "Where did each person go on his or her vacation? What do you think he or she did there?" Elicit ideas. Help with vocabulary as needed (e.g., *Xi'an, terracotta statues, yoga retreat, national park, glacier*).
- **Option:** Bring in a world map and help Ss find Xi'an, China; Miami, Florida; and Santiago, Chile. Elicit Ss' knowledge about these places.

A

- Explain the task. Remind Ss to try to guess the meanings of any words they don't know.
- Ss read the three postcards silently and complete the task individually. Then they compare answers in pairs or small groups.
- **Option:** Ask pairs or groups to find the place in each postcard where the sentences fit best.
- Elicit or explain any new vocabulary.

Vocabulary

terracotta: a kind of red clay used for sculptures and pottery

statues: stone or clay sculptures that look like people or animals

retreat: a vacation where people go to exercise and become healthier

vegetarian food: food that contains no animal products

glacier: a very large piece of ice that moves very slowly

pink flamingo: a kind of tall pink bird

wildlife: animals and birds in the place where they live

- Go over answers with the class.

Answers

3, 2, 1

B *Pair work*

- Ss discuss the questions in pairs. Go around the class and give help as needed.
- To check answers, have pairs share their responses with the class.

Answers

1. Hee-jin had a fitness vacation.
2. Rachel learned a lot on vacation.
3. Chris had a vacation that was full of adventure.
4. Answers will vary.

❗ For a new way to teach this Reading, try *Jigsaw Learning* – download it from the website.

End of Cycle 2

See the Supplementary Resources chart at the beginning of this unit for additional teaching materials and student activities related to this Cycle.

Look at the pictures. What do you think each person did on his or her vacation?

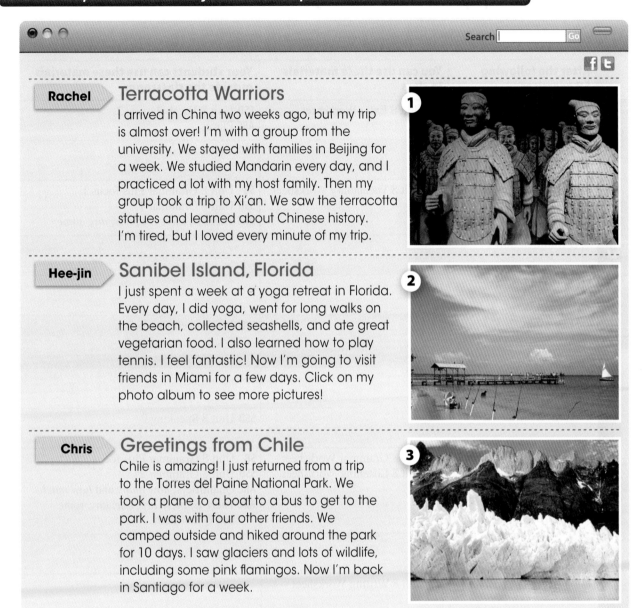

Search [ ] Go

Rachel ▸ Terracotta Warriors

I arrived in China two weeks ago, but my trip is almost over! I'm with a group from the university. We stayed with families in Beijing for a week. We studied Mandarin every day, and I practiced a lot with my host family. Then my group took a trip to Xi'an. We saw the terracotta statues and learned about Chinese history. I'm tired, but I loved every minute of my trip.

Hee-jin ▸ Sanibel Island, Florida

I just spent a week at a yoga retreat in Florida. Every day, I did yoga, went for long walks on the beach, collected seashells, and ate great vegetarian food. I also learned how to play tennis. I feel fantastic! Now I'm going to visit friends in Miami for a few days. Click on my photo album to see more pictures!

Chris ▸ Greetings from Chile

Chile is amazing! I just returned from a trip to the Torres del Paine National Park. We took a plane to a boat to a bus to get to the park. I was with four other friends. We camped outside and hiked around the park for 10 days. I saw glaciers and lots of wildlife, including some pink flamingos. Now I'm back in Santiago for a week.

A Read the online posts. Then write the number of the post where each sentence could go.

.... It was a long trip, but I was so happy after we got there!
.... I really recommend this place – it's very relaxing.
.... I had a great trip, but now I need a vacation!

B **PAIR WORK** Answer these questions.

1. Which person had a fitness vacation?
2. Who learned a lot on vacation?
3. Who had a vacation that was full of adventure?
4. Which vacation sounds the most interesting to you? Why?

Unit 8 Supplementary Resources Overview

	After the following SB exercises	You can use these materials in class	Your students can use these materials outside the classroom
CYCLE 1	1 Word Power	**TSS** Unit 8 Extra Worksheet	**SSD** Unit 8 Vocabulary 1–2 **ARC** Places
	2 Conversation		**SSD** Unit 8 Speaking 1
	3 Grammar Focus	**TSS** Unit 8 Vocabulary Worksheet	**SB** Unit 8 Grammar Plus focus 1 **SSD** Unit 8 Grammar 1 **ARC** *There is, there are; one, any, some*
	4 Pronunciation		
	5 Speaking		
	6 Listening		**WB** Unit 8 exercises 1–5
CYCLE 2	7 Snapshot		
	8 Conversation		**SSD** Unit 8 Speaking 2
	9 Grammar Focus	**TSS** Unit 8 Grammar Worksheet **TSS** Unit 8 Listening Worksheet	**SB** Unit 8 Grammar Plus focus 2 **SSD** Unit 8 Grammar 2 **ARC** Quantifiers; *how many* and *how much* **ARC** *There is, there are; one, any, some* and Quantifiers
	10 Interchange 8		
	11 Writing	**TSS** Unit 8 Writing Worksheet	
	12 Reading	**TSS** Unit 8 Project Worksheet **VID** Unit 8 **VRB** Unit 8	**SSD** Unit 8 Reading 1–2 **SSD** Unit 8 Listening 1–3 **SSD** Unit 8 Video 1–3 **WB** Unit 8 exercises 6–9

With or instead of the following SB section	You can also use these materials for assessment
Units 7–8 Progress Check	**ASSESSMENT CD** Units 7–8 Oral Quiz **ASSESSMENT CD** Units 7–8 Written Quiz **ASSESSMENT CD** Units 1–8 Test

Key
ARC: Arcade **SB**: Student's Book **SSD**: Self-study DVD-ROM **TSS**: Teacher Support Site
VID: Video DVD **VRB**: Video Resource Book **WB**: Workbook

Unit 8 Supplementary Resources Overview   *Interchange* Teacher's Edition 1 © Cambridge University Press 2013   Photocopiable

My Plan for Unit 8

Use the space below to customize a plan that fits your needs.

With the following SB exercises	I am using these materials in class	My students are using these materials outside the classroom

With or instead of the following SB section	I am using these materials for assessment	

8 What's your neighborhood like?

1 WORD POWER *Places*

A Match the words and the definitions. Then ask and answer the questions with a partner.

What's a . . . ?

1. barbershop ....
2. grocery store ....
3. laundromat ....
4. library ....
5. stationery store ....
6. theater ....
7. travel agency ....

It's a place where you . . .

a. wash and dry clothes
b. buy food
c. buy cards and paper
d. get a haircut
e. see a movie or play
f. make reservations for a trip
g. borrow books

B **PAIR WORK** Write definitions for these places.

clothing store   drugstore   Internet café   music store   post office

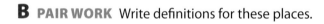

It's a place where you find new fashions. (clothing store)

C **GROUP WORK** Read your definitions. Can others guess the places?

2 CONVERSATION *I'm your new neighbor.*

▶ Listen and practice.

Jack: Excuse me. I'm your new neighbor, Jack. I just moved in.
Mrs. Day: Oh. Yes?
Jack: I'm looking for a grocery store. Are there any around here?
Mrs. Day: Yes, there are some on Pine Street.
Jack: Oh, good. And is there a laundromat near here?
Mrs. Day: Well, I think there's one across from the shopping center.
Jack: Thank you.
Mrs. Day: By the way, there's a barbershop in the shopping center, too.
Jack: A barbershop?

What's your neighborhood like?

> In Unit 8, students discuss neighborhoods. In Cycle 1, they talk about places using there is/there are *and prepositions of place. In Cycle 2, they talk about neighborhood problems using count and noncount nouns with* how many *and* how much.

 WORD POWER

Learning Objective: *learn vocabulary for discussing places in the neighborhood*

A

- Introduce the topic of neighborhoods. Ask: "What places do you need to find in a neighborhood?" Elicit Ss' answers and write them on the board.
- Elicit the names of places Ss see in the picture (e.g., *laundromat, library, barbershop*).
- Model the task. Ask "What's a barbershop?" Tell Ss to say "stop" when you read the correct definition. Read out possible answers (e.g., *It's a place where you wash and dry clothes. It's a place where you buy food.*) until the Ss say "stop."
- Ss match the words and definitions individually. Then go over answers with the class.

Answers

1. d   2. b   3. a   4. g   5. c   6. e   7. f

- Ss take turns asking and answering the questions in pairs. Go around the class and give help as needed.
- **Option:** To make the activity more challenging, Ss cover the text and use only the picture to ask and answer questions.
- Go over any errors you noticed, including pronunciation errors.

B *Pair work*

- Present the example definition for *clothing store*. Then elicit more possible definitions from the class (e.g., *It's a place where you buy jeans.*) and write them on the board.
- Ss write definitions for each place in pairs. Go around the class and give help as needed.

Possible answers

Place	It's a place where you ....
clothing store	find new fashions
drugstore	buy medicine and toiletries
Internet café	send emails and surf the net
music store	buy CDs and DVDs
post office	get stamps and mail letters

C *Group work*

- Model the task. Each pair from part B joins another pair. Pairs take turns giving definitions and guessing places.

 CONVERSATION

Learning Objectives: *practice a conversation between neighbors; see* there is/there are *and* one/any/ some *in context*

[CD 2, Track 23]

- Books closed. Write this question on the board:

  When you move to a new neighborhood, what do you need to find?

- Elicit answers from the class and write them on the board.
- Set the scene. Jack just moved into a new neighborhood, and he is looking for two things. What are they? Play the audio program.

- Go over answers with the class. (Answer: He's looking for a grocery store and a laundromat.)
- Books open. Elicit information about the picture. Ask: "What other place does Mrs. Day suggest? Why?" Then play the audio program again. Ss listen and find the answers. (Answer: She suggests a barbershop because Jack needs a haircut.)
- Play the audio program again. Ss listen and read the conversation silently.
- Ss practice the conversation in pairs.

GRAMMAR FOCUS

Learning Objectives: *ask and answer questions with there is/there are; practice using one, any, and some; practice prepositions of place*

▶ **[CD 2, Track 24]**

Is there/Are there?

- Before class, write these words on nine large cards:

is	There	a laundromat
one	are	grocery stores
any	some	near/around here

> **TIP** Cards are useful for helping Ss visualize grammar in an active way. They work well with grammar including word order and substitution.

- Focus Ss' attention on the Conversation on page 50. Ask: "What question does Jack ask beginning with *is there?*" Elicit the question. Then ask four Ss to come to the front of the class. Have them stand in line holding up these cards:
  - S1: *is*
  - S2: *there*
  - S3: *a laundromat*
  - S4: *near/around here*

- Ask: "What question does Jack ask beginning with *are there?*" Elicit the question. Then ask five Ss to stand in line holding up these cards:
  - S1: *are*
  - S2: *there*
  - S3: *any*
  - S4: *grocery stores*
  - S5: *near/around here*

- Focus Ss' attention on the two questions in the Grammar Focus box. Elicit the rule for forming questions with *is there* and *are there*.
  Is there + *a/an* + singular noun + *near/around here?*
  Are there + *any* + plural noun + *near/around here?*

One *and* some

- Ask four Ss to hold up these cards:
  - S1: *there*
  - S2: *is*
  - S3: *a laundromat*
  - S4: *near/around here*

- Point out that singular nouns and its article such as *a laundromat* can be replaced by *one*. Ask another S to take the card *one* and replace S3.

- Repeat the activity with plural nouns. This time, replace *grocery stores* with *some*.

- Play the audio program.

Prepositions

- Elicit or explain the meaning of the prepositions. Use the map. Ask: "What places are *on* Elm Street?" (Answer: King Plaza Hotel, Frank's Café, Jamison Hotel) Ask Ss about other places using prepositions.

- **Option:** For more practice visualizing the prepositions in an active way, ask Ss to stand *across from* each other, *next to* the wall, *near* the board, etc.

A

- Explain the task and read the example questions. Ss write questions individually. Point out that there should be a preposition in each question.

- Ss compare their questions in small groups. They read out their questions and check for grammatical accuracy.

- Go around the class and give help as needed. Ask three or four Ss with correct questions to write them on the board.

> **Possible answers**

All questions should follow these patterns:
Is there + a singular noun + a preposition + a place?
   (e.g., *Is there a bank across from the hotel?*)
Are there any + plural noun + a preposition + a place?
   (e.g., *Are there any hotels on Elm Street?*)

B *Pair work*

- Model the task two or three times using the map and the questions on the board:
  - T: Is there a pay phone around here?
  - S1: Yes, there is. There's one across from the gas station.
  - T: Are there any gas stations on Maple Avenue?
  - S2: No, there aren't. But there's one on Main Street.

> **TIP** To make sure that Ss understand instructions, always model the task at least twice. If possible, model it with different Ss each time.

- Ss take turns asking and answering their questions in pairs. Go around the class and give help as needed.

❗ For a new way to teach this Grammar Focus, try the *Picture Dictation* – download it from the website. Describe a town or city center to your Ss. Include streets and places.

3 GRAMMAR FOCUS

There is, there are; one, any, some ⊙

Is there a laundromat near here?
   Yes, **there is**. There's **one** across from the shopping center.
   No, **there isn't**, but there's **one** next to the library.

Are there any grocery stores around here?
   Yes, **there are**. There are **some** nice stores on Pine Street.
   No, **there aren't**, but there are **some** on Third Avenue.
   No, **there aren't any** around here.

Prepositions
on
next to
near/close to
across from/opposite
in front of
in back of/behind
between
on the corner of

A Look at the map below. Write questions about these places.

a bank	an electronics store	grocery stores	hotels	a post office
a department store	gas stations	a gym	a pay phone	restaurants

> Is there a bank around here?
>
> Are there any gas stations on Main Street?

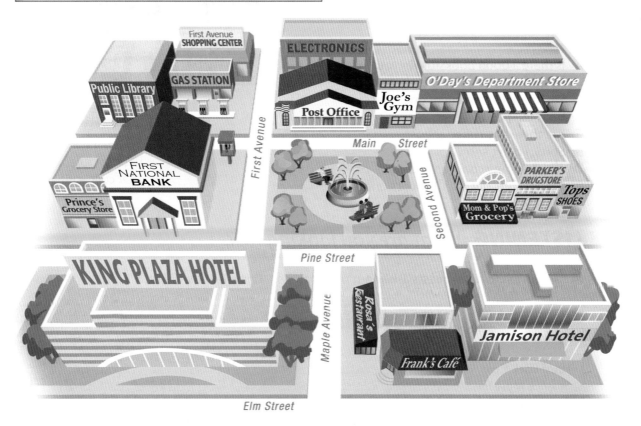

B **PAIR WORK** Ask and answer the questions you wrote in part A.

A: Is there a pay phone around here?
B: Yes, there is. There's one across from the gas station.

4 PRONUNCIATION *Reduction of there is/there are*

A Listen and practice. Notice how **there is** and **there are** are reduced in conversation, except for short answers.

Is there a laundromat near here?
   Yes, **there is**. **There's** one across from the shopping center.

Are there any grocery stores around here?
   Yes, **there are**. **There are** some on Pine Street.

B Practice the questions and answers in Exercise 3, part B again.

5 SPEAKING *My neighborhood*

GROUP WORK Take turns asking and answering questions about places like these in your neighborhood.

a bookstore	an Internet café
coffee shops	a karaoke bar
dance clubs	a library
drugstores	movie theaters
an electronics store	a park
a gym	restaurants

A: Is there a good bookstore in your neighborhood?
B: Yes, there's an excellent one across from the park.
C: Are there any coffee shops?
B: Sorry, I don't know.
D: Are there any cool dance clubs?
B: I'm not sure, but I think there's one . . .

useful expressions

Sorry, I don't know.
I'm not sure, but I think . . .
Of course. There's one . . .

 6 LISTENING *What are you looking for?*

A Listen to hotel guests ask about places to visit. Complete the chart.

Place	Location	Interesting?	
		Yes	**No**
Hard Rock Cafe	....	☐	☐
Science Museum	....	☐	☐
Aquarium	....	☐	☐

B **PAIR WORK** Which place sounds the most interesting to you? Why?

4 PRONUNCIATION

Learning Objectives: *notice the reduction of* there is/there are; *learn to sound natural when using* there is/ there are

A [CD 2, Track 25]

- Play the audio program. Point out the reduced forms. Ask Ss to practice the short conversations using the reductions. Point out that *there is* is often contracted to *there's* in writing, but *there are* is not.

B

- Go over the instructions and model the task.
- Go around the class and give individual feedback on Ss' use of reductions.

> **TIP** It's more important to recognize reductions than to produce them. Don't force Ss to produce reductions if they are not ready.

 # 5 SPEAKING

Learning Objective: *ask and answer questions about neighborhoods using* is there/are there *and* one/any/some

Group work

- Model the task. Ask a S: "Is there a good bookstore in your neighborhood?" If the S has difficulty answering, point out the *useful expressions* box for ideas.

- **Option:** Point out that people show interest in conversations by adding follow-up questions (e.g., *What's the name of the bookstore? Can you buy used books there?*).
- Ss complete the task in groups. Go around the class and note the Ss' level of fluency.

6 LISTENING

Learning Objective: *develop skills in listening for details*

A [CD 2, Track 26]

- Read out the instructions to set the scene. Then play the audio program. Ss listen and complete the *Location* column in the chart.
- Play the audio program again. Ss listen, decide if the hotel clerk thinks the places are interesting, and check (✓) *Yes* or *No*.
- Go over answers with the class.

AudioScript

Clerk Good morning. Can I help you?
Guest 1 Yes. We need some directions.
Clerk Sure. What are you looking for?
Guest 1 Well, first of all, we're looking for the Hard Rock Cafe. How far is it from here?
Clerk Oh, it's just a few minutes from here – right across from the National Bank.
Guest 2 The National Bank on Park Avenue?
Clerk Yes, that's the one.
Guest 2 Is the Hard Rock Cafe a nice place?
Clerk Well, I think so. The food is good, and there are some interesting things to look at in the restaurant – like one of Elvis's cars.
Guest 2 Great! And where is the Science Museum?
Clerk Well, that's near City Hall.
Guest 1 Near City Hall. OK, I know where that is. And what's the museum like?
Clerk Actually, it's not very good. It's small, and there isn't a lot to see there. It's really for young kids.

Guest 1 Oh, then maybe we won't go there.
Guest 2 Hmm, one last question – is there an aquarium in the city?
Clerk Yes, there's a very good one. It's only about six blocks from here. It's in the park next to the train station.
Guest 2 Oh, next to the train station.
Clerk Yes. Definitely visit the aquarium.
Guest 1 Great! Thanks a lot.
Clerk You're welcome. Have a good day.

Answers

Place	Location	Interesting?
Hard Rock Cafe	across from the National Bank on Park Avenue	Yes
Science Museum	near City Hall	No
Aquarium	in the park next to the train station	Yes

B *Pair work*

- Ss discuss the question in pairs.

End of Cycle 1

See the Supplementary Resources chart at the beginning of this unit for additional teaching materials and student activities related to this Cycle.

SNAPSHOT

Learning Objective: *learn vocabulary for talking about problems with neighbors*

- Ask pairs of Ss to brainstorm things that bad neighbors do. Elicit ideas from the class and write them on the board.
- Go over the complaints about neighbors. Elicit or explain new vocabulary.

Vocabulary

complaints: statements people make about problems
barks: makes a loud noise, like a dog
loud: noisy
garbage: trash
privacy: state of being alone or without other people
kids: children

- Ss answer the questions in small groups. Go around the groups and give help as needed.

 # CONVERSATION

Learning Objectives: *practice a conversation about a neighborhood; see* how many *and* how much *with quantifiers in context*

▶ **[CD 2, Track 27]**

- Elicit information about the picture. Ask: "What is the woman doing? What does the neighborhood look like? Does it look safe?"
- Books closed. Write these focus questions on the board:
  1. What are Nick and Pam talking about?
  2. What happens during the phone call?
- Play the audio program. Ask Ss to listen for the answers to the focus questions. Then go over the answers. (Answers: 1. Pam's new apartment and neighborhood 2. Pam's car alarm makes a loud noise.)

TIP To reduce anxiety, point out that Ss will hear the audio program several times. Remind them that they aren't expected to understand every word.

- Write these additional focus questions on the board:
  1. Where is Pam's new apartment?
  2. Which floor does she live on?
  3. What kind of restaurant is there nearby?

- Play the audio program again. Elicit Ss' answers. (Answers: 1. downtown 2. the fifth 3. Korean) Then elicit or explain any new vocabulary.

Vocabulary

downtown: the business center of a city
convenient: nearby; easy to find things
parking: places to park the car
safe: not dangerous; without crime
hold on: wait a minute

- Books open. Play the audio program again. Ss listen and read the conversation silently.
- Ss practice the conversation in pairs.
- **Option:** Ss continue the conversation in pairs. They can ask questions such as *What happened? Why did the car alarm go off?*

❗ For a new way to practice this Conversation, try the **Onion Ring** technique – download it from the website.

7 SNAPSHOT

Common Complaints About Neighbors

Noise

☐ "My neighbor's dog barks all night."

☐ "My neighbor always listens to loud music."

Cleanliness

☐ "My neighbor puts his garbage in the hall."

☐ "There are always shoes outside my door."

Pets

☐ "My neighbor's cats go everywhere."

☐ "My neighbor has six dogs. It's like a zoo!"

Privacy

☐ "My neighbor's kids visit every day. It's too much!"

☐ "My neighbor always asks me for things."

Source: Based on information from njcooperator.com

Check (✓) the complaints you have about your neighbors.
What other complaints do you have about neighbors?
What do you do when you have complaints?

8 CONVERSATION *It's pretty safe.*

▶ Listen and practice.

Nick: How do you like your new apartment?
Pam: I love it. It's downtown, so it's very convenient.
Nick: Downtown? Is there much noise?
Pam: No, there isn't any. I live on the fifth floor.
Nick: How many restaurants are there near your place?
Pam: A lot. In fact, there's an excellent Korean place just around the corner.
Nick: What about parking?
Pam: Well, there aren't many parking garages. But I usually find a place on the street.
Nick: Is there much crime?
Pam: No, it's pretty safe. Hold on. That's my car alarm! I'll call you back later.

What's your neighborhood like? ▪ 53

9 GRAMMAR FOCUS

Quantifiers; how many and how much ▶

Count nouns	Noncount nouns
Are there **many restaurants**?	Is there **much crime**?
Yes, there are **a lot**.	Yes, there's **a lot**.
Yes, there are **a few**.	Yes, there's **a little**.
No, there are**n't many**.	No, there is**n't much**.
No, there are**n't any**.	No, there is**n't any**.
No, there are **none**.	No, there's **none**.
How many restaurants are there?	**How much** crime is there?
There are ten or twelve.	There's a lot of street crime.

A Write answers to these questions about your neighborhood. Then practice with a partner.

1. Is there much parking? ....
2. Are there many apartment buildings? ....
3. How much traffic is there? ....
4. How many dance clubs are there? ....
5. Is there much noise? ....
6. Are there many pay phones? ....
7. Is there much pollution? ....
8. How many swimming pools are there? ....

B GROUP WORK Write questions like those in part A about these topics. Then ask and answer the questions.

cafés   crime   parks   pollution   public transportation   schools   traffic lights

10 INTERCHANGE 8 *Where am I?*

Play a guessing game. Go to Interchange 8 on page 122.

11 WRITING *A "roommate wanted" ad*

A Read these ads asking for roommates.

B Now write a "roommate wanted" ad. Use your real name at the end, but you can use a false phone number or email address.

C CLASS ACTIVITY Put your ads on the wall. Read the ads and choose one. Then find the person who wrote it. Ask questions to get more information.

Roommates 🏠 Wanted

Roommate needed to share large 3-bedroom apt. in nice neighborhood. Great park across the street. Only $440 a month! Parking available. Call Sheri or Jen at 352-555-8381.

Quiet student looking for roommate to share 2-bedroom house near university. Near public transportation. Pets OK. $550 a month plus utilities. Email Greg at g.adams@cup.com.

GRAMMAR FOCUS

Learning Objectives: *ask and answer questions with count and noncount nouns; practice using quantifiers*

▶ *[CD 2, Track 28]*
Count and noncount nouns
- Write this chart on the board:

Count nouns	Noncount nouns
restaurant	traffic
café	parking

- Ask: "Which nouns take a plural *-s* ending?" (Answer: restaurant and café) "Which nouns usually don't take a plural *-s* ending?" (Answer: traffic and parking) Explain that *restaurant* and *café* are count nouns because we can count them (e.g., *one restaurant, two restaurants*). However, we don't count *traffic* or *parking*.

⬚ For more practice with count and noncount nouns, play ***Tic-Tac-Toe*** – download it from the website.

How many *and* how much
- Focus Ss' attention on the Conversation on page 53. Have Ss underline questions about noise and crime (e.g., *Is there much noise? Is there much crime?*). Elicit or explain the rules:
  Is there + much + noncount noun?
  How much + noncount noun + is there?
- Have Ss underline questions with *are there* or *many*. Elicit or explain the rules:
  Are there + many + count noun?
  How many + count noun + are there?

Quantifiers
- Focus Ss' attention on the Grammar Focus box. Point out that quantifiers are used to describe different amounts of things (e.g., *a lot, a few, any, many, much, none*).

- Ask Ss to look at the Grammar Focus box. Ask "How are *a lot, any,* and *none* similar?" (Answer: They can be used with both count or noncount nouns.)
- Play the audio program.

A
- Model the first question. Ss complete the exercise individually. Then Ss compare their answers in pairs.
- Go over the answers as a class.

Possible answers

1. Yes, there's a lot. There's a little. No, there isn't much/any. No, there's none.
2. Yes, there are a lot/many. There are a few. No, there aren't any. No, there are none.
3. There's a lot/a little/none. There isn't much/any.
4. There are a lot/many. There are a few. There aren't any. There are none.
5. Yes, there's a lot. There's a little. No, there isn't much/any. No, there's none.
6. Yes, there are a lot/many. There are a few. No, there aren't any. No, there are none.
7. There is a lot/a little/none. There isn't much/any.
8. There are a lot/many. There are a few. There aren't any. There are none.

- Ss ask and answer the questions in pairs.
- **Option:** Ss repeat the task with a new partner.

B *Group work*
- Explain and model the task.
- Ss write questions individually. Then they take turns asking and answering the questions in pairs.

 # INTERCHANGE 8

See page T-122 for teaching notes.

 # WRITING

Learning Objectives: *read "roommate wanted" ads; write a "roommate wanted" ad*

A
- Ss read the example ads silently. Elicit or explain any new vocabulary.
- Point out written features of an ad (e.g., *apt.* means *apartment,* articles *a/an* and the verb *be* are usually not included).

B
- Explain the task. Ss write their ads individually. Go around the class and give help as needed.

C *Class activity*
- Explain the task. While Ss are asking questions, check for correct use of count and noncount nouns.

12 READING

Learning Objectives: *read an article; develop skills in scanning and reading for detail*

- Ss cover the text and look at the pictures. Ask: "What do you think this Toronto (Canada) neighborhood is like?" Elicit ideas from the class.
- Explain the pre-reading task. Point out that Ss should read quickly and focus on the names of countries only. Set a time limit.

> **TIP** When Ss scan an article, set a time limit. This encourages them to read quickly, focusing only on the task.

- Ss silently scan the article and check (✓) the countries that are *not* mentioned. (Answers: Greece, Spain, and Uruguay) Elicit answers from the class. Ask where they found the names of countries. (Answer: first paragraph)

A

- Model the task. Ask Ss to read the first paragraph. Then elicit the main idea.
- Ss read the next two paragraphs and write the paragraph numbers next to the main ideas.

Answers

2, 1, 3

B

- Ss read the article in detail. Elicit or explain any new vocabulary.

Vocabulary

sidewalks: places next to the street where people walk
crowded with: full of
spices: substances made from plants used to give food a special flavor
truly: really
multicultural: made up of many cultures
resident: a person who lives in a place
rent: money people pay to live in apartments
cuisine: a style of cooking

- Ss complete the exercise. Go over answers with the class.

Answers

Inexpensive stores, big apartments, great markets, good restaurants, many different cultures, good public transportation

C *Pair work*

- Go over the discussion question with the class. Encourage Ss to consider the residents, the businesses, and other neighborhood characteristics. Ss complete the task in pairs.

End of Cycle 2

See the Supplementary Resources chart at the beginning of this unit for additional teaching materials and student activities related to this Cycle and for assessment tools.

The World in One Neighborhood

Scan the article. Then check (✓) the countries that are not mentioned.
☐ Brazil ☐ China ☐ Greece ☐ India ☐ Spain ☐ Sudan ☐ Uruguay ☐ Vietnam

1 The sidewalks are crowded with people chatting in Cantonese. An Indian man sells spices from his corner shop. Brazilian music plays loudly from a café. Is it China? India? Brazil? No, it's Kensington Market, a neighborhood in Toronto, Canada. Kensington Market was once an Eastern European and Italian neighborhood, but the area changed along with its residents. First came the Portuguese, then East Asians, then people from Iran, Vietnam, Sudan, Brazil, the Caribbean, and the Middle East.

2 Today, the neighborhood is truly multicultural – you can hear more than 100 languages on its streets. New residents bring many new traditions. "What's really cool about Kensington is that as soon as you're in it, you feel as though you're not in Toronto anymore," says one resident. "I think what makes Kensington Market unique is that it's always changing," says another.

3 It isn't surprising that the area in and around Kensington Market is becoming a popular place to live. The rents are reasonable, the neighborhood is exciting, and it has good public transportation. There are apartments of every size and for every budget. It has inexpensive stores, fun cafés, fresh fruit and vegetable markets, and restaurants with almost every type of cuisine. As one resident says, "This place is the heart of Toronto."

A Read the article. Then write the number of each paragraph next to its main idea.

..... The residents and their traditions make Kensington Market a multicultural neighborhood.
.... People from all over the world live in Kensington Market.
.... The neighborhood has many good characteristics.

B Check (✓) the things you can find in Kensington Market.

☐ inexpensive stores ☐ beautiful beaches ☐ many different cultures
☐ big apartments ☐ great markets ☐ interesting old buildings
☐ good schools ☐ good restaurants ☐ good public transportation

C **PAIR WORK** Do you know of a neighborhood that is similar to Kensington Market? Describe it.

Units 7–8 Progress check

SELF-ASSESSMENT

How well can you do these things? Check (✓) the boxes.

I can	Very well	OK	A little
Understand descriptions of past events (Ex. 1)	☐	☐	☐
Describe events in the past (Ex. 1)	☐	☐	☐
Ask and answer questions about past activities (Ex. 2)	☐	☐	☐
Give and understand simple directions (Ex. 3)	☐	☐	☐
Talk about my neighborhood (Ex. 4)	☐	☐	☐

1 LISTENING *Frankie's weekend*

A A thief robbed a house on Saturday. A detective is questioning Frankie. The pictures show what Frankie really did on Saturday. Listen to their conversation. Are Frankie's answers true (**T**) or false (**F**)?

1:00 P.M. **T F**   3:00 P.M. **T F**   5:00 P.M. **T F**   6:00 P.M. **T F**   8:00 P.M. **T F**   10:30 P.M. **T F**

B PAIR WORK What did Frankie really do? Use the pictures to retell the story.

2 DISCUSSION *What do you remember?*

A Do you remember what you did yesterday? Check (✓) the things you did. Then add two other things you did.

☐ got up early   ☐ went shopping   ☐ did the dishes   ☐ went to bed late
☐ went to class   ☐ ate at a restaurant   ☐ watched TV   ☐ ....
☐ made phone calls   ☐ did the laundry   ☐ exercised   ☐ ....

B GROUP WORK Ask questions about each thing in part A.

A: Did you get up early yesterday?
B: No, I didn't. I got up at 10:00. I was very tired.

Units 7-8 Progress check

SELF-ASSESSMENT

Learning Objectives: *reflect on one's learning; identify areas that need improvement*

- Ask: "What did you learn in Units 7 and 8?" Elicit Ss' answers.
- Ss complete the Self-assessment. Encourage them to be honest, and point out they will not get a bad grade if they check (✓) *a little*.

- Ss move on to the Progress check exercises. You can have Ss complete them in class or for homework, using one of these techniques:
1. Ask Ss to complete all the exercises.
2. Ask Ss: "What do you need to practice?" Then assign exercises based on their answers.
3. Ask Ss to choose and complete exercises based on their Self-assessment.

 LISTENING

Learning Objective: *assess one's ability to understand descriptions of past events and to describe past events*

A ▶ *[CD 2, Track 29]*
- Explain the task.
- Play the audio program. Ss complete the task. Then go over answers with the class.

AudioScript

Detective Hello, Frankie. How was your weekend?
Frankie Oh, it's you, Detective. My weekend? What do you want to know about it?
Detective Now just tell the truth. Where were you at 1:00 P.M. on Saturday?
Frankie Ah . . . 1:00 P.M. . . . on Saturday? Well, oh, I remember! I was at home. I watched the baseball game on TV. Yeah, the Expos won, four to nothing. It was a great game.
Detective OK . . . OK. Where were you at 3:00 P.M.?
Frankie Ah . . . at 3:00? Ah, yeah, I went to my karate class like I always do, every Saturday at 3:00.
Detective Karate, huh? Well . . . OK. And what did you do after that? At around 5:00 P.M.?
Frankie Ah, oh, yeah, uh, after karate, I visited some old friends of mine – Tom and Mary Kent, on Front Street.
Detective Yeah? Tom and Mary Kent. We'll talk to them. Now, Frankie, 6:00. Where were you at 6:00?
Frankie Oh! Hmm . . . at 6:00? Well, I went home at 6:00 . . . yeah . . . to . . . uh . . . clean the house.
Detective Yeah, yeah, so you cleaned the house. Now,

listen carefully, Frankie. Where were you at 8:00 on Saturday night?
Frankie Uh . . . at 8:00? Uh . . . oh, yeah . . . I remember now. I was at home. I watched a terrific movie on TV. Yeah . . . it was great!
Detective Oh, you watched a movie on TV, did you? And what movie did you watch? What was the name of the movie, Frankie? Huh?
Frankie The movie? The name of the movie? Uh, let me think a minute. It was a fantastic movie.
Detective Really?
Frankie No, wait! I remember, it was, uh . . . uh . . . well, it was exciting.
Detective OK, OK, Frankie . . .
Frankie . . . and I clearly remember that I went to bed at 10:30, uh, exactly . . . Yeah. I watched the movie, and I went to bed right after . . . uh . . . the movie. Yeah, boy, I was tired – a long day, like I said.
Detective Interesting. Very interesting, Frankie. Come on, Frankie. Let's go down to the police station.
Frankie The police station? Me? Why me? I was at home on Saturday night!
Detective Sure, Frankie, sure. [*police siren*]

Answers

T, T, T, T, F, F

B *Pair work*
- Ss retell the story in pairs.

 DISCUSSION

Learning Objective: *assess one's ability to ask and answer questions about past activities*

A
- Ss check (✓) the things they did individually yesterday. Then they add two more things.

B *Group work*
- Model the conversation with a S. Then Ss ask and answer questions about the things in part A in small groups.

3 SPEAKING

Learning Objective: *assess one's ability to give and understand simple directions*

A

- Explain the task. Ss create a neighborhood. They choose five places from the list and add them to *My map*.
- For plurals, tell Ss to be sure to draw two places on their maps.
- Ss complete the task individually.
- Go around the class and give help as needed.

B *Pair work*

- Read the instructions aloud. Ask two Ss to model the example conversation. Explain that Student A draws a café on the corner of Center Street and First Avenue on *My partner's map*. Point out that Ss cannot look at their partners' maps.
- Ss take turns asking and answering questions in pairs.
- Tell Ss to ask any additional questions to find the exact location of each place (e.g., *Is it next to the grocery store?*).
- Ss then compare maps. Ask: "Did you draw the place in the correct locations?"

4 ROLE PLAY

Learning Objective: *assess one's ability to talk about neighborhoods*

- Explain the task. Ss work in pairs. Student A is a visitor in Student B's neighborhood. Student A asks questions and Student B answers them.
- Model the example conversation with a S.

- Go over the topics in the box. Explain or elicit any new vocabulary.
- Ss practice the role play in pairs. Then they change roles and practice again.
- Go around the class and check Ss' use of *how many, how much*, and quantifiers.

WHAT'S NEXT?

Learning Objective: *become more involved in one's learning*

- Focus Ss' attention on the Self-assessment again. Ask: "How well can you do these things now?"

- Ask Ss to underline one thing they need to review. Ask: "What did you underline? How can you review it?"
- If needed, plan additional activities or reviews based on Ss' answers.

3 SPEAKING *The neighborhood*

A Create a neighborhood. Add five places to "My map."
Choose from this list.

a bank   cafés   a dance club   a drugstore   gas stations   a gym   a theater

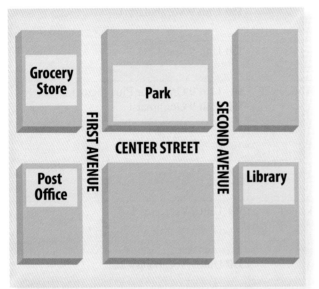

My map

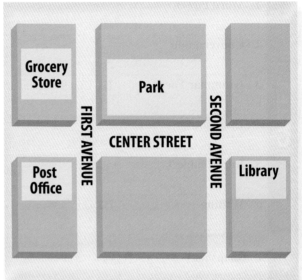

My partner's map

B **PAIR WORK** Ask questions about your partner's map. (But don't look!)
Draw the places on "My partner's map." Then compare your maps.

A: Are there any cafés in the neighborhood?
B: Yes, there's one on the corner of Center Street and First Avenue.

4 ROLE PLAY *What's it like?*

Student A: Imagine you are a visitor in Student B's neighborhood.
Ask questions about it.
Student B: Imagine a visitor wants to find out about your
neighborhood. Answer the visitor's questions.

A: How much crime is there?
B: There isn't much. It's a very safe neighborhood.
A: Is there much noise?
B: Well, yes, there's a lot. . . .

Change roles and try the role play again.

topics to ask about
crime
noise
parks
places to shop
pollution
public transportation
schools
traffic

WHAT'S NEXT?

Look at your Self-assessment again. Do you need to review anything?

Unit 9 Supplementary Resources Overview

	After the following SB exercises	You can use these materials in class	Your students can use these materials outside the classroom
CYCLE 1	1 Word Power		**SSD** Unit 9 Vocabulary 1
	2 Conversation		**SSD** Unit 9 Speaking 1
	3 Grammar Focus	**TSS** Unit 9 Vocabulary Worksheet	**SB** Unit 9 Grammar Plus focus 1 **SSD** Unit 9 Grammar 1
	4 Listening		
	5 Interchange 9		
	6 Writing	**TSS** Unit 9 Writing Worksheet	**WB** Unit 9 exercises 1–5
CYCLE 2	7 Snapshot		**SSD** Unit 9 Vocabulary 2
	8 Conversation		**SSD** Unit 9 Speaking 2
	9 Grammar Focus	**TSS** Unit 9 Grammar Worksheet	**SB** Unit 9 Grammar Plus focus 2 **SSD** Unit 9 Grammar 2–3 **ARC** Describing people and Modifiers **ARC** Modifiers with participles and prepositions 1–2
	10 Pronunciation		**ARC** Contrastive stress in responses
	11 Reading	**TSS** Unit 9 Listening Worksheet **TSS** Unit 9 Extra Worksheet **TSS** Unit 9 Project Worksheet **VID** Unit 9 **VRB** Unit 9	**SSD** Unit 9 Reading 1–3 **SSD** Unit 9 Listening 1–3 **SSD** Unit 9 Video 1–3 **WB** Unit 9 exercises 6–11

Key

ARC: Arcade	**SB:** Student's Book	**SSD:** Self-study DVD-ROM	**TSS:** Teacher Support Site
VID: Video DVD	**VRB:** Video Resource Book	**WB:** Workbook	

Unit 9 Supplementary Resources Overview   *Interchange* Teacher's Edition 1 © Cambridge University Press 2013   Photocopiable

My Plan for Unit 9

Use the space below to customize a plan that fits your needs.

With the following SB exercises	I am using these materials in class	My students are using these materials outside the classroom

With or instead of the following SB section	I am using these materials for assessment

What does she look like?

1 WORD POWER Appearance

A Look at these expressions. What are three more words or expressions to describe people? Write them in the box below.

Hair

| long brown hair | short blond hair | straight black hair | curly red hair | bald | a mustache and beard |

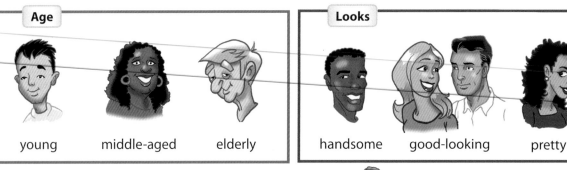

Age

young   middle-aged   elderly

Looks

handsome   good-looking   pretty

Height

short   fairly short   medium height   pretty tall   very tall

Other words or expressions

....
....
....

B PAIR WORK Choose at least four expressions to describe yourself and your partner. Then compare. Do you agree?

A: You have curly black hair. You're young and good-looking.
B: I don't agree. My hair isn't very curly.

Me	My partner
....	....
....	....
....	....
....	....

What does she look like?

Cycle 1, Exercises 1–6

In Unit 9, students describe people's appearances. In Cycle 1, they describe people's physical appearances. In Cycle 2, they identify people using modifiers with participles and prepositions to describe what they are wearing or doing.

 WORD POWER

Learning Objective: *learn vocabulary for describing people*

A

- Books closed. Explain that Ss will learn ways to describe what people look like. Ask questions about different Ss: "Is he tall or short? Does she have straight or curly hair?"
- **Option:** Ask Ss to bring pictures of friends or family members to class. Alternatively, bring magazine pictures of people to class.
- Books open. Focus Ss' attention on the expressions and pictures. Ask them to circle any words they don't know.
- Ask different Ss to read the expressions. Give help with pronunciation as needed. Point out that *handsome* usually refers to men and *pretty* to women, but *good-looking* describes both men and women. Also point out that adverbs such as *fairly* and *pretty* can modify the strength of different descriptions (e.g., *fairly short, pretty tall*).
- Write these headings across the top of the board:

  Hair   Age   Looks   Height   Other

- Ss work in groups. Ask Ss to brainstorm at least three more expressions to describe people. Then ask a S from each group to write their expressions under the correct headings on the board.

Possible answers

Hair: light brown hair, dark brown hair, gray hair, medium length hair, wavy hair, a ponytail
Age: ten, in his or her teens/twenties/thirties, old
Looks: thin, heavy, cute, beautiful, gorgeous
Height: rather short, quite tall
Other: blue eyes, green eyes, dark eyes, brown eyes

TIP Don't give your Ss too much new vocabulary. If they already know the presented vocabulary, add more. If not, add just a few extra words they want to know.

- Explain or elicit the rules for using the new words:
  be + adjective
  have + noun

Then ask Ss to write *have* or *be* next to the expressions on the board. Stress that we use *be* with age.

- **Option:** Ss write sentences about famous people using expressions from the boxes (e.g., *Robert Pattinson is handsome.*). Then they read their sentences to their classmates, who agree or disagree.

B *Pair work*

- Ss choose at least four expressions to describe themselves and their partners. They complete the chart individually. Go around the class and give help as needed.
- Ask two Ss to read the example conversation. Elicit other expressions for agreeing or disagreeing (e.g., *That's true. No way!*). Write them on the board.
- Ss compare charts in pairs. Go around the class and give help as needed.
- **Option:** Ss work with different partners. This time, they sit back-to-back and describe each other from memory.

! For a new way to review, categorize, or expand on the vocabulary in this Word Power, try *Mind Mapping* – download it from the website.

2 CONVERSATION

Learning Objectives: *practice a conversation between two people describing another person; see descriptions of people in context*

A ▶ [CD 2, Track 30]

- Ss cover the text. Ask Ss to describe the people in the picture.
- Write these focus questions on the board:
  1. Who are Randy and Emily talking about?
  2. How does Randy describe her?
  3. How old is she?
- Play the audio program and elicit the answers. (Answers: 1. Randy's new girlfriend 2. She's gorgeous and very tall. She has beautiful red hair. 3. Randy doesn't know.)
- Ss uncover the text. Play the audio program again. Ss listen and read silently.
- Elicit or explain any new vocabulary.

Vocabulary

gorgeous: very beautiful
6 feet 2: 188 centimeters
She won't tell me : She doesn't want to say.

- Ss practice the conversation in pairs. Go around the class and give help as needed.

- **Option:** Ss cover the conversation and look only at the picture. Then they practice the conversation again using their own words.

B ▶ [CD 2, Track 31]

- Read the focus question aloud. Ask Ss to make predictions. Write their predictions on the board.
- Play the audio program. Ss listen for the answer to the focus question.
- Ss compare answers in small groups. Then go over answers with the class. Was anyone's prediction correct?

AudioScript

Emily She won't tell you her age?
Randy No. But I don't care.
Emily How old do you think she is?
Randy Who knows? I think she's probably in her thirties.
Emily And how old are you?
Randy I'm 29.
Emily Oh, so she's older than you.

Possible answer

Ashley is probably in her thirties. Ashley is older than Randy. Randy doesn't care about Ashley's age.

3 GRAMMAR FOCUS

Learning Objectives: *practice describing people; ask and answer questions about appearance*

▶ [CD 2, Track 32]

- Books closed. Write these questions and statements on the board:
  1. What does she look like? a. It's medium length.
  2. How old is she? b. She's gorgeous.
  3. How tall is she? c. She's about 32.
  4. How long is her hair? d. She's 6 feet 2.
- Ask Ss to match the questions with the answers.
- Books open. Tell Ss to look at the Grammar Focus box to check their answers. Play the audio program.

A

- Explain the task. Read the first answer and elicit the question.
- Ss complete the task individually. Then they compare answers in pairs.
- Write the numbers 1 to 7 on the board. Ask different Ss to write the questions on the board. Then go over them as a class.

Answers

1. How old is your brother?
2. How tall are you?
3. What color is your mother's hair?/What color hair does your mother have?
4. Does she wear glasses?
5. What does he look like?
6. How long is your sister's hair?
7. What color are your eyes?/What color eyes do you have?

B *Pair work*

- Explain the task and model the example conversation with a S.
- Ss complete the task in pairs. Go around the class and check Ss' grammar.
- For more practice asking questions about appearance, play *Twenty Questions* – download it from the website.

2 CONVERSATION *She's very tall.*

A ▶ Listen and practice.

Emily: I hear you have a new girlfriend, Randy.
Randy: Yes. Her name's Ashley, and she's gorgeous!
Emily: Really? What does she look like?
Randy: Well, she's very tall.
Emily: How tall?
Randy: About 6 feet 2, I suppose.
Emily: Wow, that *is* tall. What color is her hair?
Randy: She has beautiful red hair.
Emily: And how old is she?
Randy: I don't know. She won't tell me.

B ▶ Listen to the rest of the conversation. What else do you learn about Ashley?

3 GRAMMAR FOCUS

Describing people ▶

General appearance	Age	Height	Hair
What does she look like?	How old is she?	How tall is she?	How long is her hair?
She's tall, with red hair.	She's about 32.	She's 1 meter 88.	It's medium length.
She's gorgeous.	She's in her thirties.	She's 6 feet 2.	
Does he wear glasses?	How old is he?	How tall is he?	What color is his hair?
Yes, and he has a beard.	He's in his twenties.	He's pretty short.	It's dark/light brown.
			He has brown hair.

A Write questions to match these statements. Then compare with a partner.

1. .... ?   My brother is 26.
2. .... ?   I'm 173 cm (5 feet 8).
3. .... ?   My mother has brown hair.
4. .... ?   No, she wears contact lenses
5. .... ?   He's tall and very good-looking.
6. .... ?   My sister's hair is medium length.
7. .... ?   I have dark brown eyes.

B **PAIR WORK** Choose a person in your class. Don't tell your partner who it is. Your partner will ask questions to guess the person's name.

A: Is it a man or a woman?
B: It's a man.
A: How tall is he?
B: . . .

4 LISTENING *Who is it?*

A ▶ Listen to descriptions of six people. Number them from 1 to 6.

B ▶ Listen again. How old is each person?

5 INTERCHANGE 9 *Find the differences*

Compare two pictures of a party. Student A go to Interchange 9A on page 123. Student B go to Interchange 9B on page 124.

6 WRITING *An email describing people*

A Imagine your e-pal is coming to visit you for the first time. You and a classmate are meeting him or her at the airport. Write an email describing yourself and your classmate. (Don't give the classmate's name.)

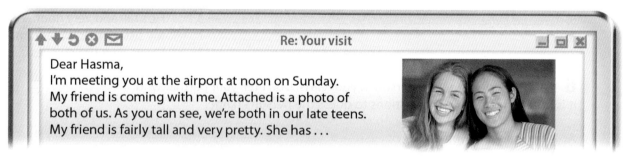

Re: Your visit

Dear Hasma,
I'm meeting you at the airport at noon on Sunday.
My friend is coming with me. Attached is a photo of
both of us. As you can see, we're both in our late teens.
My friend is fairly tall and very pretty. She has . . .

B **GROUP WORK** Read your email to the group. Can they guess the classmate you are describing?

4 LISTENING

Learning Objective: *develop skills in listening for details*

A [CD 2, Track 33]

- Focus Ss' attention on the picture. In pairs Ss brainstorm words or expressions to describe each person. Point out that they should describe the people, not their clothes.
- Each pair joins another pair and compares ideas. Go around the class and give help as needed.
- Explain the task. Tell Ss to listen for key words (e.g., *short*, *glasses*) and not worry about understanding every word.
- Play the audio program. Ss complete the task individually.
- Go over answers with the class.

AudioScript

1.
I think Brian's good-looking. He's pretty tall, with dark brown hair and a mustache. I think he's about 30.
2.
Tina's 18. She has red hair – shoulder length and very curly – and she always wears interesting glasses, just for fun.
3.
Rosie is pretty tall for her age. She has long blond hair and wears contact lenses. She just turned 10.

4.
Tim's about 23. He's fairly short and a little bit heavy. His hair isn't very long.
5.
Gary is in his fifties. He's bald and has a small moustache. He likes to wear sunglasses. And he always wears soccer shirts and jeans.
6.
Alice is very tall, and she has long black hair. She's around 25. Oh, and she's very slim. She looks like a fashion model.

Answers

2, 4, 1, 6, 5, 3

B [CD 2, Track 34]

- Ask a S to read the focus question aloud. Then play the audio program. Ss listen for the answers.
- Ss compare answers in pairs. Elicit their answers. Play the audio program again if needed.

Answers

1. 30   2. 13   3. 10   4. 23   5. 50s   6. 25

5 INTERCHANGE 9

See pages T-124 and T-125 for teaching notes.

6 WRITING

Learning Objective: *learn to write an email describing people*

A

- Set the scene. Say: "Imagine an e-pal is visiting you for the first time. You and a classmate are meeting him or her at the airport. How will your e-pal know what you look like?"
- Ask a S to read the model email. Elicit or explain any new words or expressions.
- Explain the task. Each S writes an email describing himself/herself and another classmate. Point out that Ss should not write the name of the classmate.
- **Option:** Ss write the email for homework.

B Group work

- Explain the task and read the question.
- Ss take turns reading their descriptions in small groups. Their classmates guess who they are describing

End of Cycle 1

See the Supplementary Resources chart at the beginning of this unit for additional teaching materials and student activities related to this Cycle.

7 SNAPSHOT

Learning Objective: *talk about clothing styles*

- Books closed. Ask: "What kind of clothing is in fashion now?" Help Ss with vocabulary as needed.
- Write these clothing styles on the board: *classic, cool and casual,* and *funky.* Elicit or explain their meanings.

Vocabulary

classic: always fashionable
cool: fashionable at this time
casual: not formal
funky: modern and unusual

- Ss brainstorm examples of clothing for each style.
- Books open. Ss compare their ideas with the Snapshot.
- Ask different Ss to read the questions.
- Ss complete the task individually. Then they compare answers in pairs or small groups. Elicit Ss' answers.
- **Option:** Bring fashion magazines to class. Ss discuss which styles are classic, cool and casual, or funky.
- **Option:** Assign classes of younger Ss to make their own Snapshots. Ss cut pictures of clothing from fashion magazines, put them on cards, and label the items and styles. Then display the Ss' work.

8 CONVERSATION

Learning Objectives: *practice a conversation between two people at a party; see modifiers with participles and prepositions in context*

A ▶ [CD 2, Track 35]

- Write these questions on the board:
  1. Where are these people?
  2. What are they doing?
  3. What are they wearing?
  4. What do they look like?

- Focus Ss' attention on the picture. Have Ss ask each other the questions about the people in the picture. Then elicit possible answers.

- Set the scene. Raoul comes to a party alone. He meets his friend Liz. She tells him about some people at the party.

- Write these focus questions on the board:
  1. Where's Maggie?
  2. Where's Julia?
  3. Does Julia know anyone at the party?

- Play the audio program once or twice. Elicit Ss' answers to the focus questions. (Answers: 1. She's at a concert. 2. She's standing near the window. 3. No, she doesn't.)

- Play the audio program again. Ss look at the picture and read the conversation silently.

- Elicit or explain any new vocabulary.

Vocabulary

couldn't make it: wasn't able to come

- Ss practice the conversation in pairs.

❗ For a new way to teach this Conversation, try the **Musical Dialog** – download it from the website.

B ▶ [CD 2, Track 36]

- Explain the task.
- Play the audio program. Ss listen and label the people in the picture individually.
- Ss compare answers in pairs. Then go over answers with the class. Play the audio program again if needed.

AudioScript

Liz Let's see. Who else is here? Do you know Joe? He's really nice.
Raoul No, I don't. Which one is he?
Liz He's over there. He's the one wearing white pants and . . .
Raoul . . . and a yellow polo shirt?
Liz That's right. And then there's Michiko Sasaki. She works with me at the office.
Raoul Oh? Which one is Michiko?
Liz She's the woman in black pants and a green sweater. She's wearing glasses.
Raoul Yeah, I see her. She's the one talking to Joe, right?
Liz Uh-huh.
Raoul And who are those two people dancing?
Liz Oh, that's my best friend. Her name is Rosa. She's really nice.
Raoul That's an interesting . . . purple dress.
Liz She's dancing with John DuPont, her new boyfriend.
Raoul John is Rosa's boyfriend?
Liz Yeah. Say, didn't you want to meet Julia?
Raoul Uh, I'm sorry, but which one is Julia again?

Answers

(from left to right) Joe, Michiko, Julia, John, Rosa

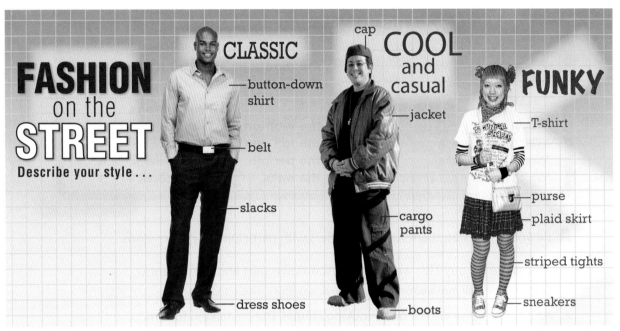

FASHION on the STREET
Describe your style . . .

CLASSIC

— button-down shirt

— belt

— slacks

— dress shoes

cap

COOL and casual

— jacket

— cargo pants

— boots

FUNKY

— T-shirt

— purse

— plaid skirt

— striped tights

— sneakers

Source: Based on an idea from *Time Out New York*

Which clothing items do you often wear? Circle the items.
What are three more things you like to wear?
What's your style? Is it classic? cool and casual? funky? something else?

8 **CONVERSATION** *Which one is she?*

A ▶ Listen and practice.

Liz: Hi, Raoul! Good to see you! Where's Maggie?
Raoul: Oh, she couldn't make it. She went to a concert with Alex.
Liz: Oh! Well, why don't you go and talk to Julia? She doesn't know anyone here.
Raoul: Julia? Which one is she? Is she the woman wearing glasses over there?
Liz: No, she's the tall one in jeans. She's standing near the window.
Raoul: Oh, I'd like to meet her.

B ▶ Listen to the rest of the conversation. Label Joe, Michiko, Rosa, and John in the picture.

Modifiers with participles and prepositions ⊙

		Participles
Who's Raoul?	He's **the man**	**wearing** a green shirt.
Which one is Raoul?	He's **the one**	**talking** to Liz.
		Prepositions
Who's Liz?	She's **the woman**	**with** short black hair.
Which one is Julia?	She's **the tall one**	**in** jeans.
Who are the Smiths?	They're **the people**	**next to** the window.
Which ones are the Smiths?	They're **the ones**	**on** the couch.

A Rewrite these statements using modifiers with participles or prepositions.

1. Clark is the tall guy. He's wearing a button-down shirt and cargo pants.
   Clark is the tall guy wearing a button-down shirt and cargo pants.

2. Adam and Louise are the good-looking couple. They're talking to Tom.
   ....

3. Lynne is the young girl. She's in a striped T-shirt and blue jeans.
   ....

4. Jessica is the attractive woman. She's sitting to the left of Antonio.
   ....

5. A.J. is the serious-looking boy. He's playing a video game.
   ....

B **PAIR WORK** Complete these questions using your classmates' names
and information. Then take turns asking and answering the questions.

1. Who's the man sitting next to .... ? 4. Which one is .... ?
2. Who's the woman wearing .... ? 5. Who are the people .... ?
3. Who is .... ? 6. Who are the ones .... ?

A ⊙ Listen and practice. Notice how the stress changes to emphasize a contrast.

A: Is Anthony the one wearing the red shirt?

B: No, he's the one wearing the black shirt.

A: Is Judy the woman on the couch?

B: No, Diana is the woman on the couch.

B ⊙ Mark the stress changes in these conversations. Listen and check.
Then practice the conversations.

A: Is Britney the one sitting next to Katy?

B: No, she's the one standing next to Katy.

A: Is Donald the one on the couch?

B: No, he's the one behind the couch.

9 GRAMMAR FOCUS

Learning Objective: *practice using modifiers with participles and prepositions*

▶ *[CD 2, Track 37]*

Modifiers with particles and prepositions

- Write these five sentences on the board:
  1. He's the man dancing in the living room.
  2. She's the one wearing a dress.
  3. She's the one with dark hair and glasses.
  4. He's the one in white pants.
  5. She's the tall person next to the window.

- Focus Ss' attention on the Conversation on page 61. Ss identify each person in pairs.

- Go over the answers as a class. (Answers: 1. John 2. Rosa 3. Michiko 4. Joe 5. Julia)

- Explain the form of a present participle (verb + -*ing*). Then elicit the participles in the sentences on the board (*dancing* and *wearing*) and underline them.

- Elicit the prepositions in the sentences on the board (*with*, *in*, and *next to*) and circle them.

- Focus Ss' attention on the Grammar Focus box. Point out that *one* replaces *man* or *woman* and *ones* refers to more than one person.

- Play the audio program. Answer any remaining questions.

A

- Explain the task and ask two Ss to read the example statement and rewritten statement.

- Ss complete the task individually. Then they compare answers in pairs.

- Ask different Ss to write the answers on the board. Then go over them with the class.

Answers

1. Clark is the tall guy wearing a button-down shirt and cargo pants.
2. Adam and Louise are the good-looking couple talking to Tom.
3. Lynne is the young girl in a striped T-shirt and blue jeans.
4. Jessica is the attractive woman sitting to the left of Antonio.
5. A.J. is the serious-looking boy playing a video game.

B *Pair work*

- Explain the task. Ss complete the task using the names of classmates.

- Ss complete the task individually. Go around the class and give help as needed.

- Ss take turns asking and answering their questions in pairs. Go around the class and note any grammar errors.

- *Option:* For more practice, Ss change partners and complete the task again.

10 PRONUNCIATION

Learning Objectives: *notice changes in stress; learn to sound natural when using contrastive stress*

A ▶ *[CD 2, Track 38]*

- Play the audio program. Ss listen for the stressed words.

- Focus Ss' attention on the conversations. Point out that people use more stress when they correct information. Ask: "What words does Student B stress?" (Answers: black, Diana)

- Play the audio program again. Ss listen and clap when they hear the stressed words.

B ▶ *[CD 2, Track 39]*

- Focus Ss' attention on the conversations. Ask them to mark the words they think Student B will stress.

- Play the audio program. Ss check and correct their guesses.

- Check answers as a class. Then Ss practice the conversations in pairs.

Answers

(Contrastive stress is in boldface.)
1. A: Is Britney the one sitting next to Katy?
   B: No, she's the one **standing** next to Katy.
2. A: Is Donald the one on the couch?
   B: No, he's the one **behind** the couch.

- *Option:* Ask Ss to write questions about classmates or classroom objects with incorrect information (e.g., *Is the teacher the one sitting in the back? Is your backpack the one on the floor?*). Then Ss ask each other the questions in pairs. Go around the class and check their use of contrastive stress.

! For a new way to teach this Pronunciation, try ● *Walking Stress* – download it from the website.

11 READING

Learning Objectives: *read and discuss an article about fashion; develop skills in scanning and reading for detail*

- Books closed. Write *Fashion: mixing and matching styles, patterns, and color* on the board. Ask Ss to write down words related to this topic in pairs. If Ss don't know anything about the topic, ask them to write questions they have about it. Elicit Ss' answers and questions.
- Books open. Ss read the pre-reading question, and scan the article to find three fashions.

Possible answers

c, a, b

A

- Ss read the article silently. Ask Ss to guess the meanings of any words they don't know.

> **TIP** Encourage Ss to guess the meaning of a new word by looking at the part of speech, its position in the sentence, and the context.

- Explain the task and model the first example. Ss find the words in italics in the article. Then they match each word with its meaning.
- Ss complete the task individually. Then they compare their answers in pairs.
- **Option:** Ss work in groups of three. Each S matches two words with their meanings. Then Ss share answers as a group.
- Go over answers with the class.

Answers

1. e   2. d   3. a   4. b   5. f   6. c

- Elicit or explain any remaining vocabulary.

Vocabulary

prints: a patterned fabric, not a solid color
trick: a clever way to do something
similarity: how things are alike
background: part of a design that is not the main feature
vintage: quality clothing from the past
modern: of the present time
outdated: no longer in style
alter: to change to fit or make stylish
tucked in: having the bottom of a shirt inside the pants

- Ask Ss what they learned or found interesting in the article.
- **Option:** Ss find the topic of each paragraph. (Answers: 1. mixing colors and patterns 2. mixing old and new 3. mixing baggy and slim)

B *Pair work*

- Ss discuss the questions in pairs. Then elicit their ideas.

End of Cycle 2

See the Supplementary Resources chart at the beginning of this unit for additional teaching materials and student activities related to this Cycle.

DEAR KEN AND PIXIE

Your style questions answered!

Look at the pictures. What is each an example of? Match the descriptions with the pictures. a. mixing old and new   b. mixing baggy and slim   c. mixing colors and patterns

All of your questions this week are about mixing and matching styles, patterns, and colors.

Dear Ken and Pixie,
I'm reading a lot about how to mix prints in the latest fashion magazines. But when I wear different prints together, I look silly. What's the trick?
– Mixed-up

Dear Mixed-up,
It's not difficult to wear different prints together. Find the similarity in each item of clothing you want to wear. Mix two or three items with the same background color, like white or another neutral color. Mix a large print with a small one. Mix similar patterns, like stripes with plaid. But if you don't feel comfortable in it, don't wear it!

Dear Ken and Pixie,
In college, I wore vintage clothes, but now I'm 30 and need a modern look. How can I wear vintage styles without looking outdated?
– Oldie but Goodie

Dear Oldie but Goodie,
Vintage clothing is always in! But mix it with something new for a modern look. Wear a vintage shirt with pants. Pair an old belt with a new bag. Wear vintage shoes with new jeans. But sometimes you need to alter the clothes. For example, take a baggy vintage skirt and make it slim, or cut the shoulder pads out of a vintage jacket.

Dear Ken and Pixie,
I'm seeing both baggy pants and skinny pants on the designer runways. Also, short pants and long pants. What's in style?
– Confused Carrie

Dear Confused Carrie,
It's all in style! For pants, anything goes this year. The trick is to wear something on top that is the opposite of the style of the pants. So, if you're wearing baggy pants, try a slim shirt. If slim pants are your thing, wear a baggy sweater. Short pants? Try funky shoes. Wear long pants with your shirt tucked in and a belt.

A Read the webpage. Find the words in *italics* in the text. Then match each word with its meaning.

...... 1. *neutral*   a. not in style
...... 2. *vintage*   b. change
...... 3. *outdated*   c. slim
...... 4. *alter*   d. from the past but still in style
...... 5. *baggy*   e. without strong color
...... 6. *skinny*   f. loose fitting

B **PAIR WORK** Answer these questions.

1. Do you mix and match patterns and colors? What does your favorite outfit look like?
2. Do you have any vintage clothing? What time period is it from?
3. Do you wear clothes because they are fashionable or because they look good on you, or both?

Unit 10 Supplementary Resources Overview

<table>
<tr><th></th><th></th><th>After the following SB exercises</th><th>You can use these materials in class</th><th>Your students can use these materials outside the classroom</th></tr>
<tr><td rowspan="3">CYCLE 1</td><td>1</td><td>Snapshot</td><td></td><td>SSD Unit 10 Vocabulary 1</td></tr>
<tr><td>2</td><td>Conversation</td><td></td><td>SSD Unit 10 Speaking 1</td></tr>
<tr><td>3</td><td>Grammar Focus</td><td></td><td>SB Unit 10 Grammar Plus focus 1
SSD Unit 10 Grammar 1
ARC Present perfect; already, yet 1–2
WB Unit 10 exercises 1–3</td></tr>
<tr><td rowspan="9">CYCLE 2</td><td>4</td><td>Conversation</td><td></td><td>SSD Unit 10 Speaking 2</td></tr>
<tr><td>5</td><td>Grammar Focus</td><td>TSS Unit 10 Extra Worksheet
TSS Unit 10 Grammar Worksheet</td><td>SB Unit 10 Grammar Plus focus 2
SSD Unit 10 Grammar 2
ARC Present perfect vs. simple past 1–2
ARC For and since</td></tr>
<tr><td>6</td><td>Pronunciation</td><td></td><td></td></tr>
<tr><td>7</td><td>Listening</td><td></td><td></td></tr>
<tr><td>8</td><td>Word Power</td><td>TSS Unit 10 Vocabulary Worksheet</td><td>SSD Unit 10 Vocabulary 2–3
ARC Activities</td></tr>
<tr><td>9</td><td>Speaking</td><td>TSS Unit 10 Listening Worksheet</td><td></td></tr>
<tr><td>10</td><td>Writing</td><td>TSS Unit 10 Writing Worksheet</td><td></td></tr>
<tr><td>11</td><td>Interchange 10</td><td></td><td></td></tr>
<tr><td>12</td><td>Reading</td><td>TSS Unit 10 Project Worksheet
VID Unit 10
VRB Unit 10</td><td>SSD Unit 10 Reading 1–2
SSD Unit 10 Listening 1–3
SSD Unit 10 Video 1–3
WB Unit 10 exercises 4–10</td></tr>
</table>

With or instead of the following SB section	You can also use these materials for assessment
Units 9–10 Progress Check	**ASSESSMENT CD** Units 9–10 Oral Quiz **ASSESSMENT CD** Units 9–10 Written Quiz

Key
ARC: Arcade **SB**: Student's Book **SSD**: Self-study DVD-ROM **TSS**: Teacher Support Site
VID: Video DVD **VRB**: Video Resource Book **WB**: Workbook

My Plan for Unit 10

Use the space below to customize a plan that fits your needs.

With the following SB exercises	I am using these materials in class	My students are using these materials outside the classroom

With or instead of the following SB section	I am using these materials for assessment

10 Have you ever ridden a camel?

1 SNAPSHOT

Entertainment Guide Fun things to do in **NEW ORLEANS**

go to a jazz club   take a riverboat tour   ride in a streetcar   visit a historic home   go to a food festival

Source: www.neworleansonline.com

Which activities have you done?
Check (✓) the activities you would like to try.

2 CONVERSATION *A visit to New Orleans*

A ▶ Listen and practice.

Jan: It's great to see you, Todd. Have you been in New Orleans long?

Todd: No, not really. Just a few days.

Jan: I can't wait to show you the city. Have you been to a jazz club yet?

Todd: Yeah, I've already been to one.

Jan: Oh. Well, how about a riverboat tour?

Todd: Uh, I've already done that, too.

Jan: Have you ridden in a streetcar? They're a lot of fun.

Todd: Actually, that's how I got here today.

Jan: Well, is there anything you want to do?

Todd: You know, I really just want to take it easy. My feet are killing me!

B ▶ Listen to the rest of the conversation. What do they plan to do tomorrow?

64

Have you ever ridden a camel?

Cycle 1, Exercises 1–3

> In Unit 10, students talk about past experiences. In Cycle 1, they talk about recent activities using the present perfect, *already*, and *yet*. In Cycle 2, they discuss experiences from the recent and distant past using the present perfect and simple past, *for*, and *since*.

1 SNAPSHOT

Learning Objective: *talk about fun activities to do*

- Books closed. Explain that this unit is about fun and unusual activities. Elicit fun or unusual activities Ss like to do and write them on the board.
- Books open. Ss look at the Snapshot and compare their ideas. Elicit or explain any new vocabulary.

Vocabulary

streetcar: a passenger train that goes along city streets
riverboat: a large passenger boat that travels on a river

2 CONVERSATION

Learning Objectives: *practice a conversation between two people in New Orleans; see the present perfect in context*

A ▶ *[CD 2, Track 40]*

- Books closed. Ask: "Where is New Orleans? What music is famous there? What festival is famous there?" (Answers: Louisiana, jazz, Mardi Gras)
- Books open. Set the scene. Todd is visiting New Orleans. His friend Jan wants to show him the city.
- Draw this chart on the board:

Activities	Yes	No
1. Go to a jazz club		
2. Take a riverboat tour		
3. Ride in a streetcar		
4. Relax		

Ask Ss to copy the chart.

- Explain the task. Ss listen to the audio program and check (✓) *Yes* if Todd has done the activities and *No* if he hasn't.
- Play the audio program and Ss complete the task. Then elicit their answers. (Answers: 1. yes 2. yes 3. yes 4. no)
- Play the audio program again. Ss listen and read along silently.
- Ask these comprehension questions: "When did Todd arrive in New Orleans? How did he get to the café?" Elicit Ss' answers. (Answers: a few days ago, by streetcar)
- Elicit or explain any new vocabulary.

Vocabulary

I can't wait to: I'm excited about; I'm looking forward to
take it easy: relax
My feet are killing me!: My feet really hurt!

- Ss practice the conversation in pairs.

B ▶ *[CD 2, Track 41]*

- Explain the task and read the focus question.
- Play the audio program. Ss listen for the answer individually. Then elicit the answer.

AudioScript

Jan So let's just stay here and relax. I know you're tired.
Todd Thanks, Jan. But we can plan something for tomorrow.
Jan Great! Have you been to the zoo?
Todd No, I haven't. But I've heard it's good. Let's go there in the afternoon.
Jan OK.
Todd Say, have you been to the French market? I'd love to go there, too.
Jan Actually, I've never been there.
Todd You're kidding! And how many years have you lived in New Orleans? We have to go there.

Answers

They plan to go to the zoo and the French market.

T-64

3 *GRAMMAR FOCUS*

Learning Objectives: *practice the present perfect with* already *and* yet; *ask and answer questions using the present perfect with regular and irregular past participles*

⏵ *[CD 2, Track 42]*

Present perfect

■ Focus Ss' attention on the Conversation on page 64. Ask: "What has Todd done in New Orleans?" Elicit Ss' answers and write them on the board:

		been	to a jazz club.
He	has	done	a riverboat tour.
		ridden	in a streetcar.

■ Ask: "When did he do these things?" (Answer: sometime in the past few days)

■ Explain that these sentences are in the present perfect. We use this tense with past actions when the exact time is not important.

■ Draw this time line on the board:

TODD ARRIVED   jazz club   NOW

Explain that Todd has been to a jazz club sometime in the past few days. We don't know the exact time, and it's not important.

■ Say: "Imagine that Todd has been to three jazz clubs this week." Draw two more *X*'s on the time line and say: "Todd has been to a jazz club three times this week."

■ Focus Ss' attention on the Grammar Focus box. Elicit or explain the rules for forming present perfect statements and yes/no questions:
Subject + *has/have* + past participle.
Has/Have + subject + past participle?

■ Point out the placement of *yet* and *already* and explain the meaning. *Yet* goes at the end of present perfect questions and at the end of negative statements. *Already* goes before the past participle and means "earlier than expected."

■ Play the audio program and answer any questions.

A

■ Explain the task and read the examples. Then ask different Ss and elicit their answers. If needed, point out the expression *once, twice*, and *a couple of times*.

■ Call on Ss to read the regular and irregular past participles. Then point out the list of irregular past participles in the appendix.

■ Ss complete the task individually and compare answers in pairs. Then ask different Ss to write their answers on the board.

Possible answers

1. I've cleaned the house once/twice this week./ I haven't cleaned the house this week.
2. I've made my bed every day/three times this week./ I haven't made my bed this week.
3. I've cooked dinner every day/four times this week./ I haven't cooked dinner this week.
4. I've done laundry once/twice this week./ I haven't done laundry this week.
5. I've washed the dishes once/five times this week./ I haven't washed the dishes this week.
6. I've gone grocery shopping once/twice this week./ I haven't gone grocery shopping this week.

B

■ Explain the task and model the first conversation with a S.

■ Ss complete the task individually. Encourage Ss to use contractions in their answers. Go around the class and give help as needed. Then elicit Ss' answers.

Answers

1. A: **Have** you **done** much exercise this week?
   B: Yes, I**'ve** already **been** to aerobics class four times.
2. A: **Have** you **played** any sports this month?
   B: No, I **haven't had** the time.
3. A: How many movies **have** you **been** to this month?
   B: Actually, I **haven't seen** any yet.
4. A: **Have** you **been** to any interesting parties recently?
   B: No, I **haven't gone** to any parties for quite a while.
5. A: **Have** you **called** any friends today?
   B: Yes, I**'ve** already **made** three calls.
6. A: How many times **have** you **gone** out to eat this week?
   B: I**'ve eaten** at fast-food restaurants a couple of times.

C *Pair work*

■ Ss take turns asking and answering the questions in part B in pairs.

🎲 For more practice with present perfect questions, play *Hot Potato* – download it from the website.

End of Cycle 1

See the Supplementary Resources chart at the beginning of this unit for additional teaching materials and student activities related to this Cycle.

Present perfect; already, yet ▶

The present perfect is formed with the verb have + the past participle.

Have you **been** to a jazz club?
  Yes, I**'ve been** to several.   No, I **haven't been** to one.
Has he **called** home lately?
  Yes, he**'s called** twice this week.   No, he **hasn't called** in months.
Have they **eaten** dinner yet?
  Yes, they**'ve** already **eaten**.   No, they **haven't eaten** yet.

Contractions

I**'ve**	=	I have
you**'ve**	=	you have
he**'s**	=	he has
she**'s**	=	she has
it**'s**	=	it has
we**'ve**	=	we have
they**'ve**	=	they have
has**n't**	=	has not
have**n't**	=	have not

A How many times have you done these things in the past week? Write your answers. Then compare with a partner.

1. clean the house
2. make your bed
3. cook dinner
4. do laundry
5. wash the dishes
6. go grocery shopping

regular past participles

call → call**ed**
hike → hike**d**
jog → jog**ged**
try → tr**ied**

I've cleaned the house once this week.
OR
I haven't cleaned the house this week.

irregular past participles

be → **been**
do → **done**
eat → **eaten**
go → **gone**
have → **had**
make → **made**
ride → **ridden**
see → **seen**

B Complete these conversations using the present perfect. Then practice with a partner.

1. A: _____Have_____ you _____done_____ much exercise this week? (do)
   B: Yes, I _____ already _____ to aerobics class four times. (be)

2. A: _____ you _____ any sports this month? (play)
   B: No, I _____ the time. (have)

3. A: How many movies _____ you _____ to this month? (be)
   B: Actually, I _____ any yet, (see)

4. A: _____ you _____ to any interesting parties recently? (be)
   B: No, I _____ to any parties for quite a while. (go)

5. A: _____ you _____ any friends today? (call)
   B: Yes, I _____ already _____ three calls. (make)

6. A: How many times _____ you _____ out to eat this week? (go)
   B: I _____ at fast-food restaurants a couple of times. (eat)

C **PAIR WORK** Take turns asking the questions in part B. Give your own information when answering.

Have you ever ridden a camel? ▪ 65

4 CONVERSATION *Actually, I have.*

A ▶ Listen and practice.

Peter: I'm sorry I'm late. Have you been here long?

Mandy: No, only for a few minutes.

Peter: Have you chosen a restaurant yet?

Mandy: I can't decide. Have you ever eaten Moroccan food?

Peter: No, I haven't. Is it good?

Mandy: It's delicious. I've had it several times.

Peter: Or how about Thai food? Have you ever had green curry?

Mandy: Actually, I have. I lived in Thailand as a teenager. I ate it a lot there.

Peter: I didn't know that. How long did you live there?

Mandy: I lived there for two years.

B ▶ Listen to the rest of the conversation. Where do they decide to have dinner?

5 GRAMMAR FOCUS

Present perfect vs. simple past ▶

Use the present perfect for an indefinite time in the past.
Use the simple past for a specific event in the past.

Have you ever **eaten** Moroccan food?	Yes, I **have**. I **ate** it once in Paris.
	No, I **haven't**. I**'ve** never **eaten** it.
Have you ever **had** green curry?	Yes, I **have**. I **tried** it several years ago.
	No, I **haven't**. I**'ve** never **had** it.

A Complete these conversations. Use the present perfect and simple past of the verbs given and short answers. Then practice with a partner.

1. A: .... you ever .... in a karaoke bar? (sing)
   B: Yes, I .... I .... in one on my birthday.

2. A: .... you ever .... something valuable? (lose)
   B: No, I .... But my brother .... his camera on a trip once.

3. A: .... you ever .... a traffic ticket? (get)
   B: Yes, I .... Once I .... a ticket and had to pay $50.

4. A: .... you ever .... a live concert? (see)
   B: Yes, I .... I .... the Black Eyed Peas at the stadium last year.

5. A: .... you ever .... late for an important appointment? (be)
   B: No, I .... But my sister .... 30 minutes late for her wedding!

B **PAIR WORK** Take turns asking the questions in part A. Give your own information when answering.

CONVERSATION

Learning Objectives: *practice a conversation about types of food; see the present perfect and simple past in context*

A ▶ *[CD 2, Track 43]*

- Set the scene. Peter and Mandy are discussing where to eat dinner. Elicit ideas and vocabulary from the picture.
- Write this focus question on the board:

  What does Peter learn about Mandy?

- Books closed. Play the audio program and Ss listen for the answer. (Answer: She lived in Thailand for two years as a teenager.)
- Books open. Play the audio program again. Ss read the conversation silently.
- Ss practice the conversation in pairs.

❗ For a new way to practice this Conversation, try the *Moving Dialog* – download it from the website.

B ▶ *[CD 2, Track 44]*

- Explain the task and read the focus question. Encourage Ss to make predictions.
- Play the audio program. Ss listen for the answer. Then elicit the answer from the class.

AudioScript

Peter So what about dinner? I'm hungry!
Mandy Have you tried Sakura? They have excellent sushi.
Peter Actually, I had Japanese food for lunch.
Mandy Well, how about Italian food? Café Roma is a great place, and it isn't far.
Peter That's fine with me. I love Italian food.

Answers

They decide to have dinner at Café Roma.

 # GRAMMAR FOCUS

Learning Objectives: *practice the present perfect and simple past; practice using expressions with* for *and* since

▶ *[CD 2, Track 45]*

Present perfect

- Write these questions on the board:

  1. Has Peter ever eaten Moroccan food?

  2 Has Mandy ever had green curry?

- Focus Ss' attention on the Conversation in Exercise 4 and elicit the answers. (Answers: 1. No, he hasn't. 2. Yes, she has.)
- Ask a few *Have you ever* questions around the class (e.g., "Have you ever eaten Moroccan food? Have you ever eaten green curry?"). Elicit Ss' answers.
- Write this on the board.

  Have you <u>ever</u> eaten green curry?

  (No,) I've <u>never</u> eaten green curry

- Point out that *ever* means "at any time in your life." We use it in present perfect questions, but not in answers. *Never* means "not ever," and we use it in present perfect statements.

Simple past

- Ask: "When did Mandy eat green curry?" Then elicit possible answers (e.g., She ate it several years ago/in 2008/as a teenager.).

- Focus Ss' attention on the Grammar Focus box. Point out that we use the simple past to talk about a specific event in the past.
- Play the audio program.

A

- Explain the task and model the first conversation with a S.
- Ss complete the task individually. Go around and encourage Ss to use contractions in short answers.
- Elicit the answers. Then Ss practice with a partner.

Answers

1. A: **Have** you ever **sung** in a karaoke bar?
   B: Yes, I **have**. I **sang** in one on my birthday.
2. A: **Have** you ever **lost** something valuable?
   B: No, I **haven't**. But my brother **lost** his camera on a trip once.
3. A: **Have** you ever **gotten** a traffic ticket?
   B: Yes, I **have**. Once I **got** a ticket and had to pay $50.
4. A: **Have** you ever **seen** a live concert?
   B: Yes, I **have**. I **saw** the Black Eyed Peas at the stadium last year.
5. A: **Have** you ever **been** late for an important appointment?
   B: No, I **haven't**. But my sister **was** 30 minutes late for her wedding!

B *Pair work*

- Explain the task. Then Ss complete it in pairs.

▶ [CD 2, Track 46]

For _and_ since

- Write this on the board:
  I lived in Thailand for two years.
  I've lived in Thailand for two years.

- Elicit or explain the difference. The first sentence is in the simple past. It means "I lived in Thailand in the past, but I don't live in Thailand now." The second sentence is in the present perfect. It means "I moved to Thailand two years ago, and I still live in Thailand now."

- Focus Ss' attention on the two expression boxes. Ask: "When do we use _for_? When do we use _since_?"

- Elicit or explain that we use _for_ with periods of time and _since_ with points in time. Elicit other expressions that go with _for_ (e.g., _a day/a week/a year_), and _since_ (_yesterday/last week/2 P.M._).

- Play the audio program.

C

- Explain the task and model the first sentence. Then Ss complete the task individually. Go over answers with the class.

> **Answers**
>
> | | | | |
> |---|---|---|---|
> | 1. for | 3. since | 5. for | 7. for |
> | 2. for | 4. for | 6. since | 8. since |

For more practice with _for_ and _since_, play **Run For It!** – download it from the website.

D Pair work

- Explain the task and ask the first question. Elicit different answers with _for_ and _since_.

- Ss complete the task in pairs. Go around the class and note any errors. Then write the errors on the board and correct them with the class.

6 PRONUNCIATION

Learning Objective: _learn to sound natural by linking final /t/ and /d/ sounds in verbs with the vowels that follow_

A ▶ [CD 2, Track 47]

- Explain the task. Focus Ss' attention on the linked sounds in the example conversations. Then play the audio program.

B Pair work

- Explain and model the task. Elicit the linked sounds in the answers (i.e., _cut it, tasted it, tried it, lost it, looked at it_). Ask Ss to repeat the linked sounds.

- Ss work in pairs. They ask and answer the questions. Go around the class and check their use of linked sounds.

7 LISTENING

Learning Objective: _develop skills in listening for main ideas_

▶ [CD 2, Track 48]

- Ask: "What's the most interesting thing you've done recently?" Elicit Ss' answers.

- Set the scene and explain the task. Ss listen to find out where Clarice and Karl went and why they liked it

- Play the audio program. Ss complete the first column of the chart individually. While they listen, draw the chart on the board. Then elicit the answers and ask Ss to write the answers on the board.

- Play the audio program again. Ss complete the second column of the chart individually. Then elicit the answers.

> **AudioScript**
>
> _Karl_ So, Clarice, what have you been up to lately?
> _Clarice_ Oh, well, . . . I tried a new restaurant last week. The Classical Café. Have you ever been there?

Karl No, I haven't. What's it like?
Clarice It's wonderful! The food is great, and the prices are reasonable. But what's really interesting are the waiters. They sing.
Karl They what?
Clarice They sing.
Karl How unusual!
Clarice And what about you, Karl? Have you done anything interesting lately?
Karl Oh, well, I went to a food festival last week
Clarice Really? I've never been to a food festival.
Karl It was really fun. It was a German food festival.
Clarice Oh, I love German food.
Karl This was the first time I had it. Everything was excellent. Now I'm learning to cook real German food.
Clarice Wow! I'm impressed!

> **Possible answers**
>
> | | Where they went | Why they liked it |
> |---|---|---|
> | Clarice | to the Classical Café | food is great; prices are reasonable; waiters sing |
> | Karl | to a German food festival | fun; food was good |

For *and* since

How long **did** you **live** in Thailand?	I **lived** there **for** two years. It was wonderful.
How long **have** you **lived** in Miami?	I'**ve lived** here **for** six months. I love it here. I'**ve lived** here **since** last year. I'm really happy here.

C Complete these sentences with *for* or *since*.
Then compare with a partner.

1. Pam was in Central America .... a month last year.
2. I've been a college student .... almost four years.
3. Hiroshi has been at work .... 6:00 A.M.
4. I haven't gone to a party .... a long time.
5. Josh lived in Venezuela .... two years as a kid.
6. My parents have been on vacation .... Monday.
7. Natalie was engaged to Danny .... six months.
8. Pat and Valeria have been best friends .... high school.

expressions with *for*

two weeks
a few months
several years
a long time

expressions with *since*

6:45
last weekend
1997
elementary school

D PAIR WORK Ask and answer these questions.

How long have you had your current hairstyle?   How long have you known your best friend?
How long have you studied at this school?   How long have you been awake today?

6 PRONUNCIATION *Linked sounds*

A ▶ Listen and practice. Notice how final /t/ and /d/ sounds in
verbs are linked to the vowels that follow them.

A: Have you cooked lunch yet?   A: Have you ever tried Cuban food?

           /t/   /d/
B: Yes, I've already cooked it.   B: Yes, I tried it once in Miami.

B PAIR WORK Ask and answer these questions. Use *it* in your
responses. Pay attention to the linked sounds.

Have you ever cut your hair?
Have you ever tasted blue cheese?
Have you ever tried Korean food?
Have you ever lost your ID?
Have you looked at Unit 11 yet?

7 LISTENING *I'm impressed!*

 Listen to Clarice and Karl talk about interesting things they've
done recently. Complete the chart.

	Where they went	Why they liked it
Clarice	....	....
Karl	....	....

8 WORD POWER Activities

A Find two phrases to go with each verb. Write them in the chart.

a camel	a costume	iced coffee	a motorcycle	your phone	a truck
chicken's feet	herbal tea	your keys	octopus	a sports car	a uniform

eat	....	....	....
drink	....	....	....
drive	....	....	....
lose	....	....	....
ride	....	....	....
wear	....	....	....

B Add another phrase for each verb in part A.

9 SPEAKING Have you ever . . . ?

A GROUP WORK Ask your classmates questions about the activities in Exercise 8 or your own ideas.

A: Have you ever ridden a camel?
B: Yes, I have.
C: Really? Where were you?

B CLASS ACTIVITY Tell the class one interesting thing you learned about a classmate.

10 WRITING An email to an old friend

A Write an email to someone you haven't seen for a long time. Include three things you've done since you last saw that person.

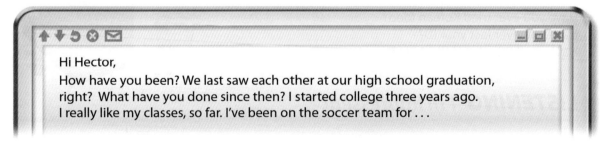

Hi Hector,
How have you been? We last saw each other at our high school graduation, right? What have you done since then? I started college three years ago. I really like my classes, so far. I've been on the soccer team for . . .

B PAIR WORK Exchange emails with a partner. Write a response to it.

11 INTERCHANGE 10 Lifestyle survey

What kind of lifestyle do you have? Go to Interchange 10 on page 125.

8 WORD POWER

Learning Objective: *learn collocations for activities with* eat, drink, drive, lose, ride, *and* wear.

A

- Explain the task. Ss find two phrases in the list that go with each verb. Model the first example (*eat + chicken's feet*). Then elicit other words or phrases that go with eat (e.g., *octopus*).
- Elicit or explain any new vocabulary.
- Ss complete the task in pairs. While they work, draw the chart on the board. Then go around the class and give help as needed.
- **Option:** Allow Ss to use their dictionaries.
- Elicit Ss' answers. Ask different Ss to write their answers on the board.

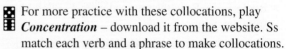

Answers

eat	chicken's feet	octopus	*steak*
drink	herbal tea	iced coffee	*soda*
drive	a sports car	a truck	*a car*
lose	your phone	your keys	*your glasses*
ride	a motorcycle	a camel	*a horse*
wear	a costume	a uniform	*an outfit*

(Note: Possible additional phrases are italicized.)

- Elicit the past participle forms of the verbs. (Answers: eaten, drunk, driven, lost, ridden, worn)
- For more practice with these collocations, play *Concentration* – download it from the website. Ss match each verb and a phrase to make collocations.

B

- Explain the task.
- Ss complete the task in pairs.
- Elicit Ss' answers.

9 SPEAKING

Learning Objective: *talk about past experiences using the present perfect and collocations*

A Group work

- Write these expressions on the board:

  Really? Wow! I'm impressed! You're kidding!

  Point out that we use these expressions to show interest or surprise. Model how to say them. Ss repeat.
- **Option:** Ss find more examples of responses in previous conversations. Practice them as a class.
- Explain the activity and model the example conversation with two Ss. Focus Ss' attention on the picture and ask: "Where was she?" Encourage Ss to make guesses.
- Elicit other follow-up questions and write them on the board.
- Ss complete the activity in small groups. Go around the class and encourage Ss to ask follow-up questions.
- **Option:** Ss get one point for each follow-up question they ask. The S in each group with the most points wins.

B Class activity

- Ss share things they learned about their classmates with the class.

10 WRITING

Learning Objective: *write a letter to an old friend using the present perfect and simple past*

A

- Ask the class: "Who haven't you seen in a long time?" Elicit Ss' answers.
- Explain the task. Then Ss read the example letter silently.
- Ss write their letters individually. Remind Ss to check their use of present perfect and simple past.

B Pair work

- Ss exchange letters in pairs. They imagine they are the "old friend" and write a response.

11 INTERCHANGE 10

See page T-123 for teaching notes.

12 READING

Learning Objectives: *read and discuss interviews about risky sports; develop skills in skimming and reading for specific information*

- Books closed. Write *Risky Sports* on the board. Elicit or explain that risky means "dangerous."
- Ss brainstorm *risky* sports in small groups. Then ask different Ss to write them on the board.

> **TIP** To prepare Ss for a Reading, ask Ss to brainstorm things they already know about the topic.

- Books open. Read the pre-reading task. Elicit ideas from the pictures.
- Ss skim the interviews and complete the task.

Answers

1. wingsuit flying   2. kiteboarding   3. ice climbing

A

- Elicit, explain, or ask Ss to look up new vocabulary.

Vocabulary

accident: something bad that happens unexpectedly
spin: to move in circles
fly like a bird: a *simile* or figure of speech comparing two things using the word *like*
conditions: the state of weather and the environment that affect someone doing sports
unpredictable: not able to tell what will happen in the future
surfer: person who surfs

> **TIP** To avoid confusing Ss, only pre-teach the words they need to complete the task. They can look up the other words later.

- Explain the task. Ss read the interviews and complete the chart. Then go over the answers with the class.

Possible answers

	Sport	What they enjoy	The danger(s)
1. Josh	wingsuit flying	flying like a bird	jumping too fast
2. Lisa	kiteboarding	the challenge, overcoming danger	hitting another surfer; the wind dropping you against something hard
3. Alex	ice climbing	feels good, beautiful view	thin air, very cold, storms

B *Pair work*

- Explain the task and read the discussion questions. Ss discuss the questions in pairs.

End of Cycle 2

See the Supplementary Resources chart at the beginning of this unit for additional teaching materials and student activities related to this Cycle and for assessment tools.

TAKING THE RISK
///////////////

Sports World magazine recently spoke with Josh Parker, Lisa Kim, and Alex Costas about risky sports.

SW: Wingsuit flying is a dangerous sport, Josh. What do you enjoy about it? And have you ever had an accident?

Josh: No, I've never been hurt. But, yes, it is dangerous, even for experienced flyers. I've been doing it for five years, but I still get a little nervous before I jump out of the plane. That's the most dangerous thing. Once, I jumped too fast, and I started to spin. That was scary! But it's amazing to be able to fly like a bird.

SW: Lisa, you've been kiteboarding for years now. What are some of the dangers?

Lisa: Oh, there are many dangers. When you're in the ocean, the conditions can be unpredictable. The wind can lift you up too fast and then drop you against something hard, like sand, or even water. You can also hit another surfer. But I like the challenge, and I like overcoming danger. That's why I do it.

SW: Alex, have you ever experienced any dangers while ice climbing?

Alex: Yes, absolutely. When you're high up on a mountain, the conditions are hard on the body. The air is thin, and it's very cold. I've seen some really dangerous storms. But the great thing about it is how you feel when you're done. Your body feels good, and you have a beautiful view of the snowy mountaintops.

▶ _____

▶ _____

///////////////

▶ _____

A Read the interviews. Then complete the chart.

	Sport	What they enjoy	The danger(s)
1. Josh	....	....	....
2. Lisa	....	....	....
3. Alex	....	....	....

B **PAIR WORK** Would you like to try any of these sports? Why or why not?

Units 9–10 Progress check

SELF-ASSESSMENT

How well can you do these things? Check (✓) the boxes.

I can	Very well	OK	A little
Ask about and describe people's appearance (Ex. 1)	☐	☐	☐
Identify people by describing what they're doing, what they're wearing, and where they are (Ex. 2)	☐	☐	☐
Find out whether or not things have been done (Ex. 3)	☐	☐	☐
Understand descriptions of experiences (Ex. 4)	☐	☐	☐
Ask and answer questions about experiences (Ex. 4)	☐	☐	☐
Find out how long people have done things (Ex. 5)	☐	☐	☐

1 ROLE PLAY Missing person

Student A: One of your classmates is lost. You are talking to a police officer. Answer the officer's questions and describe your classmate.

Student B: You are a police officer. Someone is describing a lost classmate. Ask questions to complete the form. Can you identify the classmate?

Change roles and try the role play again.

MISSING PERSON REPORT

NAME _____ # 78439122470

HEIGHT: _____   WEIGHT: _____   AGE: _____

EYE COLOR		HAIR COLOR	
☐ BLUE	☐ BROWN	☐ BLOND	☐ BROWN
☐ GREEN	☐ HAZEL	☐ RED	☐ BLACK
		☐ GRAY	☐ BALD

CLOTHING: _____

GLASSES, ETC: _____

2 SPEAKING Which one is ...?

A Look at this picture. How many sentences can you write to identify the people?

> Amy and T.J. are the people in sunglasses. They're the ones looking at the picture.

B PAIR WORK Close your books. Who do you remember? Take turns asking about the people.

A: Which one is Bill?
B: I think Bill is the guy sitting ...

Kate
Louisa
Bill
Amy and T.J.

Units 9–10 Progress check

SELF-ASSESSMENT

Learning Objectives: *reflect on one's learning; identify areas that need improvement*

- Ask: "What did you learn in Units 9 and 10?" Elicit Ss' answers.
- Ss complete the Self-assessment. Encourage them to be honest, and point out they will not get a bad grade if they check (✓) *a little*.

- Ss move on to the Progress check exercises. You can have Ss complete them in class or for homework, using one of these techniques:
  1. Ask Ss to complete all the exercises.
  2. Ask Ss: "What do you need to practice?" Then assign exercises based on their answers.
  3. Ask Ss to choose and complete exercises based on their Self-assessment.

 ROLE PLAY

Learning Objective: *assess one's ability to ask about and describe a person's appearance*

- Read the instructions aloud and explain the task. Student A makes a report about a lost classmate and Student B completes the *Missing person report*. Point out that Student A should not give the name of the classmate. Then Student B guesses the identity of the lost classmate.
- Go over the information in the report. Elicit different things Ss can write in the report.
- Write this example conversation on the board:

  A: Excuse me, Officer. Can you help me? One of my classmates is lost.

  B: Sure. Um, is the person a man or a woman?

  A: A woman.

  B: OK. I need to know her age. How old is she?

  A: I think she's 19 or 20.

  B: All right. And how tall is she?

  Model the conversation with a S. The S is person A and you are person B. Whenever the S gives additional information, pretend to write it in the report.

- Ss complete the task in pairs. Then Student B looks around the room and identifies the lost classmate.
- Set a time limit of about three minutes. Then Ss change roles. Go around the class and give help as needed.

> **TIP** If you don't have enough class time for the speaking activities, assign each S a speaking partner. Then have Ss complete the activities with their partners for homework.

 SPEAKING

Learning Objective: *assess one's ability to identify people by describing what they're doing, what they're wearing, or where they are*

A

- Focus Ss' attention on the picture. Ask a S to read the example sentences.
- Ss write sentences about each person individually.
- **Option:** Go around the class and check Ss' work.

> **Possible answers**
>
> Kate is the woman/one holding a soda/in jeans.
> Louisa is the woman/one sitting on the sofa/in the green dress.
> Bill is the man/one eating something/in a black shirt.
> Amy and T. J. are the people/ones looking at the picture/in sunglasses.

B *Pair work*

- Write the names *Kate, Louisa, Bill,* and *Amy and T.J.* on the board.
- Books closed. Explain the task. Ss ask questions about the people on the board in pairs (e.g., *Which one is Bill?*). They answer using their memory of the picture. If they have difficulty, they can look at their sentences.
- Model the example conversation with a few Ss. Elicit different ways Ss can answer.
- Ss complete the task.

SPEAKING

Learning Objective: *assess one's ability to answer questions about whether or not things have been done*

A

- Explain the task. Ss imagine they are preparing for three situations. Read the situations and the example.
- Ss list four things they need to do for each situation.

B *Pair work*

- Explain the task. Ss exchange lists. Student A asks Student B what he or she has done in each situation. Student B gives responses using *already* or *yet*.
- Ss complete the task in pairs.

 LISTENING

Learning Objectives: *assess one's ability to understand descriptions of experiences; assess one's ability to ask and answer questions about experiences*

A ⊙ [CD 2, Track 49]

- Set the scene. Jamie is on a cruise and is talking to someone about things she has done.
- Go over the chart and explain any new vocabulary. Then play the audio program. Ss complete the task.

AudioScript

Man Are you enjoying the cruise, Jamie?
Jamie Oh, yes, very much. Actually, I won a contest and this cruise was the prize.
Man That's fantastic! Hey, I've always wondered something about contests. The cruise left from Miami, so how did they get you there? Did they fly you there?
Jamie No, I live in Miami, so I didn't have to travel at all. I've never flown on a plane. But I did get to stay in an expensive hotel in Miami for a day.
Man That's nice.
Jamie Yeah, it was. Oh, and I saw Jennifer Lopez there. She was in the same hotel.
Man Jennifer Lopez? Really? Did you meet her?
Jamie No. In fact, I've never met a famous person. But I think she smiled at me.

Man Cool.
Jamie Yeah. And I got to enjoy the hotel activities. I even tried windsurfing.
Man Sounds fun.
Jamie Yeah, it was. But I did something stupid. I took my wallet with me and almost lost it. I'm always very careful with my wallet, and I have never lost it. It almost fell into the ocean. Luckily, I caught it.
Man That was lucky! Well, it sounds like you've really enjoyed this trip.
Jamie For the most part. I mean, I've been a little seasick, but I'll remember this trip forever. I've even kept a diary this whole time so I can tell my friends all about it.
Man I'm sure they'll love that. Well, enjoy the rest of the cruise.
Jamie Thanks. I will.

Answers

won a contest, stayed in an expensive hotel, gone windsurfing, been seasick, kept a diary

B *Group work*

- Ss take turns asking about the events in part A in small groups.

5 SURVEY

Learning Objective: *assess one's ability to use* how long, for, *and* since *with the present perfect*

A

- Ss complete the *My answers* column individually. Point out that they should use *for* or *since*.

B *Class activity*

- Model the task. Ask several Ss the first question until one gives the same answer. Explain that you will write that S's name in the *Classmate's name* column.
- Ss go around the room and complete the task.

WHAT'S NEXT?

Learning Objective: *become more involved in one's learning*

- Focus Ss' attention on the Self-assessment again. Ask: "How well can you do these things now?"

- Ask Ss to underline one thing they need to review. Ask: "What did you underline? How can you review it?"
- If needed, plan additional activities or reviews based on Ss' answers.

SPEAKING *Reminders*

A Imagine you are preparing for these situations. Make a list of four things you need to do for each situation.

Your first day of school is in a week.
You are moving to a new apartment.
You are going to the beach.

> "To do" list: first day of school
> 1. buy notebooks

B **PAIR WORK** Exchange lists. Take turns asking about what has been done. When answering, decide what you have or haven't done.

A: Have you bought notebooks yet?
B: Yes, I've already gotten them.

4 LISTENING *What have you done?*

A ▶ Jamie is on a cruise. Listen to her talk about things she has done. Check (✓) the correct things.

- [ ] won a contest
- [ ] flown in a plane
- [ ] stayed in an expensive hotel
- [ ] met a famous person
- [ ] gone windsurfing
- [ ] lost her wallet
- [ ] been seasick
- [ ] kept a diary

B **GROUP WORK** Have you ever done the things in part A? Take turns asking about each thing.

5 SURVEY *How long . . . ?*

A Write answers to these questions using *for* and *since*.

How long have you . . . ?	My answers	Classmate's name
owned this book		
studied English		
known your best friend		
lived in this town or city		
been a student		

B **CLASS ACTIVITY** Go around the class. Find someone who has the same answers. Write a classmate's names only once.

WHAT'S NEXT?

Look at your Self-assessment again. Do you need to review anything?

Unit 11 Supplementary Resources Overview

	After the following SB exercises	You can use these materials in class	Your students can use these materials outside the classroom
CYCLE 1	1 Word Power		**SSD** Unit 11 Vocabulary 1–2
	2 Conversation		**SSD** Unit 11 Speaking 1
	3 Grammar Focus	**TSS** Unit 11 Vocabulary Worksheet	**SB** Unit 11 Grammar Plus focus 1 **SSD** Unit 11 Grammar 1 **ARC** Adverbs before adjectives **ARC** Adverbs before adjectives and Conjunctions
	4 Listening		
	5 Writing		**WB** Unit 11 exercises 1–5
CYCLE 2	6 Snapshot		
	7 Conversation		**SSD** Unit 11 Speaking 2
	8 Grammar Focus	**TSS** Unit 11 Extra Worksheet **TSS** Unit 11 Grammar Worksheet	**SB** Unit 11 Grammar Plus focus 2 **SSD** Unit 11 Grammar 2–3 **ARC** Modal verbs *can* and *should*
	9 Pronunciation		**ARC** *Can't* and *shouldn't*
	10 Listening		
	11 Speaking	**TSS** Unit 11 Listening Worksheet **TSS** Unit 11 Writing Worksheet	
	12 Interchange 11		
	13 Reading	**TSS** Unit 11 Project Worksheet **VID** Unit 11 **VRB** Unit 11	**SSD** Unit 11 Reading 1–2 **SSD** Unit 11 Listening 1–3 **SSD** Unit 11 Video 1–3 **WB** Unit 11 exercises 6–10

Key

ARC: Arcade	**SB:** Student's Book	**SSD:** Self-study DVD-ROM	**TSS:** Teacher Support Site
VID: Video DVD	**VRB:** Video Resource Book	**WB:** Workbook	

Unit 11 Supplementary Resources Overview   *Interchange* Teacher's Edition 1 © Cambridge University Press 2013   Photocopiable

My Plan for Unit 11

Use the space below to customize a plan that fits your needs.

With the following SB exercises	I am using these materials in class	My students are using these materials outside the classroom

With or instead of the following SB section	I am using these materials for assessment

11 It's a very exciting place!

1 ## WORD POWER Adjectives

A **PAIR WORK** Match each word in column A with its opposite in column B. Then add two more pairs of adjectives to the list.

A
1. beautiful ....
2. cheap ....
3. clean ....
4. interesting ....
5. quiet ....
6. relaxing ....
7. safe ....
8. spacious ....
9. ....
10. ....

B
a. boring
b. crowded
c. dangerous
d. expensive
e. noisy
f. polluted
g. stressful
h. ugly
i. ....
j. ....

beautiful

ugly

B **PAIR WORK** Choose two places you know. Describe them to your partner using the words in part A.

2 CONVERSATION It's a fairly big city.

A ▶ Listen and practice.

Eric: So, where are you from, Carmen?
Carmen: I'm from San Juan, Puerto Rico.
Eric: Wow, I've heard that's a really nice city.
Carmen: Yeah, it is. The weather is great, and there are some fantastic beaches nearby.
Eric: Is it expensive there?
Carmen: No, It's not very expensive. Prices are pretty reasonable.
Eric: How big is the city?
Carmen: It's a fairly big city. It's not *too* big, though.
Eric: It sounds perfect to me. Maybe I should plan a trip there sometime.

B ▶ Listen to the rest of the conversation. What does Carmen say about entertainment in San Juan?

San Juan

72

It's a very exciting place!

Cycle 1, Exercises 1–5

> In Unit 11, students talk about hometowns, cities, and countries. In Cycle 1, they talk about their hometowns using adverbs, adjectives, and conjunctions. In Cycle 2, they discuss popular vacation places using can and should.

1 WORD POWER

Learning Objective: *learn vocabulary for describing places*

A *Pair work*

- Elicit adjectives that describe cities (e.g., *beautiful, ugly*) and write them on the board.
- Ss check (✓) the adjectives they listed. Then they read the other words silently.
- Elicit words Ss don't understand or know how to pronounce. Explain or pronounce these words.
- Explain the task and elicit the first example. Then Ss complete the matching task in pairs.
- Go over answers with the class.

Answers

1. h   2. d   3. f   4. a   5. e   6. g   7. c   8. b

- Pairs now add two more sets of opposites. Ss may use their dictionaries if they wish. Go over possible answers.

Possible answers

modern/traditional   large/small   hot/cold

- Ask Ss to write the new adjectives in their notebooks and check (✓) the ones that describe their city or town.
- For more practice matching opposite adjectives, play *Concentration* – download it from the website.

B *Pair work*

- Ss choose two cities or towns from any country and describe them in pairs. Encourage them to use the adjectives in part A.

2 CONVERSATION

Learning Objectives: *practice a conversation about a city; see adverbs before adjectives, and conjunctions, in context*

A ▶ *[CD 3, Track 1]*

- Books closed. Set the scene. Eric is asking Carmen about her hometown of San Juan, Puerto Rico.
- Ask: "What do you know about Puerto Rico? Where is it? What's it like?"
- Write this on the board:

  1. Weather: OK or great?
  2. Beaches: polluted or fantastic?
  3. Prices: reasonable or expensive?

- Play the audio program. Ss listen to the audio program to find the answers. Then they compare answers with a partner.
- Go over the answers with the class. (Answers: 1. great 2. fantastic 3. reasonable)
- Books open. Play the audio program again.
- Ss listen and read silently. Then they practice the conversation in pairs. Go around the class and give help as needed.

- For a new way to teach this Conversation, try the *Disappearing Dialog* – download it from the website.

B ▶ *[CD 3, Track 2]*

- Explain the task and read the focus question.
- Play the audio program. Ss listen for the answer. Then they compare answers in small groups. Go over the answer with the class.

AudioScript

Eric So what kinds of things are there to do in San Juan?
Carmen Well, there are a lot of nightclubs. Puerto Ricans love to dance!
Eric I'm not much of a dancer. Anything else?
Carmen Well, a lot of people enjoy going out to eat. There are some excellent restaurants in Old San Juan. They're popular with both locals and tourists.
Eric Now that sounds good. I love to eat!

Possible answer

There are a lot of nightclubs and some excellent restaurants.

- **Option:** Ask Ss: "Would you like to visit San Juan? Why or why not?"

Learning Objectives: *practice using adverbs before adjectives; write sentences using conjunctions*

▶ [CD 3, Track 3]
Adverbs before adjectives

- Focus Ss' attention on the Conversation on page 72. Ask: "What has Eric heard about San Juan?" (Answer: *It's really nice.*) Then ask: "How big is San Juan?" (Answer: *It's fairly big.*)

- Explain that sometimes we use adverbs like *very, really,* and *fairly* to modify adjectives.

- Ask Ss to find more examples of adverbs that modify adjectives in the Conversation and underline them (e.g., *very expensive, pretty reasonable, too big*). Elicit other adverbs.

- Focus Ss' attention on the adverbs box. Point out that they are organized from the most to the least.

- Focus Ss' attention on the Grammar Focus box. Point out the position of the adverb and elicit the rule:
  X *is* adverb + adjective.
  X *is a/an* adverb + adjective + noun.

- Explain that *too* means "more than you want," so we usually use it with negative adjectives (e.g., *too bad,* NOT *too nice*). Also, we cannot use *too* with an adverb + adjective + noun (e.g., *too expensive,* NOT *a too expensive city*).

- Play the audio program.

- **Option:** Focus Ss' attention on part B of the Word Power on page 72. Ss describe a city again, using adverbs + adjectives.

A

- Explain the task. Ss match the questions with the answers.

- Go over answers with the class. Then Ss practice the conversations in pairs.

Answers

1. e   2. d   3. a   4. b   5. c

⚃ For practice asking questions about cities, play *Twenty Questions* – download it from the website.

▶ [CD 3, Track 4]
Conjunctions

- Focus Ss' attention on the first sentence in the second Grammar Focus box. Ask: "Are *big* and *nice* positive or negative?" (Answer: Both are positive.)

- Point out that we use *and* to connect two positive or two negative ideas. Elicit a sentence with two negative ideas (e.g., *The city is ugly, and the weather is terrible.*). Ask: "What punctuation comes before *and?*" (Answer: a comma)

- Focus Ss' attention on the other three sentences. Ask: "Are they positive + positive, negative + negative, or positive + negative?" (Answer: positive + negative) Explain that we use *but, though,* and *however* to connect a positive idea with a negative idea.

- Tell Ss to look at the position of *but, though,* and *however.* Ask: "How are *though* and *however* different from *but?*" (Answer: *But* is in the middle of the sentence. *Though* and *however* are at the end.)

- Ask: "What punctuation comes before each conjunction?" (Answer: a comma) Point out that *and* and *but* connect two complete sentences.

- Play the audio program.

B

- Explain the task and model the first answer. Ss complete the task individually. Go around the class and check Ss' use of punctuation.

- Ask different Ss to write their answers on the board. Go over answers with the class.

Answers

1. Taipei is very nice, and everyone is extremely friendly.
2. The streets are crowded. It's easy to get around, though.
3. The weather is nice. Summers get pretty hot, however.
4. Shopping is great, but you have to bargain in the markets.
5. It's an amazing city, and I love to go there.

C *Group work*

- Write these topics on the board:

  | People | Food | Shopping |
  | Weather | Crime | Things to do |

- Explain the task and ask two Ss to read the example conversation. Point out that Ss can discuss the topics on the board.

- Ss complete the task. Ask Ss to name the negative statement in each description.

- Go around the class and note any errors. Then write them on the board and ask Ss to correct them.

> **TIP** To check if Ss have understood the grammar, write their errors on the board. Then ask Ss to correct them.

Adverbs before adjectives ▶

San Juan is **really** nice.   It's a **really** nice city.
It's **fairly** big.   It's a **fairly** big city.
It's not **very** expensive.   It's not a **very** expensive place.

It's **too** noisy, and it's **too** crowded for me.

adverbs

extremely
very
really
pretty
fairly
somewhat
too

A Match the questions with the answers. Then practice the conversations with a partner.

1. What's Seoul like?
   Is it an interesting place? ....

2. Do you like your hometown?
   Why or why not? ....

3. What's Sydney like?
   I've never been there. ....

4. Have you ever been to
   São Paulo? ....

5. What's the weather like
   in Chicago? ....

a. Oh, really? It's beautiful and very clean. It has a great harbor and beautiful beaches.

b. Yes, I have. It's an extremely large and crowded place, but I love it. It has excellent restaurants.

c. It's really nice in the summer, but it's too cold for me in the winter.

d. Not really. It's too small, and it's really boring. That's why I moved away.

e. Yes. It has amazing shopping, and the people are pretty friendly.

Conjunctions ▶

It's a big city, **and** the weather is nice.   It's a big city. It's not too big, **though**.
It's a big city, **but** it's not too big.   It's a big city. It's not too big, **however**.

B Choose the correct conjunctions and rewrite the sentences.

1. Taipei is very nice. Everyone is extremely friendly. (and / but)
   ....

2. The streets are crowded. It's easy to get around. (and / though)
   ....

3. The weather is nice. Summers get pretty hot. (and / however)
   ....

4. Shopping is great. You have to bargain in the markets. (and / but)
   ....

5. It's an amazing city. I love to go there. (and / however)
   ....

C **GROUP WORK** Describe three cities or towns in your country. State two positive features and one negative feature for each.

A: Lima is very exciting and there are a lot of things to do, but it's too cold.
B: The weather in Shanghai is …

LISTENING *My hometown*

Listen to Joyce and Nicholas talk about their hometowns.
What do they say? Check (✓) the correct boxes.

	Big?		Interesting?		Expensive?		Beautiful?	
	Yes	No	Yes	No	Yes	No	Yes	No
1. Joyce	☐	☐	☐	☐	☐	☐	☐	☐
2. Nicholas	☐	☐	☐	☐	☐	☐	☐	☐

5 WRITING *An interesting place*

A Write about an interesting town or city for tourists to visit in your country.

> Otavalo is a very interesting town in Ecuador. It's to the north of Quito. It has a fantastic market, and a lot of tourists go there to buy local handicrafts. The scenery around Otavalo is very pretty and . . .

B **PAIR WORK** Exchange papers and read each other's articles.
Which place sounds more interesting?

6 SNAPSHOT

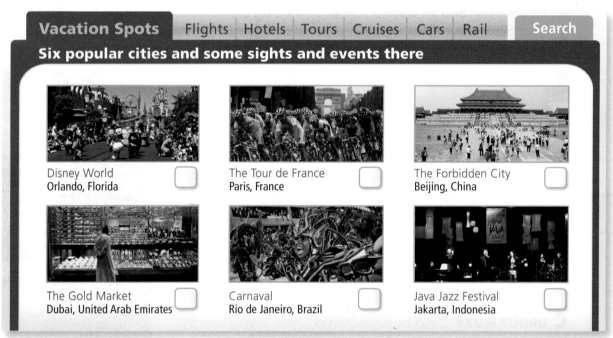

| Vacation Spots | Flights | Hotels | Tours | Cruises | Cars | Rail | Search |

Six popular cities and some sights and events there

Disney World
Orlando, Florida ☐

The Tour de France
Paris, France ☐

The Forbidden City
Beijing, China ☐

The Gold Market
Dubai, United Arab Emirates ☐

Carnaval
Rio de Janeiro, Brazil ☐

Java Jazz Festival
Jakarta, Indonesia ☐

Source: www.fodors.com

Which places would you like to visit? Why?
Put the places you would like to visit in order from most interesting to least interesting.
What three other places in the world would you like to visit? Why?

4 LISTENING

Learning Objective: *develop skills in listening for details*

▶ **[CD 3, Track 5]**

- Books closed. Set the scene. Joyce and Nicholas are talking about their hometowns.
- Books open. Explain the task. Play the audio program and Ss complete the chart.
- Ss compare answers in pairs. Then go over answers.

AudioScript

1.
Woman So tell me about your hometown, Joyce.
Joyce Well, it's a really small town.
Woman What's it like there?
Joyce Oh, I think it's boring.
Woman Really? Why?
Joyce Well, there's nothing to do. No good restaurants. No nightlife.
Woman Oh, that's too bad. But small towns are pretty inexpensive to live in.
Joyce Well, yeah, it is really cheap. And lots of people love it there because it's very pretty.
Woman Yeah?

Joyce Uh-huh. It has great scenery – lots of mountains and rivers, lakes and trees . . .
Woman Well, I don't know, Joyce. It sounds like a great place.
2.
Woman Do you come from a big city, Nicholas?
Nicholas Yeah, I guess. It's pretty big.
Woman So there's a lot to do there?
Nicholas Yeah. It's a really fun place. It has some cool art museums and great theaters and restaurants.
Woman Really? How are the prices? Is it expensive?
Nicholas I guess so. Food costs a lot in the supermarket and in restaurants. And apartments! The rents are very high.
Woman And what's it like there? What does it look like?
Nicholas Well, it's very clean, and it's really pretty, too. There are lots of parks and trees right in the center of the city.

Answers

	Big?	Interesting?	Expensive?	Beautiful?
1. Joyce	no	no	no	yes
2. Nicholas	yes	yes	yes	yes

5 WRITING

Learning Objective: *write an article about a place using adverbs before adjectives, and conjunctions*

A

- Explain the task. Then Ss read the example silently.
- Ss write their article in class or for homework.

B *Pair work*

- Explain the task. Ss complete the task in pairs.

End of Cycle 1

See the Supplementary Resources chart at the beginning of this unit for additional teaching materials and student activities related to this Cycle.

Cycle 2, Exercises 6–13

6 SNAPSHOT

Learning Objective: *talk about popular vacation spots*

- Books closed. Write the six countries from the Snapshot on the board. Ask: "Which country would you like to visit? Why?"
- Books open. Ss read the Snapshot. Elicit or explain any new vocabulary.

Vocabulary

Disney World: a famous theme park
The Tour de France: a famous bicycle race

The Forbidden City: a famous palace
The Gold Market: a famous jewelry market
Carnaval: a famous street party featuring samba music, dancing, eating and drinking
Java Jazz Festival: an annual festival featuring jazz music

- Explain the tasks. Ss complete the tasks individually. Then they discuss their answers in small groups.

7 CONVERSATION

Learning Objective: *practice a conversation about Mexico City; see modal verbs* can *and* should *in context*

A ▶ [CD 3, Track 6]

- Books closed. Set the scene. Two friends are talking about a city. Ask: "What city is it?" Play the first part of the audio program and Ss listen for the answer. (Answer: Mexico City)
- Write these focus questions on the board:
  1. What's the Palace of Fine Arts like?
  2. How are the paintings at the Museum of Modern Art?
  3. How many free things does Elena recommend?
- Play the rest of the audio program. Then elicit Ss' answers to the questions on the board. (Answers: 1. really beautiful 2. amazing 3. three)
- Books open. Play the audio program again and Ss read the conversation silently. Elicit or explain any new vocabulary.
- Ss practice the conversation in pairs.

B ▶ [CD 3, Track 7]

- Explain the task and read the focus questions. Play the audio program. Elicit Ss' answers.

AudioScript

Elena Where are you from again, Thomas?
Thomas I'm from Toronto, Canada.
Elena Oh! I've always wanted to go there. What's it like? What can you do there?
Thomas Well, there's a lot to do. But visitors should definitely spend some time in the museums. The museums there are great!

Answers

He's from Toronto, Canada. You should definitely visit the museums.

8 GRAMMAR FOCUS

Learning Objectives: *practice conversations using* can *and* should; *ask and answer questions using* can *and* should

▶ [CD 3, Track 8]

Can and should

- Focus Ss' attention on the Conversation in Exercise 7. Ask: "How does Thomas ask for advice about Mexico City?" Write his question on the board:
  Can you tell me a little about Mexico City?
- Ask: "How does Elena suggest what to see?" Elicit the answers and write them on the board:
  You should definitely visit . . .
  You shouldn't miss the . . .
  You can . . .
- Point out that *can* and *should* are modals. They show a speaker's attitude or "mood." People use *can* and *should* to ask for and give advice.
- Elicit or explain the rule for using *can* and *should* in Wh-questions and statements:
  Wh-question + modal + subject + verb?
  Subject + modal (+ *not*) verb.
  Point out that modals do not take a final *-s*.
- Focus Ss' attention on the Grammar Focus box and play the audio program.

A

- Explain the task and model the first conversation with a S. Ss complete the task individually.
- Go over answers with the class. Then Ss practice the conversations in pairs.

Answers

1. A: I **can't** decide where to go on my vacation.
   B: You **should** go to India. It's my favorite place to visit.
2. A: I'm planning to go to Bogotá next year. When do you think I **should** go?
   B: You **can** go anytime. The weather is nice almost all year.
3. A: **Should** I rent a car when I arrive in Cairo? What do you recommend?
   B: No, you **should** definitely use the subway. It's fast and efficient.
4. A: Where **can** I get some nice jewelry in Bangkok?
   B: You **shouldn't** miss the weekend market. It's the best place for bargains.
5. A: What **can** I see from the Eiffel Tower?
   B: You **can** see all of Paris, but in bad weather you **can't** see anything.

B

- Explain the task and read the questions. Ss complete the task individually. Then they compare answers in pairs.
- Elicit answers from the class.

7 CONVERSATION *What should I see there?*

A ▶ Listen and practice.

Thomas: Can you tell me a little about Mexico City?
Elena: Sure. What would you like to know?
Thomas: Well, I'm going to be there next month, but for only two days. What should I see?
Elena: Oh, you should definitely visit the Palace of Fine Arts. It's really beautiful.
Thomas: OK. Anything else?
Elena: You shouldn't miss the Museum of Modern Art. It has some amazing paintings.
Thomas: Great! And is there anything I can do for free?
Elena: Sure. You can walk in the parks, go to outdoor markets, or just watch people. It's a fascinating city!

B ▶ Listen to the rest of the conversation.
Where is Thomas from? What should you do there?

8 GRAMMAR FOCUS

> **Modal verbs can *and* should** ▶
>
> What **can** I do in Mexico City?   What **should** I see there?
>   You **can** go to outdoor markets.   You **should** visit the Palace of Fine Arts.
>   You **can't** visit some museums on Mondays.   You **shouldn't** miss the Museum of Modern Art.

A Complete these conversations using *can*, *can't*, *should*, or *shouldn't*.
Then practice with a partner.

1. A: I .... decide where to go on my vacation.
   B: You .... go to India. It's my favorite place to visit.
2. A: I'm planning to go to Bogotá next year. When do you think I .... go?
   B: You .... go anytime. The weather is nice almost all year.
3. A: .... I rent a car when I arrive in Cairo? What do you recommend?
   B: No, you .... definitely use the subway. It's fast and efficient.
4. A: Where .... I get some nice jewelry in Bangkok?
   B: You .... miss the weekend market. It's the best place for bargains.
5. A: What .... I see from the Eiffel Tower?
   B: You .... see all of Paris, but in bad weather, you .... see anything.

B Write answers to these questions about your country.
Then compare with a partner.

What time of year should you go there?   What can you do for free?
What are three things you can do there?   What shouldn't a visitor miss?

9 PRONUNCIATION Can't *and* shouldn't

A ▶ Listen and practice these statements. Notice how the *t* in **can't** and **shouldn't** is not strongly pronounced.

You can get a taxi easily.
You can**'t** get a taxi easily.
You should visit in the summer.
You shouldn**'t** visit in the summer.

B ▶ Listen to four sentences.
Circle the modal verb you hear.

1. can / can't   2. should / shouldn't   3. can / can't   4. should / shouldn't

10 LISTENING *Three capital cities*

A ▶ Listen to speakers talk about Japan, Argentina, and Egypt. Complete the chart.

	Capital city	What visitors should see or do
1. Japan		
2. Argentina		
3. Egypt		

B ▶ Listen again. One thing about each country is incorrect. What is it?

11 SPEAKING *Interesting places*

GROUP WORK Has anyone visited an interesting place in your country? Find out more about it. Start like this and ask questions like the ones below.

A: I visited Istanbul once.
B: Really? What's the best time of year to visit?
A: It's nice all year. I went in March.
C: What's the weather like then?

What's the best time of year to visit?
What's the weather like then?
What should tourists see and do there?
What special foods can you eat?
What's the shopping like?
What things should people buy?
What else can visitors do there?

Istanbul, Turkey

12 INTERCHANGE 11 *City guide*

Make a guide to fun places in your city. Go to Interchange 11 on page 126.

9 PRONUNCIATION

Learning Objective: *learn to sound natural when using* can't *and* shouldn't

A ▶ *[CD 3, Track 9]*

- Books closed. Play the audio program. Ask: "What do you notice about the pronunciation of *t* in *can't* and *shouldn't*?" (Answer: It is not strongly pronounced.)
- Books open. Play the audio program again. Ss listen and repeat. Go around the class and check their pronunciation of *can't* and *shouldn't*.

B ▶ *[CD 3, Track 10]*

- Explain the task. Play the audio program, and Ss circle the modal verb. Then elicit the correct answers.

> **Answers**

1. can't   2. should   3. can't   4. shouldn't

10 LISTENING

Learning Objective: *develop skills in listening for details*

A ▶ *[CD 3, Track 11]*

- Books closed. Write *Japan, Argentina,* and *Egypt* on the board. Ask: "What do you know about these countries?" Elicit Ss' answers.
- Explain the task. Ss listen for more information about these countries. Play the audio program, pausing after each country. Elicit Ss' answers.
- Books open. Explain the task. Play the audio program again. Ss complete the chart individually. Then they compare answers in pairs. Elicit answers from the class.

> **AudioScript**

1.
Japan has several big islands and many smaller islands. The capital city is Tokyo. The highest mountain in Japan is called Mount Everest. There are many beautiful Buddhist temples in Japan. And visitors should try Japanese food, especially sashimi, which is raw fish.
2.
Argentina is a large country in South America. The capital city is Buenos Aires. The people all speak French. People visiting Buenos Aires shouldn't miss the downtown area. Many interesting people gather in this area. Argentina is also a good place to buy leather.

3.
Egypt is famous for its many pyramids. You can see the biggest ones near its capital city, Cairo. There are many colorful markets in Cairo, and visitors should definitely buy some souvenirs there. You can often bargain for good prices. Cairo is also famous for its river, the Amazon.

> **Answers**

		Capital city	What visitors should see or do
1.	Japan	Tokyo	go to temples; eat Japanese food especially sashimi
2.	Argentina	Buenos Aires	see the downtown area; buy leather
3.	Egypt	Cairo	go to the market; buy souvenirs

B ▶ *[CD 3, Track 12]*

- Explain the task and read the focus question. Play the audio program, and Ss listen for the answers.

> **Answers**

1. Japan's highest mountain is Mount Fuji, not Everest.
2. Argentineans speak Spanish, not French.
3. Cairo's famous river is the Nile, not the Amazon.

11 SPEAKING

Learning Objective: *talk about vacations using* can, can't, should, *and* shouldn't

Group work

- Explain the task and ask three Ss to read the example conversation. Go over the discussion questions.
- **Option:** Brainstorm additional discussion questions with the class. Write them on the board.
- Ss complete the activity in small groups.

12 INTERCHANGE 11

See page T-126 for teaching notes.

It's a very exciting place! ■ T-76

13 READING

Learning Objectives: *read and discuss email messages; develop skills in predicting and reading for specific information*

- Books closed. Write these questions on the board:

  1. When on vacation, *do you ever write to people?*
  2. Do you send emails, letters, or postcards?
  3. Who do you write to?
  4. What do you write about?

  Ss discuss the questions in pairs. Then elicit their answers.

- Books open. Write *Fez, Cartagena,* and *Hanoi* on the board. Then read the pre-reading questions. Ss complete the task individually.

- Ss scan the article to check their guesses.

Answers

puppet show: Hanoi
two personalities: Cartagena
famous for leather: Fez

- Ask Ss to underline any new vocabulary and look it up before class. Elicit or explain any words Ss cannot find.

Vocabulary

crafts: objects made by hand: decorations, pottery, furniture
local: from a small area
dye: to change the color of something using a special liquid
district: a specific area of a country or town
salsa steps: the movements of the South American dance called *salsa*
mangrove: a tropical tree found near water
window-shopping: spending time looking at items in shop windows without intent to buy
pottery: objects that are made out of clay by hand

❗ For a new way to teach the vocabulary in this Reading, try *Vocabulary Mingle* – download it from the website.

A

- Explain the task and go over the activities in the chart. Tell Ss to only check (✓) the cities first. Model the first example. Tell Ss to look quickly through the emails for words related to *go shopping*. Ss complete the task individually.

- Tell Ss to look through the emails in detail for specific examples. Ss complete the task individually. Then they go over answers in pairs.

- Ask different Ss to write their answers on the board, using sentences with *can* (e.g., *You can go shopping at a local market in Vietnam.*).

Answers

Activity	Fez	Cartagena	Hanoi	Specific examples
1. go shopping	✓	✓	✓	small shops, historic district, local market
2. see old buildings	✓	✓		the medina (old city), old Spanish buildings
3. go dancing		✓		salsa
4. attend a festival	✓			World Sacred Music festival
5. take a boat trip		✓		canoe tour

B *Pair work*

- Read the discussion questions. Ss discuss them in pairs.

❗ For a new way to practice reading for specific information, try the **Reading Race** – download it from the website.

End of Cycle 2

See the Supplementary Resources chart at the beginning of this unit for additional teaching materials and student activities related to this Cycle.

Scan the email messages. What city has a puppet show? What city has two personalities? What city is famous for leather?

Fez is so interesting! I've been to the medina (the old city) every day. It has walls all the way around it, and more than 9,000 streets! It's always crowded and noisy. My favorite places to visit are the small shops where people make local crafts. Fez is famous for its leather products. I visited a place where they dye the leather in dozens of beautiful colors.

I came at the perfect time, because the World Sacred Music festival is happening right now!

Kathy

I've discovered that Cartagena has two different personalities. One is a lively city with fancy restaurants and crowded old plazas. And the other is a quiet and relaxing place with sandy beaches.

If you come here, you should stay in the historic district – a walled area with great shopping, nightclubs, and restaurants. It has some wonderful old Spanish buildings.

Last night, I learned some salsa steps at a great dance club.

Today, I went on a canoe tour of La Ciénaga mangrove forest.

Mike

Hanoi is the capital of Vietnam and its second-largest city. It's a fun city, but six days is not enough time for a visit. I'm staying near the Old Quarter of the city. It's a great place to meet people. Last night I went to a water puppet show. Tomorrow I'm going to Ha Long Bay.

I took a cooking class at the Vietnam Culinary School. I bought some fruits and vegetables at a local market and then prepared some local dishes. My food was really delicious! I'll cook you something when I get home.

Belinda

A Read the emails. Check (✓) the cities where you can do these things. Then complete the chart with examples from the emails

Activity	Fez	Cartagena	Hanoi	Specific examples
1. go shopping	☐	☐	☐	....
2. see old buildings	☐	☐	☐	....
3. go dancing	☐	☐	☐	....
4. attend a festival	☐	☐	☐	....
5. take a boat trip	☐	☐	☐	....

B **PAIR WORK** Which city is the most interesting to you? Why?

Unit 12 Supplementary Resources Overview

	After the following SB exercises	You can use these materials in class	Your students can use these materials outside the classroom
CYCLE 1	1 Snapshot		**SSD** Unit 12 Vocabulary 1 **ARC** Common health complaints
	2 Conversation		**SSD** Unit 12 Speaking 1
	3 Grammar Focus		**SB** Unit 12 Grammar Plus focus 1 **SSD** Unit 12 Grammar 1
	4 Pronunciation		
	5 Interchange 12		
	6 Discussion		**WB** Unit 12 exercises 1–4
CYCLE 2	7 Word Power	**TSS** Unit 12 Extra Worksheet **TSS** Unit 12 Vocabulary Worksheet	**SSD** Unit 12 Vocabulary 2 **ARC** Containers 1–2
	8 Conversation		**SSD** Unit 12 Speaking 2
	9 Grammar Focus	**TSS** Unit 12 Grammar Worksheet	**SB** Unit 12 Grammar Plus focus 2 **SSD** Unit 12 Grammar 2 **ARC** Suggestions 1–2
	10 Listening	**TSS** Unit 12 Listening Worksheet	
	11 Role Play		
	12 Writing	**TSS** Unit 12 Writing Worksheet	
	13 Reading	**TSS** Unit 12 Project Worksheet **VID** Unit 12 **VRB** Unit 12	**SSD** Unit 12 Reading 1–2 **SSD** Unit 12 Listening 1–3 **SSD** Unit 12 Video 1–3 **WB** Unit 12 exercises 5–8

With or instead of the following SB section	You can also use these materials for assessment
Units 11–12 Progress Check	**ASSESSMENT CD** Units 11–12 Oral Quiz **ASSESSMENT CD** Units 11–12 Written Quiz

Key **ARC**: Arcade   **SB**: Student's Book   **SSD**: Self-study DVD-ROM   **TSS**: Teacher Support Site
VID: Video DVD   **VRB**: Video Resource Book   **WB**: Workbook

My Plan for Unit 12

Use the space below to customize a plan that fits your needs.

With the following SB exercises	I am using these materials in class	My students are using these materials outside the classroom

With or instead of the following SB section	I am using these materials for assessment

12 It really works!

SNAPSHOT

Common Health Complaints

- a headache
- a backache
- sore muscles
- a stomachache
- a cold
- a cough
- the flu
- insomnia

Source: National Center for Health Statistics

Check (✓) the health problems you have had recently.
What do you do for the health problems you checked?
How many times have you been sick in the past year?

2 CONVERSATION *Health problems*

A ▶ Listen and practice.

Joan: Hi, Craig! How are you?
Craig: Not so good. I have a terrible cold.
Joan: Really? That's too bad! You should be at home in bed. It's really important to get a lot of rest.
Craig: Yeah, you're right.
Joan: And have you taken anything for it?
Craig: No, I haven't.
Joan: Well, it's sometimes helpful to eat garlic soup. Just chop up a whole head of garlic and cook it in chicken stock. Try it! It really works!
Craig: Yuck! That sounds awful!

B ▶ Listen to advice from two more of Craig's co-workers. What do they suggest?

78

It really works!

In Unit 12, students talk about health. In Cycle 1, they talk about health problems and give advice using adjective + infinitive and noun + infinitive. In Cycle 2, they ask for advice and give suggestions about health care products using the modal verbs can, could, and may.

 ## 1 SNAPSHOT

Learning Objectives: *learn vocabulary for common health problems; talk about health problems*

- Books closed. Elicit common health problems from the class and write them on the board.

- Books open. Ss compare their ideas with the Snapshot. Explain any new vocabulary, using gestures if needed.

- Explain the tasks. Ss complete the tasks in small groups. Go around the class and give help as needed.

- Ask the class: "How many of you have had a headache recently? Raise your hands." Ask about each health problem. Count the number of Ss who have had each one.

❗ For a new way to practice the vocabulary in this Snapshot, try **Vocabulary Steps** – download it from the website. Ss rank the health problems according to most/least serious or most/least common.

 ## 2 CONVERSATION

Learning Objectives: *practice a conversation about health problems; see adjective + infinitive and noun + infinitive in context*

A ▶ [CD 3, Track 13]

- Ss cover the text and look at the picture. Elicit or explain vocabulary (e.g., *tissues*). Ask: "What health problem do you think Craig has? How do you know?"

- Play the first part of the audio program. Ss listen to check the answer. (Answer: a cold)

- Write this focus question on the board:
  What does Joan suggest for Craig's cold?

- Play the audio program and ask Ss to listen for the answer. Elicit the answer. (Answer: garlic soup)

- Elicit or explain any new vocabulary.

Vocabulary

get a lot of rest: relax or sleep a lot
Have you taken anything for it?: have you taken any medicine?
chop up: cut into small pieces
chicken stock: the liquid from chicken soup
Yuck!: an expression of dislike, especially about food

- Play the audio program again. Ss listen and read silently.

- Ss practice the conversation in pairs. Go around the class and give help as needed.

> **TIP** To encourage Ss to look at each other while practicing Conversations, ask them to stand up and face each other. This also makes the conversation more active and natural.

B ▶ [CD 3, Track 14]

- Read the task and focus question. Ask Ss to make predictions. Write their ideas on the board.

- Play the audio program. Ss listen for the answers individually. Then elicit answers from the class.

AudioScript

1.
Craig [coughs]
Woman That cold sounds pretty bad, Craig!
Craig Yeah, it is. Don't get too close.
Woman Well, you know, it's important to drink a lot of liquids. I have some herbal tea. Let me make you a cup.
Craig Oh, OK. That sounds good.
2.
Man How's that cold, Craig?
Craig Not so good. [sneezes] I've still got it.
Man Oh, too bad. Well, listen, it's a good idea to take some cold medicine. And you should go home and take a long, hot bath.
Craig You're right. Maybe I should. Thanks for the advice.

Answers

The woman suggests herbal tea. The man suggests cold medicine. He also says Craig should go home and take a long, hot bath.

3 GRAMMAR FOCUS

Learning Objectives: *practice using adjective + infinitive and noun + infinitive; ask for and give advice using adjective + infinitive and noun + infinitive*

▶ *[CD 3, Track 15]*

- Books closed. Write these sentences on the board.
  You should get a lot of rest
  You should eat garlic soup.
- Point out that these sentences give suggestions with *should*. We can also give suggestions using an adjective or a noun followed by an infinitive. Cross out the words *You should* and replace them with *It's important to* and *It's helpful to*.
- Books open. Focus Ss' attention on the Grammar Focus box. Elicit the rule for forming adjective or noun + infinitive structures:
  It's important/helpful/a good idea to + verb.
- Focus Ss' attention on the Conversation on page 78. Ask Ss to underline the two examples of adjective or noun + infinitive structures.
- Play the audio program.
- **Option:** Present additional positive adjective or noun + infinitive structures (e.g., *It's useful to . . . , It's best to . . . , It's essential to . . .*) and also negative infinitives (e.g., *It's important not to . . . , It's best not to . . .*).

A

- Explain the task. Ss read the problems and advice silently. Use the picture or gestures to explain new vocabulary (e.g., *a sore throat, a fever, a toothache, a burn*).

- Read the first problem. Elicit different pieces of advice.
- Ss complete the task individually. Then go over answers with the class.

Possible answers

1. a, c, d, i, j   3. b, d, e, g, i   5. g, h, j   7. b, f, i, j
2. a, d, i, j   4. c, d, g, i, j   6. d, g, j   8. c, d, g, l, j

B *Group work*

- Explain the task. Then model the example conversation with two Ss.
- Ss take turns giving advice in small groups. Go around the class and check their use of adjective or noun + infinitive structures.

TIP Use your fingers to help Ss self-correct their errors. For example, if the error is in the fourth word in a sentence, show four fingers and point to the fourth finger.

C

- Explain the task and elicit endings for the first example. Write them on the board.
- Ss complete the task individually. Go around the class and give help as needed.

 For a new way to practice the vocabulary in this Grammar Focus, try *Mime* – download it from the website.

4 PRONUNCIATION

Learning Objectives: *notice the reduction of* to; *learn to sound natural when using* to *in conversation*

A ▶ *[CD 3, Track 16]*

- Model the reduction of *to*. Then play the audio program. Ss listen for the reduction of *to*.
- Play the audio program again. Ss take turns practicing the conversation in pairs.

TIP If you are concerned about your pronunciation and intonation, always use the audio program to present material.

B *Pair work*

- Explain the task. Ss work in pairs. They ask for and give advice using their sentences from part C of Exercise 3. Ask a few pairs of Ss to model the task.
- Ss complete the task in pairs. Go around the class and check their reduction of *to*. Then elicit the most popular advice for each problem.

3 GRAMMAR FOCUS

Adjective + infinitive; noun + infinitive ▶

What should you do for a cold?	It's **important**	**to get** a lot of rest.
	It's sometimes **helpful**	**to eat** garlic soup.
	It's a **good idea**	**to take** some vitamin C.

A Look at these health problems. Choose several pieces of good advice for each problem.

Problems
1. a sore throat ....
2. a cough ....
3. a backache ....
4. a fever ....
5. a toothache ....
6. a bad headache ....
7. a burn ....
8. the flu ....

Advice
a. take some vitamin C
b. put some ointment on it
c. drink lots of liquids
d. go to bed and rest
e. put a heating pad on it
f. put it under cold water
g. take some aspirin
h. see a dentist
i. see a doctor
j. get some medicine

a sore throat

a fever

a toothache

a burn

B **GROUP WORK** Talk about the problems in part A and give advice. What other advice do you have?

A: What should you do for a sore throat?
B: It's a good idea to get some medicine from the drugstore.
C: And it's important to drink lots of liquids and . . .

C Write advice for these problems. (You will use this advice in Exercise 4.)

a cold   sore eyes   a sunburn   sore muscles

For a cold, it's a good idea to . . .

4 PRONUNCIATION *Reduction of* to

A ▶ Listen and practice. In conversation, **to** is often reduced to /tə/.

A: What should you do for a fever?
B: It's important **to** take some aspirin. And it's a good idea **to** see a doctor.

B **PAIR WORK** Look back at Exercise 3, part C. Ask for and give advice about each health problem. Pay attention to the pronunciation of **to**.

It really works! ■ 79

5 INTERCHANGE 12 *Help!*

Play a board game. Go to Interchange 12 on page 127.

6 DISCUSSION *Difficult situations*

A GROUP WORK Imagine these situations are true for you.
Get three suggestions for each one.

I get really hungry before I go to bed.
I sometimes feel really stressed.
I need to study, but I can't concentrate.
I feel sick before every exam.
I forget about half the new words I learn.
I get nervous when I speak English to foreigners.

A: I get really hungry before I go to bed. What should I do?
B: It's a bad idea to eat late at night.
C: It's sometimes helpful to drink herbal tea.

B CLASS ACTIVITY Have any of the above situations
happened to you recently? Share what you did with the class.

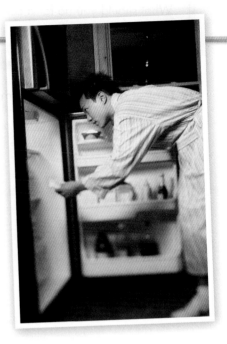

7 WORD POWER *Containers*

A Use the words in the list to complete these expressions.
Then compare with a partner.

bag   jar
bottle   pack
box   stick
can   tube

1. a .... of toothpaste
2. a .... of aspirin
3. a .... of bandages
4. a .... of shaving cream
5. a .... of tissues
6. a .... of face cream
7. a .... of cough drops
8. a .... of deodorant

B PAIR WORK What is one more thing you
can buy in each of the containers above?

"You can buy a bag of breath mints."

C PAIR WORK What are the five most
useful items in your medicine cabinet?

INTERCHANGE 12

See page T-127 for teaching notes.

 DISCUSSION

Learning Objective: *discuss difficult situations using adjective + infinitive and noun + infinitive*

A *Group work*

- Books closed. Ask: "What should you do when you forget someone's name?" Elicit Ss' answers, encouraging them to use *should,* adjective + infinitive, or noun + infinitive.

- Books open. Explain the task and ask different Ss to read the example situations. Elicit or explain any new vocabulary. Then ask three Ss to read the example conversation.

- Ss discuss the situations in small groups. Go around the class and write down any errors you hear.

- Write the most common errors on the board. Ask Ss to correct them in pairs.

Cycle 2, Exercises 7–13

7 **WORD POWER**

Learning Objective: *learn vocabulary for containers*

A

- Books closed. Write the names of the various products from the Word Power on the board. Ask Ss which ones they use. Elicit or explain any new vocabulary.

- **Option:** Bring some of the products to class (e.g., a toothbrush, deodorant). Elicit the vocabulary.

> **TIP** To teach the vocabulary for small everyday objects bring the actual objects to class.

- Books open. Focus Ss' attention on the picture. Elicit or present the words for containers.

- Ss complete the task individually.

- Go over answers with the class. Point out that we don't stress the word *of.*

Answers

1. a **tube** of toothpaste
2. a **bottle** of aspirin
3. a **box** of bandages
4. a **can** of shaving cream
5. a **pack** of tissues
6. a **jar** of face cream
7. a **bag** of cough drops
8. a **stick** of deodorant

! For a new way to practice this Discussion, try the *Onion Ring* technique – download it from the website.

B *Class activity*

- Read the question to the class. Elicit Ss' answers. Encourage Ss to ask follow-up questions.

End of Cycle 1

See the Supplementary Resources chart at the beginning of this unit for additional teaching materials and student activities related to this Cycle.

B *Pair work*

- Explain the task and ask a S to read the model sentence. Point out that Ss can include any items (e.g., foods).

- Ss work in pairs. Then Ss write their ideas on the board.

Possible answers

1. a tube of ointment/hand cream/hair gel
2. a bottle of vitamins/shampoo/juice
3. a box of herbal tea/cereal/candy
4. a can of hair spray/foot spray/soda
5. a pack of lozenges/gum/mints
6. a jar of coffee/mayonnaise/jam
7. a bag of breath mints/potato chips/rice
8. a stick of gum/butter

C *Pair work*

- Read the question. Ss complete the task in pairs.

8 CONVERSATION

Learning Objectives: *practice a conversation between a pharmacist and a customer; see modal verbs for requests and suggestions in context*

A [CD 3, Track 17]

- Books closed. Ask: "Where do you think the speakers are?" Play the audio program and Ss listen for the answer. Elicit the answer. (Answer: a pharmacy)
- Books open. Ss cover the text. Elicit the containers in the picture. Then ask: "What does the woman buy?" Encourage Ss to guess. Then play the audio program and elicit the answers. (Answers: a box of cough drops, a jar of lotion, and three bottles of multivitamins)
- Ask: "What three problems does the woman talk about?" Play the audio program again. Ss listen for the answers. Elicit the answers. (Answers: a cough/cold, dry skin, no energy.)
- **Option:** Ss work in two groups. Group A listens for the problems the woman talks about. Group B listens for the things she buys. Then they share information.
- Ss uncover the text. Then they read the conversation silently.
- Ss stand and practice the conversation in pairs.

Encourage them to role-play the conversation, as if they are in a pharmacy.

❗ For a new way to practice this Conversation, try *Say It with Feeling!* – download it from the website.

B ⏵ [CD 3, Track 18]

- Write these phrases on the board:

  tired eyes   a backache   insomnia

- Ask: "What problem does the customer have?" Play the audio program. Ss listen to find the answer. (Answer: a backache)
- Explain the task and read the focus question. Then play the audio program again. Elicit the answer.

AudioScript

Customer Excuse me.
Pharmacist Yes? How can I help you?
Customer Um, what do you suggest for a backache?
Pharmacist Well, you should take some aspirin. And it's a good idea to use a heating pad.
Customer Oh, and where is the aspirin?
Pharmacist In aisle five. Right over there.

Answer

He wants some aspirin.

9 GRAMMAR FOCUS

Learning Objective: *practice conversations using modal verbs for requests and suggestions*

⏵ [CD 3, Track 19]

- Explain that it's impolite to say *Give me* or *I want* when asking for things in a store. People usually use modal verbs such as *can, could,* and *may.*
- Focus Ss' attention on the Conversation in Exercise 8. Ask: "How did Mrs. Webb ask for things?" Ask Ss to underline the examples. (Answers: *Could I have . . . ? . . . what do you suggest? Can you suggest . . . ? May I have . . . ?*)
- Focus Ss' attention on the example questions in the first column of the Grammar Focus box. Point out that the first question (*Can/May I help you?*) is an offer of help. The other three questions are requests for help. Explain that people can use *can, could,* and *may* to make a request, but *may* is the most formal.
- Elicit the rule for questions with modals: Modal + subject + verb?
- Focus Ss' attention on the three ways to make suggestions in the second column. Ask Ss to find examples in the Conversation in Exercise 8 and underline them twice.

- Play the audio program.
- Explain the task and model the first conversation with a S.
- Ss circle the correct modal verbs individually. Then they compare answers in pairs.

Possible answers

1. A: **Can** I help you?
   B: Yes. **May** I have something for itchy eyes?
   A: You **could** try a bottle of eye drops.
2. A: What do you **suggest** for sore muscles?
   B: Why don't you **try** this ointment? It's excellent.
   A: OK. I'll take it.
3. A: Could I **have** a box of bandages, please?
   B: Here you are.
   A: And what do you **suggest** for insomnia?
   B: You **should** try some of this herbal tea. It's very relaxing.
   A: OK. Thanks.

- Ss practice the conversations in pairs.

❗ For a new way to practice the conversations in this Grammar Focus, try the *Substitution Dialog* – download it from the website. Ss replace the health problems and suggestions with ideas of their own.

8 CONVERSATION *What do you suggest?*

A ▶ Listen and practice.

Pharmacist: Hi. May I help you?

Mrs. Webb: Yes, please. Could I have something for a cough? I think I'm getting a cold.

Pharmacist: Sure. Why don't you try these cough drops? They work very well.

Mrs. Webb: OK, I'll take one box. And what do you suggest for dry skin?

Pharmacist: Well, you could get a jar of this new lotion. It's very good.

Mrs. Webb: OK. And one more thing. My husband has no energy these days. Can you suggest anything?

Pharmacist: He should try some of these multivitamins. They're excellent.

Mrs. Webb: Great! May I have three large bottles, please?

B ▶ Listen to the pharmacist talk to the next customer. What does the customer want?

9 GRAMMAR FOCUS

> ### Modal verbs can, could, may *for requests; suggestions* ▶
>
> | | |
> |---|---|
> | **Can/May** I help you? | What do you suggest/have for dry skin? |
> | **Can** I have a box of cough drops? | You could try this lotion. |
> | **Could** I have something for a cough? | You should get some skin cream. |
> | **May** I have a bottle of aspirin? | Why don't you try this new ointment? |

Circle the correct words. Then compare and practice with a partner.

1. A: **Can / Could** I help you?
   B: Yes. **May / Do** I have something for itchy eyes?
   A: Sure. You **could / may** try a bottle of eyedrops.

2. A: What do you **suggest / try** for sore muscles?
   B: Why don't you **suggest / try** this ointment? It's excellent.
   A: OK. I'll take it.

3. A: Could I **suggest / have** a box of bandages, please?
   B: Here you are.
   A: And what do you **suggest / try** for insomnia?
   B: You **should / may** try this herbal tea. It's very relaxing.
   A: OK. Thanks.

10 LISTENING *Try this!*

A ◉ Listen to four people talk to a pharmacist. Check (✓) each person's problem.

1. ☐ The man's feet are sore.
   ☐ The man's feet are itchy.
2. ☐ The woman can't eat.
   ☐ The woman has an upset stomach.

3. ☐ The man has difficulty sleeping.
   ☐ The man is sleeping too much.
4. ☐ The woman burned her hand.
   ☐ The woman has a bad sunburn.

B ◉ Listen again. What does the pharmacist suggest for each person?

11 ROLE PLAY *Can I help you?*

Student A: You are a customer in a drugstore. You need:

> something for low energy
> something for the flu
> something for a backache
> something for dry skin
> something for an upset stomach
> something for sore feet

Ask for some suggestions.

Student B: You are a pharmacist in a drugstore. A customer needs some things. Make some suggestions.

Change roles and try the role play again.

12 WRITING *A letter to an advice columnist*

A Read these letters to an online advice columnist.

Dear Fix-it Fred

Dear Fix-it Fred

I have a problem and need your advice. My parents don't like how I dress. I think I have an interesting style, but my parents say I just look strange. Weren't they ever teenagers? Can you please help?

Funky Frida

Dear Fix-it Fred

Several months ago, I started college. I study a lot and have a part-time job, so I don't have much of a social life. I haven't made many friends, but I really want to. What do you suggest?

Too Busy

B Now imagine you want some advice about a problem. Write a short letter to an advice columnist. Think of an interesting way to sign it.

C GROUP WORK Exchange letters. Read and write down some advice at the bottom of each letter. Then share the most interesting letter and advice with the class.

10 LISTENING

Learning Objective: *develop skills in listening for specific information*

A [CD 3, Track 20]

- Set the scene and explain the task. Then play the audio program. Ss listen for the answers.

AudioScript

1.
Pharmacist Can I help you?
Man Yes, I'd like something for my feet. I went on a long hike yesterday and my feet are really sore.
Pharmacist I see. Why don't you try some of this ointment? You can put it on at night. It's very good for sore feet. I use it myself, actually.

2.
Woman Excuse me. I'm looking for something for a stomachache.
Pharmacist I see. How long have you had this problem?
Woman For a few days, and it's getting worse.
Pharmacist You could try this medicine. It may help. But I think you should see a doctor.

3.
Pharmacist Can I help you?
Man Yes. I just came back from London on a long flight, and I'm having trouble sleeping.
Pharmacist We have several things for that, including sleeping pills. But try some of this herbal tea. It's very good for jet lag. Drink some before you go to bed at night.
Man Thanks. I'll try it. I don't like taking sleeping pills.

4.
Pharmacist Good morning. What can I do for you?
Woman Um, I need something for a burn. I burned my hand a little when I was cooking last night. See?
Pharmacist Oh, yes. I'll give you some cream for it. After you put on the cream, place a bandage over it for a few days. You should be fine.
Woman Thanks.

- Go over answers with the class.

Answers

1. The man's feet are sore.
2. The woman has a stomachache.
3. The man has difficulty sleeping.
4. The woman burned her hand.

B [CD 3, Track 21]

- Explain the task and read the focus question. Then play the audio program. Ss listen for the answers.
- Ss go over their answers in pairs. Then go over answers with the class.

Answers

1. ointment
2. medicine
3. herbal tea
4. cream and a bandage

11 ROLE PLAY

Learning Objective: *role-play a conversation between two people in a drugstore*

- Set the scene and explain the task. Ss work in pairs. Student A is a customer in a drugstore, and Student B is a pharmacist. The customer asks for six things and the pharmacist makes suggestions.
- **Option:** If Ss need help getting started, refer them to the first few lines of the Conversation on page 81.
- Ss complete the role play in pairs.
- Ss change roles. Go around the class and take notes on their grammar, pronunciation, fluency, and ideas.

❗ For a new way to teach this Role Play, try *Time Out!* – download it from the website.

12 WRITING

Learning Objectives: *write a letter to an online advice columnist using modal verbs for requests; write a response using suggestions*

A

- Ask: "Do you ever read advice columns online? Do you like them? Why or why not?"
- Ss read the example emails silently. Elicit or explain any new vocabulary.

B

- Explain the task. Ss complete the task individually in class or for homework.

C Group work

- Explain the task. Then Ss complete the task in small groups.

Learning Objectives: *read and discuss an article about the rain forest; develop skills in predicting, skimming, and understanding the sequence of information*

- Read the pre-reading question. Tell Ss to look at the title, pictures, and captions. Elicit Ss' predictions. (Answer: finding health remedies in the rain forest)

! For a new way to practice predicting, try *Cloud*
• *Prediction* – download it from the website.

A

- Explain the task. Tell Ss to skim the article for the answer. Point out that they shouldn't worry about any new vocabulary.
- Allow about three minutes for Ss to complete the task. Then Ss check the best description of the article. Elicit the answer.

Answer

1

- Point out that this way of ordering information is common in many magazine and online articles.

B

- Present or ask Ss to look up key vocabulary from the reading.

> **TIP** To save time, have Ss look up the vocabulary in a dictionary before class. To encourage peer teaching, assign each S a few words to look up. Then have them teach each other the words in class.

Vocabulary

rain forest: a tropical forest
medicinal: related to medicine
jungle: a tropical forest with many trees and plants
bleeding: losing blood
sources: places where things come from
researchers: people who study something
searching: looking for
produced: made; created

- Explain the task. Then answer the first question and identify the paragraph as a class.
- Ss complete the task individually and compare answers in pairs. Go around the class and check their answers. Help Ss with pronunciation as needed.

Answers

Par. 3 (from his grandmother)
Par. 5 (medical researchers)
Par. 2 (medicinal plants)
Par. 6 (none)
Par. 4 (about 50 percent)

- **Option:** Ss read the article again and underline any words they still don't know. Explain the words.

C Group work

- Ss discuss the question in small groups. Go around the class and help with vocabulary as needed. Then elicit Ss' answers. (Possible answers: They're a source of oxygen, wood, rubber, and food. They're a home for many animals.)

End of Cycle 2

See the Supplementary Resources chart at the beginning of this unit for additional teaching materials and student activities related to this Cycle and for assessment tools.

WORLD NEWS

HOME | LOG IN | SETTINGS

HOME | CURRENT ISSUE | ARCHIVES | WEB EXTRAS | RADIO | CONTACT US | SUBSCRIBE

Rain Forest Remedies?

Look at the title, pictures, and captions. What do you think the article is about?

1 Rodrigo Bonilla turns off the motor of the boat. We get off the boat and follow him along the path into the rain forest. Above us, a monkey with a baby hangs from a tree.

2 On this hot January day, Rodrigo is not looking for wild animals, but for medicinal plants – plants that can cure or treat illnesses. Medicinal plants grow in rain forests around the world.

Carol writes a column on health. Recently she took a trip to Tortuguero National Park in Costa Rica.

A broom tree

3 Rodrigo is Costa Rican. He learned about jungle medicine from his grandmother. He shows us many different plants, such as the broom tree. He tells us that parts of the broom tree can help stop bleeding.

4 People have always used natural products as medicine. In fact, about 50 percent of Western medicines, such as aspirin, come from natural sources. And some animals eat certain kinds of plants when they are sick.

5 This is why medical researchers are so interested in plants. Many companies are now working with local governments and searching the rain forests for medicinal plants.

6 So far, the search has not produced any new medicines. But it's a good idea to keep looking. That's why we are now here in the Costa Rican rain forest.

MORE >>

A Read the article. Then check (✓) the best description of the article.

☐ 1. The article starts with a description and then gives facts.
☐ 2. The article gives the writer's opinion.
☐ 3. The article starts with facts and then gives advice.

B Answer these questions. Then write the number of the paragraph where you find each answer.

.... Where did Rodrigo learn about jungle medicine?
.... Who is interested in studying medicinal plants?
.... What is Rodrigo looking for in the rain forest?
.... How many new medicines have come from Rodrigo's search?
.... How many Western medicines come from natural sources?

C GROUP WORK Can you think of other reasons why rain forests are important?

Units 11–12 Progress check

SELF-ASSESSMENT

How well can you do these things? Check (✓) the boxes.

I can	Very well	OK	A little
Understand descriptions of towns and cities (Ex. 1)	☐	☐	☐
Get useful information about towns and cities (Ex. 1, 2)	☐	☐	☐
Describe towns and cities (Ex. 2)	☐	☐	☐
Ask for and make suggestions on practical questions (Ex. 2, 3, 4)	☐	☐	☐
Ask for and give advice about problems (Ex. 3, 4)	☐	☐	☐

1 LISTENING *I'm from Honolulu.*

A Listen to Jenny talk about Honolulu. What does she say about these things? Complete the chart.

1. size of city ....
2. weather ....
3. prices of things ....
4. most famous place ....

B Write sentences comparing Honolulu with your hometown.
Then discuss with a partner.

> Honolulu isn't too big, but Seoul is really big.

2 ROLE PLAY *My hometown*

Student A: Imagine you are planning to visit Student B's hometown. Ask questions using the ones in the box or your own questions.

Student B: Answer Student A's questions about your hometown.

    A: What's your hometown like?
    B: It's quiet but fairly interesting. . . .

Change roles and try the role play again.

possible questions
What's your hometown like?
How big is it?
What's the weather like?
Is it expensive?
What should you see there?
What can you do there?

Units 11–12 Progress check

SELF-ASSESSMENT

Learning Objectives: *reflect on one's learning; identify areas that need improvement*

- Ask: "What did you learn in Units 11 and 12?" Elicit Ss' answers.

- Ss complete the Self-assessment. Encourage them to be honest, and point out they will not get a bad grade if they check (✓) *a little*.

- Ss move on to the Progress check exercises. You can have Ss complete them in class or for homework, using one of these techniques:
  1. Ask Ss to complete all the exercises.
  2. Ask Ss: "What do you need to practice?" Then assign exercises based on their answers.
  3. Ask Ss to choose and complete exercises based on their Self-assessment.

1 LISTENING

Learning Objectives: *assess one's ability to listen to and understand descriptions of cities; assess one's ability to describe places using adjectives, adverbs, and conjunctions*

A ▶ [CD 3, Track 22]

- Set the scene and explain the task. Jenny is talking about Honolulu, her hometown. Ss listen and write the size of the city, weather, prices of things, and most famous place in their chart.

- Play the audio program once or twice. Ss listen and complete the chart.

AudioScript

Man So, you're from Hawaii, Jenny.
Jenny That's right.
Man Where in Hawaii?
Jenny I'm from Honolulu – on the island of Oahu.
Man Wow! Honolulu! That's a fairly big city, isn't it?
Jenny No, not really. It's not too big.
Man The weather is great, though. Right?
Jenny Oh, yes. It is. It's very comfortable the whole year. Warm, but not too hot.
Man I've heard that Honolulu is an expensive city. Is that true?

Jenny Well, yes, it is pretty expensive. Rents are high and food is expensive, too. That's because everything comes in from the mainland.
Man What's that beach in Honolulu?
Jenny Well, the most famous place in Honolulu is probably Waikiki Beach. That's where all the tourists go.
Man Yeah, that's it. Waikiki Beach.

- Go over answers with the class.

Answers

1. not too big
2. very comfortable; warm, but not too hot
3. pretty expensive
4. Waikiki Beach

B

- Explain the task. Ss write sentences comparing Honolulu with their hometowns. Point out the conjunction, adjectives, and adverbs in the example.

- Ss write sentences individually. Then they compare their sentences in pairs.

2 ROLE PLAY

Learning Objectives: *assess one's ability to describe places using adjectives, adverbs, and conjunctions; assess one's ability to ask questions about cities and hometowns; assess one's ability to ask for and give suggestions with* can *and* should

- Explain the task. Ss work in pairs. Student A is planning to visit Student B's hometown and asks questions about it. Student B answers the questions.

- Go over the possible questions. Model the example conversation with a S.

- Ss practice the role play in pairs. Then they change roles and practice again. Go around the class and give help as needed.

3 DISCUSSION

Learning Objectives: *assess one's ability to ask for and give suggestions using* can *and* should; *assess one's ability to ask for and give advice using adjective + infinitive and noun + infinitive*

A Group work

- Explain the task and model the example conversation with two Ss.
- Ss write advice and remedies for the problems individually. Go around the class and give help as needed.

4 SPEAKING

Learning Objectives: *assess one's ability to ask for and give advice using adjective + infinitive and noun + infinitive; assess one's ability to give suggestions on a variety of problems*

A Group work

- Set the scene. The three problems are from an advice column.
- Ss read the problems silently. Then elicit or explain any new vocabulary.

- Ss compare their ideas in small groups. Encourage Ss to use expressions of advice (e.g., *it's useful to, it's helpful to, you should*).
- Go around the room and check Ss' use of adjective + infinitive and noun + infinitive.

B Group work

- Read the questions and explain the task.
- Ss discuss the questions in small groups. Encourage them to add follow-up questions.

- Explain the task. In small groups, Ss suggest advice for each problem and choose the best advice. Model the example conversation with two Ss.
- Ss complete the task.

B Class activity

- Ask different Ss to share their group's advice.

WHAT'S NEXT?

Learning Objective: *become more involved in one's learning*

- Focus Ss' attention on the Self-assessment again. Ask: "How well can you do these things now?"

- Ask Ss to underline one thing they need to review. Ask: "What did you underline? How can you review it?"
- If needed, plan additional activities or reviews based on Ss' answers.

DISCUSSION *Medicines and remedies*

A GROUP WORK Write advice and remedies for these problems. Then discuss your ideas in groups.

a stomachache

an insect bite

a nosebleed

the hiccups

For a stomachache, it's a good idea to . . .

A: What can you do for a stomachache?
B: I think it's a good idea to buy a bottle of antacid.
C: Yes. And it's helpful to drink herbal tea.

B GROUP WORK What health problems do you visit a doctor for? go to a drugstore for? use a home remedy for? Ask for advice and remedies.

4

SPEAKING *Advice column*

A GROUP WORK Look at these problems from an advice column. Suggest advice for each problem. Then choose the best advice.

I'm visiting the United States. I'm staying with a family while I'm here. What small gifts can I get for them?

My co-worker always talks loudly to her friends – during work hours. I can't concentrate! What can I do?

Our school wants to buy some new gym equipment. Can you suggest some good ways to raise money?

A: Why doesn't she give them some flowers? They're always nice.
B: That's a good idea. Or she could bring chocolates.
C: I think she should . . .

B CLASS ACTIVITY Share your group's advice for each problem with the class.

WHAT'S NEXT?

Look at your Self-assessment again. Do you need to review anything?

Unit 13 Supplementary Resources Overview

	After the following SB exercises	You can use these materials in class	Your students can use these materials outside the classroom
CYCLE 1	1 Snapshot		**SSD** Unit 13 Vocabulary 1
	2 Conversation		**SSD** Unit 13 Speaking 1
	3 Grammar Focus		**SB** Unit 13 Grammar Plus focus 1 **SSD** Unit 13 Grammar 1 **ARC** *So, too, neither, either* and Describing food **ARC** *So, too, neither, either* 1–2
	4 Pronunciation	**TSS** Unit 13 Extra Worksheet	**WB** Unit 13 exercises 1–3
CYCLE 2	5 Word Power	**TSS** Unit 13 Vocabulary Worksheet	**SSD** Unit 13 Vocabulary 2
	6 Conversation		**SSD** Unit 13 Speaking 2
	7 Grammar Focus	**TSS** Unit 13 Grammar Worksheet	**SB** Unit 13 Grammar Plus focus 2 **SSD** Unit 13 Grammar 2 **ARC** Modal verbs *would* and *will* for requests
	8 Role Play		
	9 Listening	**TSS** Unit 13 Listening Worksheet	
	10 Interchange 13		
	11 Writing	**TSS** Unit 13 Writing Worksheet	
	12 Reading	**TSS** Unit 13 Project Worksheet **VID** Unit 13 **VRB** Unit 13	**SSD** Unit 13 Reading 1–2 **SSD** Unit 13 Listening 1–3 **SSD** Unit 13 Video 1–3 **WB** Unit 13 exercises 4–8

Key

ARC: Arcade	**SB:** Student's Book	**SSD:** Self-study DVD-ROM	**TSS:** Teacher Support Site
VID: Video DVD	**VRB:** Video Resource Book	**WB:** Workbook	

My Plan for Unit 13

Use the space below to customize a plan that fits your needs.

With the following SB exercises	I am using these materials in class	My students are using these materials outside the classroom

With or instead of the following SB section	I am using these materials for assessment

13 May I take your order?

1 **SNAPSHOT**

FOOD FIRSTS

NOODLES
first made in China
around 1000 B.C.E.

COFFEE
first farmed in the
Middle East in 850

CHOCOLATE
brought to Spain
from Mexico in 1520

FRENCH FRIES
first made in Belgium
around 1680

SUSHI
modern-style sushi first
made in Japan in the 1700s

THE SANDWICH
named for the English
Earl of Sandwich in 1760

PIZZA
first pizzeria in New York
City opened in 1895

THE HAMBURGER
invented in Connecticut,
USA, in 1900

Sources: *New York Public Library Book of Chronologies;* www.digitalsushi.net; www.belgianfries.com

What are these foods made of?
Put the foods in order from your favorite to your least favorite.
What are three other foods you enjoy?

2 **CONVERSATION** *Getting something to eat*

A ▶ Listen and practice.

Jeff: Say, do you want to get something to eat?
Bob: Sure. I'm tired of studying.
Jeff: So am I. So, what do you think of Indian food?
Bob: I love it, but I'm not really in the mood for it today.
Jeff: Yeah. I'm not either, I guess. It's a bit spicy.
Bob: Do you like Japanese food?
Jeff: Yeah, I like it a lot.
Bob: So do I. And I know a great restaurant near here –
it's called Iroha.
Jeff: Oh, I've always wanted to go there.

B ▶ Listen to the rest of the conversation. What time do
they decide to have dinner? Where do they decide to meet?

May I take your order?

Cycle 1, Exercises 1–4

In Unit 13, students talk about food. In Cycle 1, they agree and disagree about food preferences using *so, too, neither,* and *either.* In Cycle 2, they order food at a restaurant using the modal verbs *would* and *will.*

1 SNAPSHOT

Learning Objectives: *read about the origins of popular foods; talk about favorite foods*

- Books closed. Write these foods on the board:

noodles	sushi
coffee	the sandwich
chocolate	pizza
french fries	the hamburger

  Ask Ss to guess where each food item is from.

- Books open. Ss check their answers with the Snapshot.

- Ask different Ss to read the facts. Elicit or explain any new vocabulary.

Vocabulary

around: about that time
B.C.E: before the common era
farmed: grown
earl: a British man of high social rank

- Point out that the Earl of Sandwich's real name was John Montague, and he loved to play cards. He created the first sandwich so he could eat neatly during card games.

- Ask: "Does any information in the Snapshot surprise you?" Elicit Ss' answers.

- Explain the tasks. Then Ss complete the tasks in pairs. Go around the class and give help as needed.

2 CONVERSATION

Learning Objectives: *practice a conversation between two people deciding where to go for dinner; see* so, too, neither, *and* either *in context*

A ▶ [CD 3, Track 23]

- Books closed. Set the scene. Jeff and Bob are discussing where to go for dinner. Write these focus questions on the board:

  1. What two kinds of food do they talk about?
  2. What kind of food do they decide to eat?

- Play the audio program. Then elicit the answers. (Answers: 1. Indian and Japanese 2. Japanese)

- Books open. Play the audio program again. Ss listen and read silently.

- Elicit or explain any new vocabulary.

Vocabulary

I'm not in the mood for: I don't really want
a bit: a little
spicy: with a hot or strong flavor, like pepper or curry

- Ss practice the conversation in pairs. Then ask Ss to role-play the conversation for the class.

! For a new way to practice this Conversation, try *Say It with Feeling!* – download it from the website.

B ▶ [CD 3, Track 24]

- Explain the task and read the focus questions. Then play the audio program. Elicit the answers.

AudioScript

Jeff So, do you want to eat early or late?
Bob Let's eat early. Then maybe we can go to a movie afterward.
Jeff Good idea! Why don't we have dinner around 6:00?
Bob Six is good. And where do you want to meet?
Jeff Let's meet at the restaurant, OK?
Bob Yeah, that's fine with me.

Answers

They decide to have dinner around 6:00. They decide to meet at the restaurant.

3 GRAMMAR FOCUS

Learning Objective: *practice agreeing and disagreeing using* so, too, neither, *and* either

⊙ *[CD 3, Track 25]*

- Focus Ss' attention on the Grammar Focus box. Ask: "Which column has positive statements? Which column has negative statements?" (Answers: The first column has positive statements, and the second column has negative statements.)

So *and* too

- Focus Ss' attention on the first column. Point out that we can use *so* or *too* to agree with a positive statement.
- Write these responses on the board:

   So do I.   So am I.   So can I.

   Ask: "When do we use each response?" Elicit or explain the rule. (Answer: The verb in each response matches that of the sentence before it.)

- Focus Ss' attention on the difference between *so* and *too*. Point out that *so* is at the beginning of the response and *too* is at the end:

   ***So** + do/am/can + I.*

   *I + do/am/can + **too**.*

- Ask Ss to find responses in the first column that disagree with positive statements. (Answers: *Really? I don't like it very much./Oh, I'm not./Really? I can't.*)
- Play the audio program for the first column.
- **Option:** Drill *So do I, So am I,* or *So can I* responses. Read a list of ten positive statements to the class (e.g., *I live near here. I am smart. I can speak English.*). Ss respond chorally and then individually.

Neither *and* either

- Focus Ss' attention on the second column of the Grammar Focus box. Elicit the rules for agreeing with a negative statement:

   ***Neither** + do/am/can + I.*

   *I **don't**/I'm **not**/I **can't** either.*

- Point out different ways to disagree with negative statements (e.g., *Oh, I like it a lot. /Really? I am.*).
- Play the audio program for the second column.
- **Option:** Drill *Neither do I, Neither am I,* or *Neither can I* responses. Read a list of ten negative statements to the class (e.g., *I don't like fish ice cream. I'm not hungry. I can't cook French food.*). Ss respond chorally and then individually.

A

- Ask different Ss to read the adjectives describing food. Help with pronunciation as needed.
- Explain the task. Ss write responses to show agreement with the statements. Point out that each statement has two correct responses.
- Read the first two statements and elicit Ss' responses. Write correct responses on the board.
- Ss complete the task individually. Then they compare answers in pairs. Go over answers with the class.

Possible answers

1. Neither am I./I'm not either.
2. So can I./I can, too.
3. So do I./I do, too.
4. Neither can I./I can't either.
5. Neither do I./I don't either.
6. So am I./I am, too.
7. So am I./I am, too.
8. Neither do I./I don't, either.
9. So do I./I do, too.
10. Neither can I./I can't either.

B *Pair work*

- Explain the task. Ss work in pairs. They take turns reading the statements in part A and responding with their own opinions.
- Go around the class and check Ss' use of grammar.
- For more practice, play **Concentration** – download it from the website. Ss match cards with the same meaning (e.g., *So do I.* and *I do, too.*).

C

- Elicit different ways to say *I like* and *I don't like*. Write them on the board:

I like	I don't like
I really like	I don't really like
I'm in the mood for	I'm not in the mood for
I like . . . very much	I don't like . . . very much
I'm crazy about	I'm not crazy about
I love	I hate

- Explain the task. Model the first example by writing two sentences on the board.
- Ss complete the task individually. Don't ask Ss to compare statements at this time. They will do this in Exercise 4.

3 GRAMMAR FOCUS

So, too, neither, either ▶

I like Japanese food a lot.
   So do I./I do, **too**.
   Really? I don't like it very much.

I'm crazy about Italian food.
   So am I./I am, **too**.
   Oh, I'm not.

I can eat really spicy food.
   So can I./I can, **too**.
   Really? I can't.

I don't like salty food.
   Neither do I./I don't **either**.
   Oh, I like it a lot.

I'm not in the mood for Indian food.
   Neither am I./I'm not **either**.
   Really? I am.

I can't stand fast food.
   Neither can I./I can't **either**.
   Oh, I love it!

healthy

salty

spicy

bland

greasy

rich

delicious

A Write responses to show agreement with these statements.
Then compare with a partner.

1. I'm not crazy about French food. ....
2. I can eat any kind of food. ....
3. I think Mexican food is delicious. ....
4. I can't stand greasy food. ....
5. I don't like salty food. ....
6. I'm in the mood for something spicy. ....
7. I'm tired of fast food. ....
8. I don't enjoy rich food very much ....
9. I always eat healthy food. ....
10. I can't eat bland food. ....

B **PAIR WORK** Take turns responding to the statements in part A again.
Give your own opinion when responding.

C Write statements about these things. (You will use the statements in Exercise 4.)

1. two kinds of food you like
2. two kinds of food you can't stand
3. two kinds of food you are in the mood for

4 PRONUNCIATION *Stress in responses*

A ⊙ Listen and practice. Notice how the last word of each response is stressed.

I do, too.	So do I.	I don't either.	Neither do I.
I am, too.	So am I.	I'm not either.	Neither am I.
I can, too.	So can I.	I can't either.	Neither can I.

B **PAIR WORK** Read and respond to the statements you wrote in Exercise 3, part C. Pay attention to the stress in your responses.

5 WORD POWER *Food categories*

A Complete the chart. Then add one more word to each category.

bread	fish	mangoes	peas	shrimp
chicken	grapes	octopus	potatoes	strawberries
corn	lamb	pasta	rice	turkey

Meat	Seafood	Fruit	Vegetables	Grains
....	....	....	....	....
....	....	....	....	....
....	....	....	....	....
....	....	....	....	....

B **GROUP WORK** What's your favorite food in each category? Are there any you haven't tried?

6 CONVERSATION *Ordering a meal*

A ⊙ Listen and practice.

Server: May I take your order?
Customer: Yes. I'd like the spicy fish and rice.
Server: All right. And would you like a salad?
Customer: Yes, I'll have a mixed green salad.
Server: OK. What kind of dressing would you like? We have blue cheese and vinaigrette.
Customer: Blue cheese, please.
Server: And would you like anything to drink?
Customer: Yes, I'd like a large iced tea, please.

B ⊙ Listen to the server talk to the next customer. What does she order?

4 PRONUNCIATION

Learning Objectives: *notice stress in responses; learn to sound natural when responding with* so, too, either, *and* neither

A ▶ [CD 3, Track 26]

- Explain the task. Then play the audio program. Point out the stress by clapping your hands on the last word of each response.
- Play the audio program again. Ss listen and practice.

Cycle 2, Exercises 5–12

5 WORD POWER

Learning Objective: *learn vocabulary for discussing food categories*

A

- Explain the task. Explain what the different food categories are and any new vocabulary.
- Ss complete the chart individually.
- Draw the chart on the board. Ask different Ss to complete the chart.

6 CONVERSATION

Learning Objectives: *practice a conversation between a server and a customer; see modal verbs* would *and* will *for requests in context*

A ▶ [CD 3, Track 27]

- Ss cover the text. Elicit ideas and vocabulary from the picture. Ask: "What kind of restaurant is this? What kinds of food do they serve?"
- Set the scene. A server is taking a customer's order. Write this summary sentence on the board:

  The customer orders spicy fish/spicy chicken and rice, a salad with blue cheese/vinaigrette dressing, and an iced coffee/tea

- Play the audio program. Ss listen for the correct answers. Ask different Ss to circle the correct answers on the board. (Answers: spicy fish, blue cheese, tea)
- Ss uncover the text. Play the audio program again. Ss listen and read silently.
- Ss practice the conversation in pairs.

B *Pair work*

- Explain the task. Then Ss complete the task in pairs. Go around the class and check Ss' pronunciation.

End of Cycle 1

See the Supplementary Resources chart at the beginning of this unit for additional teaching materials and student activities related to this Cycle.

Answers

Meat	Seafood	Fruit	Vegetables	Grains
chicken	fish	grapes	corn	bread
lamb	octopus	mangoes	peas	pasta
turkey	shrimp	strawberries	potatoes	rice
beef	*salmon*	*apples*	*broccoli*	*cereal*
hot dog	*ceviche*	*bananas*	*spinach*	*muffin*

(Note: Possible answers are italicized.)

B *Group work*

- Ss discuss the questions in small groups.

B ▶ [CD 3, Track 28]

- Explain the task and read the focus question. Then play the audio program. Elicit the answer.

AudioScript

Server Are you ready to order?
Woman Yes, I think so. I'd like a cheeseburger, please.
Server Would you like today's special, a cheeseburger and fries?
Woman Uh, no fries for me. But I'll take a small potato salad.
Server OK. Anything to drink?
Woman Yeah. I'll have a large iced coffee, please.
Server And how about some dessert? We have pie, cake, and ice cream.
Woman No, thanks. I'm trying to watch my weight.

Answers

a cheeseburger, a small potato salad, and a large iced coffee

7 GRAMMAR FOCUS

Learning Objective: *practice conversations using modal verbs* would *and* will *for requests*

 [CD 3, Track 29]

Modal verbs would ***and*** will

- Write these sentences on the board:
  1. What kind of dressing *do you* <u>want</u>?
  2. And do you <u>want</u> anything to drink?
  3. I <u>want</u> a mixed green salad.
  4. I <u>want</u> a large iced tea, please

  Explain that people don't usually say *want* in formal situations.

- Focus Ss' attention on the Conversation on page 88. Ss find and underline sentences and questions with the same meaning as those on the board. Ask different Ss to write them on the board. (Answers: 1. What kind of dressing would you like? 2. And would you like anything to drink? 3. I'll have a mixed green salad. 4. I'd like a large iced tea, please.)

- Focus Ss' attention on the Grammar Focus box. Elicit the structure for making Wh- and yes/no questions with *would*:

  Wh-question + *would* + subject + verb?

  Would + subject + verb?

  Point out that the word *would* does not have strong stress.

- Elicit or explain that we can order in a restaurant with *I'd like* or *I'll have*. Point out the contractions. Play the audio program.

- Explain the task and model the first two lines of the conversation. Ss complete the conversation individually. Then they compare answers in pairs.
- Go over answers by asking different Ss to read the conversation.

Answers

Server: What **would** you like to order?
Customer: I**'ll** have the spicy chicken.
Server: **Would** you like rice or potatoes?
Customer: I**'d** like rice, please.
Server: OK. And **would** you like anything to drink?
Customer: I**'ll** just have a glass of water.
Server: Would you **like** anything else?
Customer: No, that**'ll** be all for now, thanks.
(*Later*)
Server: Would you **like** dessert?
Customer: Yes, I**'d** like ice cream.
Server: What flavor **would** you like?
Customer: Hmm. I**'ll** have strawberry, please.

! For a new way to practice the conversations in this
• Grammar Focus, try the ***Substitution Dialog*** – download it from the website. Ss replace the food and drink items with their own ideas.

 **8 ROLE PLAY**

Learning Objective: *role-play a conversation between a customer and a server in a coffee shop*

- Ss work in pairs. Set the scene and explain the task. Student A is a customer in a coffee shop. Student B is a server. Student A orders lunch and Student B takes the order. If possible, Student A sits at a table and Student B stands. Model the pronunciation of the things if needed.

- Model taking the order with a S. Show how to add follow-up questions (e.g., *Would you like dressing on your salad? Would you like anything else?*). Ss complete the role play in pairs.

- Provide useful feedback. Then ask Ss to change roles and use their own information. Go around the class and encourage Ss to ask follow-up questions.

- **Option:** Ss complete the role play in small groups. One S is the server and the other Ss are customers.

> **TIP** To make role plays more authentic, bring props to class. For example, in a restaurant role play you can bring real menus, pens, and notepads.

! For a new way to practice this Role Play, try
• ***Time Out!*** – download it from the website.

7 GRAMMAR FOCUS

Modal verbs would and will for requests ▶

What **would** you **like**?	I**'d like** the fish and rice.	**Contractions**
	I**'ll have** a small salad.	I**'ll** = I will
What kind of dressing **would** you **like**?	I**'d like** blue cheese, please.	
	I**'ll have** vinaigrette.	I**'d** = I would
What **would** you **like** to drink?	I**'d like** an iced tea.	
	I**'ll have** coffee.	
Would you **like** anything else?	Yes, please. I**'d like** some water.	
	No, thank you. That**'ll be** all.	

Complete this conversation. Then practice with a partner.

Server: What .... you like to order?
Customer: I .... have the spicy chicken.
Server: .... you like rice or potatoes?
Customer: I .... like rice, please.
Server: OK. And .... you like anything to drink?
Customer: I .... just have a glass of water.
Server: Would you .... anything else?
Customer: No, that .... be all for now, thanks.

Later

Server: Would you .... dessert?
Customer: Yes, I .... like ice cream.
Server: What flavor .... you like?
Customer: Hmm. I .... have strawberry, please.

8 ROLE PLAY *In a coffee shop*

Student A: You are a customer in a coffee shop. Order what you want for lunch.
Student B: You are the server. Take your customer's order.

Today's Lunch Specials

Spicy beef and potatoes   Vegetable curry and rice
Lamb with french fries   Chicken salad sandwich
Shrimp pizza and salad   Sushi plate with miso soup

DRINKS
Coffee   Tea   Soda   Milk   Fresh juice

DESSERTS
Ice cream   Chocolate cake   Apple pie   Fresh fruit

Change roles and try the role play again.

9 LISTENING Let's order.

A ▶ Listen to Rex and Hannah order in a restaurant.
What did each of them order? Fill in their check.

Phil's DINER   No. 399825

....

....

....

....

....

....

Thank You!   **TOTAL** _____

B ▶ Listen to the rest of the conversation. Circle the two items that the server forgot to bring.

10 INTERCHANGE 13 Plan a menu

Create a menu of dishes to offer at your very own restaurant. Go to Interchange 13 on page 128.

11 WRITING A restaurant review

A Have you eaten out recently? Write a restaurant review.
Answer these questions and add ideas of your own.

What's the name of the restaurant?
When did you go there?
What did you have?
What did/didn't you like about it?
Would you recommend it? Why or why not?

Overview   Review   Menu   Photos   Search

Luigi's ★★★★☆

Last week, I had lunch at Luigi's, a new Italian restaurant in my neighborhood.
I had a green salad and a cheese pizza. For dessert, I had chocolate cake.
The pizza was excellent, but the salad wasn't very good. The lettuce wasn't
very fresh. The cake was rich and delicious. I would recommend this restaurant
because the pizza is great and not very expensive.

B **GROUP WORK** Take turns reading your reviews.
Which restaurant would you like to try?

9 LISTENING

Learning Objective: *develop skills in listening for details*

A ▶ [CD 3, Track 30]

- Set the scene and explain the task. Point out the picture and ask "What foods and drinks do you see?"
- Play the audio program. Ss fill in the check individually.
- Ss compare answers in pairs. Play the audio program again if needed. Then go over answers with the class.

For a new way to practice this Listening, try *Prediction Bingo* – download it from the website.

AudioScript

Server Hi. May I take your order?
Rex Yes. I'll have a cup of coffee.
Server Cream and sugar?
Rex Oh, yes, please.
Server And you?
Hannah I'd like a chicken sandwich. And I'll have some chips . . . oh, you call them french fries here. Right. I'll have some french fries, please.
Server All right. One coffee with cream and sugar, and a chicken sandwich with french fries. Uh, anything else?
Hannah Yes, I'd like an iced tea, please.
Server One iced tea. Thank you.
Rex Oh, wait a minute! What kind of desserts do you have?
Server Well, we have pie, cake, ice cream, chocolate mousse . . .
Rex Oooo! What kind of pie do you have?
Server I think today we have apple, cherry, lemon . . .
Rex Hmm, I think I'll have a piece of apple pie with my coffee. How about you, Hannah?
Hannah Oh, maybe I'll have a piece later . . . or . . . I'll have some of yours! [*laughs*]
Server Then it's one coffee, one apple pie, one chicken sandwich, an order of french fries, and an iced tea. Right?
Rex Yes, thank you.
Hannah Thanks.

Answers

Rex's order: coffee with cream and sugar, a piece of apple pie
Hannah's order: a chicken sandwich, french fries, iced tea

B ▶ [CD 3, Track 31]

- Ask: "Has a server ever made a mistake with your order? What happened?" Elicit Ss' answers.
- Play the audio program. Ss complete the task individually. Then go over answers with the class.

AudioScript

Hannah Oh, here comes our server!
Rex Yeah, I wondered what took so long.
Server Whew! Here you are!
Hannah Uh, I ordered french fries with my chicken sandwich, and you brought me . . . noodles?
Server Oh, you ordered french fries?
Hannah Yes.
Rex Uh, and could I have the apple pie I ordered?
Server What apple pie? Did you order apple pie?
Rex Uh-huh, yeah, I did, with my coffee.
Server Really? Gee, how did I forget that?
Hannah Uh, can I ask you a question?
Server Yes?
Hannah How long have you been a server?
Server Who, me? Oh, uh, today is my first day. [*all laugh*] Well, I'll get your apple pie and the french fries right away. Sorry about that.
Rex Oh, that's OK.
Hannah Yeah, thanks. Good luck.
Server Thanks.

Answers

He forgot to bring the french fries and apple pie.

10 INTERCHANGE 13

See page T-120 for teaching notes.

11 WRITING

Learning Objective: *write a restaurant review*

A

- Explain the task and read the questions. Ss read the example review silently. Ss then discuss the questions in pairs.
- Ss complete the task individually in class or for homework.

For a new way to teach this Writing, try *Mind Mapping* – download it from the website.

B Group work

- Explain the task. Ss read their reviews in small groups. Then they choose a restaurant they would like to try.
- **Option:** Put the reviews on the walls around the class. Ss read them and choose one they would like to try.

12 READING

Learning Objectives: *read and discuss an article about tipping in the United States; develop skills in scanning and guessing meaning from context*

- Focus Ss' attention on the picture. Ask: "Who are the people on the left? What do they want? Elicit Ss' answers and explain new vocabulary. (Answers: They are a chef, parking valet, maid, barber/hair stylist, taxi driver, server, and bellhop/hotel assistant. They all want a tip.)

- Explain that this article is about tipping in the U.S. Ss read the first paragraph silently. Ask: "Where do Americans usually give tips?" (Answers: in restaurants, airports, hotels, and hair salons)

- Explain the task and read the pre-reading questions. Ss scan the article for the answers.

- Go over answers with the class. Ask: "What helped you find the answers?" (Answer: The jobs are in boldface.)

Answers

Someone who carried your suitcase: $1 or $2
    for each suitcase
Someone who parks your car: $2
Someone who serves you in a fast food
    restaurant: nothing

- **Option:** Ask Ss if they think each tip is reasonable, too little, or too much.

! For a new way to teach this Reading, try
- *Running Dictation* – download it from the website. Use the first paragraph only.

A

- Explain the task. Encourage Ss to guess the answers by choosing the meaning of each word that best fits the sentence in the article.

- Ss complete the task individually. Then they compare answers in pairs.

- Go over answers with the class. Elicit or explain any new vocabulary.

Vocabulary

slang: informal spoken language
service: help that someone gives a customer
size: amount
parking valets: restaurant or hotel employees who park your car for you
bellhops: hotel employees who carry your bags for you
guidelines: general rules about how to do something
porters: people who carry your bags for you at an airport or railway station
service providers: people in the service industry

Answers

1. regular pay for a job
2. happy or satisfied
3. change according to
4. a way of acting
5. act toward
6. courtesy

B

- Explain the task. Point out that Ss must do some math to complete the task. Ss complete the task individually and compare answers in pairs.

- Ask different Ss to write the answers on the board. Then ask the class to correct the answers if needed.

Answers

1. at least $6
2. ✓
3. ✓
4. at least $14
5. at least $3.10

C *Group work*

- Ss discuss the questions in small groups. Then they share their information with the class.

End of Cycle 2

See the Supplementary Resources chart at the beginning of this unit for additional teaching materials and student activities related to this Cycle.

To Tip or Not to Tip?

Scan the article. How much should you tip someone in the United States who: carries your suitcase at a hotel? parks your car? serves you in a fast-food restaurant?

The word *tip* comes from an old English slang word that means "to give." It's both a noun and a verb. People in the U.S. usually tip people in places like restaurants, airports, hotels, and hair salons. People who work in these places often get paid low wages. A tip shows that the customer is pleased with the service.

Sometimes it's hard to know how much to tip. The size of the tip usually depends on the service. People such as parking valets or bellhops usually get smaller tips. The tip for people such as taxi drivers and servers is usually larger. Here are a few guidelines for tipping in the United States:

Taxi drivers: 15 percent of the bill; more if they help you with bags
Servers: 15 to 20 percent of the bill (There is no tipping in fast-food restaurants.)
Barbers or hairstylists: 15 percent of the bill
Airport porters or hotel bellhops: $1 or $2 for carrying each suitcase
Hotel door attendants: $1 or $2 for getting a taxi
Parking valets: $2 for parking a car
Hotel maids: $2 to $5 per night

When you're not sure about how much to tip, do what feels right. You don't have to tip for bad service. And you can give a bigger tip for very good service. Remember, though, your behavior is more important than your money. Always treat service providers with respect.

A Read the article. Find the words in italics in the article. Then check (✓) the meaning of each word.

1. *wages*
   - ☐ regular pay for a job
   - ☐ tips received for a job

2. *pleased*
   - ☐ happy or satisfied
   - ☐ annoyed or bothered

3. *depend on*
   - ☐ be the same as
   - ☐ change according to

4. *behavior*
   - ☐ a way of acting
   - ☐ a way of feeling

5. *treat*
   - ☐ ignore
   - ☐ act toward

6. *respect*
   - ☐ courtesy
   - ☐ rudeness

B Check (✓) the statements that describe appropriate tipping behavior. For the other items, what is acceptable?

- ☐ 1. Your haircut costs $40. You love it. You tip the stylist $3.
- ☐ 2. A porter at the airport helps you with three suitcases. You tip him $6.
- ☐ 3. Your fast-food meal costs $8. You don't leave a tip.
- ☐ 4. You stay in a hotel for a week. You leave a $10 tip for the hotel maid.
- ☐ 5. Your taxi ride costs $14. The driver carries your bag. You tip him $3.

C **GROUP WORK** Is tipping customary in your country? Do you like the idea of tipping? Why or why not?

Unit 14 Supplementary Resources Overview

	After the following SB exercises	You can use these materials in class	Your students can use these materials outside the classroom
CYCLE 1	1 Word Power		**SSD** Unit 14 Vocabulary 1–2
	2 Conversation		**SSD** Unit 14 Speaking 1
	3 Grammar Focus	**TSS** Unit 14 Vocabulary Worksheet	**SB** Unit 14 Grammar Plus focus 1 **SSD** Unit 14 Grammar 1 **ARC** Geography **ARC** Comparisons with adjectives 1–3
	4 Pronunciation	**TSS** Unit 14 Grammar Worksheet	
	5 Speaking		
	6 Listening		
	7 Interchange 14		**WB** Unit 14 exercises 1–5
CYCLE 2	8 Snapshot		
	9 Conversation		**SSD** Unit 14 Speaking 2
	10 Grammar Focus	**TSS** Unit 14 Extra Worksheet **TSS** Unit 14 Listening Worksheet	**SB** Unit 14 Grammar Plus focus 2 **SSD** Unit 14 Grammar 2–3 **ARC** Questions with *how*
	11 Writing	**TSS** Unit 14 Writing Worksheet	
	12 Reading	**TSS** Unit 14 Project Worksheet **VID** Unit 14 **VRB** Unit 14	**SSD** Unit 14 Reading 1–2 **SSD** Unit 14 Listening 1–2 **SSD** Unit 14 Video 1–3 **WB** Unit 14 exercises 6–8

With or instead of the following SB section	You can also use these materials for assessment
Units 13–14 Progress Check	**ASSESSMENT CD** Units 13–14 Oral Quiz **ASSESSMENT CD** Units 13–14 Written Quiz

Key **ARC:** Arcade   **SB:** Student's Book   **SSD:** Self-study DVD-ROM   **TSS:** Teacher Support Site
VID: Video DVD   **VRB:** Video Resource Book   **WB:** Workbook

My Plan for Unit 14

Use the space below to customize a plan that fits your needs.

With the following SB exercises	I am using these materials in class	My students are using these materials outside the classroom

With or instead of the following SB section	I am using these materials for assessment

14 The biggest and the best!

1 WORD POWER *Geography*

A Label the picture with words from the list. Then compare with a partner.

a. beach
b. desert
c. forest
d. hill
e. island
f. lake
g. mountain
h. ocean
i. river
j. valley
k. volcano
l. waterfall

B **PAIR WORK** What other geography words can you think of? Do you see any of them in the picture above?

C **GROUP WORK** Try to think of famous examples for each item in part A.

A: A famous beach is Waikiki in Hawaii.
B: And the Sahara is a famous . . .

The biggest and the best!

> In Unit 14, students talk about world geography. In Cycle 1, they talk about geography using the comparative and superlative forms of adjectives. In Cycle 2, they discuss distances, measurements, and places using questions with how.

 WORD POWER

Learning Objective: *learn vocabulary for discussing geography*

A

- **Option:** Bring in a world map, globe, or atlas to class.
- Explain that this unit is about world geography.
- Explain the task. Ss label the picture with words from the list. Go around the class and give help as needed.
- Ss compare their pictures in pairs. Elicit or explain any new vocabulary or pronunciation.

Answers

(from left to right)
k, c, e, f, b, a, j, g, l, i, h, d

B *Pair work*

- Ss brainstorm to see how many words they can think of that relate to geography. Ask different Ss to write their words on the board under these headings:

  Water-related words   Land-related words
  Climate-related words   Other
- Go over the words and ask Ss to copy them into their vocabulary notebooks.

Possible answers

Water-related: sea, stream, coast, pond, coral reef
Land-related: continent, plateau, canyon, rain forest
Climate-related: weather, storm, rain, snow, cloud, fog
Other: country, city, town, village

> **TIP** Create a Vocabulary Box. As a new word is taught, a S writes the word on a slip of paper and puts it in the box. Review words as a warm-up activity in future classes, or use them in games.

- **Option:** Review vocabulary with **Odd Man Out**. List geography words, and ask Ss to find which word is different from the others (e.g., *hill, mountain, volcano, ocean*; ocean is the only water-related word).

C *Group work*

- Explain the task. Read the example conversation. Point out that the words *Mount* and *Lake* come before the name (e.g., **Mount** Fuji, **Lake** Victoria). The other terms come after the name (e.g. Waikiki **Beach**, the Nile **River**, the Sahara **Desert**).
- Ss work in small groups to think of other examples. Ask groups to share their examples with the class.
- Point out that seas, rivers, and mountain ranges (but not most lakes) use the definite article (e.g., *the Black Sea, the Rhine River, the Himalayas*), but bring this up only if Ss ask you.

Possible answers

beach – Waikiki, Copacabana, Bondi
desert – Sahara, Atacama, Gobi
forest – Black Forest, Sherwood Forest
hill – Capitol Hill, Bunker Hill, Beverly Hills
island – Puerto Rico, Java, Hokkaido
lake – Titicaca, Superior, Baikal
mountain – Aconcagua, Everest, Kilimanjaro
ocean – Atlantic, Indian, Arctic
river – Amazon, Rhine, Mekong
valley – Silicon, Loire, Death
volcano – Cotopaxi, Etna, Pinatubo
waterfall – Angel Falls, Iguaçú Falls, Niagara Falls

❗ For a new way to practice this vocabulary, try ● *Picture Dictation* – download it from the website. Describe a scene similar to the one in the picture.

2 CONVERSATION

Learning Objectives: *practice a conversation about geography; see comparisons with adjectives in context*

A [CD 3, Track 32]

- Set the scene. Mike is asking Wendy some questions from a geography quiz. Point out that Wendy gets some answers wrong.
- Play the audio program. Ss listen to Wendy's answers and underline them in the conversation.
- Ask: "How many questions do you think Wendy got right? One? Two? Three? All four?"

B [CD 3, Track 33]

- Play the audio program. Ss listen for the correct answers.
- Ask: "How many answers did Wendy get right?" (Answer: two)

AudioScript

Mike So let's see how you did on this quiz. The first question: Which is larger, China or Canada? You said . . .
Wendy Canada.
Mike And you're right! Both are large, but Canada is larger. Next: What's the longest river in the Americas? You said the Mississippi. Sorry, no. It's the Amazon.
Wendy Oh, of course.
Mike This next question I didn't know. Monaco is more crowded than Singapore.
Wendy So I got it right? I just guessed.
Mike And finally, you said that Bogotá is the highest capital city in South America.
Wendy Yeah, I remember hearing that somewhere.
Mike Sorry, Wendy, but you're wrong. La Paz in Bolivia is the highest.
Wendy Really? Gee, I guess I didn't do so well – two right but two wrong!

Answers

Canada, Amazon, Monaco, La Paz

3 GRAMMAR FOCUS

Learning Objective: *ask and answer questions using comparisons with adjectives*

 [CD 3, Track 34]

Comparative and superlative forms of adjectives

- Focus Ss' attention on the Conversation in Exercise 2. Ask Ss to identify the first two questions that compare things. (Answers: Which country is larger, China or Canada? What's the longest river in the Americas?)
- Ask Ss to make sentences comparing two things in their country (e.g., *mountains, rivers, cities*). If necessary, review comparative adjectives using Exercise 10 in Unit 3.
- Draw a chart on the board, like this:

- Explain the reasons for the numbers 1, 2, 3+ (e.g., *3+ is used when we are comparing three or more things*).
- Elicit or explain the rules for forming the superlative:
  1. use the definite article (e.g., *the largest country*)
  2. when the adjective has only one syllable or two syllables ending in *y*, use: *the* + adjective + *-est* + noun (e.g., *the longest river, the prettiest lake*)
  3. when the adjective has two or more syllables, use: *the most* + adjective + noun (e.g., *the most crowded country*)

- Refer Ss to the appendix on page T–164 for spelling rules. Go over with the class.
- Give Ss a list of adjectives. Ss write comparative and superlative forms in the circles on the board.
- Point to the examples in the Grammar Focus box. Play the audio program.

A

- Go over the task. Ss complete the sentences individually. Then they ask and answer the questions in pairs.
- Elicit the Ss' answers.

Answers

1. Which country is **smaller**, Monaco or <u>Vatican City</u>?
2. Which waterfall is **higher**, Niagara Falls or <u>Victoria Falls</u>?
3. Which city is **more crowded**, <u>Hong Kong</u> or Cairo?
4. Which lake is **larger**, the <u>Caspian Sea</u> or Lake Superior?
5. Which is **the highest**: Mount Aconcagua, <u>Mount Everest</u>, or Mount Fuji?
6. What is **the longest** river in the world, the Mekong, <u>the Nile</u>, or the Amazon?
7. Which city is **the most expensive**: London, <u>Tokyo</u>, or Moscow?
8. What is **the deepest** ocean in the world, <u>the Pacific</u>, the Atlantic, or the Arctic?

(Note: Answers to questions are <u>underlined</u>.)

B *Class activity*

- Explain the task. Ss write four questions and take turns asking them around the class.

T-93 ▪ *Unit 14*

2 CONVERSATION *Which is larger?*

A ⊙ Listen and practice.

Mike: Here's an interesting geography quiz.
Wendy: Oh, I love geography. Ask me the questions.
Mike: Sure, first question. Which country is larger, China or Canada?
Wendy: I know. Canada is larger than China.
Mike: OK, next. What's the longest river in the Americas?
Wendy: Hmm, I think it's the Mississippi.
Mike: Here's a hard one. Which country is more crowded, Monaco or Singapore?
Wendy: I'm not sure. I think Monaco is more crowded.
Mike: OK, one more. Which South American capital city is the highest: La Paz, Quito, or Bogotá?
Wendy: Oh, that's easy. Bogotá is the highest.

B ⊙ Listen to the rest of the conversation. How many questions did Wendy get right?

3 GRAMMAR FOCUS

Comparisons with adjectives ⊙

Which country is **larger**, Canada or China?
 Canada is **larger than** China.

Which city has **the largest** population:
Tokyo, Mexico City, or São Paulo?
 Tokyo has **the largest** population of the three.

What is **the most beautiful** mountain in the world?
 I think Mount Fuji is **the most beautiful**.

Adjective	Comparative	Superlative
long	longer	the longest
dry	drier	the driest
big	bigger	the biggest
famous	more famous	the most famous
beautiful	more beautiful	the most beautiful
good	better	the best
bad	worse	the worst

A Complete questions 1 to 4 with comparatives and questions 5 to 8 with superlatives. Then ask and answer the questions.

1. Which country is ...., Monaco or Vatican City? (small)
2. Which waterfall is ...., Niagara Falls or Victoria Falls? (high)
3. Which city is ...., Hong Kong or Cairo? (crowded)
4. Which lake is ...., the Caspian Sea or Lake Superior? (large)
5. Which is ....: Mount Aconcagua, Mount Everest, or Mount Fuji? (high)
6. What is .... river in the world, the Mekong, the Nile, or the Amazon? (long)
7. Which city is ....: London, Tokyo, or Moscow? (expensive)
8. What is .... ocean in the world, the Pacific, the Atlantic, or the Arctic? (deep)

B CLASS ACTIVITY Write four questions like those in part A about your country or other countries. Then ask your questions around the class.

4 PRONUNCIATION *Questions of choice*

A ▶ Listen and practice. Notice how the intonation in questions of choice drops, then rises, and then drops.

Which city is more crowded, Hong Kong or Cairo?

Which city is the most expensive: London, Tokyo, or Moscow?

B **PAIR WORK** Take turns asking these questions. Pay attention to your intonation. Can you guess the answers?

Which desert is bigger, the Gobi or the Sahara?
Which city is higher, Denver or New Orleans?
Which ocean is the smallest: the Arctic, the Indian, or the Atlantic?
Which mountains are the highest: the Alps, the Rockies, or the Himalayas?

5 SPEAKING *Our recommendations*

GROUP WORK Imagine these people are planning to visit your country. What would they enjoy doing? Agree on a recommendation for each person.

Molly

"I really like quiet places where I can relax, hike, and enjoy the views. I can't stand big crowds."

Rod

"I love to eat in nice restaurants, go dancing, and stay out late at night. I don't like small towns."

Teresa

"My favorite activity is shopping. I love to buy gifts to take home. I don't like modern shopping malls."

A: Molly should go to . . . because it has the best views in the country, and it's very quiet.
B: Or what about . . . ? I think the views there are more beautiful.
C: She also likes to hike, so . . .

6 LISTENING *Game show*

▶ Listen to three people on a TV game show. Check (✓) the correct answers.

1. ☐ the Statue of Liberty
   ☐ the Eiffel Tower
   ☐ the Panama Canal

2. ☐ Niagara Falls
   ☐ Angel Falls
   ☐ Victoria Falls

3. ☐ gold
   ☐ butter
   ☐ feathers

4. ☐ the U.S.
   ☐ China
   ☐ Canada

5. ☐ India
   ☐ Russia
   ☐ China

6. ☐ Australia
   ☐ Argentina
   ☐ Brazil

4 PRONUNCIATION

Learning Objective: *learn to sound natural when asking questions of choice*

A [CD 3, Track 35]

- Point out that intonation changes in questions of choice. Play the audio program.

- **Option:** Model the intonation by humming. Ss repeat.
- Play the audio program again. Ss listen and practice.

B *Pair work*

- Explain the task. Then Ss complete the task in pairs. Go around the class and check Ss' pronunciation.

5 SPEAKING

Learning Objective: *give visitors recommendations using comparisons with adjectives*

Group work

- Set the scene. Ss imagine that three people are planning to visit their country.
- Ask a S to read Molly's statement. Elicit recommendations from the class. Ask: "Where do you

think Molly should go? What should she do?"

- Model the example conversation with two Ss.

> **TIP** Discussions are difficult for many Ss. Allow Ss time to plan what they are going to say.

- Ss from the same countries should work in groups if possible. Ss discuss where the visitors should go and why. Go around the class and give help as needed.

6 LISTENING

Learning Objective: *develop skills in listening for details*

 [CD 3, Track 36]

- Set the scene. Explain that Ss are going to hear three people on a TV game show.
- Write these focus questions on the board:
  1. Which is the _____ ?
  2. What is the _____ building in the world?
  3. Which is the _____ ?
  4. Which country is the _____ ?
  5. Which country has the _____ population?
  6. Which is the _____ ?

- Play the audio program. Ss listen for the game show questions and fill in the blanks. (Answers: oldest, tallest, heaviest, largest, largest, smallest)
- Play the audio program again. Ss check their answers.

AudioScript

Hostess [music and applause] Our contestants this evening are Jack, Susan, and Jonathan. And now, contestants, let's get right to our first question. Question number one: Which is the oldest: the Statue of Liberty, the Eiffel Tower, or the Panama Canal? [buzzer] Jack?

Jack The Statue of Liberty is the oldest. They built it in 1886. They didn't build the Eiffel Tower until 1889, and the Panama Canal until 1914.

Hostess That's correct! [applause] Question number two: What is the tallest waterfall in the world? Is it Niagara Falls, Angel Falls, or Victoria Falls? [buzzer] Susan.

Susan Angel Falls is the highest. It's over 1,000 meters high.

Hostess That's right! [applause] Question number three: Which is the heaviest: a pound of gold, a pound of butter, or a pound of feathers? [buzzer] Jonathan.

Jonathan They all weigh the same.

Hostess Yes! [applause] Question number four: Which country is the largest: the U.S., China, or Canada? Nobody knows? Does anybody want to guess? [buzzer] Jack.

Jack Uh . . . China is the largest. [audience laughs]

Hostess No, sorry!

Jack Oh, shoot!

Hostess [buzzer] Jonathan.

Jonathan Canada is the largest.

Hostess Correct! [applause] Question number five: Which country has the largest population: India, Russia, or China? [buzzer] Susan.

Susan China has the largest.

Hostess Very good! [applause] Question number six: Which is the smallest: Australia, Argentina, or Brazil? [buzzer] Susan.

Susan Argentina is the smallest of the three.

Hostess That's right! [applause and music] OK, contestants, the winner is . . .

Answers

1. the Statue of Liberty	4. Canada
2. Angel Falls	5. China
3. They all weigh the same.	6. Argentina

INTERCHANGE 14

See page T-129 for teaching notes.

End of Cycle 1

Cycle 2, Exercises 8–12

See the Supplementary Resources chart at the beginning of this unit for additional teaching materials and student activities related to this Cycle.

 SNAPSHOT

Learning Objective: *read real-world facts that present the superlative in context*

- Books closed. As a warm-up, ask some questions about items in the Snapshot (e.g., *What's the most popular country to visit in the world?*). Ss guess the answers in teams.

- Books open. Ss read the Snapshot individually. Help Ss with vocabulary.

- Read the questions to the class. Have a brief class discussion.

- **Option:** Ss underline all the superlative forms of adjectives in the Snapshot. (Answers: *most popular, most-watched, busiest, longest, largest, coldest, windiest, highest, strongest*)

9 CONVERSATION

Learning Objectives: *practice a conversation about distances and measurements; see questions with* **how** *in context*

A ▶ *[CD 3, Track 37]*

- Books closed. Ask: "What do you know about New Zealand? What would you like to know about New Zealand?" Ss work in small groups to discuss the questions.

- Play the audio program. Ss listen for information about New Zealand.

- **Option:** If any of the Ss' questions were not answered, tell them to find out the answers for the next class.

- Write these focus questions on the board:
  1. Where is Scott going next year?
  2. Where is Beth from?
  3. How far is Auckland from Sydney?

- Books open. Play the audio program again. Ss read the conversation silently. They write down the answers. (Answers: 1. Australia 2. Auckland, New Zealand 3. about 2,000 kilometers)

- Ss practice the conversation in pairs.

! For a new way to practice this Conversation, try
• *Look Up and Speak!* – download it from the website.

B ▶ *[CD 3, Track 38]*

- Write the following on the board:

great beaches	coral reef	surfing
boating and sailing	waterfalls	jet boating
volcanoes	good skiing	deserts

- Play the audio program. Ss listen to find the things mentioned in the conversation.

- Elicit answers from around the class. Then have a brief follow-up discussion. Ask: "Would you like to visit New Zealand? Why or why not?"

AudioScript

Scott Tell me a little more about New Zealand, Beth.
Beth Well, it has some great beaches. There are some excellent surfing beaches in the North Island.
Scott Well, I don't really like surfing, but I love boating.
Beth Really? You can go boating in Auckland. It's one of the most popular places for sailing. And you should definitely try jet boating in the South Island.
Scott Oh, I'd love to do that! It sounds really exciting.
Beth It is. And there's good skiing in New Zealand. Lots of people go there to ski.
Scott It sounds perfect for me. Now I have to go!

Answers

New Zealand is famous for great beaches, surfing, boating, sailing, jet boating, and skiing.

INTERCHANGE 14 *How much do you know?*

You probably know more than you think! Take a quiz.
Go to Interchange 14 on page 129.

 SNAPSHOT

The World We Live In

- France is the most popular country to visit. It has about 78 million visitors a year.
- The most-watched World Cup was in the United States in 1994. It had an average attendance of 70,000 fans a day.
- The largest clock is in Mecca, Saudi Arabia. Each of its four faces is 43 meters (141 feet).
- The busiest airport in the world is Hartsfield-Jackson International Airport, in Atlanta, Georgia, United States. It has more than 88 million passengers a year.

- *Avatar* is the most popular movie ever. It has made more than $2.4 billion.
- The longest nonstop flight is from New York to Singapore. It's 18.5 hours long.
- Antarctica is the largest desert on earth at 14 million square kilometers (5.4 million square miles). It's also the coldest, windiest continent.
- The highest price for a book at an auction is $11.5 million for *Birds of America* by John Audubon.
- The strongest animal is the rhinoceros beetle. It can lift 850 times its own weight.

Source: *The Top 10 of Everything;* www.extremescience.com

Which facts do you find surprising?
What's the tallest building in your country? the most popular city to visit?
the busiest airport?

9 **CONVERSATION** *Distances and measurements*

A ⏵ Listen and practice.

Scott: I'm going to Australia next year. Aren't you from Australia, Beth?
Beth: Actually, I'm from New Zealand.
Scott: Oh, I didn't know that. So what's it like there?
Beth: Oh, it's beautiful. There are lots of farms, and it's very mountainous.
Scott: Really? How high are the mountains?
Beth: Well, the highest one is Mount Cook. It's about 3,800 meters high.
Scott: Wow! So how far is New Zealand from Australia?
Beth: Well, I live in Auckland, and Auckland is about 2,000 kilometers from Sydney.
Scott: Maybe I should visit you next year, too!

Mount Cook

B ⏵ Listen to the rest of the conversation.
What else is New Zealand famous for?

10 GRAMMAR FOCUS

Questions with how ▶

How far is New Zealand from Australia?	It's about 2,000 kilometers.	(1,200 miles)
How big is Singapore?	It's 710 square kilometers.	(274 square miles)
How high is Mount Cook?	It's 3,740 meters **high**.	(12,250 feet)
How deep is the Grand Canyon?	It's about 1,900 meters **deep**.	(6,250 feet)
How long is the Mississippi River?	It's about 5,970 kilometers **long**.	(3,710 miles)
How hot is Auckland in the summer?	It gets up to about 23° Celsius.	(74° Fahrenheit)
How cold is it in the winter?	It goes down to about 10° Celsius.	(50° Fahrenheit)

A Write the questions to these answers. Then practice with a partner.

1. A: .... ?
   B: Niagara Falls is 52 meters (170 feet) high.
2. A: .... ?
   B: California is about 403,970 square kilometers (155,973 square miles).
3. A: .... ?
   B: The Nile is 6,670 kilometers (4,145 miles) long.
4. A: .... ?
   B: Osaka is about 400 kilometers (250 miles) from Tokyo.
5. A: .... ?
   B: Mexico City gets up to about 28° Celsius (82° Fahrenheit) in the spring.

B GROUP WORK Think of five questions with *how* about places in your country or other countries you know. Ask and answer your questions.

11 WRITING *An article*

A Write an article to promote a place in your country. Describe a place in the list.

a beach
a desert
an island
a lake
a mountain
a river
a volcano
a waterfall

Web   Location   Photos   News   Ask

Jeju Island, South Korea

Tweet   Like

JEJU ISLAND

One of the most interesting places to go in South Korea is Jeju Island. Many people go there for its warm climate and beautiful beaches. I think one of the best places to visit there is Halla Mountain, or Halla-san. It's an old volcano and you can climb it in a day, but you should go early.

B PAIR WORK Read your partner's article. Ask questions to get more information.

10 GRAMMAR FOCUS

Learning Objective: *ask and answer questions with* how

 [CD 3, Track 39]

How + *adjective*

- **Option:** Find out which systems Ss are familiar with for distances (e.g., *meters and kilometers* or *feet and miles*) and for temperature (*Celsius* or *Fahrenheit*). Use the most suitable system during the class.

- Write this on the board:

How far is NZ from Australia?	It's 3,740 meters high.
How big is Singapore?	It's 1,900 meters deep.
How high is Mount Cook?	It's about 2,000 kilometers.
How deep is the Grand Canyon?	It's 648 square kilometers.

- Ask Ss to match the questions with the correct answers. Ss check their answers in the Grammar Focus box.

- Point out the use of *how* + adjective (e.g., *how far, how big*) in questions. Elicit more examples. Ask Ss to write them on the board in visual form:

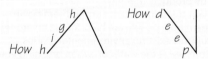

> **TIP** Visual and spatial Ss find structures and vocabulary easier to remember if they store the language in a pictorial form.

- Focus Ss' attention on the answers in the Grammar Focus box. Ask: "What is different about *high, deep,* and *long*?" (Answer: They are repeated in the answer.)
- Use the audio program to present the questions and answers.
- **Option:** Give your Ss practice with large numbers by having them repeat the answers line by line.

A

- Explain the task. Ss complete the task individually. Check Ss' answers before they work in pairs to practice the conversations.

> **Answers**
> 1. How high is Niagara Falls?
> 2. How big is California?
> 3. How long is the Nile?
> 4. How far is Osaka from Tokyo?
> 5. How hot is Mexico City in the spring?

B Group work

- **Option:** Ss can find facts in advance of this activity from the Internet, an atlas, or a guidebook.
- Explain the task. Elicit an example question. Ss write five questions with *how.*
- Ss work individually to write the questions. Go around the class and give help as needed.
- Ss ask and answer questions in groups.
- **Option:** Organize the class into teams and prepare a class game show using the Ss' questions.

11 WRITING

Learning Objective: *write an article to promote a place in your country*

A

- **Option:** Ss check the Internet or other sources for information about their country. Tell Ss to look at real examples of country websites.
- Explain the task. Ss write about their country and places to visit.
- Ss read the example article silently. Elicit the topics included in the article.
- Ss choose a place in their country to write about. Brainstorm with the class details to include in the articles (e.g., location, landscape, weather, history, how to get there, and when to go).

- Ss compose their first drafts. Then ask Ss to correct their grammar and spelling after writing the content.
- **Option:** Ss prepare attractive articles and display them on the wall for others to read.

B Pair work

- Explain the task. Ss work in pairs. They exchange articles and read them silently. Then the reader asks questions to get more information (e.g., *What else is it famous for?*).
- Encourage Ss to give each other helpful peer feedback. Then Ss revise their articles.

Learning Objectives: *read and discuss an article about the environment; develop skills in recognizing sources and understanding details*

- Books closed. Write these questions on the board:

  Do you like to take long showers? How long do you spend in the shower?

  Do you usually walk, ride a bicycle, take public transportation, or use a car?

- Ss discuss the questions in pairs.

- Books open. Explain that this article is about the environment. Ss look at the pictures and decide which show environmental problems and which show solutions. Help Ss with vocabulary.

Answers

problems: 1, 4, 5, 8
solutions: 2, 3, 6, 7

A

- Explain the task. Ss read the article. Then they guess where the article is from. (Answer: a magazine) Ask: "How do you know? What clues tell you the answer?" (Answer: photos, design, title)

- Elicit or explain any new vocabulary.

Vocabulary

SUVs: sport utility vehicles
vehicles: machines used for transporting people or things
tuned up: adjusted so it works as effectively as possible
throws away: disposes of; gets rid of
landfills: places where large amounts of garbage are buried
over and over again: repeatedly
recycled: collected and treated to be used again
"low-flow" showerhead: a device that controls or restricts the movement of water
leaky: allowing water to escape, even when turned off

B

- Explain the task. Read aloud the first statement in part B. Ask: "Where should we look for advice about this?" (Answer: the section about water) Ask a S to describe how to find the answer. Ask another S to write the advice on the board.

- Ss continue the task individually. Go over answers with the class.

Possible answers

1. Stephanie should buy a low-flow showerhead and take shorter showers.
2. Ralph should turn down the heat during the day.
3. Matt should think before he buys it.
4. Stuart should walk or bicycle to work.
5. Sheila should buy bulbs that use less energy and remember to turn lights off.

C *Group work*

- Ss work in groups to discuss the question. Go around the class and give help as needed.

- Groups share their suggestions with the class. Groups choose a S to write their suggestions on the board.

Possible answers

Buy products that have the recycling symbol on them.
Plant trees, instead of cutting them down.
Learn how people are helping the environment.
Support existing environmental groups.
Don't leave the water on when brushing your teeth.

End of Cycle 2

See the Supplementary Resources chart at the beginning of this unit for additional teaching materials and student activities related to this Cycle and for assessment tools.

Things You Can Do to Help the Environment

Look at the pictures. Which show environmental problems? Which show solutions?

CARS

Cars are getting bigger. SUVs—large, truck-like vehicles—are now the most popular cars in the United States. Bigger vehicles burn more gas and increase air pollution. So try to walk, bicycle, or use public transportation. If you drive a car, keep it tuned up. This saves gas and reduces pollution.

ENERGY

The biggest use of home energy is for heating and cooling. So turn up your air conditioner and turn down the heat, especially at night. Replace regular lightbulbs with bulbs that use less energy. And remember to turn lights off.

PRODUCTS

Each American throws away about 1.8 kilograms (4 pounds) of garbage every day. Most of it goes into landfills. Reduce waste before you buy by asking yourself: Do I need this? Is it something I can only use once? Buy products that you can use over and over again. And try to buy products made from recycled materials.

WATER

Showers use a lot of water. In one week, a typical American family uses as much water as a person drinks in three years! Buy a special "low-flow" showerhead or take shorter showers. This can cut water use in half. Also, fix any leaky faucets.

A Read the article. Where do you think it is from? Check (✓) the correct answer.

☐ a textbook ☐ an encyclopedia ☐ a magazine ☐ an advertisement

B Read these statements. Then write the advice from the article that each person should follow.

1. Stephanie always takes long showers in the morning. ....
2. In the winter, Ralph keeps the heat turned up all day. ....
3. Matt buys a newspaper every day, but never reads it. ....
4. Stuart drives to work, but his office is near his home. ....
5. Sheila leaves the lights on at home all the time. ....

C **GROUP WORK** What other ways do you know about to help the environment?

Units 13–14 Progress check

SELF-ASSESSMENT

How well can you do these things? Check (✓) the boxes.

I can	Very well	OK	A little
Say what I like and dislike (Ex. 1)	☐	☐	☐
Agree and disagree with other people (Ex. 1)	☐	☐	☐
Understand a variety of questions in a restaurant (Ex. 2)	☐	☐	☐
Order a meal in a restaurant (Ex. 3)	☐	☐	☐
Describe and compare things, people, and places (Ex. 4, 5)	☐	☐	☐
Ask questions about distances and measurements (Ex. 5)	☐	☐	☐

1 SURVEY Food facts

A Answer these questions. Write your responses under the column "My answers."

	My answers	Classmate's name
What food are you crazy about?	....	....
What food can't you stand?	....	....
Do you like vegetarian food?	....	....
Can you eat very rich food?	....	....
What restaurant do you like a lot?	....	....
How often do you go out to eat?	....	....

B CLASS ACTIVITY Go around the class. Find someone who has the same opinions or habits.

A: I'm crazy about Korean food.
B: I am, too./So am I. OR Oh, I'm not. I'm crazy about . . .

2 LISTENING In a restaurant

▶ Listen to six requests in a restaurant. Check (✓) the best response.

1. ☐ Yes. This way, please.
   ☐ Yes, please.

2. ☐ No, I don't.
   ☐ Yes, I'll have tea, please.

3. ☐ I'd like a steak, please.
   ☐ Yes, I would.

4. ☐ I'll have a cup of coffee.
   ☐ Italian, please.

5. ☐ Carrots, please.
   ☐ Yes, I will.

6. ☐ Yes, I'd like some water.
   ☐ No, I don't think so.

Units 13–14 Progress check

SELF-ASSESSMENT

Learning Objectives: *reflect on one's learning; identify areas that need improvement*

- Ask: "What did you learn in Units 13 and 14?" Elicit Ss' answers.
- Ss complete the Self-assessment. Encourage them to be honest, and point out they will not get a bad grade if they check (✓) *a little*.

- Ss move on to the Progress check exercises. You can have Ss complete them in class or for homework, using one of these techniques:
  1. Ask Ss to complete all the exercises.
  2. Ask Ss: "What do you need to practice?" Then assign exercises based on their answers.
  3. Ask Ss to choose and complete exercises based on their Self-assessment.

 SURVEY

Learning Objectives: *assess one's ability to express likes and dislikes; assess one's ability to agree and disagree*

A
- Ss write answers to the questions in the *My answers* column individually.

B *Class activity*
- Explain the task. Then model the example conversation with a few Ss. Point out that the S begins the conversation by making a statement.

- Elicit how to make statements from the remaining questions in the chart.
- Explain that Ss write the name of a classmate with the same opinion or habit in the *Classmate's name* column. Then they move on and talk to another classmate.
- Ss complete the task. Encourage them to respond with expressions of agreement or disagreement (e.g., *So am I. Oh, I'm not.*).
- Go around the class and note any grammar, vocabulary, or pronunciation errors.

 LISTENING

Learning Objectives: *assess one's ability to understand questions in a restaurant; assess one's ability to make requests*

▶ *[CD 3, Track 40]*
- Explain the task. Ss listen to restaurant requests and check (✓) the correct responses.
- Play the audio program once or twice. Ss complete the task individually.
- Go over answers with the class.

AudioScript

1. Could I have a table for two, please?
2. Can I get you anything to drink?
3. What would you like for dinner?
4. What kind of dressing would you like?
5. What vegetable would you like?
6. Would you like dessert?

Answers

1. Yes. This way, please.
2. Yes, I'll have tea, please.
3. I'd like a steak, please.
4. Italian, please.
5. Carrots, please.
6. No, I don't think so.

ROLE PLAY

Learning Objective: *assess one's ability to order a meal in a restaurant*

- Set the scene and explain the task. Ss work in pairs. Student A is a server in a restaurant and Student B is a hungry customer. Student B orders a meal and Student A writes the order on the check.

- Ss practice the role play in pairs. Then they change roles.
- Go around the class and check Ss' use of *would* and *will*.

 SPEAKING

Learning Objective: *assess one's ability to describe and compare things, people, and places*

A *Pair work*

- Explain the task and read the example fact and question.
- Ss write six facts and six related Wh-questions in pairs. Encourage Ss to use comparisons with adjectives.

B *Group work*

- Explain the task. Each pair joins another pair. Ss take turns asking and answering their questions. Tell each pair to write down how many questions the other pair answers correctly.
- Ss complete the task in groups. Go around the class and check Ss' use of comparisons with adjectives. Then ask which pair got the most correct answers.
- *Option:* Ask Ss to share their facts. Find out who has the most unusual facts.

5 **GAME**

Learning Objectives: *assess one's ability to describe and compare things, people, and places; assess one's ability to ask questions about distances and measurements*

A

- Explain the task and ask different Ss to read the example statements.
- Point out that all the statements can be answers for Wh- or *how* questions. Elicit possible questions (e.g., *How far is your house from the school? Which ocean is bigger, the Pacific or the Atlantic? Who has the longest hair in our class?*).

- Ss complete the task. Go around the class and give help as needed.

B *Class activity*

- Explain the task and model the example conversation with a S.
- Ss play the game as a class.

WHAT'S NEXT?

Learning Objective: *become more involved in one's learning*

- Focus Ss' attention on the Self-assessment again. Ask: "How well can you do these things now?"

- Ask Ss to underline one thing they need to review. Ask: "What did you underline? How can you review it?"
- If needed, plan additional activities or reviews based on Ss' answers.

ROLE PLAY *What would you like?*

Student A: Imagine you are a server and
Student B is a customer. Take his or her order
and write it on the check.

Student B: Imagine you are a hungry customer and can
order anything you like. Student A
is a server. Order a meal.

Change roles and try the role play again.

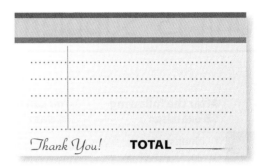

Thank You!   **TOTAL** _____

4 **SPEAKING** *City quiz*

A **PAIR WORK** Write down six facts about your city using comparatives or superlatives. Then write six Wh-questions based on your facts.

> 1. The busiest street is Market Drive.
> What's the busiest street in our city?

B **GROUP WORK** Join another pair. Take turns asking the other pair your questions. How many can they answer correctly?

5 **GAME** *What's the question?*

A Think of three statements that can be answered with *how* questions or Wh-questions with comparatives and superlatives. Write each statement on a separate card.

B **CLASS ACTIVITY** Divide into Teams A and B. Shuffle the cards together. One student from Team A picks a card and reads it to a student from Team B. That student tries to make a question for it.

A: The Pacific Ocean is bigger than the Atlantic Ocean.
B: Which ocean is bigger, the Pacific or the Atlantic?

Keep score. The team with the most correct questions wins.

> *It's about four kilometers
> from my house to the school.*

> *The Pacific Ocean is bigger
> than the Atlantic Ocean.*

> *Ana has the longest hair in
> our class.*

WHAT'S NEXT?

Look at your Self-assessment again. Do you need to review anything?

Unit 15 Supplementary Resources Overview

	After the following SB exercises	You can use these materials in class	Your students can use these materials outside the classroom
CYCLE 1	1 Snapshot		**SSD** Unit 15 Vocabulary 1
	2 Conversation		**SSD** Unit 15 Speaking 1
	3 Grammar Focus		**SB** Unit 15 Grammar Plus focus 1 **SSD** Unit 15 Grammar 1 **ARC** Future with present continuous and *be going to* 1–2
	4 Word Power	**TSS** Unit 15 Vocabulary Worksheet	**SSD** Unit 15 Vocabulary 2
	5 Role Play		
	6 Interchange 15	**TSS** Unit 15 Listening Worksheet	**WB** Unit 15 exercises 1–6
CYCLE 2	7 Conversation	**TSS** Unit 15 Extra Worksheet	**SSD** Unit 15 Speaking 2
	8 Grammar Focus	**TSS** Unit 15 Grammar Worksheet	**SB** Unit 15 Grammar Plus focus 2 **SSD** Unit 15 Grammar 2 **ARC** Messages with *tell* and *ask* 1–3
	9 Writing	**TSS** Unit 15 Writing Worksheet	
	10 Pronunciation		
	11 Listening		
	12 Role Play		
	13 Reading	**TSS** Unit 15 Project Worksheet **VID** Unit 15 **VRB** Unit 15	**SSD** Unit 15 Reading 1–2 **SSD** Unit 15 Listening 1–3 **SSD** Unit 15 Video 1–3 **WB** Unit 15 exercises 7–11

Key
  ARC: Arcade   **SB:** Student's Book   **SSD:** Self-study DVD-ROM   **TSS:** Teacher Support Site
  VID: Video DVD   **VRB:** Video Resource Book   **WB:** Workbook

My Plan for Unit 15

Use the space below to customize a plan that fits your needs.

With the following SB exercises	I am using these materials in class	My students are using these materials outside the classroom

With or instead of the following SB section	I am using these materials for assessment

15 I'm going to a soccer match.

1 SNAPSHOT

Making Excuses

Some common excuses for not accepting an invitation

I can't. I have to wash my hair.

- ☐ I'm busy that night.
- ☐ I can't find a babysitter.
- ☐ I'm not feeling well.
- ☐ I have to work then.
- ☐ I have class that night.
- ☐ My parents are visiting from out of town.
- ☐ I need to stay home with my new puppy.
- ☐ My favorite TV show is on that night.
- ☐ I have to get up early the next morning.

Sources: www.excuses.co.uk; interviews with people aged 18–45

Have you ever used any of these excuses? Have you ever heard any of them?
Which are good excuses and which are bad excuses? Check (✓) the good ones.
What other excuses can you make for not accepting an invitation?

2 CONVERSATION *Making plans*

A ▶ Listen and practice.

Lynn: Say, Miguel, what are you doing tonight? Do you want to go bowling?

Miguel: I'd love to, but I can't. I'm going to a soccer match with my brother.

Lynn: Oh, well, maybe some other time.

Miguel: Are you doing anything tomorrow? We could go then.

Lynn: Tomorrow sounds fine. I'm going to work until five.

Miguel: So let's go around six.

Lynn: OK. Afterward, maybe we can get some dinner.

Miguel: Sounds great.

B ▶ Listen to the rest of the conversation.
When are they going to have dinner? Who are they going to meet after dinner?

100

I'm going to a soccer match.

> In Unit 15, students talk about activities and plans. In Cycle 1, they discuss future activities and plans using the present continuous, be going to, and time expressions. In Cycle 2, they leave messages using tell and ask.

1 SNAPSHOT

Learning Objective: *read and talk about common excuses for not accepting an invitation*

- Books closed. Write the following excuses on the board. Ask Ss to guess what this Snapshot is about. Elicit or explain that these are all excuses.

  I'm sorry, I can't.   I'm busy that night.
  I have to work.   I'm too tired.

- Books open. Call on Ss to read the excuses.
- Elicit or explain any new vocabulary.

Vocabulary

babysitter: a person who takes care of someone else's baby or child for a short time
puppy: a young dog

- Explain the tasks. For the second task, ask Ss to imagine they are having a party, but some people can't come. Tell Ss to check (✓) the excuses they would find acceptable.
- Ss work in pairs to complete the tasks. Go around the class and give help as needed.
- Ask Ss for feedback on the second task. Which excuses are rude? Which ones are acceptable?
- Elicit Ss' ideas for the third task (e.g., *I have a headache.*).

2 CONVERSATION

Learning Objectives: *practice a conversation between two people making plans; see future with present continuous and* be going to *in context*

A ▶ [CD 3, Track 41]

- Ask Ss to look at the picture and invent a story about the two people. To guide Ss, ask: "Who are they? Where are they? What is their relationship? What is she asking him? What is he saying?"

▪ For more practice with vocabulary, play ***Picture It!*** – download it from the website.

- Set the scene. Lynn and Miguel are co-workers. Lynn is asking Miguel out on a date.
- Books closed. Write these focus questions on the board:

  1. What is Lynn inviting Miguel to do?
  2. Why can't Miguel go?
  3. When are they going to meet?

- Play the audio program. Then elicit the answers. (Answers: 1. go bowling 2. He's going to a soccer match that night. 3. tomorrow night)
- Books open. Play the audio program again. Ss listen and read along silently.

❗ For a new way to practice this Conversation, try ***Say It with Feeling!*** – download it from the website.

B ▶ [CD 3, Track 42]

- Read the focus questions aloud. Ask Ss to guess the answers. Write some of their ideas on the board.
- Play the audio program. Ss work individually. Then go over answers with the class.

AudioScript

Lynn After we're done bowling, do you want to go to the Chinese Palace for dinner?
Miguel Sure. I love their food. We can go around 8:00. That's not too late. You know, maybe Jason can join us.
Lynn Yeah. Hey, Jason, what are you doing tomorrow night? Do you want to join Miguel and me for dinner? We're going to the Chinese Palace at 8:00.
Jason I have to work till 8:30. But why don't I meet you afterward?
Miguel That'd be great, Jason.

Answers

They're going to have dinner at 8:00. Jason is going to meet them afterward.

- ***Option:*** Have a brief class discussion. Ask: "Do young people go on dates in your country? Where do people usually go on dates? Do you think it's OK for co-workers to date? Why or why not?"

3 GRAMMAR FOCUS

Learning Objective: *practice using future with the present continuous and be going to*

▶ **[CD 3, Track 43]**

Present continuous with future meaning

- Focus Ss' attention on the Conversation on page 100. Write these sentences on the board:

  Lynn: What _____ you _____ tonight?
  Miguel: _____ you _____ anything tomorrow?

- Call on Ss to fill in the blanks. (Answers: are/doing, Are/doing) Ask: "Do you recognize this tense?"

- Explain that earlier we used this tense to talk about what is happening right now. Now we are going to use it to talk about the future.

- Point to the first column in the Grammar Focus box. Elicit the rule for forming the present continuous:
  Question: (Wh) + *be* + subject + verb + *-ing* + ?
  Statement: Subject + *be* + verb + *-ing*.

Be going to

- Explain that we can also use *be going to* + verb for future plans. Focus Ss' attention on the second column in the Grammar Focus box.

- Draw a calendar for the week, and point to today's date. Ask questions like these:

  T: Are you going to do anything on Friday? (pointing to Friday)

  S1: Yes. I'm going to study.

  T: What about you, Pablo? What are you doing on Friday?

- Play the audio program. Ask Ss to repeat or mouth the words as they hear them.

A

- Explain the task. Model the first answer in both columns.

- Ss complete the conversations individually. Ask early finishers to write their answers on the board.

Answers

1. What **are** you **doing** tonight? Would you like to go out?
2. **Are** you **doing** anything on Friday night? Do you want to see a movie?
3. We**'re having** friends over for a barbecue on Sunday. Would you and your parents like to come?
4. **Are** you **staying** in town next weekend? Do you want to go for a hike?

a. I**'m going to be** here on Saturday, but not Sunday. Let's try and go on Saturday.
b. Well, my father **is going to visit** my brother at college. But my mother and I **are going to be** home. We'd love to come!
c. Sorry, I can't. I**'m going to work** overtime tonight. How about tomorrow night?
d. Can we go to a late show? I**'m going to stay** at the office till 7:00.

B

- Explain the task. Ss match the invitations to the responses. Go over answers with the class.

Answers

1. c   2. d   3. b   4. a

- Ss practice the invitations in pairs.

4 WORD POWER

Learning Objective: *learn vocabulary for discussing leisure activities*

A

- Explain the task. Model with several words from the list.

- Ss work in pairs. Go around the class, giving help with vocabulary.

- Ss add one more example to each category. To check answers, write the chart on the board.

Answers

Spectator sports
baseball game   volleyball tournament
bicycle race   *soccer match*
tennis match   *football game*

Friendly gatherings
barbecue   picnic
beach party   *dinner party*
birthday party   *wedding*

Live performances
dance performance   singing contest
play   *ballet*
rock concert   *opera*

(Note: Additional examples are italicized.)

B *Pair work*

- Explain the task. Ss talk about the activities in pairs. Go around the class and give help as needed.

 To review the vocabulary in this Word Power, play *Vocabulary Tennis* – download it from the website.

Future with present continuous and be going to ▶

With present continuous	**With be going to + verb**	**Time expressions**
What **are** you **doing** tonight?	What **is** she **going to do** tomorrow?	tonight
I**'m going** to a soccer match.	She**'s going to work** until five.	tomorrow
Are you **doing** anything tomorrow?	**Are** they **going to go** bowling?	on Friday
No, I'm not.	Yes, they are.	this weekend
		next week

A Complete the invitations in column A with the present continuous used as future.
Complete the responses in column B with *be going to*.

A

1. What .... you .... (do) tonight?
   Would you like to go out?

2. .... you .... (do) anything on
   Friday night? Do you want to see a movie?

3. We .... (have) friends over for a
   barbecue on Sunday. Would you and your
   parents like to come?

4. .... you .... (stay) in town next
   weekend? Do you want to go for a hike?

B

a. I .... (be) here on Saturday, but not
   Sunday. Let's try and go on Saturday.

b. Well, my father .... (visit) my brother at
   college. But my mother and I .... (be)
   home. We'd love to come!

c. Sorry, I can't. I .... (work) overtime
   tonight. How about tomorrow night?

d. Can we go to a late show? I .... (stay)
   at the office till 7:00.

B Match the invitations in column A with the responses in column B. Then practice with a partner.

4 **WORD POWER** *Leisure activities*

A Complete the chart with words and phrases from the list.
Then add one more example to each category.

barbecue	bicycle race	picnic	singing contest
baseball game	birthday party	play	tennis match
beach party	dance performance	rock concert	volleyball tournament

Spectator sports	Friendly gatherings	Live performances
....	....	....
....	....	....
....	....	....
....	....	....
....	....	....

B **PAIR WORK** Are you going to do any of the activities in part A?
When are you doing them? Talk with a partner.

5 ROLE PLAY Accept or refuse?

Student A: Choose an activity from Exercise 4 and invite a partner to go with you. Be ready to say where and when the activity is.

> A: Say, are you doing anything on . . . ?
>   Would you like to . . . ?

Student B: Your partner invites you out. Either accept the invitation and ask for more information, or say you can't go and give an excuse.

Accept	Refuse
B: OK. That sounds fun. Where is it?	B: Oh, I'm sorry, I can't. I'm . . .

Change roles and try the role play again.

6 INTERCHANGE 15 Weekend plans

Find out what your classmates are going to do this weekend.
Go to Interchange 15 on page 130.

7 CONVERSATION Can I take a message?

A Listen and practice.

Secretary: Good morning, Parker Industries.
 Mr. Kale: Hello. May I speak to Ms. Graham, please?
Secretary: I'm sorry. She's not in. Can I take a message?
 Mr. Kale: Yes, please. This is Mr. Kale.
Secretary: Is that G-A-L-E?
 Mr. Kale: No, it's K-A-L-E.
Secretary: All right.
 Mr. Kale: Please tell her our meeting is on Friday at 2:30.
Secretary: Friday at 2:30.
 Mr. Kale: And could you ask her to call me this afternoon? My number is (646) 555-4031.
Secretary: (646) 555-4031. Yes, Mr. Kale. I'll give Ms. Graham the message.
 Mr. Kale: Thank you. Good-bye.
Secretary: Good-bye.

B Listen to three other calls. Write down the callers' names.

5 ROLE PLAY

Learning Objective: *role-play a conversation between two people making plans*

- Divide the class into groups A and B. Ask Students B to look at the excuses in the Snapshot on page 100 while you explain the task to Students A.
- Explain the task to Students A. Model the example questions. Elicit additional questions that Ss can use to invite someone out (e.g., *What are you doing on . . . ? Are you busy on . . . ?*). Write these cues on the board for Student As to use in their invitations: *activity/event   day/date/time   place*

- While Students A plan their invitations, explain the task to Students B. Model how to accept or refuse an invitation. Elicit more examples from Ss (e.g., *Wow! That sounds great! Thanks, I've really wanted to do that!*).
- Model the role play with Ss. Show Ss how to elaborate and use their own words.
- Ss work in pairs to do the role play. Remind Ss to use the cues in the book and on the board.
- Provide feedback. Then Ss change roles and do the activity again.

6 INTERCHANGE 15

See page T-130 for teaching notes.

See page T-130 for teaching notes.

End of Cycle 1

See the Supplementary Resources chart at the beginning of this unit for additional teaching materials and student activities related to this Cycle.

Cycle 2, Exercises 7–13

7 CONVERSATION

Learning Objectives: *practice a conversation between two people talking on the phone; see messages with* tell *and* ask *in context*

A ▶ [CD 3, Track 44]

- Ask Ss to cover the text. Have Ss describe the picture. Then ask: "Have you ever taken a message? Who for? Where?"
- Write this focus question on the board:
  What are Mr. Kale's two messages for Ms. Graham?
- Play the audio program. Then elicit the answers. (Answers: The meeting is on Friday at 2:30. Call him this afternoon.)
- Ask Ss to uncover the text. Play the audio program again. Ss read the conversation silently, paying attention to how the telephone numbers are said.
- Ss practice the conversation in pairs. Tell Ss to sit back-to-back.

B ▶ [CD 3, Track 45]

- Explain the task. Ss listen to find out the names of the three callers. Play the audio program.
- Elicit answers from around the class.

AudioScript

Secretary [phone rings] Good morning, Parker Industries.
Mr. Lee Hello. May I speak to Ms. Graham, please?
Secretary I'm sorry. She's not in. Can I take a message?
Mr. Lee Yes, this is Tom Lee from the Beijing office. Can you ask her to call me back? She has the number.
Secretary Of course, Mr. Lee.

Secretary [phone rings] Good morning, Parker Industries.
Ms. Brown Hello. Is Ms. Graham there?
Secretary I'm afraid she's not in. Can I take a message?
Ms. Brown Yes, this is Susan Brown. Please have her call me back as soon as possible. The number is (846) 555-9037.
Secretary Yes, Ms. Brown. I'll give her the message.

Secretary [phone rings] Good morning, Parker Industries.
Kelly Hi. Is Mom there? This is Kelly.
Secretary Oh, hi, Kelly. How's it going?
Kelly Pretty good.
Secretary Listen, your mom isn't here right now, but I'll tell her you called.
Kelly OK.

Answers

Tom Lee, Susan Brown, Kelly

8 GRAMMAR FOCUS

Learning Objective: *practice writing and giving messages with* tell *and* ask

 [CD 3, Track 46]

Tell *with statements*

- Focus Ss' attention on the "statement" part of the Grammar Focus box. Ask these four questions:
  1. "What is the message?" (The meeting is on Friday.)
  2. "Do we use *tell* or *ask* with statements?" (*tell*)
  3. "Does the message change when we use *tell*?" (no)
  4. "What are three ways to ask someone to relay a message?" (Please tell X . . . /Could you tell him/her . . . ?/Would you tell him/her . . . ?)
- Elicit the rule for forming messages with a statement:

  Tell + person + (*that*) + the statement.

Ask *with requests*

- Repeat the above steps for requests with the "request" part of the Grammar Focus box.
  1. "What is the message?" (Call me this afternoon.)
  2. "Do we use *tell* or *ask* with requests?" (*ask*)
  3. "Does the message change when we use *ask*?" (no, but we use *to*)
  4. "What are three ways to ask someone to relay a message?" (Please ask X . . . /Could you ask him/her . . . ?/Would you ask him/her . . . ?)

- Elicit the rule for forming messages with a request: *Ask* + person + *to* + the request.
- Focus Ss' attention on the Conversation on page 102. Ask: "What structures does Mr. Kale use when he gives his two messages?" (Answers: Please tell her . . . , Could you ask her to . . . ?)
- Use the audio program to present the language.
- Present messages 1–6. Model how to unscramble the first sentence. Point out that both statements and requests begin with the words *please, could,* or *would.*
- Ss complete the task individually.
- **Option:** If Ss have difficulty with the patterns for *tell* and *ask,* ask them to read each message and find the *ask* examples (2, 5, 6). Ask Ss "Are these requests?" (yes)
- Ss compare messages in pairs. Then elicit and check Ss' answers around the class.

Answers

1. Please tell Ryan that the barbecue is on Saturday.
2. Could you ask Patrick to call me at 12:00?
3. Could you tell Amy that the dance performance is tonight?
4. Would you tell Celia that the picnic is in the park?
5. Would you ask Noriko to meet me at the stadium?
6. Please ask Jason to bring the tickets to the rock concert.

9 WRITING

Learning Objective: *write a note asking someone to pass on messages with* tell *and* ask

A Pair work

- Explain the task. Ask Ss to read the example message silently. Using the example message, demonstrate with a S.

  The writer's tasks:
  1. The writer writes a note to his or her partner. The note should include three messages to other people in the class.
  2. Then the writer gives the note with three messages to his or her partner.

  The partner's tasks:
  1. The partner reads the note and then gets up to tell the messages to the three people named in the note.
  2. The partner goes to the first person in the note and tells him or her the writer's message. Then the partner goes to the second person in the note and tells the writer's message. Finally, the partner goes to the third person in the note and tells him or her the writer's message.

> **TIP** For long instructions, it helps to write them on the board so Ss can follow them as the activity develops.

- Ss write their notes individually. Remind Ss to include messages for three people. Encourage Ss to write interesting or unusual messages.
- Give Ss five to ten minutes to write their messages.
- **Option:** Assign this writing task for homework.
- Ss exchange their notes with a partner. Then everyone gets up to deliver each message.

B Group work

- Ss work in groups to compare answers. Allow about five minutes for discussion. Remind Ss to decide who has the most unusual message. Groups share their most unusual message with the class.

8 GRAMMAR FOCUS

Messages with *tell* and *ask* ⏵

Statement	**Messages with a statement**
The meeting is on Friday.	**Please tell her (that)** the meeting is on Friday.
	Could you tell her (that) the meeting is on Friday?
	Would you tell her (that) the meeting is on Friday?
Request	**Messages with a request**
Call me this afternoon.	**Please ask him to** call me this afternoon.
	Could you ask him to call me this afternoon?
	Would you ask him to call me this afternoon?

Unscramble these messages. Then compare with a partner.

1. tell / that / is / please / Ryan / the barbecue / on Saturday

   ....

2. call me / at 12:00 / you / Patrick / could /ask / to

   .... ?

3. is / that / Amy / tonight / could / you / the dance performance / tell

   .... ?

4. tell / is / Celia / in the park / would / you / that / the picnic

   .... ?

5. meet me / to / you / would / Noriko / ask / at the stadium

   .... ?

6. ask / to the rock concert / please / bring / Jason / to / the tickets

   ....

9 WRITING *Unusual favors*

A **PAIR WORK** Think of unusual messages for three people in your class.
Write a note to your partner asking him or her to pass on the messages.

Dear Rachel,
Could you tell Brian to wear two different color
socks tomorrow?

Please tell Jeff that our class tomorrow is at midnight.

Would you ask Sun-hee to bring me a hamburger
and french fries for breakfast tomorrow?

Thanks!
David

B **GROUP WORK** Compare your messages.
Which is the most unusual?

10 PRONUNCIATION *Reduction of* could you *and* would you

A ▶ Listen and practice. Notice how **could you** and **would you** are reduced in conversation.

[cʊdʒə]
Could you tell her the meeting is on Friday?

[wʊdʒə]
Would you ask him to call me this afternoon?

B PAIR WORK Practice these questions with reduced forms.

Could you tell them I'll be late?
Would you ask her to be on time?

Could you ask her to return my dictionary?
Would you tell him there's a picnic tomorrow?

11 LISTENING *Taking a message*

▶ Listen to telephone calls to Mr. Lin and Ms. Carson. Write down the messages.

1

To: Mr. _____
Date: _____ Time: _____
WHILE YOU WERE OUT
From: _____
of: City _____
Phone: _____ ext: _____
Message:
Call Mrs. _____
_____
Taken by: _____

2

To: Wendy _____
Date: _____ Time: _____
WHILE YOU WERE OUT
From: _____
of: National _____
Phone: _____ ext: _____
Message:
_____
_____
Taken by: _____

12 ROLE PLAY *Who's calling?*

Student A: Call your friend Andrew to tell him this:

There's a party at Ray's house on Saturday night.
Ray's address is 414 Maple St., Apt. 202. Pick me up at 8:00 P.M.

Student B: Someone calls for your brother Andrew. He isn't in.
Take a message for him.

Change roles and try another role play.

Student A: You are a receptionist at Systex Industries. Someone calls for your boss, Ms. Park.
She isn't in. Take a message for her.

Student B: Call Ms. Park at Systex Industries to tell her this:

You can't make your lunch meeting at 12:00. You want to meet at 12:30 at the same place
instead. Call her to arrange the new time.

useful expressions
May I speak to . . . ?
Sorry, but . . . isn't here.
Can I leave a message?
Can I take a message?
I'll give . . . the message.

10 PRONUNCIATION

Learning Objective: *notice the reduced forms of* could you *and* would you

A [CD 3, Track 47]

- Play the audio program. Model the consonant sounds *d* + *y* in *could you* and *would you*. Ss repeat.
- Call on different Ss to try the reductions.

B Pair work

- Read out the four questions for the class. Ask Ss to repeat.
- For a new way to practice this Pronunciation, try **Walking Stress** – download it from the website.

11 LISTENING

Learning Objective: *develop skills in listening for details*

▶ [CD 3, Track 48]

- Explain the task. Point out the different parts of the message slips.
- Play the audio program. Ss listen and write down the messages. Then Ss compare answers with a partner.
- Play the audio program again. Break up the two listenings into smaller segments. Pause after every few lines to give Ss time to complete the messages.

AudioScript

1.
Receptionist [*phone rings*] Good afternoon, MBI. May I help you?
Mrs. Paris Hello. I want to speak to Mr. Lin, please.
Receptionist I'm sorry. Mr. Lin is in a meeting right now. Would you like to leave a message?
Mrs. Paris Yes, please. This is Mrs. Paris of City Car Center.
Receptionist Mrs. Paris. Is that P-A-R-I-S?
Mrs. Paris Yes, that's right. Please ask him to call me at the City Car Center before 3:30 this afternoon. It's very important.
Receptionist All right. And your number, please?
Mrs. Paris 718-555-3290.
Receptionist 718-555-3290?
Mrs. Paris That's it.
Receptionist OK. I'll ask him to call you before 3:30, Mrs. Paris.

Mrs. Paris Thank you. Good-bye.
Receptionist Good-bye.
2.
Receptionist [*phone rings*] This is Software Systems. Good morning.
Sam Good morning. May I speak to Ms. Carson, please?
Receptionist Hmm . . . do you mean Mrs. Carter?
Sam No, Carson, Ms. Wendy Carson. She's new there.
Receptionist Let me check. Oh, yes, let me try to connect you. Hold on. [*phone rings three times*] I'm sorry. There's no answer. May I take a message?
Sam Yes. Would you please ask her to call Sam at First National Bank?
Receptionist Sam . . . at First National Bank.
Sam The number is 914-555-1187, extension 313.
Receptionist 914-555-1187, extension 313?
Sam That's right.
Receptionist OK. I'll give her the message.
Sam Thanks so much. Bye.
Receptionist Good-bye.

- Call on Ss to write their answers on the board.

Answers

1. To: Mr. **Lin**
   From: **Mrs. Paris**
   of: City **Car Center**
   Phone: **718-555-3290**
   Message: Call Mrs.
   Paris before 3:30 this afternoon. Important!

2. To: Wendy **Carson**
   From: **Sam**
   of: **First** National **Bank**
   Phone: **914-555-1187**
   ext. **313**
   Message: **Call Sam at the bank.**

12 ROLE PLAY

Learning Objective: *role-play a conversation between two people talking on the phone*

- Divide the class into pairs and assign A/B roles. Explain the roles and go over the A/B cues.
- Model the role play with a S. Have Ss sit back-to-back. Change roles if necessary.
- **Option:** Before starting the activity, tell Ss to reread the Conversation on page 102. Or Ss can listen again to the audio program in Exercise 11 to review phone

etiquette. Ask Students A to find expressions callers use and Students B to find expressions receptionists use.

- Ss do the first role play, sitting back-to-back. Provide feedback after they finish.
- Explain the second role play and go over the A/B cues. Pairs change roles and do the new role play.

TIP To maintain interest it's best to ask only one pair to demonstrate the role play to the class.

13 READING

Learning Objectives: *read and discuss an article about cell phone etiquette; develop skills in scanning, summarizing, and recognizing points of view*

- Books closed. To set the scene, ask Ss to brainstorm things that cell phone users do that are dangerous or rude (e.g., *They talk too loudly. They take calls in movie theaters.*).

- Books open. Call on a S to read the title aloud. Elicit or explain that *etiquette* means "manners."

- Tell Ss to read the cell phone article quickly. Ask Ss to find the answers to the pre-reading questions. (Answers: It's not OK to use a cell phone in a movie theater. It's not OK to use a cell phone in a restaurant if there is a sign saying "turn off cell phones." It's not OK to use a cell phone on the street if you talk loudly or if you don't watch where you're going.)

A

- Explain the task. Ss read the article silently. Remind Ss to try to guess the meanings of any words they don't know.

- Elicit or explain any new vocabulary.

Vocabulary

happens: occurs; takes place
day-to-day: ordinary; regular
beeping: a short, high-pitched sound
take calls: answer the phone
ringer: device that creates the ring-tone on a cell phone
You get the picture.: You understand what I am talking about.
nuisance: something that is annoying

❗ For a new way to teach the vocabulary in this Reading, try *Vocabulary Mingle* – download it on the website.

- Ss complete the summary. Then go over answers with the class.

- **Option:** If the summary seems too difficult for your Ss, include the words in a cloud summary on the board, like this:

off   can't
   never
loudly   softly

Many people don't practice good cell phone **etiquette**. They talk too **loudly**, listen to **loud** music, or check their email while **crossing** the street. To be a better cell phone user, follow a few simple rules. For example: Turn **off** your phone in public places that don't allow cell phones; speak **softly** on phone calls; and don't talk, text, play games, or listen to music while **driving** or crossing the street.

B

- Ask the following question: "Is the writer against cell phones, for cell phones, or for cell phones only if they're used in a way that doesn't bother other people?"

- Elicit examples in the article that show the writer's opinion.

- Explain the task. Ss imagine they are the writer of the article. They check (✓) the sentences the writer would agree with.

- Ss complete the task individually. Then they compare answers with a partner.

- Go over answers with the class.

The writer would probably agree with 3, 7, 8.

C *Pair work*

- Explain the task. Ss work in pairs. They discuss which opinions they agree or disagree with and why.

End of Cycle 2

See the Supplementary Resources chart at the beginning of this unit for additional teaching materials and student activities related to this Cycle.

Cell Phone Etiquette

Scan the article. Is it OK to use a cell phone in a movie theater? in a restaurant? on the street?

What do these things have in common: a stranger's personal problems, details about a business meeting, the food in someone's refrigerator, someone's medical issues, and a private argument? These are all things you hear about when the people around you don't practice good cell phone etiquette!

Most people find cell phones a necessity in their day-to-day lives. But we've all sat next to someone talking too loudly, listening to loud music, or playing a loud beeping game on a

cell phone. But a recent report shows that while most people are annoyed by cell phone rudeness, most admit to doing it, too. What can you do to practice better etiquette? Here are a few rules:

> **Off means off!** Respect the rules of restaurants and other public places. If a sign says "No cell phones," don't use your phone – for anything.

> **Keep private conversations private!** Speak softly and for a short time. Observe the 3-meter (10-feet) rule – stay away from other people.

> **Lights off, phone off!** Never take calls or send text messages in a theater, at the movies, or at a performance. Turn your phone or your ringer off.

> **Pay attention!** Talking or texting while driving is dangerous. Listening to music with headphones while driving is dangerous. Crossing the street while playing a game or checking your email is dangerous. You get the picture.

Cell phones have become mini-computers that people depend on 24 hours a day. But don't let yours become a nuisance – or a danger – to others! Next time you're getting ready to use yours, stop and consider the people around you.

A Read the article. Then complete the summary with information from the article.

Many people don't practice good cell phone .... They talk too .... , listen to .... music, or check their email while .... the street. To be a better cell phone user, follow a few simple rules. For example: Turn .... your phone in public places that don't allow cell phones; speak .... on phone calls; and don't talk, text, play games, or listen to music while .... or crossing the street.

B Check (✓) the statements the writer would probably agree with.

- ☐ 1. You should never use a cell phone in public.
- ☐ 2. Cell phone users are very rude people.
- ☐ 3. Turn off your cell phone if someone asks you to.
- ☐ 4. You can talk loudly if you're more than 3 meters away from someone.
- ☐ 5. It's OK to send text messages while driving a car.
- ☐ 6. You can use a cell phone at a dance performance if you speak quietly.
- ☐ 7. Don't play games on your phone in restaurants.
- ☐ 8. Don't check your email while crossing the street.

C **PAIR WORK** Do you agree with the writer's opinions? Why or why not?

Unit 16 Supplementary Resources Overview

	After the following SB exercises	You can use these materials in class	Your students can use these materials outside the classroom
CYCLE 1	1 Snapshot		**SSD** Unit 16 Vocabulary 1–2 **ARC** Things that bring about changes in our lives
	2 Conversation		**SSD** Unit 16 Speaking 1
	3 Grammar Focus		**SB** Unit 16 Grammar Plus focus 1 **SSD** Unit 16 Grammar 1 **ARC** Describing changes
	4 Listening	**TSS** Unit 16 Listening Worksheet **TSS** Unit 16 Extra Worksheet	
	5 Word Power		**SSD** Unit 16 Vocabulary 3 **WB** Unit 16 exercises 1–5
CYCLE 2	6 Conversation		**SSD** Unit 16 Speaking 2
	7 Grammar Focus	**TSS** Unit 16 Vocabulary Worksheet **TSS** Unit 16 Grammar Worksheet	**SB** Unit 16 Grammar Plus focus 2 **SSD** Unit 16 Grammar 2 **ARC** Verb + infinitive 1–2
	8 Pronunciation		**ARC** Vowel sounds /ou/ and /ʌ/
	9 Interchange 16		
	10 Speaking		
	11 Writing	**TSS** Unit 16 Writing Worksheet	
	12 Reading	**TSS** Unit 16 Project Worksheet **VID** Unit 16 **VRB** Unit 16	**SSD** Unit 16 Reading 1–2 **SSD** Unit 16 Listening 1–3 **SSD** Unit 16 Video 1–3 **WB** Unit 16 exercises 6–10

With or instead of the following SB section	You can also use these materials for assessment
Units 15–16 Progress Check	**ASSESSMENT CD** Units 15–16 Oral Quiz **ASSESSMENT CD** Units 15–16 Written Quiz **ASSESSMENT CD** Units 9–16 Test

Key   **ARC**: Arcade   **SB**: Student's Book   **SSD**: Self-study DVD-ROM   **TSS**: Teacher Support Site
       VID: Video DVD   **VRB**: Video Resource Book   **WB**: Workbook

My Plan for Unit 16

Use the space below to customize a plan that fits your needs.

With the following SB exercises	I am using these materials in class	My students are using these materials outside the classroom

With or instead of the following SB section	I am using these materials for assessment

16 A change for the better!

1 SNAPSHOT

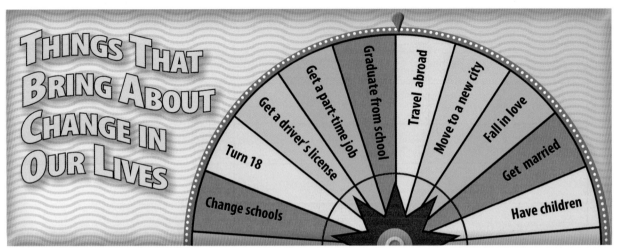

THINGS THAT BRING ABOUT CHANGE IN OUR LIVES

- Change schools
- Turn 18
- Get a driver's license
- Get a part-time job
- Graduate from school
- Travel abroad
- Move to a new city
- Fall in love
- Get married
- Have children

Source: Based on interviews with people between the ages of 16 and 50

Which of these events are the most important changes?
Have any of these things happened to you recently?
What other things bring about change in our lives?

2 CONVERSATION *Catching up*

A ▶ Listen and practice.

Diane: Hi, Kerry. I haven't seen you in ages. How have you been?

Kerry: Pretty good, thanks.

Diane: Are you still in school?

Kerry: No, not anymore. I graduated last year. And I got a job at Midstate Bank.

Diane: That's great news. You know, you look different. Have you changed your hair?

Kerry: Yeah, it's shorter. And I wear contacts now.

Diane: Well, you look fantastic!

Kerry: Thanks, so do you. And there's one more thing. Look! I got engaged.

Diane: Congratulations!

B ▶ Listen to the rest of the conversation. How has Diane changed?

106

A change for the better!

In Unit 16, students talk about changes in a person's life. In Cycle 1, they discuss changes using the comparative and the present, past, and present perfect tenses. In Cycle 2, they talk about plans for the future using verb + infinitive.

1 SNAPSHOT

Learning Objective: *read and talk about things that change our lives*

- Books closed. Write the unit title on the board. Elicit or explain the meaning of *a change for the better* and also *a change for the worse*. Explain that this unit is about important changes in our lives.
- Ss brainstorm things that change our lives (e.g., *get married, have a child, change schools*). Help with vocabulary as needed.
- Books open. Ss compare their ideas with those in the Snapshot.
- Elicit or explain any new vocabulary.

Vocabulary

driver's license: a document that proves you are legally allowed to drive a car
graduate: complete your studies
abroad: to a foreign country

- Explain the tasks. Ss discuss the questions in pairs or small groups. Remind Ss they don't have to share personal information. They can respond by saying "I prefer not to talk about that."
- Have a brief class discussion about changes that have occurred in Ss' lives.

2 CONVERSATION

Learning Objectives: *practice a conversation between two people catching up; see descriptions of changes in context*

A ▶ [CD 3, Track 49]

- Set the scene. Two old friends run into each other and "catch up" on changes in their lives.
- Books closed. Play the audio program. Ask: "Has Kerry's life changed for the better or for the worse?" (Answer: for the better)
- Write these focus questions on the board:
  <u>True or false?</u>
  1. Kerry is still in school.
  2. Her hair is shorter than before.
  3. She got married.
- Play the audio program again. Then elicit the answers. (Answers: 1. false 2. true 3. false) For the false ones, ask Ss what really happened.
- Books open. Play the audio program again. Ss listen and read along silently. Elicit or explain any new vocabulary.

Vocabulary

contacts: short for contact lenses
got engaged: formally agreed to marry someone

❗ For a new way to practice this Conversation, try *Say It With Feeling!* – download it from the website.

- Ss practice the conversation in pairs. Go around the class and give help as needed.
- **Option:** Ss write their own conversation, based on the one in the book. They practice the new conversation in pairs.

B ▶ [CD 3, Track 50]

- Play the audio program once or twice. Ss listen to find out how Diane has changed.
- Ss compare answers in small groups. Then go over answers with the class.

AudioScript

Kerry So tell me, Diane, what have you been up to?
Diane Well, let's see. I've changed jobs.
Kerry Really? You don't work at the hospital anymore?
Diane No, I left last year. I'm still a nurse, but I work in a private clinic. My job is less stressful now.
Kerry Do you still live downtown?
Diane Oh, no. I moved to a new place. I'm in the suburbs now. I live in Parkview, just outside the city.
Kerry Parkview? That's where I live! That means we're neighbors!

Possible answer

Diane changed jobs, works now in a private clinic, and moved to the suburbs.

3 GRAMMAR FOCUS

Learning Objective: *practice describing changes with the present tense, the past tense, the present perfect, and comparatives*

 [CD 3, Track 51]

- **Option:** Ask Ss to bring in some old photos that show how they have changed. Ss can show each other their photos and discuss them.
- Write these four categories on the board:

Present tense   Present perfect
Past tense   Comparative

- Focus Ss' attention on the Conversation on page 106. Ask Ss to find examples in each category. Call on Ss to write them on the board.
- **Option:** Divide the class into four groups and assign each group a different tense.

Possible answers

Present tense
Are you still in school?
That's great news.
You look different.
I wear contacts now.
You look fantastic!
There's one more thing.

Present perfect
I haven't seen you in ages.
How have you been?
Have you changed your hair?

Past tense
I graduated last year.
I got a job.
I got engaged.

Comparative
It's shorter.

- Play the audio program to present the grammar. Then ask Ss to describe the changes to the man in the picture (e.g., *He wears different clothes now. He has grown taller. His hair is shorter now.*).
- **Option:** If needed, review the tenses. For the past tense, see Unit 7; for the present perfect, see Unit 10; and for comparatives, see Unit 14.

A

- Explain the task. Ss check (✓) true statements and correct any false statements. Put this example on the board:

✓ 1. I've changed my hairstyle.
  2. I dress differently now.   I dress the same.

- Ss complete the task individually. Go around the class and give help as needed.

B *Pair work*

- Explain the task. Then Ss work in pairs to compare their part A responses. Ask the class: "Who has changed in similar ways?"

C *Group work*

- Explain the task. Ss work individually. They write five sentences describing other changes in their lives.
- Ss work in groups to compare answers. Allow about five minutes for discussion. Remind Ss to decide who in the group has changed the most.

4 LISTENING

Learning Objective: *develop skills in listening for details*

 [CD 3, Track 52]

- Set the scene. Linda and Scott are looking through a photo album and discussing how they have changed over the years.
- Play the audio program. Ss listen and take notes on three changes they hear. Go over answers with the class.

AudioScript

Linda What are you looking at, Scott?
Scott Oh, just one of our photo albums.
Linda Oh, look – it's our wedding picture.
Scott Yeah. Just think, we'll be celebrating our fifth wedding anniversary this month.
Linda Yeah, and I remember we didn't get along so well when we first met. But a year later, we fell in love and got married.

Scott And here's a picture of our honeymoon. Wow! We sure look different now, don't we?
Linda Yes. My hair is much shorter now. And you wore glasses back then. You were always too thin. Oh, and look. Here's a picture of the day we brought Maggie home from the hospital.
Scott She's so cute. And now we have two kids. Who would have guessed?
Linda Yeah. We're just lucky that they look like me.

Possible answers

They didn't get along when they first met.
They're married now.
Linda's hair is shorter.
Scott doesn't wear glasses.
They have two kids now.

3 GRAMMAR FOCUS

Describing changes ▶

With the present tense
I'**m not** in school anymore.
I **wear** contacts now.

With the past tense
I **got** engaged.
I **moved** to a new place.

With the present perfect
I'**ve changed** jobs.
I'**ve fallen** in love.

With the comparative
My hair is **shorter** now.
My job is **less stressful**.

A How have you changed in the last five years?
Check (✓) the statements that are true for you.
If a statement isn't true, give the correct information.

1. I've changed my hairstyle.
2. I dress differently now.
3. I've made some new friends.
4. I got a pet.
5. I've joined a club.
6. I moved into my own apartment.
7. I'm more outgoing than before.
8. I'm not in high school anymore.
9. My life is easier now.
10. I got married.

B PAIR WORK Compare your responses in
part A. Have you changed in similar ways?

C GROUP WORK Write five sentences describing
other changes in your life. Then compare in groups.
Who in the group has changed the most?

4 LISTENING *Memory lane*

 Linda and Scott are looking through a photo album.
Listen to their conversation. How have they changed?
Write down three changes.

Changes

5 WORD POWER

A Complete the word map with phrases from the list. Then add two more examples to each category.

dye my hair
get a bank loan
get a credit card
grow a beard
improve my English vocabulary
learn a new sport
learn how to dance
open a savings account
pierce my ears
start a new hobby
wear contact lenses
win the lottery

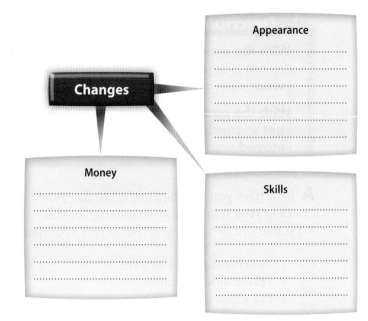

Changes

Appearance
....
....
....
....
....

Money
....
....
....
....
....
....

Skills
....
....
....
....
....

B **PAIR WORK** Have you changed in any of these areas? Tell your partner about a change in each category.

A: I opened a savings account last year. I've already saved $500.
B: I got my first credit card last month. Can I borrow … ?

6 CONVERSATION *Planning your future*

A Listen and practice.

Alex: So, what are you going to do after graduation, Susan?
Susan: Well, I've saved some money, and I think I'd really like to travel.
Alex: Lucky you. That sounds exciting!
Susan: Yeah. Then I plan to get a job and my own apartment.
Alex: Oh, you're not going to live at home?
Susan: No, I don't want to live with my parents – not after I start to work.
Alex: I know what you mean.
Susan: What about you, Alex? Any plans yet?
Alex: I'm going to get a job *and* live at home. I'm broke, and I want to pay off my student loan!

B Listen to the rest of the conversation. What kind of job does Alex want? Where would Susan like to travel?

5 WORD POWER

Learning Objective: *learn vocabulary for discussing changes*

A

- Explain the task. Ss complete the word map with phrases from the list.
- Call on Ss to read the phrases. Explain any vocabulary.
- Ss complete the word map. Remind them to add two more examples to each category.
- Draw the word map on the board. Ask Ss to write answers and add more examples to each category.

Answers

Appearance	Money	Skills
dye my hair	get a bank loan	improve my English
grow a beard	get a credit card	vocabulary
pierce my ears	open a savings	learn a new sport
wear contact	account	learn how to dance
lenses	win the lottery	start a new hobby

lose weight	get a mortgage	learn how to paint
dress better	support a charity	take an art class

(Note: Additional examples are italicized.)

B *Pair work*

- Explain the task and model the example with a S. Elicit additional responses and write them on the board.
- Ss discuss their changes in each category.

End of Cycle 1

See the Supplementary Resources chart at the beginning of this unit for additional teaching materials and student activities related to this Cycle.

Cycle 2, Exercises 6–12

6 CONVERSATION

Learning Objectives: *practice a conversation between two people planning their futures; see verb + infinitive in context*

A ▶ [CD 3, Track 53]

- Have Ss cover the text. Use the picture to set the scene. Ask: "What's happening? What do you think they are discussing?" Elicit ideas.
- Write this chart on the board (without the answers). Ask Ss to listen for three future plans for each person.

<u>Future plans</u>
Susan: travel, get a job, get her own apartment
Alex: get a job, live at home, pay off his student loan

- Play the audio program. Ss write their answers. Ss compare answers in pairs. Then go over answers with the class.
- Have Ss uncover the text. Play the audio program again. Ss read the conversation silently.
- Elicit or explain any new vocabulary.

Vocabulary

graduation: the ceremony at which a person who has completed a course of study gets a diploma
I'm broke: I don't have any money.
pay off: make the final payment for something
student loan: money given to a student that must be paid back after graduating

- Ss practice the conversation in pairs.

B ▶ [CD 3, Track 54]

- Play the audio program. Ss listen to find out the answers to the focus questions.
- Elicit answers from around the class.

AudioScript

Susan What kind of job are you looking for?
Alex Well, I've thought a lot about it, and I'd like to do computer programming. So I hope to get a job with a big computer company.
Susan That sounds really interesting.
Alex Yeah, I've got an interview next week.
Susan Well, good luck!
Alex And where do you plan to travel to, Susan?
Susan Well, I'd like to travel around the United States a bit. There are so many places that I've never seen.
Alex Well, please send me a lot of postcards while you're away.
Susan All right, I will. And I hope you get the job.
Alex Me, too!

Possible answers

Alex wants a job as a computer programmer with a big company. Susan wants to travel around the U.S.

7 GRAMMAR FOCUS

Learning Objectives: *practice using verb + infinitive; ask and answer questions about the future using verb + infinitive*

▶ **[CD 3, Track 55]**

- Books closed. Write these sentences on the board:
  Susan: I'd really _____ _____ travel.
  Susan: I _____ _____ get a job and my own apartment.
  Susan: I don't _____ _____ live with my parents.
  Alex: I'm _____ _____ get a job and live at home.

- Books open. Focus Ss' attention on the Conversation on page 108. Call on Ss to find the answers and to fill in the blanks on the board. (Answers: *like to, plan to, want to, going to*)

- Ask Ss to look at the Grammar Focus box.

- Ask: "What do these structures have in common? What other structures follow this pattern?" (Answers: All are verb + infinitive; *hope to, would like to*)

- Play the audio program. Then have Ss make sentences of their own (e.g., *I don't plan to get married this year.*).

For more practice with verb + infinitive, play **Line Up!** – download it from the website. Ss line up according to the age when they hope to marry, how many children they hope to have, etc.

A

- Explain the task. Tell Ss to write true information about themselves. Encourage Ss to use each verb from the Grammar Focus box at least once.

- Ss work individually to complete the sentences. Remind Ss to add two more statements for numbers 7 and 8. Go around the class and give help. (Note: Don't check Ss' answers until the end of part B.)

- **Option:** Tell Ss to look at the photos. As a class, discuss the aspects of people's lives that the photos represent (e.g., *traveling overseas, families, working parents, getting married, becoming successful*).

B Pair work

- Ss work in pairs to discuss their responses. Tell pairs to check (✓) the statements on their lists that are the same and to put an X next to the ones that are different.

- Elicit some "same" and "different" responses from pairs.

C Group work

- Explain the task. Call on Ss to read the questions. Check for correct intonation.

- Ss work in small groups. They take turns asking and answering the questions. Tell Ss to ask the questions in any order they want. Also encourage Ss to ask follow-up questions and to respond to group members' plans.

- **Option:** Ss earn one point for every follow-up question they ask.

 8 PRONUNCIATION

Learning Objective: *notice the difference between the vowel sounds /oʊ/ and /ʌ/*

A ▶ **[CD 3, Track 56]**

- Explain that words spelled with *o* are pronounced in different ways in English. Point out the two examples in the book.

- Play the audio program and let Ss listen to the two sounds and practice.

- Elicit more words that contain the two sounds (e.g., *lot, job, grow, oh*).

- **Option:** If Ss are having problems, ask them to find words spelled with *o* in the unit. Say the words, and ask Ss which have the /oʊ/ sound, which have the /ʌ/ sound, and which have some other sound.

For more practice with this Pronunciation, play **Bingo** – download it from the website.

B ▶ **[CD 3, Track 57]**

- Explain the task. Model the first word.

- Play the audio program. Ss check (✓) the sound they hear.

- **Option:** Ss first check (✓) the sound they think is represented by the letter *o*. Then play the audio program. Ss check if their guesses were right or wrong.

- Check Ss' answers on the board.

Answers

/oʊ/	both	cold	home	over
/ʌ/	come	honey	money	mother

- **Option:** Ss work in pairs. They write a conversation with at least five words from part A or B. Then Ss practice the conversation.

> **TIP** Each week, select a "sound of the week" and focus specifically on that (or, in this case, the two sounds).

7 GRAMMAR FOCUS

Verb + infinitive

What **are** you **going to do** after graduation?
I'm (not) **going to get** a job right away.
I (don't) **plan to get** my own apartment.
I (don't) **want to live** with my parents.

I hope to get a new car.
I'd like to travel this summer.
I'd love to move to a new city.

A Complete these statements so that they are true for you. Use information from the grammar box. Then add two more statements of your own.

1. I .... travel abroad.
2. I .... live with my parents.
3. I .... get married.
4. I .... have a lot of children.
5. I .... make a lot of money!
6. I .... become very successful.
7. ....
8. ....

B **PAIR WORK** Compare your responses with a partner. How are you the same? How are you different?

C **GROUP WORK** What are your plans for the future? Take turns asking and answering these questions.

What are you going to do after this English course is over?
Do you plan to study here again next year?
What other languages would you like to learn?
What countries would you like to visit? Why?
Do you want to get a (new) job in a few years?
What kind of future do you hope to have?

8 PRONUNCIATION Vowel sounds /oʊ/ and /ʌ/

A Many words spelled with *o* are pronounced /oʊ/ or /ʌ/. Listen to the difference and practice.

/oʊ/ =	don't	smoke	go	loan	own	hope
/ʌ/ =	month	love	some	does	young	touch

B Listen to these words. Check (✓) the correct pronunciation.

	both	cold	come	home	honey	money	mother	over
/oʊ/	☐	☐	☐	☐	☐	☐	☐	☐
/ʌ/	☐	☐	☐	☐	☐	☐	☐	☐

INTERCHANGE 16 *My possible future*

Imagine you could do anything, go anywhere, and meet anybody.
Go to Interchange 16 on page 131.

 ## SPEAKING *A class party*

A **GROUP WORK** Make plans for a class party.
Talk about these things and take notes.

Date	Transportation	Place	Food and drink
Time	Entertainment	Activities	Cost (if any)

A: When are we going to have our party?
B: I'd like to have it on Saturday.
C: That sounds fine. Let's plan to have it in the afternoon.
D: Can we start the party at noon?

B **GROUP WORK** Decide what each person is going
to bring to the party.

A: I can bring the drinks.
B: And I can bring some snacks.
C: Hey, why don't you bring
   your guitar?

 ## WRITING *Party plans*

A **GROUP WORK** Work with your same group from Exercise 10.
As a group, write about your plans for the class party.

> Baseball Fun in the Sun!
> 1.   Date and Time: We'd like to have our end-of-the-class party
>   next Saturday, on June 18th, from 12:00 – 4:00 p.m.
> 2.   Place: We plan to meet at City Park near the baseball field.
>   If it rains, meet on Sunday at the same time and place.
> 3.   Activities: We're going to play a class baseball game. The
>   game can start after lunch. Other activities are . . .

B **CLASS ACTIVITY** Present your plans to the class. Each person in
your group should present a different part. Then choose the best plan.

INTERCHANGE 16

See page T-131 for teaching notes.

 SPEAKING

Learning Objective: *talk about plans for a class party using verb + infinitive*

A *Group work*

- Explain the task. Ss make plans for a class party. Go over the issues they need to think about (e.g., *date, time, place, transportation*). Model the conversation with three Ss.
- Encourage Ss to use a variety of verb + infinitive forms.
- Ss work in small groups to discuss their plans. Set a time limit of about ten minutes. Tell groups to choose one person to take notes.

> **TIP** If you notice that you always monitor groups in the same order (e.g., you always start at the front of the class), change your routine. Try starting from another direction so that some Ss do not get ignored.

B *Group work*

- Explain the task. Ss decide what each person is going to bring to the party. Model the conversation with two Ss.
- Ss discuss their plans in their groups. Then Ss can report their plans orally to the class.

 WRITING

Learning Objective: *learn how to write a plan using verb + infinitive.*

A *Group work*

- Explain the task. Ask Ss to read the example plan silently. Ss write a similar plan, based on their discussion in Exercise 10.
- Ss form the same small groups as in Exercise 10. They write their plan for an end-of-the-class party. Go around the groups and give help as needed.

B *Class activity*

- Explain the task. Each S in the group chooses a different section (e.g., *date and time, place*) to present to the class.
- Groups take turns presenting their ideas to the class. While a group presents its plan, the other groups take notes so that they can vote afterward.
- ***Option:*** After Ss vote on the best plan, have the party!

12 READING

Learning Objectives: *read and discuss an article about setting personal goals; develop skills in recognizing audience and reading for specific information*

- Go over the pre-reading question. Ask Ss to scan the list to find the areas for change or improvement. (Note: The list has bullet points and boldface words.)
- Ss read the list of areas individually. Then pairs discuss which aspects of their lives they would like to change or improve.

A

- Explain the task. Ss read the article silently. Remind Ss to try to guess the meanings of any words they don't know.
- Ask: "Who do you think the article was written for?" Go over the answer with the class.

Answer

people who are looking for direction

- Elicit or explain any remaining new vocabulary.

Vocabulary

setting goals: choosing specific objectives for what you would like to do or change in your life
motivate: provide a stimulation for doing something
achieve: accomplish; reach
fields: areas of activity or interest
community service: work done without payment to help others
realistic: likely to happen in the future; reasonable
manageable: easy or possible to deal with; controllable
adjust: change slightly

B

- Read aloud the questions in part B. Then ask Ss to look for the answers. (Encourage Ss to look for the information quickly, without reading the whole article again.) Give Ss a time limit.

- Ss compare answers in pairs or groups. Have the Ss who finish first write their responses on the board.

Answers

1. Top athletes and successful business people in all fields set personal goals.
2. People set goals because they need more direction in life.
3. You should divide your goals into steps because one big goal is more manageable to achieve in small tasks.
4. It is important to adjust your goals because your goals can change with time.

C *Pair work*

- Explain the task. Ss work in pairs to discuss one of their personal goals and the steps they will take to achieve them.
- **Option:** Draw this diagram on the board. Label the circles (from outside to in): five-year goal, one-year goal, three-month goal, one-month goal. Label the center circle *Major Goal*. Ss copy the diagram and complete it. Then they discuss the goals in pairs.

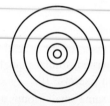

End of Cycle 2

See the Supplementary Resources chart at the beginning of this unit for additional teaching materials and student activities related to this Cycle and for assessment tools.

Goal Setting

Setting Personal Goals

Look at the list in the article. Which of these areas of your life would you like to change or improve?

Ask any top athlete or successful businessperson and they will tell you the importance of setting goals. Goal setting can motivate you and give your life direction. It seems easy, right? Just write down a list of things you want to achieve and then do them. Well, it's not that easy!

Effective goal setting happens on several levels. First, you create a big picture of what you want to do with your life. At this point, you decide what large-scale goals you want to achieve. Second, you divide these into smaller and smaller tasks. Third, you put the smaller tasks into a rough time line. Finally, once you have your plan, you start working to achieve it.

How do you know what your large-scale goals are? These questions can help you get started.

- **Career**
What level do you want to reach in your career?

- **Family**
What kind of relationship do you want with the people in your family?

- **Community Service**
How do you want to give back to your community?

- **Financial**
How much money do you want to earn? How much do you want to save?

- **Creative**
Do you want to achieve any artistic goals?

- **Physical**
How will you stay in good physical shape throughout your life?

- **Education**
What do you want to learn? How will you learn it?

- **Recreation**
How do you want to enjoy yourself?

PROCESS

Write down your goals and think about them carefully. Are they realistic?

How important are they?

Rank them in order from most important to least important.

Then follow the process above to make your long-term plan. Remember, your goals can change with time.

Look at them regularly and adjust them if necessary. And be sure your goals are things you hope to achieve, not things others want.

A Read the article. Who do you think the article was written for? Check (✓) the correct answer.

People who...

☐ have very clear goals ☐ are looking for direction ☐ don't care about their future

B Answer these questions.

1. What kinds of people set personal goals? ....
2. Why do people set personal goals? ....
3. Why should you divide your goals into steps? ....
4. Why is it important to adjust your goals? ....

C **PAIR WORK** What is one of your personal goals? What steps will you take to achieve it?

Units 15–16 Progress check

SELF-ASSESSMENT

How well can you do these things? Check (✓) the boxes.

I can	Very well	OK	A little
Discuss future plans and arrangements (Ex. 1)	☐	☐	☐
Make and respond to invitations (Ex. 2)	☐	☐	☐
Understand and pass on telephone messages (Ex. 3)	☐	☐	☐
Ask and answer questions about changes in my life (Ex. 4)	☐	☐	☐
Describe personal goals (Ex. 5)	☐	☐	☐
Discuss and decide how to accomplish goals (Ex. 5)	☐	☐	☐

 1 **DISCUSSION** *The weekend*

A **GROUP WORK** Find out what your classmates are doing this weekend.
Ask for two details about each person's plans.

Name	Plans	Details
....	....	....
....	....	....
....	....	....

A: What are you going to do this weekend?
B: I'm seeing a rock concert on Saturday.
C: Which band are you going to see?

B **GROUP WORK** Whose weekend plans sound the best? Why?

2 **ROLE PLAY** *Inviting a friend*

Student A: Invite Student B to one of the events from
Exercise 1. Say where and when it is.

Student B: Student A invites you out. Accept and ask for
more information, or refuse and give an excuse.

Change roles and try the role play again.

Units 15–16 Progress check

SELF-ASSESSMENT

Learning Objectives: *reflect on one's learning; identify areas that need improvement*

- Ask: "What did you learn in Units 15 and 16?" Elicit Ss' answers.
- Ss complete the Self-assessment. Encourage them to be honest, and point out they will not get a bad grade if they check (✓) *a little*.

- Ss move on to the Progress check exercises. You can have Ss complete them in class or for homework, using one of these techniques:
  1. Ask Ss to complete all the exercises.
  2. Ask Ss: "What do you need to practice?" Then assign exercises based on their answers.
  3. Ask Ss to choose and complete exercises based on their Self-assessment.

DISCUSSION

Learning Objective: *assess one's ability to discuss future plans and arrangements*

A *Group work*

- Explain the task. Ss work in groups of four. Each S writes the names of the other three Ss in the first column. Ss then ask each other about their weekend plans. Encourage them to ask follow-up questions to find out details. Model the example with two Ss.

- Ss complete the task. Go around the class and check their use of the present continuous and *be going to*.

B *Group work*

- Explain the task. Ss discuss the questions in groups and share their results with the class.

ROLE PLAY

Learning Objectives: *assess one's ability to make and respond to invitations*

- Elicit different ways to make invitations, accept invitations, refuse invitations, and make excuses. Write them on the board.

- Explain the task. Ss work in pairs. Student A invites Student B to an event from Exercise 1. Student B accepts or refuses.
- Model the role play with a S.
- Ss complete the role play in pairs. Then they change roles and practice again. Go around the class and give help as needed.

3 LISTENING

Learning Objective: *assess one's ability to understand and pass on phone messages*

 [CD 3, Track 58]

- Set the scene and explain the task. Ss will hear two telephone calls. They listen and write the name of the person the message is for, the caller, and the message.
- Play the audio program once or twice. Ss listen and complete the messages.

AudioScript

1.
Man [*phone rings*] Hello.
Lisa Hi. Could I speak to Paul, please?
Man I'm sorry. Paul isn't home right now. May I take a message?
Lisa Oh, um. Sure. This is Lisa. Would you tell him to meet me at the theater at 7:00? The play starts at 7:30.
Man Meet Lisa at the theater at 7:00. The play is at 7:30. Got it.
Lisa Thanks. Bye.
Man Bye-bye.

2.
Man [*phone rings*] Hello.
Ann Hi. Brian?
Man No, sorry. Brian isn't here right now. Can I take a message?
Ann Yes, thanks. Do you have a pencil?
Man Yeah. Go ahead.
Ann OK. This is Ann. Could you tell him that I'm still at the barbecue? Please ask him to pick me up here. Not at home.
Man You're still at the barbecue. He should pick you up there. Not at home.
Ann That's it. Thanks.
Man No problem.

- Go over answers with the class.

Possible answers

1. Message for: **Paul**
   Caller: **Lisa**
   Message: **Play is at 7:30. Meet her at theater at 7:00.**
2. Message for: **Brian**
   Caller: **Ann**
   Message: **Pick her up at barbecue, not at home.**

4 SURVEY

Learning Objective: *assess one's ability to ask and answer questions about changes in one's life*

A Class activity

- Explain the task and go over the chart. Explain any new vocabulary. Then elicit how to make questions with the phrases in the chart (e.g., *Did you get your hair cut last week?*).

- Set a time limit of about ten minutes. Ss complete the task. Go around the class and note any grammar or vocabulary errors.

B Class activity

- Ss compare their information as a class. Ask: "Who has changed the most?"

5 SPEAKING

Learning Objective: *assess one's ability to describe personal goals; assess one's ability to discuss and decide on how to accomplish goals*

- Ss check (✓) the goals they want to accomplish individually. Then they add two more goals.

- Explain the task. Each S chooses one goal. Then they plan how to achieve the goal in pairs.
- Model the example conversation with a S. Then Ss complete the task in pairs. Go around the class and check their use of verb + infinitive.

WHAT'S NEXT?

Learning Objective: *become more involved in one's learning*

- Focus Ss' attention on the Self-assessment again. Ask: "How well can you do these things now?"

- Ask Ss to underline one thing they need to review. Ask: "What did you underline? How can you review it?"
- If needed, plan additional activities or reviews based on Ss' answers.

3 LISTENING *Telephone messages*

▶ Listen to the telephone conversations. Write down the messages.

1
Message for: _____
Caller: _____
Message: _____
_____
_____
_____

2
Message for: _____
Caller: _____
Message: _____
_____
_____
_____

4 SURVEY *Changes*

A CLASS ACTIVITY Go around the class and find this information. Write a classmate's name only once! Ask follow-up questions.

Find someone who	Name
1. got his or her hair cut last week	....
2. doesn't wear glasses anymore	....
3. has changed schools recently	....
4. goes out more often these days	....
5. got married last year	....
6. has started a new hobby	....
7. is happier these days	....
8. has gotten a part-time job recently	....

last week

this week

B CLASS ACTIVITY Compare your information. Who in the class has changed the most?

5 SPEAKING *Setting goals*

Check (✓) the goals you have and add two more. Then choose one goal. Plan how to accomplish it with a partner.

- ☐ own my own computer
- ☐ move to a new city
- ☐ have more free time
- ☐ have more friends
- ☐ get into a good school
- ☐ travel a lot more
- ☐ live a long time
- ☐ ....
- ☐ ....

A: I'd like to travel a lot more.
B: How are you going to do that?

WHAT'S NEXT?

Look at your Self-assessment again. Do you need to review anything?

Interchange activities

interchange 1

Learning Objective: *find out more about classmates in interviews*

A Class activity

- As a warm-up, stand next to different Ss. For each S, ask the class: "What is his/her name? Where is he/she from?"
- Ask Ss to look at the picture. If needed, explain that Lady Gaga is a popular singer and that Lady Gaga is not her real name.
- Go over the questions in the chart. Help Ss with vocabulary and pronunciation. If necessary, review hobbies and the months of the year.
- Explain the task. Model the questions with a S. Point out that Ss will interview three classmates.
- Ss complete the task. Go around the class and give help as needed. Write down any grammar or vocabulary errors and go over them after Ss complete the task.

B Group work

- Explain the task. Go over the questions and review the vocabulary if needed.
- Ss discuss the questions as a group.
- **Option:** Elicit interesting information that Ss found out about their classmates.

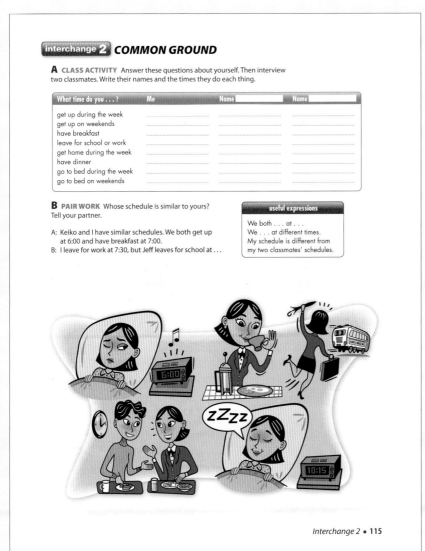

interchange 2 *COMMON GROUND*

A CLASS ACTIVITY Answer these questions about yourself. Then interview two classmates. Write their names and the times they do each thing.

What time do you . . . ?	Me	Name	Name
get up during the week			
get up on weekends			
have breakfast			
leave for school or work			
get home during the week			
have dinner			
go to bed during the week			
go to bed on weekends			

B PAIR WORK Whose schedule is similar to yours? Tell your partner.

A: Keiko and I have similar schedules. We both get up at 6:00 and have breakfast at 7:00.
B: I leave for work at 7:30, but Jeff leaves for school at . . .

useful expressions
We both . . . at . . .
We . . . at different times.
My schedule is different from my two classmates' schedules.

Interchange 2 ▪ 115

---

interchange 2

Learning Objective: *find out more about classmates using a survey about schedules*

A *Class activity*

- Focus Ss' attention on the pictures at the bottom of the page. Ask: "What does the woman do every day? What time does she do each thing?"

- Go over any new vocabulary in the chart. Teach or review how to write times.
- Explain the first part of the task. Ask Ss: "What time do you get up during the week?" Ss complete the first line in the *Me* column. Then they complete the rest of the column individually. Allow about three minutes. Go around the class and give help as needed.

- Explain the rest of the task. Ss go around the class and interview two classmates. They write each classmate's name at the top of the column and ask the questions in the chart. They write a time for each response.
- Model the task with a S.

TIP At beginning levels, sometimes instructions are difficult to understand. It is much more effective to model the task than to explain it.

- Set a time limit of about 15 minutes. Then Ss complete the task. Go around the class and give help as needed. Write down any errors you hear for Ss to correct later.

B *Pair work*

- Explain the task. Go over the useful expressions and model the example conversation with a S.
- Ss complete the task in pairs. Encourage them to explain why.
- Elicit answers from the class.

Learning Objectives: *ask for and give prices; practice bargaining*

A

- Point out the title. Explain that a *flea market* is a place where people sell used things. Sellers have an "asking price," but people bargain.
- Ask: "Are there flea markets in your country? Do people bargain for better prices?" Encourage discussion.
- Focus Ss' attention on the pictures on both pages. Ask: "What do you see here? What are these people doing?"
- Divide the Ss into pairs and assign pages A and B. Explain the task.
- Focus Ss' attention on the TV. Ask: "What is a good price for a used TV?" Tell Ss with page A to choose an "asking price" and write it down. Then focus Ss' attention on the painting. Ask: "What is a good price for the painting?" Tell Ss with page B to choose an "asking price" and write it down.
- Ss work individually to make up prices for the remaining four items.

TIP If Ss have difficulty with a specific task, try a different grouping for the task. For example, have them work in small groups instead of pairs.

B *Pair work*

- Explain the task. Ss work in pairs. Students A and B take turns as buyer and seller. The buyers choose three things they want to buy from their partner's page. Buyers decide on a good price for each thing.

interchange 3 **FLEA MARKET**

Student A

A You want to sell these things. Write your "asking price" for each item.

116 ■ *Interchange 3*

- Model the example conversation with a few Ss, showing that A is the buyer and B is the seller. Remind the class to vary the conversation and to bargain.
- Give Ss a time limit of about ten minutes. Explain that partners need to take turns starting the conversation so that each S is both buyer and seller.

- Continue until both partners buy and sell at least three things. Tell the Ss to write down the prices they bought the things for.
- Go around the class and give help as needed.
- **Option:** Ask a pair of Ss to perform their role play for the class. Alternatively, Ss can change partners and try the activity again.

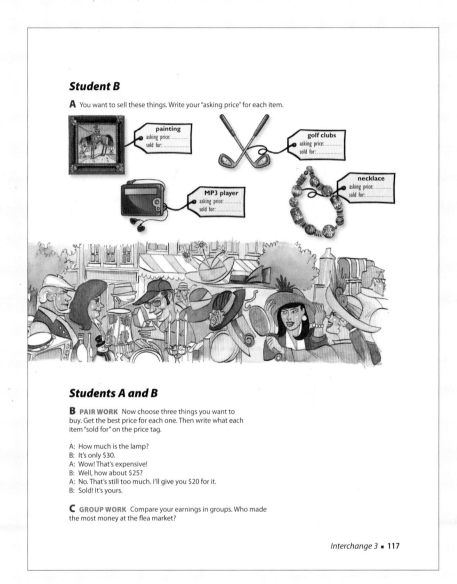

Student B

A You want to sell these things. Write your "asking price" for each item.

painting
asking price: ....
sold for: ....

golf clubs
asking price: ....
sold for: ....

MP3 player
asking price: ....
sold for: ....

necklace
asking price: ....
sold for: ....

Students A and B

B PAIR WORK Now choose three things you want to buy. Get the best price for each one. Then write what each item "sold for" on the price tag.

A: How much is the lamp?
B: It's only $30.
A: Wow! That's expensive!
B: Well, how about $25?
A: No. That's still too much. I'll give you $20 for it.
B: Sold! It's yours.

C GROUP WORK Compare your earnings in groups. Who made the most money at the flea market?

Interchange 3 ▪ 117

- **Option:** Ss make a list of six to eight things to sell at a flea market. They can also bring in two or three things and role-play a sale at a flea market.

C Group work

- Ss look at the "sold for" part of their page and add up the amount of money they made individually.

- Ss work in groups to take turns making and responding to invitations. Go around the room and encourage Ss to respond politely.
- **Option:** Elicit interesting refusals that Ss made.

interchange 4

Learning Objective: *to make weekend plans with classmates*

A

- Explain the task. Ss read the directions. Ss write two tasks they need to do this weekend and the times. Model an example for the class.
- Ss complete the task individually.

B

- Explain the task. Ss read the events page to learn what is happening in the city this weekend. Ss choose three things they would like to do. Model an example for the class.
- Ss read the events page and make their choices individually. Explain any vocabulary they need help with.

C *Group work*

- Explain the task. Model the example with a S. Review invitations and polite refusals if necessary.
- Ss work in groups to take turns making and responding to invitations. Go around the room and encourage Ss to respond politely.
- **Option:** Elicit interesting refusals that Ss made.

interchange 4 *ARE YOU FREE THIS WEEKEND?*

A Write two things you need to do this weekend. Include the times.

Saturday	Sunday

B Read the events page from your city's website. Choose three things you'd like to do.

On The Town

HOME · Log In · Register · Contact Us

Search the Calendar · What do you want to do? · GO

RESTAURANTS | LATE NIGHT | MUSIC | THEATER | MUSEUMS | OUTDOORS | KIDS | MOVIES | CALENDAR

TOP PICKS What's on this weekend

Saturday, May 21

Community Art Fair
See the work of local artists at the Community Art Fair! More than 200 artists, plus food, drinks, and music. Fun for the whole family!
11:00–5:00

Play Tennis!
Free tennis lessons for all ages. Central Park Tennis Courts. Bring a partner!
2:00–4:00

Bike Now's Ride Around the City
Once a year, this group organizes a bike ride around the city. Free food and drinks for cyclists from local restaurants.
Ride starts at 4:30.

Movies at Green Park
This Saturday's movie: *Avatar.* Bring your dinner, sit on the grass, and enjoy a movie under the stars.
Movie starts at 8:30.   MORE

Sunday, May 22

Concerts on the River
Come hear your favorite music next to the White River. A different kind of music from a different country every week. Concert starts at 1:00.

Chess in the Park
Bring a partner or find a partner at the city's biggest chess-a-thon. All levels and ages welcome. City Park, next to Park Café.
2:00–7:00

Free Tango Lessons
Learn to dance the tango! Live music and dancing. All levels. Beginners welcome. Center Street Activity Center.
5:30–7:00

City Baseball League
Green Park Team vs. the Lions. Come cheer for your favorite team! Come early to win prizes for the biggest fans!
Game at 7:30   MORE

C **GROUP WORK** Take turns inviting your classmates to the events. Say yes to one invitation and no to two invitations. Give a polite excuse.

A: Would you like to play tennis on Saturday? We can play from 2:00 to 4:00.
B: I'd like to, but I can't. I have to clean my room on Saturday afternoon.
A: Well, are you free in the morning?

118 ■ *Interchange 4*

 **FAMILY FACTS**

A CLASS ACTIVITY Go around the class and find this information.
Write a classmate's name only once. Ask follow-up questions of your own.

Find someone	Name
1. who is an only child **"Do you have any brothers or sisters?"**	....
2. who has two brothers **"How many brothers do you have?"**	....
3. who has two sisters **"How many sisters do you have?"**	....
4. whose brother or sister is living abroad **"Are any of your brothers or sisters living abroad?"**	....
5. who lives with his or her grandparents **"Do you live with your grandparents?"**	....
6. who has a grandparent still working **"Is your grandmother or grandfather still working?"**	....
7. who has a family member with an unusual job **"Does anyone in your family have an unusual job?"**	....
8. whose mother or father is studying English **"Is either of your parents studying English?"**	....

B GROUP WORK Compare your information.

Interchange 5 ▪ 119

---

interchange 5

Learning Objective: *gain fluency asking questions about classmates' families*

A Class activity

- Focus Ss' attention on the pictures. Point out that they show three different families. Ask: "What can you tell me about each family?"
- Go over the chart and explain the task.

- Model the first question with several Ss. Ask the question until you find a S who is an only child. Write that S's name in the *Name* column.
- Elicit possible follow-up questions for the first question. Write them on the board.
- Point out that Ss can make up responses or say "Sorry, I'd rather not say" if they don't want to give true information.

- Set a time limit of 10 to 15 minutes. Ss complete the activity.
- Go around the room and encourage Ss to move around and talk to other classmates. Note any errors, such as question formation.

B Group work

- Ss compare their answers in small groups. Then elicit interesting things they learned about their classmates.
- Go over any errors you noticed in part A and ask Ss to correct them.

Learning Objective: *speak more fluently about leisure activities*

A Class activity

- Focus Ss' attention on the picture. Ask: "What is a talent show?" Elicit ideas. If needed, explain that it is a contest in which people sing, dance, or play an instrument.

- Explain the task. Ss ask each other who does these activities, how often they do them, and how well they do them. Point out that Ss must try to find one person who does each thing. Also, they cannot use the same name twice.

- Model the task with a S at the front of the class, using the example conversation.

- Set a time limit of 10 to 15 minutes. Ss go around the room and complete the activity.

B Group work

- Explain the task. Tell Ss to imagine the class is participating in a talent show. Ss choose three people from the class to enter in the contest. Ask: "What will each person do in the contest? Why?"

- Model the conversation with two Ss. Then Ss complete the task in small groups.

- Ask the groups to share and explain their choices with the class.

---

interchange 6 **DO YOU DANCE?**

A CLASS ACTIVITY Does anyone in your class do these things? How often and how well? Go around the class and find one person for each activity.

	Name	How often?	How well?
dance			
play an instrument			
sing			
act			
tell jokes			
do gymnastics			
do magic tricks			

A: Do you dance?
B: Yes, I do.
A: How often do you go dancing?
B: Every weekend.
A: Really? And how well do you dance?

B GROUP WORK Imagine there's a talent show this weekend. Who do you want to enter? Choose three people from your class. Explain your choices.

A: Let's enter Adam in the talent show.
B: Why Adam?
A: Because he dances very well.
C: Yes, he does. And Yvette is very good at playing the guitar. Let's enter her, too!

120 • *Interchange 6*

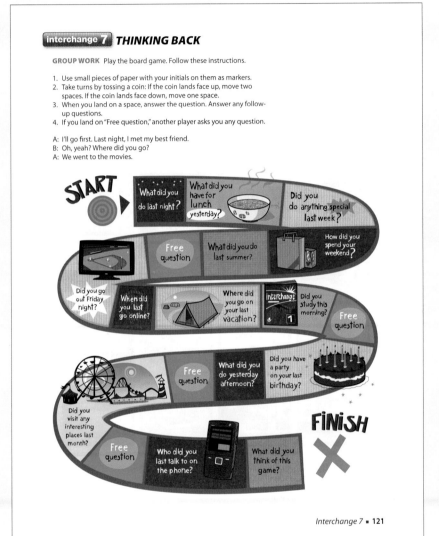

Interchange 7 ▪ 121

interchange 7

Learning Objective: *speak more fluently about events in the past by playing a board game*

Group work
- Focus Ss' attention on the board game and read the instructions. Show Ss how to write their initials on small pieces of paper and use them as markers.

- **Option:** Ss can use other small items as markers (e.g., pen caps or erasers).
- Show Ss how to toss a coin. Point out which side is face up and which side is face down.
- Have different Ss read the questions in each space. Explain that a "free question" can be any question another player wants to ask you. Remind Ss they can make up an answer if they don't want to answer truthfully.

- Then ask two Ss to model the example conversation. Point out that Ss should ask follow-up questions.
- Show how to play the game with a group of three Ss.

TIP In low-level classes, it is more effective to model a game or activity than to explain it.

- Ss play the game in small groups. Go around the class and encourage Ss to ask follow-up questions.
- **Option:** Ask Ss to share any interesting information they learned about their classmates.

Learning Objective: *discuss neighborhood places and use* there is/ there are + *quantifiers by playing a guessing game*

Class activity

- Explain Ss will play a guessing game. Read the locations. Elicit or explain any location meanings.

- Read the instructions. Put Ss into two teams, A and B. Explain that one S from each team will go to the front of the class.

- Those two Ss choose a location from the list and give four clues to their own team. Point out Ss will use *there is/there are* and use quantifiers. Model an example: "There are a lot of people waiting at this place. There are a lot of suitcases. There are a lot of planes. There aren't any bicycles. Where am I?"

- The first S to guess the location correctly goes to the front of the class, too. That S chooses a different location to give clues.

- The first team with all of its members at the front wins.

- Have two Ss model the example conversation at the bottom of the page.

- Show how to play the game with a group of three Ss.

> **TIP** In low-level classes, it is more effective to model a game or activity than to explain it.

- Put the class into two teams to play. Listen to make sure that Ss give four clues and use *there is/there are* + quantifiers. Give help as needed.

---

interchange 8 **WHERE AM I?**

CLASS ACTIVITY Play a guessing game. Follow these instructions.

1. Get into two teams, A and B. One student from each team goes to the front of the class.
2. These two students choose a location and give four clues, using *There is/are* plus a quantifier.
3. The first student to guess the location correctly joins his or her team-mate at the front.
4. The new student chooses a different location and gives clues. His or her team answers.
5. The first team with all of its members in the front wins.

A: There isn't any food in this place. There's a lot of coffee. There are a few computers. There are many emails. Where am I?
B: In an Internet café!
A: Correct! Now you come to the front.

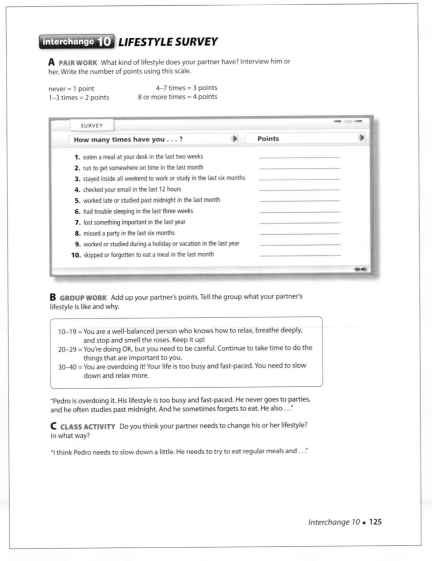

 **LIFESTYLE SURVEY**

A PAIR WORK What kind of lifestyle does your partner have? Interview him or her. Write the number of points using this scale.

never = 1 point   4–7 times = 3 points
1–3 times = 2 points   8 or more times = 4 points

SURVEY

How many times have you . . . ?	Points
1. eaten a meal at your desk in the last two weeks	
2. run to get somewhere on time in the last month	
3. stayed inside all weekend to work or study in the last six months	
4. checked your email in the last 12 hours	
5. worked late or studied past midnight in the last month	
6. had trouble sleeping in the last three weeks	
7. lost something important in the last year	
8. missed a party in the last six months	
9. worked or studied during a holiday or vacation in the last year	
10. skipped or forgotten to eat a meal in the last month	

B GROUP WORK Add up your partner's points. Tell the group what your partner's lifestyle is like and why.

10–19 = You are a well-balanced person who knows how to relax, breathe deeply, and stop and smell the roses. Keep it up!
20–29 = You're doing OK, but you need to be careful. Continue to take time to do the things that are important to you.
30–40 = You are overdoing it! Your life is too busy and fast-paced. You need to slow down and relax more.

"Pedro is overdoing it. His lifestyle is too busy and fast-paced. He never goes to parties, and he often studies past midnight. And he sometimes forgets to eat. He also . . ."

C CLASS ACTIVITY Do you think your partner needs to change his or her lifestyle? In what way?

"I think Pedro needs to slow down a little. He needs to try to eat regular meals and . . ."

Interchange 10 ▪ 125

---

interchange 10

Learning Objective: *Ss complete a survey about his or her lifestyle*

A Pair Work
- Focus S's attention on the survey. Then write *easygoing and relaxed* and *busy and fast-paced* on the board. Explain that these are different lifestyles. Elicit different activities and write them on the board under each lifestyle.

- Explain the task. Then Ss read the questions silently. Elicit or explain any new vocabulary.
- Model the activity by asking a S the first interview question. Explain that the S should answer with the number of times he or she has done the thing asked about.
- Show how to use the chart at the top to calculate the number of times into points. based on Ss responses Show where to write the number of points.

- Ss complete the survey in pairs. Go around the class and give help as needed.
- ***Option:*** To make Ss listen more carefully, tell them to ask the questions in a different order.

B Group work
- Explain the task and demonstrate how to add up the points. Then ask a few S to read the results chart and the example reading. Point out that Ss will use the results chart to create their own explanation about their partner's lifestyle.
- Ss use their surveys to make notes about their partner's lifestyle.
- In groups, Ss take turns talking about their partner's lifestyle.

C Class activity
- Explain the task and read the example.
- Ask the class: "Who has an easygoing and relaxed lifestyle? Why? Who has a busy and fast-paced lifestyle? Why?" Elicit Ss' answers.

Interchange activities ▪ **T-123**

interchange 9A/B

Learning Objective: *speak more fluently about differences in people's appearances*

A *Pair Work*

- Ss work in pairs. One S looks at Interchange 9A and the other S looks at Interchange 9B.
- Explain the task. Both Ss have pictures of a party, but there are some differences in the pictures. Ss ask each other questions to find the differences without looking at their partners' picture.
- Ask different Ss to read the questions at the top of the page. Point out that Ss can use these questions to find the differences.
- Model the task with one pair. Ask: "What is Dave wearing in Picture 1? in Picture 2?" Elicit answers. (Answers: Student A: In Picture 1, Dave's wearing a blue shirt. Student B: In Picture 2, he's wearing a white shirt.)

> **TIP** With information gap activities, tell Ss to sit across from their partners and put a textbook between them. That way, they can hear each other but not see each other's pictures.

- Ss complete the task in pairs. Go around the class and give help as needed.

B *Class activity*

- Tell pairs to look over their answers (i.e., the differences between the two pictures) and to choose one to write on the board. Encourage them to come to the board quickly by making it a rule that no answer can be written twice.

---

interchange 9A *FIND THE DIFFERENCES*

Student A

A **PAIR WORK** How many differences can you find between your picture here and your partner's picture? Ask questions like these to find the differences.

How many people are standing / sitting / wearing . . . / holding a drink? Who?
What color is . . . 's T-shirt / sweater / hair?
Does . . . wear glasses / have a beard / have long hair?
What does . . . look like?

B **CLASS ACTIVITY** How many differences are there in the pictures?

"In picture 1, Dave's T-shirt is . . . . In picture 2, it's . . ."

- To check the answers written on the board, ask the pair who wrote an answer to read it aloud for the class. Then find out if other Ss agree. If they do agree, go on to the next answer until all of them have been checked. If Ss don't agree, ask the class to look at both pictures again to check it.

interchange 9B *FIND THE DIFFERENCES*

Student B

A PAIR WORK How many differences can you find between your picture here and your partner's picture? Ask questions like these to find the differences.

How many people are standing / sitting / wearing . . . / holding a drink? Who?
What color is . . . 's T-shirt / sweater / hair?
Does . . . wear glasses / have a beard / have long hair?
What does . . . look like?

Picture 2

Patrick

Neil

Dave

Fiona

Kate

Anna

B CLASS ACTIVITY How many differences are there in the pictures?

"In picture 1, Dave's T-shirt is . . . . In picture 2, it's . . ."

124 ▪ *Interchange 9B*

Possible Answers

1. In Picture 1, Dave is wearing a blue shirt. In Picture 2, he's wearing a white shirt.
2. In Picture 1, Anna's hair is long. In Picture 2, it's short.
3. In Picture 1, Anna is sitting. In Picture 2, she's standing.
4. In Picture 1, Fiona's sweater is green. In Picture 2, it's purple.
5. In Picture 1, Kate has curly red hair. In Picture 2, she has straight brown hair.
6. In Picture 1, Neil is standing. In Picture 2, he's sitting.
7. In Picture 1, there are three gifts on the table. In Picture 2, there are two gifts on the table.

interchange 11

Learning Objective: *speak more fluently about cities by discussing a guide found on a city's website*

A

- Ask: "Where are some different places to find out information about a city?" Elicit Ss' answers.

> **TIP** To get Ss' attention, give them instructions from different places. Sometimes give them from the back of the classroom; other times give them from the middle of the classroom.

- Explain the task. Ss make a city guide for a website. Have them choose a city they know well or a city they want to learn about.

- Go over the questions and chart. Point out that this guide is from a city's website. Elicit or explain any new vocabulary.

Vocabulary

souvenirs: things you buy to help you remember a place you visit
inexpensive: cheap
historical sights: important places in a city's or country's past
bargain clothing stores: stores that have cheap clothes
free: costing no money

- Ss complete the guide individually in class or for homework.

B Group work

- Explain the task. Ask different Ss to read the questions aloud. Then elicit additional questions and ask a S to write them on the board.

- Ss compare their city guides in small groups. (If possible, Ss should work with classmates who wrote about different cities.)

- Go around the class and encourage Ss to ask follow-up questions.

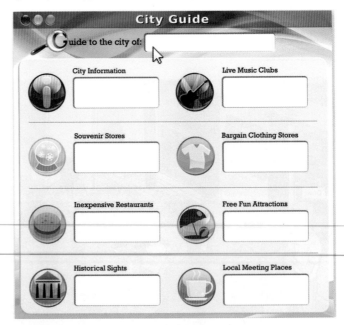

interchange 11 *CITY GUIDE*

A Where can you get information about a city? buy souvenirs? see historical sights? Complete the city guide with information about a city of your choice.

City Guide

Guide to the city of:

City Information	Live Music Clubs
Souvenir Stores	Bargain Clothing Stores
Inexpensive Restaurants	Free Fun Attractions
Historical Sights	Local Meeting Places

B **GROUP WORK** Compare your city guide in groups. Ask these questions and questions of your own. Add any additional or interesting information to your guide.

Where can you get information about your city?
Where's a good place to buy souvenirs?
Where's an inexpensive place to eat?
What historical sights should you visit?
Where's the best place to hear live music?
Where's a cheap place to shop for clothes?
What fun things can you do for free?
Where's a popular place to meet?

126 ▪ *Interchange 11*

A GROUP WORK Play the board game. Follow these instructions.

1. Use small pieces of paper with your initials on them as markers.
2. Take turns by tossing a coin:
   If the coin lands face up, move two spaces.
   If the coin lands face down, move one space.
3. When you land on a space, ask two others in your group for advice.

A: I have a terrible headache. Akira, what's your advice?
B: Well, it's important to get a lot of rest.
A: Thanks. What about you, Jason? What do you think?
C: You should take two aspirin. That always works for me.

useful expressions
You should . . .
You could . . .
It's a good idea to . . .
It's important to . . .
I think it's useful to . . .

B CLASS ACTIVITY Who gave the best advice in your group? Tell the class.

Interchange 12 ▪ **127**

interchange 12

Learning Objective: *speak more fluently about health problems and medical advice by playing a board game*

A Group work

- Focus Ss' attention on the board game and read the instructions. Show Ss how to write their initials on small pieces of paper and use them as markers.

- **Option:** Ss can use other small items as markers (e.g., pen caps or erasers).
- Show Ss how to toss a coin. Point out which side is face up and which side is face down.
- Have different Ss read the problems in each space. Elicit or explain any vocabulary. Then ask three Ss to model the example conversation.
- Show how to play the game with a group of three Ss.

TIP In low-level classes, it is more effective to model a game or activity than to explain it.

- Ss play the game in small groups. Go around the class and encourage Ss to use the expressions in the useful expressions box.

B Class activity

- Read the question. Elicit information from each group. Encourage them to give examples.

interchange 13

Learning Objective: *discuss and create a menu for a new restaurant*

A Group work

- Write these words on the board:
  soups   salads   main dishes
  desserts beverages

- In small groups, Ss discuss their favorite dishes in each category. Then elicit their answers and write them on the board.

- Set the scene and explain the task. Explain that a *kid's menu* has dishes children like. They are usually cheaper and smaller than dishes on the regular menu. Elicit possible dishes for this menu.

- Ss complete the task in small groups. Go around the class and give help with vocabulary, spelling, or prices.

B Group work

- In the same groups, Ss choose a name for their restaurant and write it at the top of the menu. To help Ss think of ideas, ask these questions: "Where is the restaurant? What's special about it?"

C Class activity

- Collect each group's menu. Then put them around the class so each group can see the other groups' menus.

- Read the instructions and explain the task. Ss go around the class and compare the menus. Then they write a name of the restaurant next to each phrase.

- Elicit answers from the class. Encourage Ss to explain their reasons.

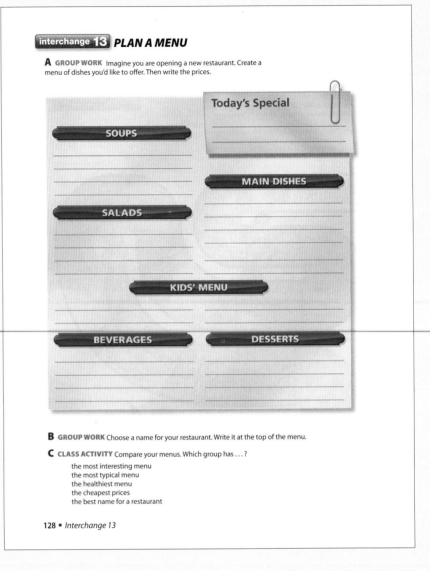

interchange 13 **PLAN A MENU**

A GROUP WORK Imagine you are opening a new restaurant. Create a menu of dishes you'd like to offer. Then write the prices.

Today's Special

SOUPS

MAIN DISHES

SALADS

KIDS' MENU

BEVERAGES   DESSERTS

B GROUP WORK Choose a name for your restaurant. Write it at the top of the menu.

C CLASS ACTIVITY Compare your menus. Which group has . . . ?
  the most interesting menu
  the most typical menu
  the healthiest menu
  the cheapest prices
  the best name for a restaurant

128 ▪ *Interchange 13*

interchange 14 *HOW MUCH DO YOU KNOW?*

A PAIR WORK Take turns asking and answering these questions. Check (✓) the answer you think is correct for each question.

World Knowledge Quiz

1.	Which animal lives the longest?	☐ a whale	☐ an elephant	☐ a tortoise
2.	Which one is the tallest?	☐ an elephant	☐ a giraffe	☐ a camel
3.	Which of these is the heaviest?	☐ the brain	☐ the heart	☐ the liver
4.	Which planet is the smallest?	☐ Mercury	☐ Venus	☐ Earth
5.	Which planet is the largest?	☐ Jupiter	☐ Saturn	☐ Neptune
6.	Which metal is the heaviest?	☐ gold	☐ silver	☐ aluminum
7.	Which country is the driest?	☐ Egypt	☐ Peru	☐ Chile
8.	Which is closest to the equator?	☐ Malaysia	☐ Colombia	☐ India
9.	Which place is the wettest?	☐ Kauai, Hawaii	☐ Bogor, Indonesia	☐ Manaus, Brazil
10.	Which ocean is the deepest?	☐ the Pacific	☐ the Arctic	☐ the Indian

Correct answers 1. a tortoise 2. a giraffe 3. the liver 4. Mercury 5. Jupiter 6. gold 7. Egypt 8. Colombia 9. Kauai, Hawaii 10. the Pacific

How many did you get correct?

10 Perfect! Brilliant! You should be a teacher.   **2–5** Just OK. How often do you go to the library?
6–9 Very good! Do you watch lots of TV game shows?   **0–1** Oh, dear. You should never be on a quiz show

B PAIR WORK Create your own quiz. Write 3 to 5 questions. Then ask the questions to another pair.

Interchange 14 ▪ 129

---

interchange 14

Learning Objective: *speak more fluently about general knowledge facts by asking and answering quiz questions*

A Pair Work

- Write these subjects on the board:

biology   geography
science   history
chemistry   foreign languages

- As a warm-up, ask: "Do you watch quiz shows on TV? How well would you do with these subjects?" Encourage discussion.

- Explain the task. Model the first question with its three choices.

- Call on Ss to read the questions and the three choices. (It's best not to explain new words at this time as this might give away the answer.)

- Model this possible conversation with a S:

T: Which animal lives the longest, a whale, an elephant, or a tortoise?

S: I think a whale lives the longest.

T: Hmm. I think a tortoise lives the longest.

S: I don't agree. I think a whale lives the longest.

T: OK, I guess we disagree here. So I'll check the *tortoise* and you check the *whale*. We'll find out later who got the correct answer for this one.

S: Now it's my turn. Let's go on to question 2. Which one . . . ?

- Ss work in pairs. Ss take turns asking and answering the questions. Tell Ss to cover the answers.

- Allow five to ten minutes for the activity. When time is up, pairs check their answers in the *Correct answers* box, total their scores, and read the description of the scores.

B Pair work

- Explain the task. Ss work in pairs to write their own quiz. Ask them to include an answer key and score chart.

- Each pair joins another pair. Ss take turns asking and answering the other pair's questions.

interchange 15

Learning Objective: *speak more fluently about plans for the weekend*

A Class activity

- As a warm-up, ask: "What are you doing this weekend?"
- **Option:** Let the class ask you about your weekend plans.
- Ask Ss to look at the items in the chart. Elicit or explain any new vocabulary. Call on Ss to form the questions from the phrases (e.g., *Are you going to go out of town this weekend?*).
- Model by asking different Ss: "Are you going to meet friends this weekend?" When a S says "no," go on to the next person until you find someone who says "yes." Write that person's name in the chart, and ask at least two follow-up questions. Write the details in the *Notes* column.
- Ask two Ss to model the conversation.
- Model how to react to hearing about someone's plans (e.g., *Really? That sounds great! Wow! That sounds like fun!*). Ss practice the expressions.
- Ss move around the class to do the activity.

> **TIP** It's best not to interrupt Ss during a fluency exercise. For this type of activity communication of real information is more important than grammatical or lexical accuracy.

- After the activity, go over any common errors.

B Pair work

- Ss work in pairs to discuss the questions.

interchange 15 **WEEKEND PLANS**

A CLASS ACTIVITY What are your classmates' plans for the weekend? Go around the class and find people who are going to do these things. For each question, ask for further information.

Find someone who is going to . . .	Name	Notes
go out of town		
meet friends		
stay out late		
visit relatives		
go to a party		
see a live performance		
play video games		
study for a test		
exercise		
buy something for someone		

A: Omar, are you going to go out of town this weekend?
B: Yes, I am.
A: What are you going to do?
B: My friend Tom and I are going to go camping in the mountains.

B PAIR WORK Compare your information with a partner. Who is going to do something fun? physical? serious?

130 ▪ *Interchange 15*

---

interchange 16 *MY POSSIBLE FUTURE*

A Complete this chart with information about yourself.

My possible future	
What are two things you plan to do next year?	....
What are two things you aren't going to do next year?	....
What is something you hope to buy in the next year?	....
What would you like to change about yourself?	....
Where would you like to visit someday?	....
What city would you like to live in someday?	....
What kind of job would you like to have?	....
What career goals do you hope to achieve?	....
What famous person would you like to meet?	....

B GROUP WORK Compare your information in groups.
Be prepared to explain the future you have planned.

A: What are two things you plan to do next year?
B: Well, I'm going to take a cooking class, and I'm also going to
go to Italy.
C: Oh, really? What part of Italy are you going to visit?
B: I'm not sure yet! What about you? What are two things you plan
to do next year?

Interchange 16 ▪ 131

---

interchange 16

Learning Objective: *speak more fluently about possibilities for the future*

A

- Focus Ss' attention on the picture. Elicit what kind of dreams and plans the woman has.
- Explain the task. Ss answer each question in the chart with information about themselves.

- ***Option:*** Have Ss ask you the questions in the chart. Reply with your own information. If there are any problems with pronunciation or intonation of questions, review briefly.
- Ss complete the chart individually. Go around the class and give help as needed.

B *Group work*

- Explain the task. Model the example conversation with Ss.
- Ss form groups and take turns explaining their possible future plans.
- ***Option:*** Ask each group to choose the most interesting or unusual future plans that someone talked about. Then that S tells the rest of the class about his or her plans.

Grammar plus

Unit 1

1 Statements with *be*; possessive adjectives (page 3)

▶ Don't confuse contractions of *be* with possessive adjectives: **You're** a student. **Your** class is English 1. (NOT: ~~You're class is English 1.~~) **He's** my classmate. **His** name is Roberto. (NOT: ~~He's name is Roberto.~~)

Circle the correct words.

1. This **is** / **are** Delia Rios. **She's** / **Her** a new student from Peru.
2. My name **am** / **is** Sergio. **I'm** / **He's** from Brazil.
3. My brother and I **is** / **are** students here. **Our** / **We're** names are Dave and Jeff.
4. **He's** / **His** Yoshi. **He's** / **His** 19 years old.
5. **They're** / **Their** in my English class. **It's** / **Its** a big class.

2 Wh-questions with *be* (page 4)

▶ Use *What* to ask about things: **What's** in your bag? Use *Where* to ask about places: **Where's** your friend from? Use *Who* to ask about people: **Who's** your teacher? Use *What . . . like?* to ask for a description: **What's** your friend **like**?

Match the questions with the answers.

1. Who's that? ....f....
2. Where's your teacher? ....
3. What are your friends like? ....
4. Where's she from? ....
5. Who are they? ....
6. What's his name? ....

a. They're really nice.
b. She's from Japan.
c. They're my brother and sister.
d. His name is Carlos.
e. He's in class.
f. That's our new classmate.

3 Yes/No questions and short answers with *be* (page 5)

▶ Use short answers to answer yes/no questions. Don't use contractions with short answers with *Yes*: **Are you** from Mexico? Yes, **I am**. (NOT: ~~Yes, I'm.~~)

Complete the conversations.

1. A: _Are they_ in your class?
   B: No, ... They're in English 2.
2. A: Hi! .... in this class?
   B: Yes, ... I'm a new student here.
3. A: .... from the United States?
   B: No, ... We're from Montreal, Canada.
4. A: Hi, Sonia. .... free?
   B: No, ... I'm on my way to class.
5. A: That's the new student. .... from Puerto Rico?
   B: No, ... He's from Costa Rica.
6. A: .... from Thailand?
   B: Yes, ... She's from Bangkok.

Unit 2

1 Simple present Wh-questions and statements (page 10)

Statements
- ► Verbs with he/she/it end in –s: He/She **walks** to school. BUT I/You/We/They **walk** to school.
- ► *Have, go,* and *do* are irregular with he/she/it: She **has** a class at 1:00. He **goes** to school at night. She **does** her homework before school.

Wh-questions
- ► Use *does* in questions with he/she/it and *do* with all the others: Where *does* he/she/it live? Where *do* I/you/we/they live?
- ► Don't add –s to the verb: Where does she **live**? (NOT: Where does she lives?)

Complete the conversations with the correct form of the verbs in parentheses.

1. A: I ....*have*........ (have) good news! Dani .... (have) a new job.
   B: How .... she .... (like) it?
   A: She .... (love) it. The hours are great.
   B: What time .... she .... (start)?
   A: She .... (start) at nine and .... (finish) at five.
2. A: What .... you .... (do)?
   B: I'm a teacher.
   A: What .... you .... (teach)?
   B: I .... (teach) Spanish and English.
   A: Really? My sister .... (teach) English, too.

2 Time expressions (page 12)

- ► Use *in* with *the morning/afternoon/evening.* Us *at* with *night*: He goes to school **in** the afternoon and works **at** night. BUT: **on** *Friday night.*
- ► Use *at* with clock times: She gets up **at** 7:00.
- ► Use *on* with days: He gets up early **on** weekdays. She has class **on** Mondays.

Complete the conversation with time expressions from the box. You can use some words more than once.

at	early	in	on	until

A: How's your new job?
B: I love it, but the hours are difficult. I start work .... 7:30 A.M., and I work .... 3:30.
A: That's interesting! I work the same hours, but I work .... night. I start .... 7:30 .... the evening and finish .... 3:30 .... the morning.
B: Wow! What time do you get up?
A: Well, I get home .... 4:30 and go to bed .... 5:30. And I sleep .... 2:00. But I only work .... weekends, so it's OK. What about you?
B: Oh, I work .... Monday, Wednesday, and Friday. And I get up .... – around 6:00 A.M.

Unit 3

1 Demonstratives; *one, ones* (page 17)

> ▶ With singular nouns, use *this* for a thing that is nearby and *that* for a thing that is not nearby: How much is **this** cap here? How much is **that** cap over there?
>
> ▶ With plural nouns, use *these* for things that are nearby and *those* for things that are not nearby: How much are **these** earrings here? How much are **those** earrings over there?
>
> ▶ Use *one* to replace a singular noun: I like the red <u>hat</u>. → I like the red **one**. Use *ones* to replace plural nouns: I like the green <u>bags</u>. → I like the green **ones**.

Circle the correct words.

1. A: Excuse me. How much are **this / these** shoes?
   B: **It's / They're** $279.
   A: And how much is **this / that** bag over there?
   B: **It's / They're** only $129.
   A: And are the two gray **one / ones** $129, too?
   B: No. **That / Those** are only $119.
   A: Oh! **This / That** store is really expensive.

2. A: Can I help you?
   B: Yes, please. I really like **these / those** jeans over there. How much **is it / are they**?
   A: Which **one / ones**? Do you mean **this / these**?
   B: No, the black **one / ones**.
   A: Let me look. Oh, **it's / they're** $35.99.
   B: That's not bad. And how much is **this / that** sweater here?
   A: **It's / They're** only $9.99.

2 Preferences; comparisons with adjectives (page 20)

> ▶ With adjectives of one or two syllables, add *–er* to form the comparative: cheap → cheaper; nice → nicer; pretty → prettier; big → bigger.
>
> ▶ With adjectives of three or more syllables, use *more* + adjective to form the comparative: expensive → more expensive.

A Write the comparatives of these adjectives.

1. attractive   ....*more attractive*..........   5. interesting   ....
2. boring   ....   6. reasonable   ....
3. exciting   ....   7. sad   ....
4. friendly   ....   8. warm   ....

B Answer the questions. Use the words in parentheses in your answer. Then write another sentence with the second word.

1. Which pants do you prefer, the cotton ones or the wool ones? (wool / attractive)
   I prefer the wool ones. They're more attractive than the cotton ones

2. Which ring do you like better, the gold one or the silver one? (silver / interesting)
   ....

3. Which one do you prefer, the silk jacket or the wool jacket? (silk / pretty)
   ....

4. Which ones do you like more, the black shoes or the purple ones? (purple / exciting)
   ....

Unit 4

1 Simple present questions; short answers (page 23)

▶ Use *do* + base form for yes/no questions and short answers with I/you/we/they: **Do** I/you/we/they **like** rock? Yes, I/you/we/they **do**. No, I/you/we/they **don't**.

▶ Use *does* in yes/no questions and short answers with he/she/it: **Does** he/she **like** rock? Yes, he/she **does**. No, he/she **doesn't**.

▶ Use *don't* and *doesn't* + base form for negative statements: I **don't like** horror movies. He **doesn't like** action movies.

▶ Remember: Don't add –*s* to the base form: Does she **like** rock? (NOT: ~~Does she likes rock?~~)

▶ Subject pronouns (*I, you, he, she, it, we, they*) usually come before a verb. Object pronouns (*me, you, him, her, it, us, them*) usually come after a verb: He likes **her**, but she doesn't like **him**.

A Complete the questions and short answers.

1. A: <u>Do you play</u> (play) a musical instrument?
   B: Yes, <u>I do</u>. I play the guitar.
2. A: .... (like) Taylor Swift?
   B: No, ... Joe doesn't like country music.
3. A: .... (like) talk shows?
   B: Yes, ... Lisa is a big fan of them.
4. A: .... (watch) the news on TV?
   B: Yes, ... Kevin and I watch the news every night.
5. A: .... (like) hip-hop?
   B: No, ... But I love R&B.
6. A: .... (listen to) jazz?
   B: No, ... But my parents listen to a lot of classical music.

B Complete the sentences with object pronouns.

1. We don't listen to hip-hop because we really don't like <u>it</u> .
2. We love your voice. Please sing for ....
3. These sunglasses are great. Do you like .... ?
4. Who is that man? Do you know .... ?
5. Beth looks great in green. It's a really good color for ....

2 *Would*; verb + *to* + verb (page 26)

▶ Don't use a contraction in affirmative short answers with *would*. **Would** you **like to go to** the game? Yes, I **would**. (NOT: ~~Yes, I'd.~~)

Unscramble the questions and answers to complete the conversation.

A: tonight   to see   would you like   with me   a movie
.... ?

B: I would.   yes,   what   to see   would you like
.... ?

A: the new Halle Berry movie   to see   I'd like
....

B: OK. That's a great idea!

Unit 5

1 Present continuous (page 32)

▶ Use the present continuous to talk about actions that are happening now: What **are** you **doing (these days)**? I'**m studying** English.

▶ The present continuous is present of *be* + *-ing*. For verbs ending in *e*, drop the *e* and add *-ing*: have → having, live → living.

▶ For verbs ending in vowel + consonant, double the consonant and add *-ing*: sit → sitting.

Write questions with the words in parentheses and the present continuous. Then complete the responses with short answers or the verbs in the box.

live	study	take	✓ teach	work

1. A: (what / your sister / do / these days) *What's your sister doing these days?*
   B: *She's teaching* English.
   A: Really? (she / live / abroad) ....
   B: Yes, ... She .... in South Korea
2. A: (how / you / spend / your summer) ....
   B: I .... part-time. I .... two classes also.
   A: (what / you / take) ....
   B: My friend and I .... photography and Japanese. We like our classes a lot.

2 Quantifiers (page 34)

▶ Use *a lot of, all, few, nearly all* before plural nouns: **A lot of/All/Few/Nearly all** families are small. Use *no one* before a verb: **No one** gets married before the age of 18.

▶ *Nearly all* means "almost all."

Read the sentences about the small town of Monroe. Rewrite the sentences using the quantifiers in the box. Use each quantifier only once.

a lot of	all	few	nearly all	✓ no one

1. In Monroe, 0% of the people drive before the age of 16.
   In Monroe, no one drives before the age of 16.
2. Ninety-eight percent of students finish high school.
   ....
3. One hundred percent of children start school by the age of six.
   ....
4. Eighty-nine percent of couples have more than one child.
   ....
5. Twenty-three percent of families have more than four children.
   ....

Unit 6

1 Adverbs of frequency (page 37)

> ▶ Adverbs of frequency (*always, almost always, usually, often, sometimes, hardly ever, almost never, never*) usually come before the main verb: She **never plays** tennis. I **almost always eat** breakfast. BUT Adverbs of frequency usually come after the verb *be*: I**'m always** late.
>
> ▶ *Usually* and *sometimes* can begin a sentence: **Usually** I walk to work. **Sometimes** I exercise in the morning.
>
> ▶ Some frequency expressions usually come at the end of a sentence: *every day, once a week, twice a month, three times a year:* Do you exercise **every day**? I exercise **three times a week**.

Put the words in order to make questions. Then complete the answers with the words in parentheses.

1. you   what   weekends   usually   do   do   on
   Q: *What do you usually do on weekends?* ....
   A: I .... (often / play sports)
2. ever   you   go jogging   do   with a friend
   Q: ....
   A: No, ... (always / alone)
3. you   play   do   tennis   how often
   Q: ....
   A: I .... (four times a week)
4. do   you   what   in the evening   usually   do
   Q: ....
   A: My family and I .... (almost always / watch TV)
5. go   how often   you   do   to the gym
   Q: ....
   A: I .... (never)

2 Questions with *how*; short answers (page 40)

> ▶ Don't confuse *good* and *well*. Use the adjective *good* with *be* and the adverb *well* with other verbs: How **good** are you at soccer? BUT How **well** do you play soccer?

Complete the questions with *How* and a word from the box. Then match the questions and the answers.

> good   long   often   well

1. .... do you lift weights? ....   a. Not very well, but I love it.
2. .... do you play tennis? ....   b. About six hours a week.
3. .... are you at aerobics? ....   c. Not very often. I prefer aerobics.
4. .... do you spend at the gym? ....   d. Pretty good, but I hate it.

Unit 7

1 Simple past (page 45)

> ▶ Use *did* with the base form – not the past form – of the main verb in questions: How **did** you **spend** the weekend? (NOT: How did you spent . . .?)
> ▶ Use *didn't* with the base form in negative statements: We **didn't go** shopping. (NOT: . . . we didn't went shopping.)

Complete the conversation.

A: ....Did.... you ...have... (have) a good weekend?

B: Yes, I .... I .... (have) a great time. My sister and I .... (go) shopping on Saturday. We .... (spend) all day at the mall.

A: .... you .... (buy) anything special?

B: I .... (buy) a new laptop. And I .... (get) some new clothes, too.

A: Lucky you! What clothes .... you .... (buy)?

B: Well, I .... (need) some new boots. I .... (find) some great ones at Luff's Department Store.

A: What about you? What .... you .... (do) on Saturday?

B: I .... (not do) anything special. I .... (stay) home and .... (work) around the house. Oh, but I .... (see) a really good movie on TV. And then I .... (make) dinner with my mother. I actually .... (enjoy) the day.

2 Past of *be* (page 47)

▶ Present		Past
am/is	→	**was**
are	→	**were**

Rewrite the sentences. Find another way to write each sentence using *was, wasn't, were,* or *weren't* and the words in parentheses.

1. Tony didn't come to class yesterday. (in class)
   Tony wasn't in class yesterday.

2. He worked all day. (at work)
   ....

3. Tony and his co-workers worked on Saturday, too. (at work)
   ....

4. They didn't go to work on Sunday. (at work)
   ....

5. Did Tony stay home on Sunday? (at home)
   ....

6. Where did Tony go on Sunday? (on Sunday)
   ....

7. He and his brother went to a baseball game. (at a baseball game)
   ....

8. They stayed at the park until 7:00. (at the park)
   ....

Unit 8

1 *There is, there are; one, any, some* (page 51)

> ▶ Don't use a contraction in a short answer with *Yes*: Is there a hotel near here? Yes, **there is**. (NOT: ~~Yes, there's.~~)
> ▶ Use *some* in affirmative statements and *any* in negative statements: There are **some** grocery stores in my neighborhood, but there aren't **any** restaurants. Use *any* in most questions: Are there **any** nice stores around here?

Complete the conversations. Circle the correct words.

1. A: **Is / Are** there any supermarkets in this neighborhood?
   B: No, there **isn't / aren't**, but there are **one / some** on Main Street.
   A: And **is / are** there a post office near here?
   B: Yes, **there's / there is**. It's across from the bank.
2. A: **Is / Are** there a gas station around here?
   B: Yes, **there's / there are** one behind the shopping center.
   A: Great! And are there **a / any** coffee shops nearby?
   B: Yes, there's a good **one / some** in the shopping center.

2 Quantifiers; *how many* and *how much* (page 54)

> ▶ Use *a lot* with both count and noncount nouns: Are there many traffic lights on First Avenue? Yes, there are **a lot**. Is there much traffic? Yes, there's **a lot**.
> ▶ Use *any* – not *none* – in negative statements: How much traffic is there on your street? There **isn't any**. = There**'s none**. (NOT: ~~There isn't none.~~)
> ▶ Use *How many* with count nouns: **How many books** do you have?
> ▶ Use *How much* with noncount nouns: **How much traffic** is there?

A Complete the conversations. Circle the correct words.

1. A: Is there **many / much** traffic in your city?
   B: Well, there's **a few / a little**.
2. A: Are there **many / much** public telephones around here?
   B: No, there aren't **many / none**.
3. A: **How many / How much** restaurants are there in your neighborhood?
   B: There **is / are** a lot.
4. A: **How many / How much** noise **is / are** there in your city?
   B: There's **much / none**. It's very quiet.

B Write questions with the words in parentheses. Use *much* or *many*.

1. A: Is there much pollution in your neighborhood? .... (pollution)
   B: No, there isn't. My neighborhood is very clean.
2. A: .... (parks)
   B: Yes, there are. They're great for families.
3. A: .... (crime)
   B: There's none. It's a very safe part of the city.
4. A: .... (laundromats)
   B: There aren't any. A lot of people have their own washing machines.

Unit 9

1 Describing people (page 59)

> ▶ Use *have* or *is* to describe eye and hair color: I **have** brown hair. = My hair **is** brown.
> He **has** blue eyes. = His eyes **are** blue.
> ▶ Don't confuse *How* and *What* in questions: **How** tall are you? (NOT: ~~What tall are you?~~) **What** color is your hair? (NOT: ~~How color is your hair?~~)

Unscramble the questions. Then write answers using the phrases in the box.

blond	brown eyes	contact lenses
✓ tall and good-looking	5 feet 11	26 – two years older than me

A: brother   like   look   what   your   does
  <u>What does your brother look like?</u>
B: <u>He's tall and good-looking.</u>
A: tall   is   how   he

....
B: ....
A: he   does   glasses   wear

....
B: ....
A: what   hair   color   his   is

....
B: ....
A: he   does   blue   have   eyes

....
B: ....
A: old   he   how   and   is

....
B: ....

2 Modifiers with participles and prepositions (page 62)

> ▶ Don't use a form of *be* in modifiers with participles: Sylvia is the woman **standing**
> near the window. (NOT: ~~Sylvia is the woman is standing near the window.~~)

Rewrite the conversations. Use the words in parentheses and *one* or *ones*.

1. A: Who's Carla?
   B: She's the woman in the red dress.
2. A: Who are your neighbors?
   B: They're the people with the baby.
3. A: Who's Jeff?
   B: He's the man wearing glasses.

A: <u>Which one is Carla?</u> (which)
B: .... (wearing)
A: .... (which)
B: .... (walking)
A: .... (which)
B: .... (with)

Unit 10

1 Present perfect; *already, yet* (page 65)

▶ Use the present perfect for actions that happened some time in the past.
▶ Use *yet* in questions and negative statements: Have you checked your email **yet**?
No, I haven't turned on my computer **yet**. Use *already* in affirmative statements:
I've **already** checked my email.

A Complete the conversations with the present perfect of the verbs in parentheses
and short answers.

1. A: ......*Has*...... Leslie ......*called*...... (call) you lately?
   B: No, she .... (not call) me, but I .... (get) some emails from her.
2. A: .... you and Jan .... (have) lunch yet?
   B: No, we .... We're thinking of going to Tony's. .... you
   .... (try) it yet? Come with us.
   A: Thanks. I .... (not eat) there yet, but I .... (hear) it's pretty good.

B Look at things Matt said. Put the adverb in the correct place in the second sentence.

1. I'm very hungry. I haven't eaten. (yet) *yet*
2. I don't need any groceries. I've gone shopping. (already)
3. What have you done? Have you been to the zoo? (yet)
4. I called my parents before dinner. I've talked to them. (already)

2 Present perfect vs. simple past (page 66)

▶ Don't mention a specific time with the present perfect: I've **been** to a jazz club.
Use the simple past to say when a past action happened: I **went** to a jazz club
last night.

Complete the conversation using the present perfect or the simple past of the verbs in
parentheses and short answers.

1. A: ......*Did*...... you ......*see*...... (see) the game last night? I really .... (enjoy) it.
   B: Yes, I .... It .... (be) an amazing game. .... you ever .... (go) to a game?
   A: No, I .... I .... never .... (be) to the stadium. But I'd love to go!
   Maybe we can go to a game next year.
2. A: .... you ever .... (be) to Franco's Restaurant?
   B: Yes, I .... My friend and I .... (eat) there last weekend. How about you?
   A: No, I .... But I .... (hear) it's very good.
   B: Oh, yes – it's excellent!

3 *For* and *since* (page 67)

▶ Use *for* + a period of time to describe how long a present condition has been true:
We've been in New York **for two months**. (= We arrived two months ago.)
▶ Use *since* + a point in time to describe when a present condition started: We've
been here **since August**. (= We've been here from August to now.)

Circle the correct word.

1. I bought my car almost 10 years ago. I've had it **for / since** almost 10 years.
2. The Carters moved to Seattle six months ago. They've lived there **for / since** six months.
3. I've wanted to see that movie **for / since** a long time. It's been in theaters **for / since** March.

Unit 11

1 Adverbs before adjectives (page 73)

> ▶ Use *a/an* with (adverb) + adjective + singular noun: It's a **very modern city**.
> It's **an expensive city**. Don't use *a/an* with (adverb) + adjective:
> It's **really interesting**. (NOT: ~~It's a really interesting.~~)

Read the sentences. Add *a* or *an* where it's necessary to complete the sentences.

1. Brasília is ^an^ extremely modern city.

2. Seoul is very interesting place.

3. Santiago is pretty exciting city to visit.

4. Montreal is beautiful city, and it's fairly old.

5. London has really busy airport.

2 Conjunctions (page 74)

> ▶ Use *and* for additional information: The food is delicious, **and** it's not expensive.
> ▶ Use *but, though*, and *however* for contrasting information: The food is delicious, **but**
> it's very expensive. / The food is delicious. It's expensive, **though/however**.

Circle the correct word.

1. Spring in my city is pretty nice, **and / but** it gets extremely hot in summer.
2. There are some great museums. They're always crowded, **and / however**.
3. There are a lot of interesting stores, **and / but** many of them aren't expensive.
4. There are many amazing restaurants, **and / but** some are closed in August.
5. My city is a great place to visit. Don't come in summer **but / though**!

3 Modal verbs *can* and *should* (page 75)

> ▶ Use *can* to talk about things that are possible: Where **can** I get some nice souvenirs?
> Use *should* to suggest things that are good to do: You **should** try the local
> restaurants.
> ▶ Use the base form with *can* and *should* – not the infinitive: Where **can** I ~~to~~ get some
> nice souvenirs? You **should** ~~to~~ try the local restaurants.

Complete the conversation with *can, can't, should*, or *shouldn't*.

A: I .... *can't* .... decide where to go on vacation. .... I go to Costa Rica
or Hawaii?
B: You .... definitely visit Costa Rica.
A: Really? What can I see there?
B: Well, San Jose is an exciting city. You .... miss the Museo del Oro. That's
the gold museum, and you .... see beautiful animals made of gold.
A: OK. What else?
B: Well, you .... visit the museum on Mondays. It's closed then. But you
.... definitely visit the rain forest. It's amazing!

Unit 12

1 Adjective + infinitive; infinitive + noun (page 79)

> ▶ In negative statements, *not* comes before the infinitive: With a cold, it's important **not to exercise** too hard. (NOT: ~~With a cold, it's important **to not exercise** too hard.~~)

Rewrite the sentences using the words in parentheses. Add *not* when necessary.

1. For a bad headache, you should relax and close your eyes. (a good idea)
   It's a good idea to relax and close your eyes when you have a headache.
2. You should put some cold tea on that sunburn. (sometimes helpful)
   ....
3. For a fever, you should take some aspirin. (important)
   ....
4. For a cough, you shouldn't drink milk. (important)
   ....
5. For sore muscles, you should take a hot bath. (sometimes helpful)
   ....
6. When you feel stressed, you shouldn't drink a lot of coffee. (a good idea)
   ....

2 Modal verbs *can, could, may* for requests; suggestions (page 81)

> ▶ In requests, *can, could,* and *may* have the same meaning. *May* is a little more formal than *can* and *could*.

Number the lines of the conversation. Then write the conversation below.

.... Yes, please. What do you suggest for itchy skin?
.... Here you are. Can I help you with anything else?
.... Sure I can. You should see a dentist!
...1... Hello. May I help you?
.... You should try this lotion.
.... Yes. Can you suggest something for a toothache?
.... OK. And could I have a bottle of aspirin?

A: Hello. May I help you?
B: ....
A: ....
B: ....
A: ....
B: ....
A: ....

Unit 13

1 *So, too, neither, either* (page 87)

> ▶ Use *so* or *too* after an affirmative statement: I'm crazy about sushi. **So** am I./I am, **too**.
> ▶ Use *neither* or *not either* after a negative statement: I don't like fast food. **Neither** do I./I don't **either**.
> ▶ With *so* and *neither*, the verb comes before the subject: **So am I.** (NOT: ~~So I am.~~)
> **Neither do I.** (NOT: ~~Neither I do.~~)

A Choose the correct response to show that B agrees with A.

1. A: I'm in the mood for something salty.
   B: **I am, too.** / **I do, too.**
2. A: I can't stand fast food.
   B: **Neither do I. / I can't either.**
3. A: I really like Korean food.
   B: **So do I. / I am, too.**
4. A: I don't eat Italian food very often.
   B: **I do, too. / I don't either.**
5. A: I'm not crazy about pizza.
   B: **I am, too. / Neither am I.**

B Write responses to show agreement with these statements.

1. A: I'm not a very good cook.
   B: ....
2. A: I love french fries.
   B: ....
3. A: I can't eat very spicy food.
   B: ....
4. A: I never eat bland food.
   B: ....
5. A: I can make delicious desserts.
   B: ....

2 Modal verbs *would* and *will* for requests (page 89)

> ▶ Don't confuse *like* and *would like*. *Would like* means "want."
> ▶ You can also use *I'll have . . .* when ordering in a restaurant to mean *I will have . . . .*

Complete the conversation with *would, I'd,* or *I'll*.

A: Would .... you like to order now?
B: Yes, please. .... have the shrimp curry.
A: .... you like noodles or rice with that?
B: Hmm, ... have rice.
A: And .... you like a salad, too?
B: No, thanks.
A: .... you like anything else?
B: Yes, ... like a cup of green tea.

Unit 14

1 Comparisons with adjectives (page 93)

> ▶ Use the comparative form (adjective + -er or more + adjective) to compare two people, places, or things: Which river is **longer**, the Nile or the Amazon? The Nile is **longer than** the Amazon. Use the superlative form (the + adjective + -est or the most + adjective) to compare three or more people, places, or things: Which river is **the longest**: the Nile, the Amazon, or the Mississippi? The Nile is **the longest** river in the world.
>
> ▶ You can use a comparative or superlative without repeating the noun: Which country is **larger**, Canada or China? Canada is **larger**. What's the highest waterfall in the world? Angel Falls is **the highest**.

Write questions with the words. Then look at the underlined words, and write the answers.

1. Which desert / dry / the Sahara or <u>the Atacama</u>?
   Q: _Which desert is drier, the Sahara or the Atacama?_
   A: _The Atacama is drier than the Sahara._
2. Which island / large / <u>Greenland</u>, New Guinea, or Honshu?
   Q: ....
   A: ....
3. Which island / small / New Guinea or <u>Honshu</u>?
   Q: ....
   A: ....
4. Which U.S. city / large / Los Angeles, Chicago, or <u>New York</u>?
   Q: ....
   A: ....
5. Who / older / your father or your <u>grandfather</u>?
   Q: ....
   A: ....

2 Questions with *how* (page 96)

> ▶ Use *high* to describe mountains and waterfalls: How **high** is Mount Fuji? Angel Falls is 979 meters **high**. Use *tall* to describe buildings: How **tall** is the Empire State Building? (NOT: ~~How high is the Empire State Building?~~)

Complete the questions with the phrases in the box. There is one extra phrase.

How big	How cold	✓ How deep	How high	How tall

1. Q: _How deep_ .... is Lake Baikal?   A: It's 1,642 meters (5,387 feet) at its deepest point.
2. Q: .... is Alaska?   A: It's 586,412 square miles (1,518,800 kilometers).
3. Q: .... is Mount McKinley?   A: It's 20,300 feet (6,194 meters) high.
4. Q: .... is the CN Tower?   A: It is 553 meters (1,814 feet) tall.

Unit 15

1 Future with present continuous and *be going to* (page 101)

> Use the present continuous to talk about something that is happening now:
> What **are** you **doing**? I**'m studying**. You can also use the present continuous
> with time expressions to talk about the future: What **are** you **doing tomorrow**?
> I**'m working.**

A Read the sentences. Are they present or future? Write P or F.

1. Why are you wearing shorts? It's cold. ....P....
2. What are you wearing to the party on Friday? ....
3. Where are you going this weekend? ....
4. Where are you going? ....
5. Are you going to watch TV tonight? ....

B Complete the conversations. Use the present continuous and *be going to.*

1. A: What ....*are*.......... you and Tony ....*doing*.......... (do) tonight?
   B: We .... (try) the new Chinese restaurant. Would you like to come?
   A: I'd love to. What time .... you .... (go)?
   B: We .... (meet) at Tony's house at 7:00. And don't forget an umbrella.
      It .... (rain) tonight.
2. A: Where .... you .... (go) on vacation this year?
   B: I .... (visit) my cousins in Paris. It .... (be) great!
   A: Well, I .... (not go) anywhere this year. I .... (stay) home.
   B: That's not so bad. Just think about all the money you .... (save)!

2 Messages with *tell* and *ask* (page 103)

> In messages with a request, use the infinitive of the verb: Please ask her **to meet** me
> at noon. (NOT: Please ask her meet me at noon.)
> In messages with negative infinitives, *not* goes before to in the infinitive: Could you
> ask him **not to be** late? (NOT: Could you ask him to not be late?)

Read the messages. Ask someone to pass them on. Use the words in parentheses.

1. Message: Patrick – We don't have class tomorrow. (please)
   Please tell Patrick that we don't have class tomorrow. ....
2. Message: Ana – Call me tonight on my cell phone. (would)
   ....
3. Message: Alex – The concert on Saturday is canceled. (would)
   ....
4. Message: Sarah – Don't forget to return the book to the library. (could)
   ....

Unit 16

1 Describing change (page 107)

> ▶ You can use several tenses to describe change – present tense, past tense, and present perfect.

A Complete the sentences with the information in the box. Use the present perfect of the verbs given.

buy a house	change her hairstyle	join a gym	start looking for a new job

1. Pedro and Debbie .... Their apartment was too small.
2. Allen .... The one he has now is too stressful.
3. Sandra .... Everyone says it's more stylish.
4. Kevin .... He feels healthier now.

B Rewrite the sentences using the present tense and the words in parentheses.

1. Joy doesn't wear jeans anymore. *She wears dresses* .... (dresses)
2. They don't live in the city anymore. .... (suburbs)
3. Carol isn't shy anymore. .... (outgoing)
4. I quit eating greasy food. .... (healthier)

2 Verb + infinitive (page 109)

> ▶ Use the infinitive after a verb to describe future plans or things you want to happen: I **want to learn** Spanish.

Complete the conversation with the words in parentheses and a verb from the box. You can use some verbs more than once.

be	do	drive	go	live	make	stay	work

A: Hey, Steven. What .....*are you going to do*..... (go) after graduation?
B: Well, I .... (plan) here in the city for a few months.
A: Really? I .... (want) home. I'm ready for my mom's cooking.
B: I understand that, but my boss says I can keep my job for the summer. So I .... (want) a lot of hours because I .... (hope) enough money for a new car.
A: But you don't need a car in the city.
B: I .... (not plan) here for very long. In the fall, I .... (go) across the country. I really .... (want) in California.
A: California? Where in California .... (like)?
B: In Hollywood, of course. I .... (go) a movie star!

Unit 1 Language summary

Vocabulary

Nouns

actor
athlete
birthday
bow
brother
cafeteria
character
chemistry
city
class
classmate
club
English
family
(best) friend
future
greeting
hobby
identity
member
name
opinion
parents
person
semester
sister
student
survey
teacher
tradition
university
vacation
year

Greetings

bow
fist bump
handshake
hug
kiss (on the cheek)
pat (on the back)

Pronouns

Subject pronouns

I
you
he
she
it
we
they

Titles

Miss
Mr.
Mrs.

Adjectives

Possessives

my
your
his
her
its
our
their

Other

adventurous
athletic
average
beautiful
big
boring
common
cool
creative
exciting
famous
favorite
friendly
good
good-looking
interesting
negative
nerdy
new
next
nice
old-fashioned
ordinary
particular
plain
(un)popular
positive
recent
same
serious
shy
typical
unusual

Articles

a
an
the

Verbs

agree
am
are
has
interview
is
love
spell

Adverbs

Responses

no
yes

Other

actually
here
(over) there
not
now
really/too/very
    (+ adjective)
surprisingly

Prepositions

at (10:00/City
    College)
from (Seoul/South
    Korea)
in (the morning/the
    same class)
on (my way to. . .)

Conjunctions

and
but
or

Expressions

Saying hello
Good morning.
Hi.
Hey.
Hello.
How are you?/How's it
    going?
    (I'm) fine, thanks.
    Pretty good.
    OK.
What's up?

Saying good-bye
Bye.
Good-bye.
Good night.
Have a good day.
See you later.
See you tomorrow.
Talk to you later.

**Exchanging personal
    information**
What's your name?
    I'm. . . /My name is. . .
What's your first/last
    name?
    It's. . .
What are your hobbies?
    My hobbies are. . .
When's your birthday?
    It's. . .
What's. . . like?
    He's/She's/It's. . .
What are. . . like?
    They're. . .
Where are you from?
    I'm/We're from. . .

Introducing someone
This is. . . /These are. . .
    Nice to meet you.

Asking about someone
Who's that?
    That's. . .
    His/Her name is. . .
Who are they?
    They're. . .
    Their names are. . .
    and. . .
Where's your friend?
    He's/She's. . .

Thanking someone
Thanks.
Thank you.

Checking information
How do you spell. . . ?
Sorry, what's your name
    again?
    It's. . .
What do people call you?
    Everyone calls me. . .
    Please call me. . .

Making suggestions
Let's. . .

Apologizing
(I'm) sorry.

Agreeing
OK.
Sure.
That's right.

Interchange Teacher's Edition 1 © Cambridge University Press 2013 Photocopiable

Unit 2 Language summary

Vocabulary

Nouns

Jobs/Professions
accountant
caregiver
carpenter
cashier
chef
dancer
director
dishwasher
fitness instructor
flight attendant
mechanic
musician
nurse
pilot
receptionist
reporter
salesperson
server
singer
team assistant
tour guide
tutor
usher
website designer

Types of jobs
entertainment business
food service
office work
travel industry

Workplaces
airline

(computer/construction)
    company
garage
hospital
newspaper
office
restaurant
school
(department/clothing) store
university

Other
allowance
breakfast
clothes
country
dinner
drink
experience
fashion design
food
heaven
house
job
music
passenger
patient
phone
schedule
snack
thing
time
work

Adjectives
bad
better

busy
different
difficult
expensive
fantastic
fast
favorite
full-time
great
part-time
similar
worse
worst

Verbs
answer
build
care for
cook
do
earn
fix
get (home)
go (to bed/to school/to
    work)
have (a job/lunch)
know
leave (work/for work)
like
live
own
save
sell
sleep
start
stay up

study
take (care of)
teach
wake up
watch
work (in an office/
    for an airline)
write

Adverbs

Response
yeah

Other
a lot
early
exactly
home
late
only
usually

Prepositions
after (midnight)
around/about (10:00/noon)
at (6:00/night/midnight)
at (a travel agency/a
    fast-food restaurant)
before (noon)
in (an office)
in (the morning/the
    afternoon/the evening)
like (= for example)
on (weekdays/Fridays)
until (midnight)

Expressions

*Talking about school/
    work*
What do you do (exactly/
    there)?
    I'm a/an. . .
Where does he work?
    He works in/at/for. . .
How do you like your job/
    classes?
    I like it/them a lot.
    I love it/them.

Where do you go to
    school?
    I go to. . .
What's your favorite. . . ?
    My favorite. . . is. . .

*Asking for more
    information*
What time. . . ?
Which. . . ?
Why?

*Talking about daily
    schedules*
What time do you go to
    work?
I start work at. . .
When do you get home?
    I usually get home at. . .

Expressing interest
How interesting!
Oh? (Oh.)
Oh, really?
Really?

Expressing surprise
Oh!
Wow!

Starting a sentence
Well,. . .
By the way,. . .

Unit 3 Language summary

Vocabulary

Nouns

Clothes and jewelry
backpack
bag
boots
bracelet
dress
earrings
gloves
jacket
jeans
necklace
ring
scarf
shirt
socks
sunglasses
sweater
tie
T-shirt
wallet
watch

*Materials**
cotton
gold
leather
plastic
polyester

rubber
silk
silver
wool

Other
bargains
cent(s)
clerk
(golf) clubs
coffee
compare
cost
cup
customer
decisions
design
dollar
(at one's) fingertips
flea market
item
lamp
MP3 player
notebook
opinions

painting
paperback (book/
  novel)
phone
price
review(s)
smartphone
speakers
social networking
style
TV
(price) tag

Pronouns
one
ones

Adjectives

Colors
black
blue
brown
gray
green
orange
pink
purple
red

white
yellow

Other
attractive
boring
cheap
each
expensive
fun
happy
jealous
large
light
loving
medium
mysterious
perfect
powerful
pretty
pure
reasonable
sad
small
stylish
truthful
warm

Verbs

Modal
can

Other
ask
buy
connect
help
let (me) + verb
look (= seem)
look at
mean
pay (for)
prefer
say

Adverbs
almost
directly
else
more
(shop) online

*Names of materials can be used as nouns or adjectives.

Expressions

Talking about prices
How much is this/that
  scarf?
  It's. . . .
  That's not bad.
How much are these/those
  gloves?
  They're. . .
  That's expensive.

Comparing
The silk dress is prettier/
  more expensive than the
  polyester dress.

**Getting someone's
  attention**
Excuse me.
Look!
Look at. . .
Oh,. . .

Offering help
Can I help you?

Identifying things
Which one?
  The blue one.
Which ones?
  The yellow ones.

**Talking about
  preferences**
Which one do you prefer?
  I prefer the. . . one.
Which ones do you like
  better/more?
  I like the. . . one better/
  more.

**Requesting an
  alternative**
Do they come in (black)?

**Making and declining an
  offer**
Would you like to. . . ?
  Uh, no. That's OK.

Thanking someone
Thanks anyway.
  You're welcome.

Expressing doubt
Hmm.
I'm not sure.
Uh,. . .
Let's see. . .

Unit 4 Language summary

Vocabulary

Nouns

Movies
3-D
action
horror
musical
science fiction

TV programs
game show
reality show
soap opera
talk show

Music*
classical
country
electronic
gospel
heavy metal
hip-hop
jazz
New Age
pop
R&B (rhythm and
   blues)

reggae
rock
salsa

Musical instruments
guitar
piano

Entertainers
actor
actress
group
rapper
singer
songwriter

Other
album
award
concert
cyclists
date
(art) fair
fan
fashion designer

(baseball) game
gate
grass
highlight(s)
(musical) instrument
kind (of)
level
(soccer) match
(text) message
stadium
tango
ticket
video game
voice

Pronouns

Object pronouns
me
you
him
her
it
us
them

Verbs

Modal
would

Other
cheer
come
dream
go out
guess
have to (+ verb)
know
listen to
meet
miss
need to (+ verb)
play (an instrument)
visit
win

Adjectives
famous
free (=not have plans)
glamorous
local

welcome
whole
worldwide

Adverbs
especially
just
never
pretty (+ adjective)
still
tomorrow
under the stars
   (=outside)
(not) very much

Prepositions
about (it)
for (dinner)
from. . . until. . . /
   from . . . to. . .
with (me)

*Names of musical styles can be used as nouns or adjectives.

Expressions

Talking about likes and dislikes
Do you like. . . ?
   Yes, I do. I like. . . a lot./I love. . .
   No, I don't. I don't like. . .
   very much.
What kind of. . . do you like?
Who's/What's your favorite. . . ?

Inviting someone
Would you like to. . . ?
Do you want to. . . ?
Why don't we. . . ?

Accepting an invitation
Yes, I would.
Thanks. I'd love to.
That sounds great.

Refusing an invitation
I'd like to, but I have to. . .
I'd like to, but I need to. . .
I'd like to, but I want to. . .

Asking about events
When is it?
Where is it?
What time does it start/end?

Unit 5 Language summary

Vocabulary

Nouns
Family/Relatives
aunt
brother
children
cousin
dad
daughter
father
grandfather
grandmother
husband
mom
mother
nephew
niece
sister
sister-in-law
son
uncle
wife
Other
adult
age
attention
challenge
college
couple
elevator
email

fact
family tree
foreign language
freedom
government
household
housework
men
money
only child
people
percent
(wildlife) photographer
population
(birthday) present
project
pros and cons
women

Pronouns
anyone
no one

Adjectives
Quantifiers
all
nearly all
most
many
a lot of/lots of
some

not many
a few
few
Other
average
dear (+ name)
elderly
lonely
married
one-on-one
related
secret
single
stay-at-home (mom/dad)
stressful
stuck
urban
young

Verbs
enjoy
get (married)
grow(ing) up
move
spend (money)
stand
tell
travel
vote
wait

Adverbs
Time expressions
(almost) always
right now
these days
this week/month/year
Other
abroad
alone
away
together

Preposition
of

Conjunction
because

Expressions

Asking about family
Tell me about your family.
Do you have any brothers and sisters?
How many brothers and sisters do you have?
   I have. . . brother(s) and. . . sister(s).
   I'm an only child.
How old is your sister?

**Exchanging information
   about the present**
Are you living at home?
   Yes, I am./No, I'm not.
What is your brother doing?
   He's traveling in. . . .
Is anyone in your family. . . right now?
   Yes, my. . . is. . .

Expressing interest
What an interesting. . .

Expressing relief
Thank goodness!

    Interchange Teacher's Edition 1 © Cambridge University Press 2013 Photocopiable

Unit 6 Language summary

Vocabulary

Nouns

Sports and fitness activities
aerobics
baseball
basketball
bicycling
bowling
football
golf
gymnastics
jogging
karate
running
soccer
softball
stretching
swimming
tennis
volleyball
walking
weight training
yoga

Other
athlete
couch potato
country
fitness
fitness freak
free time
gym
gym rat
joke
meal
physical (exam)
serving (= portion of food)
sports nut
teen (= teenager)
tip
treadmill
vitamin(s)

Pronoun
nothing

Adjectives
above/below average
both
either
fit
good at (something)

middle-aged
real
regular
tired

Verbs
act
chat
dance
eat
enter
exercise
keep (fit/up the good work)
lift weights
play (cards/a sport)
relax
sing
spend (time)
talent
(magic) tricks
work out

Adverbs

Frequency
always
almost always
usually
often
sometimes
hardly ever
almost never
never
every. . .
once a. . .
twice a. . .
three times a. . .
not very often/much

Other
sometime
then

Prepositions
in (my free time/great shape)
like (that)

Expressions

Talking about routines
How often do you. . . ?
  Every. . .
  Once/Twice/Three times a. . .
  Not very often.
Do you ever. . . ?
  Yes, I always/often/sometimes. . .
  No, I never/hardly ever. . .
How long do you spend. . . ?
  Thirty minutes a day./Two hours a week.

Talking about abilities
How well do you. . . ?
  Pretty well./About average.
  Not very well.
How good are you at. . . ?
  Pretty good./OK.
  Not so good.

Asking for more information
What else. . . ?

Expressing surprise/disbelief
Seriously?

Agreeing
All right.
No problem!

Unit 7 Language summary

Vocabulary

Nouns
adventure
city
congratulations
contest
dishes
fishing
flamingo
food
glaciers
homework
host family
initials
karaoke bar
lake
laundry
neighbor
noise
party
(air)plane
retreat
ruins
statues
surfing
test
tour

trip
vacation
waves
weather
wildlife

Pronouns
anybody
anything
something

Adjectives
amazing
awful
broke
cloudy
cold
cool
excellent
foggy
full
hot
incredible
leisure-time (activities)
lucky
special

terracotta
vegetarian
whole

Verbs
arrive
call
cook
drive
forget
happen
invite
make (a phone call)
rain
read
stay (home)
stop
take (a day off)
worry

Adverbs
Time expressions
again
all day/night/weekend
as usual

last night/Saturday/
  weekend
the whole time
today
yesterday

Other
also
anywhere
downtown
first of all
unfortunately

Prepositions
on (business/vacation)
over (the weekend)

Expressions

Asking about past activities
Did you go anywhere last weekend?
  Yes, I did. I . . .
  No, I didn't.
How did you spend. . . ?
How long were you. . . ?
What did you do. . . ?
What time did you. . . ?
Where did you. . . ?
Who did you. . . with?

Giving opinions about past experiences
How did you like. . . ?/How was. . . ?
  It was. . .
What was the best thing about. . . ?
Was the. . . OK?

Unit 8 Language summary

Vocabulary

Nouns

Neighborhood/
  Recreational facilities
airport
apartment (building)
aquarium
avenue
bank
barbershop
bookstore
clothing store
coffee shop
dance club
drugstore
electronics store
gas station
grocery store
hospital
hotel
Internet café
laundromat
library
(shopping) mall
(outdoor) market
movie theater
(science) museum
pay phone
park
post office
shopping center

stationery store
swimming pool
theater
train station
(public) transportation
travel agency
zoo

Other
(car) alarm
balcony
bedroom
budget
card
cat
cleanliness
crime
cuisine
dog
door
fashion
floor
garbage
haircut
hall(way)
kid
(traffic) light
parking
pet
pollution
privacy

rent
reservations
resident
roommate
sidewalk
traffic
utilities

Adjectives
available
convenient
crowded
fresh
inexpensive
loud
multicultural
quiet
reasonable
unique

Verbs
bark
borrow
call back
dry
find
hold on
look for
share
wash

Adverbs

Responses
of course

Other
anymore
around the corner
in fact
first of all
too (= also)

Prepositions
on
next to
near(by)/close to
across from/opposite
in front of
in back of/behind
between
on the corner of

Conjunction
so

Expressions

Asking for and giving locations
Is there a/an. . . near here?
  No, there isn't, but there's one. . .
Are there any. . . around here?
  Yes, there are. There are some. . .
  No, there aren't, but there are some. . .
  No, there aren't any. . . around here.

Asking about quantities
Are there many. . . ?
  Yes, there are a lot.
  Yes, there are a few.
  No, there aren't many.
  No, there aren't any.
  No, there are none.
Is there much. . . ?
  Yes, there's a lot.
  Yes, there's a little.
  No, there isn't much.
  No, there isn't any.
  No, there's none.

Unit 9 Language summary

Vocabulary

Nouns

appearance
beard
belt
boyfriend
cargo pants
contact lenses
couple
e-pal
eye(s)
feet
girlfriend
glasses
hair
height
length
looks
meter
(fashion) model
mustache

outfit
patterns
(time) period
picture
plaid
polo (shirt)
prints
(fashion) runway
shoulder pads
similarity
stripe(s)
trick
window

Adjectives

attached
background (color)
baggy
bald
blond

button-down (shirt)
casual
classic
comfortable
curly
dark
elderly
fashionable
funky
good-looking
gorgeous
handsome
heavy
in style
late (teens/twenties)
latest (fashions)
long
medium
middle aged
mixed-up
modern

neutral
outdated
short
silly
skinny
slim
straight
striped
tall
tucked in
vintage

Verbs

alter
describe
learn
mix
pair
sit
wear

Adverbs

fairly (+ adjective)

Prepositions

for (her age)
in (a T-shirt/jeans/her thirties)
on (the couch)
to the left/right of
with (red hair)

Expressions

Asking about appearance

What does she look like?
  She's tall.
  She has red hair.
How old is she?
  She's about 32.
  She's in her thirties.
How tall is she?
  She's 1 meter 88.
  About 6 feet 2, I suppose.
How long is her hair?
  It's medium length.
What color is her hair?
  It's dark/light brown.
Does he wear glasses?
  Yes, he does./No, he doesn't.

Identifying someone

Who's Raoul?
  He's the man wearing a green shirt/talking to Liz.
Which one is Julia?
  She's the one in jeans/near the window.

Making suggestions

Why don't you. . . ?

Interchange Teacher's Edition 1 © Cambridge University Press 2013 Photocopiable

Unit 10 Language summary

Vocabulary

Nouns

appointment
blue cheese
camel
(weather) condition(s)
costume
curry
danger
(food) festival
hairstyle
ice climbing
iced coffee
jazz club
key(s)
ID (= identification)
kiteboarding
lifestyle
magazine
mountaintop(s)

octopus
point(s)
risk
riverboat tour
sand
sports car
storm
streetcar
surfer
(herbal) tea
(traffic/speeding)
  ticket
truck
uniform
view
wedding
wingsuit

Adjectives

awake

current
experienced
fast-paced
hard
historic
important
live (concert)
nervous
scary
several
unpredictable
valuable
well-balanced

Verbs

be engaged (to
  someone)
breathe
clean
cut

drop
have trouble (doing
  something)
hike
jump
kill
lift
lose
overcome
overdo
read
ride
skip
slow down
spin
take it easy
taste
try

Adverbs

ago
already
lately
in the past (few days/
  week/year)
recently
somewhere
yet

Prepositions

for (six months/two
  years)
since (6:45/
  last weekend/
  elementary school)

Expressions

Talking about past experiences
Have you ever. . . ?
Have you. . . recently/lately. . .
  this week?
  Yes, I have./No, I haven't.
Have you/they. . . yet?
  Yes, I have. I've (already). . .
  No, they haven't. They haven't. . .
  (yet).

How many times have you. . . ?
  I've. . . once/a couple of times.
How long have you lived here?
  I've lived here for/since. . .
How long did you live there?
  I lived there for. . .

Expressing uncertainty
I can't decide.

Apologizing
I'm sorry (I'm late).

Unit 11 Language summary

Vocabulary

Nouns

beach
canoe
(handi)crafts
district
event
(city) guide
harbor
hometown
island
mangrove
nightlife
personality
plaza
pottery
pyramid
scenery
sight
souvenir
spices

spot (=place)
subway
summer
taxi
temple
town
visitor
window-shopping

Pronoun

you (= anyone)

Adjectives

best
delicious
efficient
fascinating
forbidden
lively
noisy
polluted

raw
sacred
safe
spacious
stressful
ugly
walled (city/area)

Verbs

Modal

should

Other

bargain
dye
move away
plan to (+ verb)
recommend
rent
tell (someone) about
  (something)
use

Adverbs

all year
anytime
definitely
easily
extremely (+ adjective)
somewhat (+ adjective)

Prepositions

in (the center of) town/the
  city

Conjunctions

however
though

Expressions

Describing something

What's. . . like?
  It's. . . and. . .
  It's. . . , but (it's not). . .
  It's. . . It's not (too). . . , though.
  It's. . . It's not (too). . . , however.

Asking for information

Can you tell me about. . . ?

Talking about advisability

What can you do. . . ?
  You can. . .
  You can't. . .
Can I. . . ?
  Yes, you can./No, you can't.

Asking for and giving suggestions

What should I. . . ?
  You should. . .
  You shouldn't. . .

Interchange Teacher's Edition 1 © Cambridge University Press 2013 Photocopiable

Unit 12 Language summary

Vocabulary

Nouns
Health problems
backache
bleeding
burn
cold
cough
dry skin
fever
(the) flu
headache
(the) hiccups
homesick
illness
insomnia
itchy eyes
mosquito bite(s)
sore muscles/throat
stomachache
sunburn
toothache
upset stomach
Containers
bag
bottle
box

can
jar
pack
stick
tube
Pharmacy items
aspirin
bandages
breath mints
cough drops
deodorant
eyedrops
face cream
heating pad
lotion
medicine
multivitamin
ointment
shaving cream
tissues
toothpaste
vitamin C
Other
advice
chicken stock

(newspaper/advice)
  column
complaint
dentist
energy
garlic
hand
head
idea
jungle
liquid
medicine cabinet
monkey
motor
muscle
plant(s)
rain forest
researcher
rest
social life
(chicken/garlic/onion)
  soup
source
throat

Adverb
deeply

Adjectives
helpful
hungry
itchy
medicinal
natural
sick
sore
strange
stressed (out)
terrible

Verbs
Modal
could
may
Other
burn
chop up
concentrate
cure
get (a cold/some rest)
hang (from a tree)

hurt
rest
put (= apply directly,
  as ointment)
search
see (a doctor/dentist)
sneeze
suggest
take (medicine/
  something for. . .)
treat
work (= succeed)

Prepositions
in (bed)
under (cold water)

Expressions

Talking about health problems
How are you?
  Not so good. I have. . .
That's too bad.

Offering and accepting assistance
Can/May I help you?
  Yes, please.
Can/Could/May I have. . . ?

Asking for and giving advice
What should you do. . . ?
  It's important/helpful/a good idea to. . .
What do you suggest/have for. . . ?
  Try/I suggest/You should/You could. . .

Expressing dislike
Yuck!

Agreeing
You're right.

Unit 13 Language summary

Vocabulary

Nouns

Food and beverages
beef
bread
cake
(blue) cheese
chicken
chocolate
corn
curry
dessert
(main) dish
dressing
fish
flavor
french fries
grapes
hamburger
ice cream
lamb
lemon
lettuce
mangoes
meat
miso
noodle
octopus
pasta
peas
(apple) pie
pizza
potatoes
rice
salad
sandwich
seafood
shrimp
soup
strawberries
sushi
turkey
vinaigrette
water

Other
barber
bellhops
coffee shop
door attendants
guidelines
hairstylist
maid
menu
order
parking valets
review
waiter

Adjectives
bland
bothered
fresh
greasy
healthy
mixed
rich
salty
slang
sour
spicy

Verbs

Modals
will
would

Other
bring
order
take (an order)
tip

Adverbs
a bit (+ adjective)
either
neither
tonight

Expressions

Expressing feelings
I'm (not) crazy about. . .
I'm (not) in the mood for. . .
I can't stand. . .

Agreeing and disagreeing
I like. . .
   So do I.
I don't like. . .
   Neither do I./I don't either.
I'm crazy about. . .
   So am I./I am, too.
I'm not in the mood for. . .
   Neither am I./I'm not either.
I can. . .
   So can I./I can, too.
I can't. . .
   Neither can I./I can't either.

Ordering in a restaurant
May I take your order?
What would you like (to. . .)?
   I'd like/I'll have a/an/the. . .
What kind of. . . would you like?
   I'd like/I'll have. . . , please.
Would you like anything else?
   Yes, please. I'd like. . .
   No, thank you. That'll be all.

Interchange Teacher's Edition 1 © Cambridge University Press 2013 Photocopiable

Unit 14 Language summary

Vocabulary

Nouns

Geography
canal
capital (city)
continent
desert
earth
(the) equator
(the) falls
forest
hill
island
lake
mountain
ocean
river
sea
valley
volcano
waterfall
world

*Distance and
   measurements*
degree (Celsius/
   Fahrenheit)
(square) kilometer
meter
(square) mile
pound

Other
airport
auction
(rhinoceros) beetle
boating
climate
cooling
environment
farm
faucet
feather
flight
gift
heating

landfill
lightbulbs
million
planet
(air/water) pollution
population
quiz
tower
waste
winter

Adjectives

deep
far
heavy
high
leaky
mountainous
nonstop
recycled
tuned up
wet

windy
worse

Verbs

get up (to)
go down (to)
reduce

Prepositions

in (the summer/the world/
   the Americas)
of (the three)
on (the island/earth)
from. . . to. . .

Expressions

Talking about distances and measurements

How far is. . . from. . . ?
  It's about. . . kilometers/miles.
How big is. . . ?
  It's. . . square kilometers/miles.
How high is (are). . . ?
  It's (They are). . . meters/feet high.
How deep is. . . ?
  It's. . . meters/feet deep.
How long is. . . ?
  It's. . . kilometers/miles long.
How hot is. . . in the summer?
  It gets up to. . . degrees.
How cold is. . . in the winter?
  It goes down to. . . degrees.

Making comparisons

Which country is larger, . . . or. . . ?
  . . . is larger than. . .
Which country is the largest: . . . , . . . , or. . . ?
  . . . is the largest of the three.
Which country has the largest. . . ?
  . . . has the largest. . .
What's the longest. . . in. . . ?
  . . . is the longest.
What is the most beautiful. . . in the world?
  I think. . . is the most beautiful.

Unit 15 Language summary

Vocabulary

Nouns

Leisure activities
barbecue
(rock) concert
(singing) contest
gathering
(tennis/soccer) match
(dance) performance
picnic
play
(bicycle) race
(volleyball) tournament

Other
address
babysitter
cell (phone)

etiquette
excuse
extension
favor
headphones
invitation
issue(s)
meeting
message
nuisance
(phone) number
puppy
request
ringer
rudeness
rule
statement
stranger

Adjectives
beeping
day-to-day
rude
spectator

Verbs
accept
admit
annoy
consider
give
have in common
observe
pass on
practice
refuse

return
speak

Adverbs
afterward
as soon as possible
on time
out of town
overtime

Expressions

Talking about plans
What are you doing tonight?
  I'm going. . .
Are you doing anything tomorrow?
  No, I'm not.
What is she going to do tomorrow?
  She's going. . .
Are they going to. . . ?
  Yes, they are.

Apologizing and giving reasons
I'd love to, but I can't. I. . .
Sorry, I can't. . .

Making a business call
May I speak to. . . ?
  . . .'s not in. Can I take/leave a message?
Yes, please. This is. . . Would you ask. . . to call me?
This is. . .
  I'll give. . . the message.

Asking for and giving suggestions
Can/May I take a message?
  Please tell. . . (that). . .
  Please ask. . . to. . .
  Would you tell. . . to. . . ?
  Would you ask. . . to. . . ?

Unit 16 Language summary

Vocabulary

Nouns

(savings) account
(photo) album
(a/the) big picture
    (= full view)
career
change
course
credit card
goal
graduation
(driver's) license
life
(bank/car/student) loan
lottery
skill
suburb(s)

task
time line
vocabulary

Adjectives

broke
large-scale
long-term
outgoing
own
possible
successful

Verbs

achieve
adjust
become
bring about

catch(ing) up
change
divide
dress
dye
fall (in love)
gct along (with)
graduate
hope (+ verb)
improve
join
motivate
pay off
pierce
rank
set (a goal)

Adverbs

a bit
differently
less
overseas

Prepositions

in (ages/a few years)
into (my own apartment)
throughout

Expressions

Describing changes
I'm not in school anymore.
I wear contact lenses.
I got engaged.
I moved to a new place.
I've changed jobs.
My hair is shorter now.
My job is less stressful.

Talking about future plans
What are you going to do?
I'm (not) going to. . .
I (don't) plan/want to. . .
I hope to. . .
I'd like/love to. . .

Expressing congratulations
Congratulations!

Appendix

Countries and nationalities

This is a partial list of countries, many of which are presented in this book.

Argentina	Argentine	Germany	German	the Philippines	Filipino
Australia	Australian	Greece	Greek	Poland	Polish
Austria	Austrian	Hungary	Hungarian	Russia	Russian
Bolivia	Bolivian	India	Indian	Saudi Arabia	Saudi Arabian
Brazil	Brazilian	Indonesia	Indonesian	Singapore	Singaporean
Canada	Canadian	Ireland	Irish	South Korea	South Korean
Chile	Chilean	Italy	Italian	Spain	Spanish
China	Chinese	Japan	Japanese	Switzerland	Swiss
Colombia	Colombian	Lebanon	Lebanese	Thailand	Thai
Costa Rica	Costa Rican	Malaysia	Malaysian	Turkey	Turkish
Ecuador	Ecuadorian	Mexico	Mexican	the United Kingdom	British
Egypt	Egyptian	Morocco	Moroccan	the United States	American
England	English	New Zealand	New Zealander	Uruguay	Uruguayan
France	French	Peru	Peruvian	Vietnam	Vietnamese

Irregular verbs

Present	Past	Participle	Present	Past	Participle
(be) am/is, are	was, were	been	make	made	made
bring	brought	brought	meet	met	met
buy	bought	bought	put	put	put
come	came	come	quit	quit	quit
cut	cut	cut	read	read	read
do	did	done	ride	rode	ridden
drink	drank	drunk	run	ran	run
drive	drove	driven	see	saw	seen
eat	ate	eaten	sell	sold	sold
fly	flew	flown	set	set	set
fall	fell	fallen	sit	sat	sat
feel	felt	felt	sleep	slept	slept
get	got	gotten	speak	spoke	spoken
give	gave	given	spend	spent	spent
go	went	gone	take	took	taken
grow	grew	grown	teach	taught	taught
have	had	had	tell	told	told
hear	heard	heard	think	thought	thought
keep	kept	kept	wear	wore	worn
lose	lost	lost	write	wrote	written

Comparative and superlative adjectives

Adjectives with -er and -est

big	deep	heavy	nice	small
busy	dirty	high	old	tall
cheap	dry	hot	pretty	thin
clean	easy	large	quiet	ugly
cold	fast	light	safe	warm
cool	friendly	long	short	wet
dark	funny	new	slow	young

Adjectives with more and most

attractive	dangerous	expensive	outgoing
beautiful	delicious	famous	popular
boring	difficult	important	relaxing
crowded	exciting	interesting	stressful

Irregular adjectives

good → better → the best
bad → worse → the worst

    Interchange Teacher's Edition 1 © Cambridge University Press 2013 Photocopiable

Workbook answer key
1 *Please call me Beth.*

Exercise 1

Answers will vary.

Exercise 2

2. A: What's her first name?
   B: Her first name is. . .
3. A: Where is your teacher from?
   B: My teacher is from. . .
4. A: How is your English class?
   B: My English class is. . .
5. A: What are your classmates like?
   B: My classmates are. . .

Exercise 3

2. A: My name is Young-hoon Park.
   B: <u>Nice to meet you, Young-hoon.</u>
3. A: Hello. I'm a new club member.
   B: <u>Welcome.</u>
4. A: I'm sorry. What's your name again?
   B: <u>Joe King.</u>
5. A: How do you spell your first name?
   B: <u>A-N-T-O-N-I-O.</u>
6. A: What do people call you?
   B: <u>Everyone calls me Ken.</u>

Exercise 4

2. JIM: What<u>'s your last name?</u>
   BOB: My last name's Hayes.
3. JIM: Who<u>'s that?</u>
   BOB: That's my wife.
4. JIM: What<u>'s her name?</u>
   BOB: Her name is Rosa.
5. JIM: Where<u>'s she from?</u>
   BOB: She's from Mexico.
6. JIM: Who <u>are they?</u>
   BOB: They're my wife's parents.

Exercise 5

2.	Our	4.	He	6.	Her	8.	It
3.	your	5.	My	7.	They		

Exercise 6

AMY: Oh, they <u>are</u> on the volleyball team. Let me introduce you. Hi, Surachai, this <u>is</u> Lisa Neil.
SURACHAI: Nice to meet you, Lisa.
LISA: Nice to meet you, too. Where <u>are</u> you from?
SURACHAI: I <u>am</u> from Thailand.
AMY: And this <u>is</u> Mario. He <u>is</u> from Brazil.
LISA: Hi, Mario.

Exercise 7

A

Name	Where from?	Languages	Sports?
1. *Mario*	Cali, Colombia	Spanish and French	volleyball
2. Charlotte	*Brussels, Belgium*	French and Dutch	
3. Su-yin	Wuhan, China	*Chinese and English*	volleyball
4. Ahmed	Luxor, Egypt	Arabic and English	*soccer*

B

Answers will vary.

Exercise 8

SARAH: Pretty good, thanks. Are you a student here?
RICH: <u>No, I'm not. I'm on vacation. Are you a student?</u>
SARAH: Yes, I am.
RICH: <u>What are your classmates like?</u>
SARAH: They're really interesting.
RICH: <u>Oh, really? Is Susan Miller in your class?</u>
SARAH: Yes, she is. Is she your friend?
RICH: <u>No, she's not. She's my sister!</u>

Exercise 9

TINA: Hi. <u>I'm</u> Tina Fernandez.
AMY: Are you from South America, Tina?
TINA: Yes, <u>I am.</u> <u>I'm</u> from Argentina. Where are you and your sister from, Alex?
ALEX: <u>We're</u> from Taiwan.
TINA: Are you from Taipei?
ALEX: No, <u>we're not.</u> <u>We're</u> from Tainan. Say, are you in English 101?
TINA: No, <u>I'm not.</u> I'm in English 102.

Exercise 10

2. A: <u>Are you free?</u>
   B: No, I'm not. I'm very busy.
3. A: <u>Are you from Spain?</u>
   B: No, we're not from Spain. We're from Mexico.
4. A: <u>Is your teacher Mr. Brown?</u>
   B: No, my teacher isn't Mr. Brown. I'm in Ms. West's class.
5. A: <u>Are Natalie and Mika in your class?</u>
   B: Yes, Natalie and Mika are in my class.
6. A: <u>Is it an interesting class?</u>
   B: Yes, it's an interesting class.
7. A: <u>Are they on the same baseball team?</u>
   B: No, they're not on the same baseball team. They're on the same volleyball team.

Exercise 11

	Hello	Good-bye
2. See you tomorrow.		✓
3. Good night.		✓
4. Good morning.	✓	
5. Talk to you later.		✓
6. How's it going?	✓	
7. Have a good day.		✓
8. What's up?	✓	

Exercise 12

Answers will vary.

2 What do you do?

Exercise 1

2. fitness instructor
3. flight attendant
4. newspaper reporter
5. tour guide
6. website designer

Exercise 2

1. *He*'s a website designer. He works in an office.
   He likes computers a lot.
2. *She* works in a gym. She's a fitness instructor.
   She teaches aerobics.
3. *He*'s a tour guide. He takes people on tours.
   He travels a lot.
4. *She* works for an airline. She assists passengers.
   She's a flight attendant.

Exercise 3

2. She works for a travel company. She arranges tours.
   She's a travel agent.
3. He has a difficult job. He's a cashier. He works in
   a supermarket.
4. She's an architect. She works for a large company. She
   designs houses. It's an interesting job.
5. He works with cars in a garage. He's a mechanic. He's
   also a part-time student. He takes a business class in
   the evening.

Exercise 4

Answers will vary.

Exercise 5

Tom: What *does* your husband *do* exactly?

Liz: He *works* for a department store. He's a
store manager.

Tom: How *does* he *like* it?

Liz: It's an interesting job. He *likes* it very much.
But he *works* long hours. And what *do* you *do*?

Tom: I'm a student. I *study* architecture.

Liz: Oh, really? Where *do* you *go* to school?

Tom: I go to Lincoln University. My girlfriend *goes*
there, too.

Liz: Really? And what *does* she *study*?

Tom: She *studies* hotel management.

Liz: That sounds interesting.

Exercise 6

Victor: I work for Cybotics Industries.

Mark: And what *do you do* there?

Victor: I'm in management.

Mark: How *do you like it*?

Victor: It's a great job. And what *do you do*?

Mark: I'm a salesperson.

Victor: Really? What *do you sell*?

Mark: I sell computers. Do you want to buy one?

Exercise 7

1. *He*'s a chef.
2. He practices cooking new things, and then he
   writes cookbooks.
3. He makes TV programs about Thai cooking.
4. *She*'s a lifeguard.
5. She works at the city pool.
6. She finishes work at noon.

Exercise 8

Answers will vary. Possible answers:
2. Where does he work?
3. When does he start work?
4. How does he like his job?

Exercise 9

Everyone knows Pat at the hospital. Pat is a part-time
nurse. He works at night on weekends. <u>On</u> Saturdays and
Sundays, Pat sleeps most of the day and wakes up a little
<u>before</u> nine <u>in</u> the evening, usually at 8:45 or 8:50. He has
breakfast very late, <u>around</u> 9:30 or 10:00 P.M.! He watches
television <u>until</u> eleven o'clock, and then starts work <u>at</u>
midnight. <u>Early</u> in the morning, usually around 5:00 A.M.,
he leaves work, has a little snack, goes home, goes to
bed, and sleeps <u>late</u>. It's a perfect schedule for Pat. He's a
premed student on weekdays at a local college.

Exercise 10

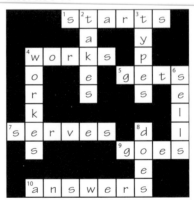

Exercise 11

2. What does he do?
3. She fixes cars.
4. He goes to the university.
5. She stays up late.
6. He works part time.

Exercise 12

1. New York Hospital needs <u>nurses</u>. Work during the day
   or <u>at night</u>, weekdays or <u>weekends</u>, full time or
   <u>part time</u>. Call 614-555-1191.
2. <u>Interesting</u> job for a language <u>student</u>. Mornings only.
   Take people on <u>tours</u>. Need good English and <u>Spanish</u>
   skills. Email Dave at dave189@cup.org.
3. No need to work <u>long hours</u>! Only work from 6:00 <u>until</u>
   11:00 four evenings a week. Our <u>restaurant</u> serves great
   food! Work as our <u>manager</u>. Call 308-555-6845.

3 How much is it?

Exercise 1

SAM: The light blue ones over there. They're nice.

REBECCA: <u>Yes. But I don't really like light blue.</u>

SAM: Hmm. Well, what about that sweater? It's perfect for you.

REBECCA: <u>Which one?</u>

SAM: This red one.

REBECCA: <u>Well, I like it, but it's expensive.</u>

SAM: Hey, let me buy it for you. It's a present!

REBECCA: <u>Oh, Sam. Thank you very much.</u>

Exercise 2

2. A: <u>How much are those</u> bracelets?
   B: They're $29.
3. A: <u>How much are these</u> shoes?
   B: They're $64.
4. A: <u>How much is that</u> cat?
   B: That's *my* cat, and he's not for sale!

Exercise 3

1. *backpacks*
2. boxes
3. companies
4. days
5. dresses
6. gloves
7. hairbrushes
8. necklaces
9. rings
10. scarves
11. sweaters
12. ties

Exercise 4

Answers will vary. Possible answers:
2. That's cheap.
3. That's pretty expensive!
4. That's reasonable.
5. That's not bad.
6. That's cheap.
7. That's not bad.

Exercise 5

1. CLERK: <u>It's</u> $195.
   LUIS: And how much is that <u>one</u>?
   CLERK: <u>It's</u> $255.
   LUIS: Oh, really? Well, thanks, anyway.
2. MEG: Excuse me. How much are <u>those</u> jeans?
   CLERK: <u>They're</u> only $59.
   MEG: And how much is <u>this</u> sweater?
   CLERK: Which <u>one</u>? They're all different.
   MEG: This green <u>one</u>.
   CLERK: <u>It's</u> $34.
3. SONIA: I like <u>those</u> sunglasses over there.
   CLERK: Which <u>ones</u>?
   SONIA: The small brown <u>ones</u>.
   CLERK: <u>They're</u> $199.
   SONIA: Oh, they're expensive!

Exercise 6

Cotton	Gold	Leather	Plastic	Silk	Wool
gloves	bracelet	boots	boots	pants	pants
pants	ring	pants	bracelet	gloves	gloves
shirt	necklace	gloves	ring	shirt	shirt
jacket		jacket	necklace	jacket	jacket

Exercise 7

1. B: Yes, but the leather ones are <u>nicer</u>.
   A: They're also <u>more expensive</u>.
2. A: Those silk jackets look <u>more attractive than</u> the wool ones.
   B: Yes, but the wool ones are <u>warmer</u>.
3. A: This purple shirt is an interesting color!
   B: Yes, but the color is <u>prettier than</u> the design.
   A: The design isn't bad.
   B: I think the pattern on that red shirt is <u>better than</u> the pattern on this purple one.
4. A: Hey, look at this silver ring! It's nice. And it's <u>cheaper than</u> that gold ring.
   B: But it's <u>smaller than</u> the gold one.
   A: Well, yeah. The gold one is <u>bigger than</u> the silver one. But look at the price tag. One thousand dollars is a lot of money!

Exercise 8

Clothing	Electronics	Jewelry
boots	DVD player	bracelet
cap	MP3 player	earrings
dress	television	necklace
T-shirt	video camera	ring

Exercise 9

Answers will vary. Possible answers:
2. Which cap do you like more, the wool one or the leather one?
   <u>I like the wool one more.</u> *or* <u>I like the leather one more.</u>
3. Which ones do you like more, the high-tops or the sandals?
   <u>I like the high-tops more.</u> *or* <u>I like the sandals more.</u>
4. Which one do you prefer, the laptop computer or the desktop computer?
   <u>I prefer the laptop computer.</u> *or* <u>I prefer the desktop computer.</u>
5. Which necklace do you like better, the silver one or the gold one?
   <u>I like the gold one better.</u> *or* <u>I like the silver one better.</u>

Exercise 10

A
1. d   2. c   3. a   4. b

B
1. False
2. True
3. True
4. False

C
Answers will vary.

4 I really like hip-hop.

Exercise 1
Answers will vary.

Exercise 2
Answers will vary. Possible answers:
2. Do you like Usher? Yes, I do. I love <u>him</u>.
3. Do you like romantic comedies? No, I don't. I can't stand <u>them</u>.
4. Do you like Adele? Yes, I do. I like <u>her</u> a lot.
5. Do you like video games? No, I don't. I don't like <u>them</u> very much.
6. Do you like science fiction books? Yes, I do. I like <u>them</u> a lot.

Exercise 3
1. Katy Perry is a <u>singer</u>.
2. The Kings of Leon are <u>a rock band</u>.
3. Colin Firth is <u>an actor</u>.
4. Nani is <u>a soccer player</u>.

Exercise 4
1. SARAH: Yes, I <u>like</u> it a lot. I'm a real fan of Keith Urban.
   ED: Oh, <u>does</u> he play the guitar?
   SARAH: Yes, he <u>does</u>. He's my favorite musician.
2. ANNE: <u>What</u> kind of music <u>do</u> your parents <u>like</u>, Jason?
   JASON: They <u>like</u> classical music.
   ANNE: Who <u>do</u> they <u>like</u>? Mozart?
   JASON: No, they <u>don't</u> like him very much. They prefer Beethoven.
3. SCOTT: Teresa, <u>do</u> you <u>like</u> Beyonce?
   TERESA: No, I don't. I can't stand her. I like Alicia Keys.
   SCOTT: I don't know her. What kind of music <u>does</u> she sing?
   TERESA: She <u>sings</u> R&B. She's really great!

Exercise 5
Responses will vary.
1. <u>What kinds</u> of movies do you like? | <i>I like</i> comedies and musicals.
2. <u>What</u> is your favorite movie? | <i>My favorite</i> movie is <i>Avatar</i>.
3. <u>What kind/kinds</u> of movies do you dislike? | I dislike animated movies.
4. <u>What kind/kinds</u> of TV shows do you like? | I like reality shows.
5. <u>Who</u> is your favorite actor or actress? | My favorite actor is Matt Damon.
6. <u>What</u> is your favorite song? | My favorite song is "Let It Be."
7. <u>Who</u> is your favorite rock band? | My favorite rock band is U2.
8. <u>What</u> is your favorite video game? | My favorite video game is Limbo.

Exercise 6
Answers will vary. Possible answers:
1. Which movies are more interesting, musicals or science fiction films?
   <u>Science fiction films are more interesting than musicals.</u>
2. Which films are scarier, horror films or thrillers?
   <u>Horror films are scarier than thrillers.</u>
3. Which do you like more, animated films or historical dramas?
   <u>I like historical dramas more.</u>
4. Which do you prefer, romantic comedies or action films?
   <u>I prefer action films.</u>
5. Which films are more exciting, westerns or crime thrillers?
   <u>Crime thrillers are more exciting than westerns.</u>

Exercise 7
A
Answers will vary. Possible answers:

Listen to	Play	Watch
jazz	the piano	videos
music	the guitar	a sports match
the radio	the trumpet	a movie

B
Answers will vary.

Exercise 8
A
1. Ahead of Time 2. House of Laughs 3. Coming Up for Air
B
1. a science fiction film
2. a comedy
3. a crime thriller

Exercise 9
2. A: Do you like country music?
   B. <u>I can't stand it.</u>
3. A: There's a baseball game tonight.
   B. <u>Great. Let's go.</u>
4. A: Would you like to see a movie this weekend?
   B: <u>That sounds great!</u>

Exercise 10
A
2. No   4. No
3. Yes   5. Yes
B
Answers will vary.

Exercise 11
1. KATE: Yes, I do. <u>I like</u> it a lot.
   ROBIN: There's a Linkin Park concert on Friday. <u>Would you like</u> to go with me?
   KATE: Yes, <u>I'd love to</u>. Thanks.
2. CARLOS: There is a basketball game on TV tonight. <u>Would you like</u> to come over and watch it?
   PHIL: <u>I'd like to</u>, but I have to study tonight.
   CARLOS: Well, <u>do you like</u> soccer?
   PHIL: Yes, <u>I do</u>. I love it!
   CARLOS: There's a match on TV tomorrow at 3:00. <u>Would you like</u> to watch that with me?
   PHIL: <u>I'd love to</u>. Thanks.

Exercise 12
2. Richard can't stand classical music.
3. I love horror films!
4. Celia is not a fan of pop music.
5. Would you like to go to a baseball game?

5 I come from a big family.

Exercise 1

Males	Females
brother	*aunt*
father	daughter
husband	mother
nephew	niece
son	sister
uncle	wife

Exercise 2

DON: No, I'm not. My brother and sister <u>are staying</u> with me right now. We go to bed after midnight every night.

JOEL: Really? What <u>are they doing</u> this summer? <u>Are they taking</u> classes, too?

DON: No, they aren't. My brother is on vacation now, but he<u>'s looking</u> for a part-time job here.

JOEL: What about your sister? <u>Is she working</u>?

DON: Yes, she is. She has a part-time job at the university. What about you, Joel? Are you in school this summer?

JOEL: Yes, I am. <u>I'm studying</u> two languages.

DON: Oh, <u>are you taking</u> French and Spanish again?

JOEL: Well, I'm taking Spanish again, but <u>I'm starting</u> Japanese.

DON: Really? That's exciting!

Exercise 3

2. *Peter is* Liz's husband.
3. Frank and Liza are Isabel's grandparents.
4. We have a son and (a) daughter.
5. My father-in-law is a painter.
6. Michael is looking for a job right now.

Exercise 4

CHRIS: Wow! Do you like it?

PHILIP: <u>Yes, I do. I like it a lot.</u>

CHRIS: And is your brother still working in Hong Kong?

PHILIP: <u>Yes, he is. He loves it there.</u>

CHRIS: And how about your parents? Are they still living in Florida?

PHILIP: <u>No, they aren't. They're living in New York these days.</u> How about you and your family, Chris? Are you still living here?

CHRIS: <u>Yes, we are. We really love San Francisco.</u>

Exercise 5

1. This is my aunt Barbara. She <u>*lives*</u> in Rome, but she<u>'s visiting</u> Chile this summer. She<u>'s taking</u> some summer classes there.
2. And these are my parents. They <u>work</u> in London. They<u>'re</u> on vacation right now.
3. And here you can see my grandparents. They <u>aren't working</u> *or* They<u>'re not working</u> now. They<u>'re</u> retired.
4. This is my brother-in-law Edward. He <u>wants</u> to be a company director. He<u>'s studying</u> business in Canada right now.

5. And this is my niece Christina. She <u>goes</u> *or* She<u>'s going</u> to high school. She <u>likes</u> mathematics, but she <u>doesn't like</u> English.

Exercise 6

Answers will vary.

Exercise 7

A

Answers will vary.

B

1. False: Many college students live in university housing.
2. True
3. False: Few young people in the United States live with their parents.
4. False: Nearly all university students live with their parents.
5. True
6. False: (Rents in the city are very expensive.) Many young people continue to live with their parents after they marry.

Exercise 8

1. *all*
2. nearly all
3. most
4. many
5. a lot of
6. some
7. not many
8. few
9. *no*

Exercise 9

1. Most <u>*children go to public schools.*</u>
   Few <u>children go to private schools.</u>
2. Many <u>young people go to college after they finish high school.</u>
   Some <u>young people look for work after they finish high school.</u>
3. Not many <u>people over 65 like to use the Internet.</u>
   A lot of <u>people over 65 like to spend time on a hobby.</u>
   Nearly <u>all people over 65 like to talk to family and friends.</u>

Exercise 10

In my country, some <u>*couples*</u> get married fairly young. Not many marriages <u>break up</u>, and nearly all <u>divorced</u> people remarry. Elderly couples often <u>live at home</u> and take care of their grandchildren.

Exercise 11

Answers will vary.

6 How often do you exercise?

Exercise 1

Team sports	Individual sports	Exercise
baseball	swimming	swimming
basketball	jogging	jogging
football	bicycling	aerobics
soccer	tennis	bicycling
volleyball	yoga	tennis
swimming		stretching
tennis		yoga

Exercise 2

2. They hardly ever play tennis.
3. How often do you go jogging?
4. We often do yoga on Sunday mornings.
5. Does Charlie ever do aerobics?
6. What do you usually do on Saturdays?

Exercise 3

2. A: <u>What do you usually do on weekends?</u>
   B: Well, I usually do karate on Saturdays and yoga on Sundays.
3. A: <u>Do you ever go to the gym after work?</u>
   B: No, I never go to the gym after work.
4. A: <u>How often do you exercise?</u>
   B: I don't exercise very often at all.
5. A: <u>Do you ever play sports on weekends?</u>
   B: Yes, I sometimes play sports on weekends –usually baseball.
6. A: <u>What do you usually do in your free time?</u>
   B: I usually play tennis in my free time.

Exercise 4

A
Answers will vary.
B
Answers will vary.

Exercise 5

JERRY: I always go jogging <u>at</u> 7:00. How about you, Susan?

SUSAN: I usually go jogging <u>around</u> noon. I jog <u>for</u> about an hour.

JERRY: And do you also play sports <u>in</u> your free time?

SUSAN: No, I usually go out with my classmates. What about you?

JERRY: I go to the gym <u>on</u> Mondays and Wednesdays. And sometimes I go bicycling <u>on</u> weekends.

SUSAN: Wow! You really like to stay in shape.

Exercise 6

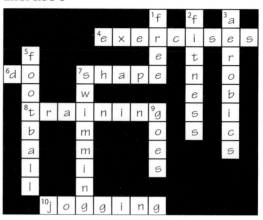

Exercise 7

A
Hiking Club: go to myhikingclub.cup.org
Adult Education Program: pick up a brochure at any Star Supermarket or the public library
Community Center: call 888-555-9916

B

	Hiking Club	Adult Education Program	Community Center
play indoor sports			✓
do outdoor activities	✓		
take evening classes		✓	
go dancing			✓
learn to cook		✓	
meet new people	✓	✓	✓

Exercise 8

2. A: How long do you spend in the pool?
   B: <u>About 45 minutes.</u>
3. A: And how well do you swim?
   B: <u>I'm about average.</u>
4. A: How good are you at other sports?
   B: <u>Not very good, actually.</u>

Exercise 9

2. A: <u>How often do you go for a walk?</u>
   B: Almost every day. I really enjoy it.
3. A: <u>How long do you spend jogging?</u>
   B: I spend about an hour jogging.
4. A: <u>How good are you at soccer?</u>
   B: I'm pretty good at it. I'm on the school team.
5. A: <u>How well do you play basketball?</u>
   B: Basketball? Pretty well, I guess. I like it a lot.

Exercise 10

2. Tom doesn't exercise very often.
3. Philip tries to stay in shape.
4. Jill often works out at the gym.
5. I always go jogging with my wife.
6. How well do you play tennis?

Exercise 11

Answers will vary.

7 *We had a great time!*

Exercise 1

A

2. enjoyed
3. invited
4. loved
5. studied
6. tried
7. visited
8. washed
9. watched

B

2. give
3. meet
4. see
5. sleep
6. spend
7. take
8. go

C

Answers will vary.

Exercise 2

2. Who did you meet at the party?
   I met someone very interesting.
3. What time did you and Eva get home?
   We got home a little after 1:00.
4. How did you and Bob like the art exhibition?
   We liked the art exhibition a lot.
5. What did you buy?
   I bought some new leather boots.
6. Where did Jeff and Joyce spend their vacation?
   They spent their vacation in the country.

Exercise 3

Answers will vary.

Exercise 4

A: What did you do?
B: Well, on Saturday, we went shopping.
A: And did you do anything special in the evening?
B: No, nothing special.
A: Where did you go on Sunday?
B: We went to the amusement park.
A: How did you like it?
B: We had a great time. In fact, we stayed there all day.
A: Really? What time did you get home?
B: We got home very late, around midnight.

Exercise 5

2. A: I stayed home from work all day yesterday. Did you take the day off, too?
   B: No, I didn't. I worked all day until six o'clock.
3. A: I worked all weekend on my research paper. Did you spend the weekend at home, too?
   B: No, I didn't. I went out with friends.
4. A: I studied all weekend. Did you and John have a lot of homework, too?
   B: No, we didn't. We finished our homework on Saturday.
5. A: Carl drove me to work yesterday morning. Did you drive to work?
   B: No, I didn't. I took the bus.
6. A: Kathy went to the baseball game last night. Did you and Bob go to the game?
   B: No, we didn't. We watched it on TV.

Exercise 6

2. d. He took a day off.
3. e. He did housework.
4. c. He didn't do the laundry.
5. a. He had people over.
6. b. He had a good time.

Exercise 7

A

Both William and Sue visited Bangkok for the first time.

C

	William	Sue
2. visited the floating market	✓	✓
3. bought fruit		✓
4. saw some historic ruins		✓
5. traveled on the river	✓	✓
6. loved the food the most	✓	
7. enjoyed everything		✓

Exercise 8

B: It was great. I really enjoyed it.
A: How long were you there?
B: We were there for two weeks.
A: Were you in Lima all the time?
B: No, we weren't. We were in the mountains for a few days.
A: And how was the weather? Was it good?
B: No, it wasn't good at all. In fact, it was terrible. The city was very hot, and the mountains were really cold!

Exercise 9

B: It was a great trip. I really enjoyed South Africa and Namibia.
A: How long were you in South Africa?
B: For ten days.
A: And how long were you in Namibia?
B: I was in Namibia for about five days.
A: Wow, that's a long time. How was the weather?
B: It was hot and sunny the whole time.
A: And what was the best part?
B: It was definitely the natural parks and wildlife in Namibia. And we saw some meerkats!

Exercise 10

1. I'm sorry I was late. I had to make a phone call.
2. My friends and I really enjoyed your party. We all had a good time.
3. I stayed home last night and did the laundry.
4. We didn't see very much in the mountains. The weather was pretty foggy.
5. I worked really hard in Switzerland last week. I was there on business.

Exercise 11

A

Answers will vary.

B

Answers will vary.

8 What's your neighborhood like?

Exercise 1

A

2. gas station
3. grocery store
4. Internet café
5. karaoke bar
6. movie theater
7. pay phone
8. post office
9. travel agency

B

2. A: I want to check my email. <u>Are there any Internet cafés</u> near here?
   B: No, there aren't, but there are some near the university.
3. A: I want to mail this package. <u>Is there a post office</u> around here?
   B: Yes, there's one next to the laundromat.
4. A: I need to make a phone call. <u>Are there any pay phones</u> around here?
   B: Yes, there are some across from the library.
5. A: We need some gas. <u>Are there any gas stations</u> on this street?
   B: No, there aren't, but there are a couple on Second Avenue.
6. A: We need to make a reservation for a trip. <u>Is there a travel agency</u> near here?
   B: Yes, there's one near the Prince Hotel.

Exercise 2

Possible answers:

3. There's a laundromat on the corner of 1st Street and Oak in Avery, but there isn't one in Bailey. There's a hospital.
4. There's a grocery store on Elm Street in Bailey, but there isn't one in Avery.
5. There's a restaurant on the corner of 3rd Street and Oak in Avery, but there isn't one in Bailey. There's a drugstore.
6. There's a bank on the corner of 2nd Street and Oak in Avery, but there isn't one in Bailey. There's a department store.
7. There's a post office on the corner of 3rd and Birch in Avery, but there isn't one in Bailey. There's a movie theater.
8. There's a supermarket on the corner of 2nd and Elm in Avery, but there isn't one in Bailey.
9. There are some houses on 3rd Street in Avery, but there aren't any in Bailey. There are some apartments.
10. There's a barbershop on 4th Street in Avery, but there isn't one in Bailey. There's a coffee shop.

Exercise 3

Answers will vary. Possible answers:
2. Is there a post office near here?
   Yes. There<u>'s one on the corner of Lincoln Street and 3rd Avenue.</u>
3. I'm looking for a drugstore.
   <u>There's one opposite the gas station.</u>
4. Is there a laundromat in this neighborhood?
   <u>Yes. There's one next to the park.</u>
5. Is there a department store on Lincoln Street?
   <u>Yes. There's one between the travel agency and the gym.</u>

6. Are there any pay phones around here?
   <u>Yes. There are some in front of the post office.</u>

Exercise 4

Answers will vary.

Exercise 5

A

Diana would like to live in the suburbs. Victor would like to live downtown.

B

	Advantages	Disadvantages
Downtown	*near the shopping center* near the bus station	very noisy, streets full of people traffic is terrible parking is a big problem
Suburbs	safe a lot of parks good schools very little crime	too quiet not many shops, no clubs or movie theaters takes a long time to drive anywhere nothing ever really happens

C

Answers will vary.

Exercise 6

Count nouns		Noncount nouns	
bank	people	crime	pollution
hospital	school	noise	traffic
library	theater	parking	water

Exercise 7

2. How many buses are there?   There aren't any.
3. How much traffic is there?   There's only a little.
4. How many banks are there?   There are a couple.
5. How many people are there?   There are a few.
6. How much crime is there?   There's a lot.

Exercise 8

ALEX: Sure. There are <u>a lot</u>. There's a great club <u>across from</u> the National Bank, but it's expensive.

LUIS: Well, are there <u>any</u> others?

ALEX: Yeah, there are <u>a few</u>. There's a nice one near here. It's called Sounds of Brazil.

LUIS: That's perfect! Where is it exactly?

ALEX: It's on Third Avenue, <u>between</u> the Royal Theater and May's Restaurant.

LUIS: So let's go!

Exercise 9

1. I'm going to the stationery store to get a <u>birthday card</u>.
2. We're taking a long drive. We need to go to the <u>gas station</u>.
3. I live on the 8th floor of my <u>apartment building</u>.
4. Our apartment is in the center of the city. We live <u>downtown</u>.

9 What does she look like?

Exercise 1
2. light
3. young
4. short
5. tall

Exercise 2
A
2. fairly long
3. goodlooking
4. medium height
5. middle aged

B
2. A: How long is his hair?
   B: It's fairly long.
3. A: What color is his hair?
   B: It's dark brown.
4. A: How old is he?
   B: He's middle aged.
5. A: How tall is he?
   B: He's medium height.

Exercise 3
JIM: And how long is her hair?
STEVE: It's medium length.
JIM: How tall is she?
STEVE: She's fairly tall.
JIM: And how old is she?
STEVE: She's in her early twenties.
JIM: Does she wear glasses?
STEVE: Sometimes. I think she's wearing them now.
JIM: I think I see her over there. Is that her?

Exercise 4
Answers will vary.

Exercise 5
1. George is in his late sixties. He's pretty tall. He has a mustache, and he's bald. He's wearing a shirt, jeans, and boots.
   He isn't bald. He has short, curly hair.
2. Sophie is about 25. She's very pretty. She's medium height. Her hair is long and blond. She's wearing a black sweater, a jacket, and sneakers. She's standing next to her motorcycle. She isn't wearing sneakers. She's wearing boots. She isn't standing next to her motorcycle. She's sitting on her motorcycle.
3. Lucinda is in her early twenties. She's pretty serious-looking. She has glasses and curly dark hair. She's fairly tall, and she's wearing a nice-looking jacket and jeans.
   She doesn't have glasses. She isn't wearing jeans. She's wearing a skirt.

Exercise 6
Formal	Casual
shirt	boots
dress	jeans
scarf	shorts
skirt	sneakers
suit	T-shirt
necktie	cap

Exercise 7
2. Alice is the woman talking to the man.
3. Mandy is the tall woman carrying a jacket.
4. Edward and Kate are the ones wearing sunglasses.
5. William is the one wearing a suit and tie.

Exercise 8
Possible answers:
2. A: Who's Carlos?
   B: He's the one behind the couch.
3. A: Who are Dan and Cindy?
   B: They're the ones dancing.
4. A: Which one is Angela?
   B: She's the one on the couch.
5. A: Who's Ken?
   B: He's the one with short black hair.

Exercise 9
2. A: Which ones are the teachers?
      Who are the teachers?
   B: They're the ones on the couch.
      They're the ones sitting on the couch.
3. A: Which one is Larry?
      Who is Larry?
   B: He's the guy wearing the coat.
      He's the guy in the coat.

Exercise 10
Yeah, classes start tomorrow. What am I doing? Let's see. . . . I'*m looking* out my window right now. There's a middle-aged woman walking with her baby. Some people are waiting at the bus stop. A serious-looking man is asking for directions. A young guy is using his cell phone. Two people are standing next to him. Hey! The one wearing a baseball cap is my classmate! And hey, here comes a really cute girl carrying a backpack. Wait a minute! I know her. That's my old friend. I have to go now! Bye.

Exercise 11
2. A: Who's Sam?
   B: The handsome guy near the door.
3. A: Is she the one on the couch?
   B: That's right.
4. A: How tall is she?
   B: Pretty short.

10 *Have you ever ridden a camel?*

Exercise 1

2. e. called
3. b. done
4. j. eaten
5. a. gone
6. h. had
7. g. made
8. f. run
9. c. seen
10. i. tried

Exercise 2

2. A: <u>Have you done</u> your homework yet?
   B: Yes, I have. I did it last night.
3. A: How many phone calls <u>have you made</u> today?
   B: I made only one – to call you!
4. A: How long <u>have you had</u> those sunglasses?
   B: I've had them for a few weeks.
5. A: <u>Have you eaten</u> at Rio Café?
   B: Yes, we've already eaten there. It's very good but a little expensive.
6. A: How many times <u>have you gone</u> shopping at the mall this month?
   B: Actually, I haven't gone at all. Why don't we go later today?

Exercise 3

A
Answers will vary.

B
Answers will vary.

Exercise 4

2. I have been a nurse <u>for</u> several years.
3. Masayuki was an exchange student in Spain <u>for</u> a whole semester.
4. I'm so sleepy. I've been awake <u>since</u> 4:00 this morning.
5. Mr. and Mrs. Chang have been married <u>for</u> nearly 40 years.
6. Maggie has had the same hairstyle <u>since</u> high school.
7. How are you? I haven't seen you <u>since</u> your wedding.
8. Where have you been? I've been here <u>for</u> over an hour!
9. I haven't had this much fun <u>since</u> I was a kid.

Exercise 5

Answers will vary.

Exercise 6

A
The first writer went to Switzerland. He or she wanted to go skiing.
The second writer went to Taiwan. He or she wanted to go fishing.

B

<u>2</u>	lost a wallet
<u>1</u>	enjoyed the view
<u>1 and 2</u>	got no exercise
<u>2</u>	spent time on a boat
<u>1</u>	waited for help
<u>2</u>	went swimming
<u>1 and 2</u>	had a terrible day

C
Answers will vary.

Exercise 7

2. A: <u>Have you ever seen a sumo wrestling match?</u>
   B: Actually, I saw a sumo wrestling match last month on TV. It was terrific!
3. A: <u>Have you ever eaten oysters?</u>
   B: No, I haven't. I've never eaten oysters.
4. A: <u>Have you ever been wall climbing?</u>
   B: No, I've never been wall climbing.
5. A: <u>Have you ever ridden in a sports car?</u>
   B: Yes, I rode in a sports car last month.
6. A: <u>Have you ever been camping?</u>
   B: No, I haven't. I've never been camping.
7. A: <u>Have you ever ridden a motorcycle?</u>
   B: Yes, I have. I once rode my brother's motorcycle.

Exercise 8

Answers will vary.

Exercise 9

B: Yes, I <u>lost</u> my cell phone last month.
A: <u>Have</u> you <u>found</u> it yet?
B: No. Actually, I<u>'ve</u> already <u>bought</u> a new one. Look!
A: Oh, that's nice. Where <u>did</u> you <u>buy</u> it?
B: I <u>got</u> it at Tech Town last weekend. What about you? <u>Have</u> you ever <u>lost</u> anything valuable?
A: Well, I <u>left</u> my leather jacket book in a coffee shop a couple of months ago.
B: Oh no! <u>Did</u> you <u>go</u> back and look for it?
A: Well, I <u>called</u> them but it was gone.

Exercise 10

2. A: Are you having a good time?
   B: <u>Yes, really good.</u>
3. A: How long did Joe stay at the party?
   B: <u>For two hours.</u>
4. A: Have you had lunch?
   B: <u>Yes, I've already eaten.</u>
5. A: How many times has Gina lost her keys?
   B: <u>Twice.</u>
6. A: What about a tour of the city?
   B: <u>Sure. I hear it's great.</u>
7. A: Have you been here long?
   B: <u>No, just a few minutes.</u>
8. A: Have you seen Chad today?
   B: <u>Yes, I saw him this morning.</u>

11 *It's a very exciting place!*

Exercise 1
2. Florence is a beautiful old city. There are not many <u>modern</u> buildings.
3. My hometown is not an exciting place. The nightlife there is pretty <u>boring</u>.
4. Some parts of our city are fairly dangerous. They're not very <u>safe</u> late at night.
5. Athens is a very quiet city in the winter. The streets are never <u>crowded</u> at that time of the year.

Exercise 2
A: <u>Is it big?</u>
B: No, it's fairly small, but it's not too small.
A: <u>What's the weather like?</u>
B: The winter is wet and really cold. It's very nice in the summer, though.
A: <u>Is the nightlife exciting?</u>
B: No! It's really boring. There are no good restaurants or nightclubs.

Exercise 3
2. Sapporo is a very nice place. The winters are terribly cold, though.
3. Marrakech is an exciting city, and it's a fun place to sightsee.
4. My hometown is a great place for a vacation, but it's not too good for shopping.
5. Our hometown is somewhat ugly. It has some beautiful old homes, however.

Exercise 4
2. _____ Restaurants are very cheap in Ecuador.
3. ✓ Copenhagen is a clean city.
4. _____ The buildings in Paris are really beautiful.
5. _____ Apartments are very expensive in Hong Kong.
6. ✓ Dubai is a very hot city in the summer.
7. _____ Mexico City has excellent museums.
8. ✓ Rio de Janeiro is an exciting place to visit.

Exercise 5
Ever-Popular London
London <u>is</u> Britain's biggest city. It <u>has</u> a very old capital and dates back to the Romans. It <u>is</u> a city of interesting buildings and churches, and it <u>has</u> many beautiful parks. It also <u>has</u> some of the best museums in the world. London <u>is</u> very crowded in the summer, but it <u>is</u> not too busy in the winter. It <u>is</u> a popular city with foreign tourists and <u>has</u> millions of visitors a year. The city <u>is</u> famous for its shopping and <u>has</u> many excellent department stores. London <u>has</u> convenient trains and buses that cross the city, so it <u>is</u> easy for tourists to get around.

Exercise 6
A
Helsinki is in Finland, on the Baltic Sea.
Vancouver is on the west coast of Canada.
Salvador da Bahia is in northeast Brazil.

B

City	Date founded	Population	Weather	Attractions
Helsinki	*1550*	Nearly 600,000	very cold in the winter	walking and bicycling; cruises
Vancouver	1870s (or 1886)	Over 2 million	fairly mild	restaurants, nearby mountains, and skiing
Salvador da Bahia	1549	about 2.6 million	hot and humid with sea breezes	beaches architecture African food and music

C
2. <u>Vancouver</u> has many Chinese speakers.
3. <u>Helsinki</u> is the coldest of the three cities.
4. <u>Helsinki and Salvador da Bahia</u> were both founded in the mid-sixteenth century.

Exercise 7
2. You <u>shouldn't stay</u> near the airport. It's too noisy.
3. You <u>shouldn't miss</u> the museum. It has some new exhibits.
4. You <u>can take</u> a bus tour of the city if you like.
5. You <u>shouldn't walk</u> alone at night. It's too dangerous.
6. You <u>can get a</u> taxi if you're out late.

Exercise 8
B: <u>You shouldn't miss</u> Yogyakarta, the old capital city. There are a lot of beautiful old buildings. For example, <u>you should</u> see the temple of Borobudur.
A: Sounds great. Bali is very popular, too. <u>Should I</u> go there?
B: Yes, <u>you should</u>. It's very interesting.
A: <u>Should I</u> take a lot of money with me?
B: No, <u>you shouldn't</u>. Indonesia is not an expensive country to visit.
A: So when <u>should I</u> go there?
B: Anytime. The weather's always nice.

Exercise 9
Possible questions:
2. What can you see and do there?
3. What shouldn't you do there?
4. What special foods should you try?
5. What fun things can you buy there?
6. What other interesting things can you do?

Exercise 10
2. The streets are always crowded.
3. It's a fairly ugly city.
4. When's a good time to visit the city?
5. You really shouldn't miss the weekend market.

Interchange Teacher's Edition 1   *Workbook answer key* ▪ **T-175**

12 ■ *It really works!*

Exercise 1

A

Suggested answers:
2. a bad cold: go to bed and rest
3. a burn: put it under cold water
4. a headache: take some aspirin
5. an insect bite: apply anti-itch cream
6. sore muscles: use some ointment

B

Possible answers:
2. A: What should you do for a bad cold?
   B: It's important to go to bed and rest.
3. A: What should you do for a burn?
   B: It's important to put it under cold water.
4. A: What should you do for a headache?
   B: It's sometimes helpful to take some aspirin.
5. A: What should you do for an insect bite?
   B: It's a good idea to apply anti-itch cream.
6. A: What should you do for sore muscles?
   B: It's helpful to use some ointment.

Exercise 2

Possible answers:
2. For a sore throat, it's a good idea not to talk too much.
3. For a burn, it's important not to put ice on it.
4. For insomnia, it's sometimes helpful not to drink coffee at night.
5. For a fever, it's important not to get out of bed.

Exercise 3

Answers will vary.

Exercise 4

A

some medicines, stress

B
1. False
2. False
3. True
4. True
5. False
6. True
7. True
8. True

Exercise 5

A

Bottle	Box	Can	Tube
ear drops	cough drops	insect spray	anti-itch cream
eyedrops	bandages	sunburn spray	muscle ointment

B

Possible answers:
2. Mary has a bad cough.
   She should buy a box of cough drops.

3. David has a terrible earache.
   He should buy a bottle of ear drops.
4. There may be mosquitoes where Ed's camping.
   He should get a can of insect spray.
5. Manuel has dry, itchy skin.
   He should buy a tube of anti-itch cream.
6. Susan has a cut on her hand.
   She should get a box of bandages.
7. Jin Sook and Brandy got burned at the beach.
   They should get a can of sunburn spray.
8. Mark's shoulders are sore after his workout.
   He should buy a tube of muscle ointment.

Exercise 6

1. CUSTOMER: Yes. Can I have a bottle of aspirin?
   PHARMACIST: Here you are.
   CUSTOMER: And what do you have for a sunburn?
   PHARMACIST: I suggest this lotion.
   CUSTOMER: Thanks.
2. PHARMACIST: Hi. Can I help you?
   CUSTOMER: Yes. Could I have something for sore muscles?
   PHARMACIST: Sure. Try this ointment.
   CUSTOMER: Thanks. And what do you suggest for the flu?
   PHARMACIST: Try some of these tablets. They really work.
   CUSTOMER: OK, thanks. I'll take them. And could I have a box of tissues?
   PHARMACIST: Sure. Here you are.

Exercise 7

A: Wow, you don't look very good! Do you feel OK?
B: No, I think I'm getting a cold. What should I do <u>for</u> it?
A: You should stay <u>at</u> home and go <u>to</u> bed.
B: You're probably right. I've got a really bad cough, too.
A: Try drinking some hot tea <u>with</u> honey. It really helps.
B: Anything else?
A: Yeah, I suggest you get a big box <u>of</u> tissues!

Exercise 8

Possible answers:
2. I think I'm getting a cold.
   You should get a bottle of vitamin C.
3. I can't stop sneezing.
   Try and hold your breath.
4. I don't have any energy.
   I suggest some multivitamins.
5. I'm stressed out!
   You should work less and play more.
6. I can't get to sleep.
   Try going to bed at the same time every night.

T-176 ■ *Workbook answer key*

Interchange Teacher's Edition 1

13 *May I take your order?*

Exercise 1

2. A: I really like Chinese food.
   B: <u>So do I.</u>
3. A: I'm in the mood for Italian food.
   B: <u>I am, too.</u>
4. A: I can't stand spicy food.
   B: <u>Neither can I.</u>
5. A: I don't like bland food very much.
   B: <u>I don't either.</u>
6. A: I think Japanese food is delicious.
   B: <u>I do, too.</u>

Exercise 2

A
Answers will vary.
B
Answers will vary.

Exercise 3

A
1. Camille   ★ Awful!
2. Luke   ★★★★★ Fantastic!!
3. Adam   ★★★ Pretty good.

B

	Trattoria Romana	*Dynasty*	*Beirut Café*
Food	*Italian*	American	Lebanese
Atmosphere	*quiet and relaxing*	boring	lively
Specialties	desserts	steak and potatoes	meze
Service	very good	slow and unfriendly	pretty friendly
Price/person	about $32	$36	about $18
Reservation	yes	no	yes

Exercise 4

Possible answers:
2. peas (others are fruit)
3. octopus (others are grains)
4. chicken (others are vegetables)
5. ice cream (others are drinks)
6. sushi (others are sandwiches)

Exercise 5

SERVER: What kind of dressing <u>would you like</u> on your salad – French, blue cheese, or vinaigrette?
CUSTOMER: <u>I'd</u> like French, please.
SERVER: And would you like <u>anything</u> to drink?
CUSTOMER: Yes. <u>I'll</u> have iced coffee.
SERVER: With milk and sugar?
CUSTOMER: Yes, <u>please</u>.
SERVER: Anything else?
CUSTOMER: No, <u>thanks</u>. That'll <u>be</u> all.
SERVER: OK. I'll bring it right away

Exercise 6

2. A: Would you like french fries or salad?
   B: <u>I'd like french fries, please.</u>
3. A: What kind of soda would you like?
   B: <u>I'll have a cola.</u>
4. A: Would you like anything to drink?
   B: <u>No, thanks.</u>
5. A: What flavor ice cream would you like?
   B: <u>Chocolate, please.</u>
5. A: Would you like anything else?
   B: <u>That'll be all, thanks.</u>

Exercise 7

2. In a restaurant, the server takes your <u>order</u>.
3. Many people like <u>dressing</u> on their salad.
4. Some people rarely cook with spices. They prefer <u>bland</u> food.
5. Strawberry is a popular ice cream <u>flavor</u>.

Exercise 8

SHERRY: It's delicious! I <u>like it a lot</u>!
WHITNEY: I do, <u>too</u>. It's my <u>favorite kind of food</u>. Let's call Chiang Mai restaurant for home delivery.
SHERRY: Great idea! Their food is always good. I eat there a lot.
WHITNEY: <u>So do I</u>. Well, what <u>would</u> you like tonight?
SHERRY: I'm in the mood for some soup.
WHITNEY: So <u>am</u> I. And I think I <u>will</u> have spicy chicken and special Thai rice.
SHERRY: OK, let's order. Oh, wait a minute, I don't have any money with me.
WHITNEY: Neither <u>do</u> I. What should we do?
SHERRY: Well, let's look in the refrigerator. Hmm. Do you like boiled eggs?
WHITNEY: I <u>can't stand them</u>!
SHERRY: Actually, neither <u>can</u> I.

Exercise 1

A

2. b. forest
3. a. valley
4. a. lake
5. c. volcano
6. a. desert

B

2. Amazon <u>River</u>
3. <u>Lake</u> Superior
4. <u>Mount</u> Fuji
5. Mediterranean <u>Sea</u>
6. Angel <u>Falls</u>
7. Pacific <u>Ocean</u>
8. Sahara <u>Desert</u>

Exercise 2

2. cooler   the coolest
3. friendlier   the friendliest
4. heavier   the heaviest
5. nicer   the nicest

6. noisier   the noisiest
7. older   the oldest
8. safer   the safest
9. smaller   the smallest
10. wetter   the wettest

Exercise 3

IAN: Well, it certainly has some of <u>the most famous</u> cities in the world – Rome, Milan, and Venice.

VAL: Yeah. I had <u>the best</u> time in Venice. It's <u>the most beautiful</u> city I've ever seen. Of course, it's also one of <u>the most popular</u> tourist attractions. It was <u>the most crowded</u> city I visited this summer, and there weren't even any cars!

IAN: I've always wanted to visit Venice. What's it like in the winter?

VAL: Actually, that's <u>the worst</u> time to visit unless you want to avoid the summer crowds. Venice is one of <u>the coldest and foggiest</u> places in Italy in the winter.

Exercise 4

3. The Suez Canal joins the Mediterranean and Red seas. It is 190 kilometers (118 miles) long. It is <u>longer than</u> the Panama Canal.
4. Canada and Russia are <u>the largest</u> countries in the world.
5. Russia is <u>larger than</u> Canada.
6. <u>The highest</u> waterfall in the world is in Venezuela.
7. The Atacama Desert in Chile is <u>the driest</u> place in the world.
8. Mount Walialeale in Hawaii gets 1,170 centimeters (460 inches) of rain a year. It is <u>the wettest</u> place on earth!
9. The continent of Antarctica is <u>colder than</u> any other place in the world.

10. The Himalayas are some of <u>the most dangerous</u> mountains to climb.
11. Badwater, in California's Death Valley, is <u>the lowest</u> point in North America.
12. The Pacific Ocean is <u>deeper than</u> the Atlantic Ocean. At one place, the Pacific Ocean is 11,033 meters (36,198 feet) deep.

Exercise 5

A

Possible answers

Antarctica is the most southern continent. It is the coldest and windiest place in the world. Most of it is covered in ice. It is a desert. Very few plants grow there. In the summer, the sun shines for 24 hours a day.

B

1. False
2. False
3. False
4. True
5. False
6. False
7. True

Exercise 6

2. How far is New Zealand from Australia?
   a. It's about 2,000 kilometers (1,200 miles).
3. How long is the Yangtze River?
   a. It's 6,300 kilometers (3,917 miles) long.
4. How cold is Antarctica?
   b. It gets down to -88.3 degrees Celsius (-126.9 degrees Fahrenheit).
5. How big is the Amazon Rain Forest?
   a. It's 6 million square kilometers (2.5 million miles).
6. How deep is the Grand Canyon?
   b. It's about 1.6 kilometers (1 mile) deep.

Exercise 7

Answers will vary.

Exercise 8

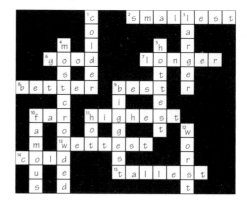

15 I'm going to a soccer match.

Exercise 1

2. beach party
3. bicycle race
4. dance contest/performance
5. rock concert
6. singing contest/tournament
7. tennis match/tournament
8. volleyball game/tournament

Exercise 2

Possible answers:

2. On Monday, she's working overtime to finish the report.
3. On Tuesday evening at 7:00, she's seeing a play with Tony.
4. On Wednesday night, she's watching the tennis match with Kate and Sam.
5. On Thursday, she's having lunch with Candy at noon.
6. On Friday, she's staying home and watching the baseball game on TV.
7. On Saturday evening, she's going to a dance performance with Maria.

Exercise 3

Mark: I'm going to go to a rock concert on Saturday.
Marta: That sounds interesting.
Mark: Yeah. There's a free concert in the park. And how about you, Marta?
Marta: Well, Brian and I are going to see a basketball game in the afternoon.
Mark: And what are you going to do in the evening?
Marta: Brian's going to visit his mother in the hospital. But I'm not going to do anything really.
Mark: Well, I'm going to have some friends over for a barbecue. Would you like to come?
Marta: Thanks. I'd love to!

Exercise 4

2. A: Would you like to have dinner at Rosa's tonight?
   B: Great! But it's my turn to pay.
3. A: Do you want to go on a picnic tomorrow?
   B: Sure. I'd love to.
4. A: How about going to a movie on Saturday?
   B: Oh, I'm sorry. I can't.

Exercise 5

Answers will vary.

Exercise 6

Answers will vary.

Exercise 7

A

Text messages are short, typed messages of up to about 150 characters. They include letters, numbers, and spaces. They can also include images, videos, and sound.

B

2. e
3. f
4. i
5. j
6. b
7. a
8. g
9. c
10. d

Exercise 8

Possible answers:

1. Could you ask her to bring the Henderson file?
2. Could you tell Mr. Alvarez that we need the report by noon? Please ask him to call Ms. James as soon as possible.
3. Would you tell Miss Lowe that the new laptop is ready? Could you tell her to pick it up this afternoon?

Exercise 9

Possible answers:

1. Please ask Michael not to meet me at the airport until midnight. Would you tell him that the plane is going to be late?
2. Please tell Lucy that we're meeting at Dino's house before the concert. Could you ask her not to forget the tickets?
3. Could you tell Christopher that the beach party starts at noon? Please ask him not to be late.

Exercise 10

SECRETARY: I'm sorry. She's not in. Can I take a message?

Ms. CURTIS: Yes, please. This is Ms. Curtis. Would you tell her that I'm staying at the Plaza Hotel? The number is 555-9001, Room 605. Could you ask her to call me?

SECRETARY: OK, Ms. Curtis. I'll give her the message.

Ms. CURTIS: Thank you very much. Good-bye.

Exercise 11

2. Could I ask her to call you back?
   Yes. My number is (303) 555-3241.
3. Who's calling, please?
   My name's Graham. Graham Lock.
4. Can I take a message?
   Yes, please. Could you tell him Roz called?
5. Could I speak to Paul, please?
   Let me see if he's in.
6. I'm sorry. She's busy at the moment.
   That's OK. I'll call back.

16 *A change for the better!*

Exercise 1

2. A: I haven't seen you for ages.
   B: I know. How have you been?
3. A: You know, I have three kids now.
   B: That's terrific!
4. A: How are you?
   B: I'm doing really well.

Exercise 2

1. Judy has moved to a new apartment. Her old one was too small.
2. Kim and Anna have stopped eating in restaurants. Now they cook dinner at home every evening. It's much cheaper.
3. Alex has started going to the gym. He looks healthier, and he has more energy.

Exercise 3

Answers will vary. Possible answers:

2. Elena doesn't wear glasses. *or* Elena wore glasses before.
3. Mr. and Mrs. Jones have a new daughter. *or* Mr. and Mrs. Jones had another baby.
4. Eddie is thinner now. *or* Eddie lost a lot of weight.

Exercise 4

Possible answers:

2. James was heavier before.
3. Mary has changed schools.
4. Tess isn't married anymore.
5. My hair is longer now.
6. We don't go to the gym anymore.

Exercise 5

A

1. Luis had an interesting job two years ago.
2. Rosie had a money problem two years ago.
3. Aki was a student two years ago.

B

1. Aki   c
2. Luis   a
3. Rosie   b

C

1. Aki
   Now I actually look forward to getting up early.
   I dress up now.
   My hair is shorter.
2. Luis
   I got married!
   My wife and I often have friends over for dinner.
   We're taking evening classes.
3. Rosie
   Now I work as a computer programmer.
   I've gained several kilos.
   I feel much happier and healthier.

Exercise 6

2. What career do you think you're most interested in pursuing?
3. I go to school, and I have a family and a part-time job. I have a lot of responsibilities.
4. Lucy wants to pay off her student loan before she buys a car.
5. Marie lost her job. Now she's broke and can't pay her rent.
6. I'd like to be successful in my first job. Then I can get a better job and a raise.

Exercise 7

LEO: I want to get a summer job. I'd like to save money for a vacation.

MELISSA: Really? Where would you like to go?

LEO: I'd love to travel to Latin America. What about you, Melissa?

MELISSA: Well, I'm not going to get a job right away. First, I want to go to Spain and Portugal.

LEO: Sounds great, but how are you going to pay for it?

MELISSA: I hope to borrow some money from my brother. I have a good excuse. I plan to take courses in Spanish and Portuguese.

LEO: Oh, I'm tired of studying!

MELISSA: So am I. But I also hope to take people on tours to Latin America. Why don't you come on my first tour?

LEO: Count me in!

Exercise 8

Answers will vary. Possible answers:

1. I hope to find a new job.
   I want to make more money.
   I plan to take a computer class.
2. I'm going to go to a gym.
   I'd like to eat healthier food.
   I'd love to get more sleep.
3. I'm going to join a singles club.
   I want to be more outgoing.
   I plan to find a hobby.

Exercise 9

2. Heather's salary is much lower than before. She had to take a pay cut.
3. After graduation, Jack plans to work for an international company.
4. This job is more stressful than my last job.
5. Mel hopes to move to a small town.
6. William and Donna got engaged last summer. The wedding will be in April.

Exercise 10

Answers will vary.

Credits

Illustrations

Photos